for you.

...ed to hop into an ...cab after I got off ...other day. I told the ...age and the kind of ...ke, and he said, "I ...these just for you, ...n he started playing the music I used to listen to in high school. It was so cool. I guess it's a famous cab that's been featured on TV. I'm sorry I didn't have time to give you an autograph, driver. The manga artist you picked up at Gaien-Nishi in early spring was me.

—Tite Kubo

BLEACH is author Tite Kubo's second title. Kubo made his debut with ZOMBIEPOWDER., a four-volume series for WEEKLY SHONEN JUMP. To date, BLEACH has been translated into numerous languages and has also inspired an animated TV series that began airing in the U.S. in 2006. Beginning its serialization in 2001, BLEACH is still a mainstay in the pages of WEEKLY SHONEN JUMP. In 2005, BLEACH was awarded the prestigious Shogakukan Manga Award in the shonen (boys) category.

BLEACH
Vol. 39: EL VERDUGO
SHONEN JUMP Manga Edition

STORY AND ART BY
TITE KUBO

English Adaptation/Lance Caselman
Translation/Joe Yamazaki
Touch-up Art & Lettering/Mark McMurray
Design/Yukiko Whitley, Kam Li
Editor/Alexis Kirsch

Printed in the U.S.A.

Published by VIZ Media, LLC
P.O. Box 77010
San Francisco, CA 94107

10 9 8 7 6 5 4 3 2 1
First printing, April 2012

To err is human.
To kill is evil.

BLEACH 39 EL VERDUGO

Shonen Jump Manga

STARS AND

松本乱菊

Rangiku Matsumoto

Genryusai Shigekuni
Yamamoto

Apache

アパッチ

山本元柳斎重國

★ plot

When high school student Ichigo Kurosaki meets Soul Reaper Rukia Kuchiki his life is changed forever. Soon Ichigo is a soul-cleansing Soul Reaper too, and he finds himself having adventures, as well as problems, that he never would have imagined. Now Ichigo and his friends must stop renegade Soul Reaper Aizen and his army of Arrancars from destroying the Soul Society and wiping out KarakuraTown as well.

The battle finally begins! The Thirteen Court Guard Companies head to Karakura while Ichigo remains in Hueco Mundo to rescue Orihime. Meanwhile Aizen's forces, led by Barragan's Fracciónes, launch their attack on Karakura and soon find themselves locked in mortal combat with the Soul Reapers. But as the battle progresses, the question remains: who will prevail?

BLEACH ALL

黒崎一護
Ichigo Kurosaki

ミラ・ローズ
Mila Rose

Sun-Sun

スンスン

STORIES

BLEACH 39

EL VERDUGO

Contents

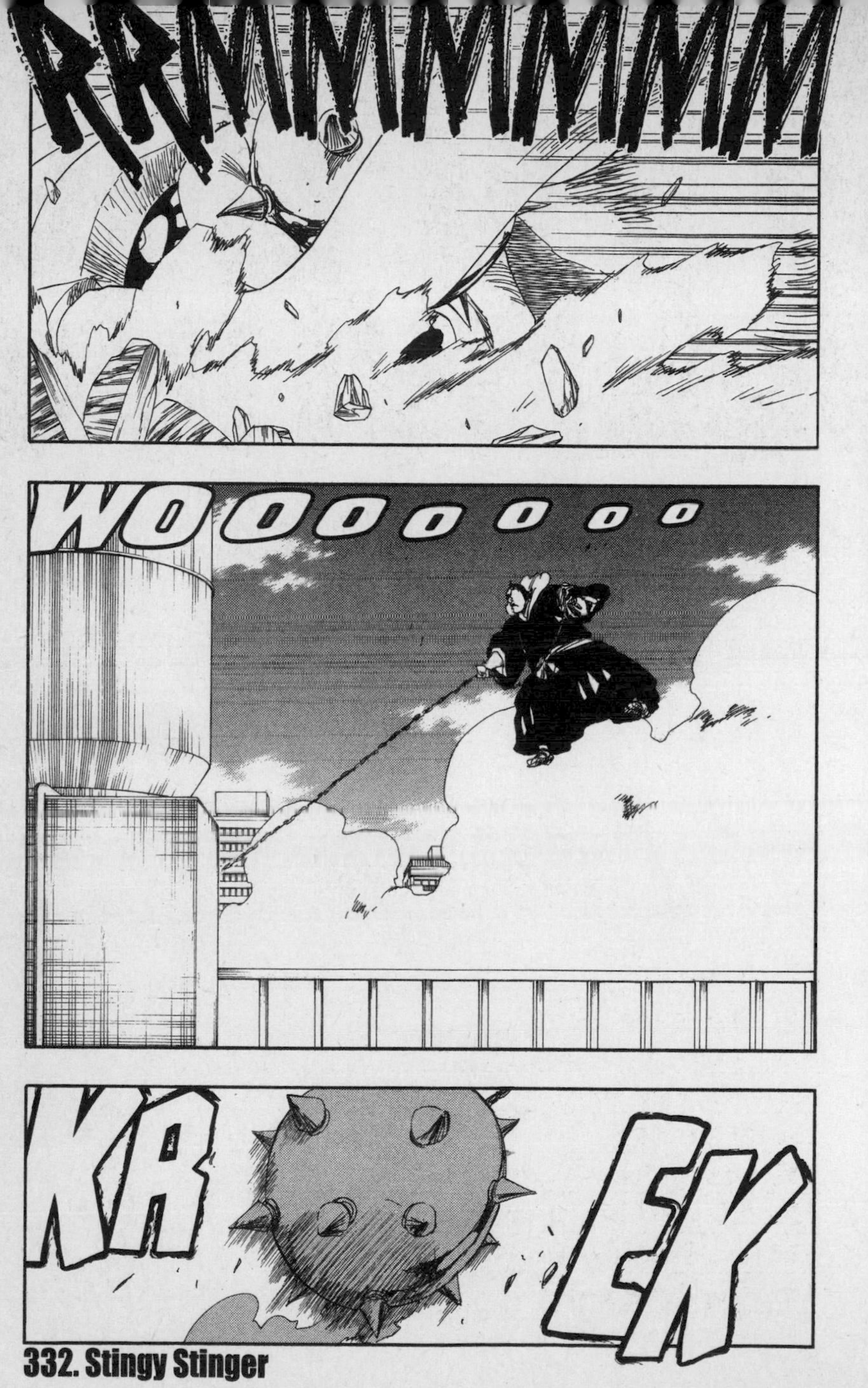
RRMMMMMM
WOOOOOOO
KRA
EK

332. Stingy Stinger

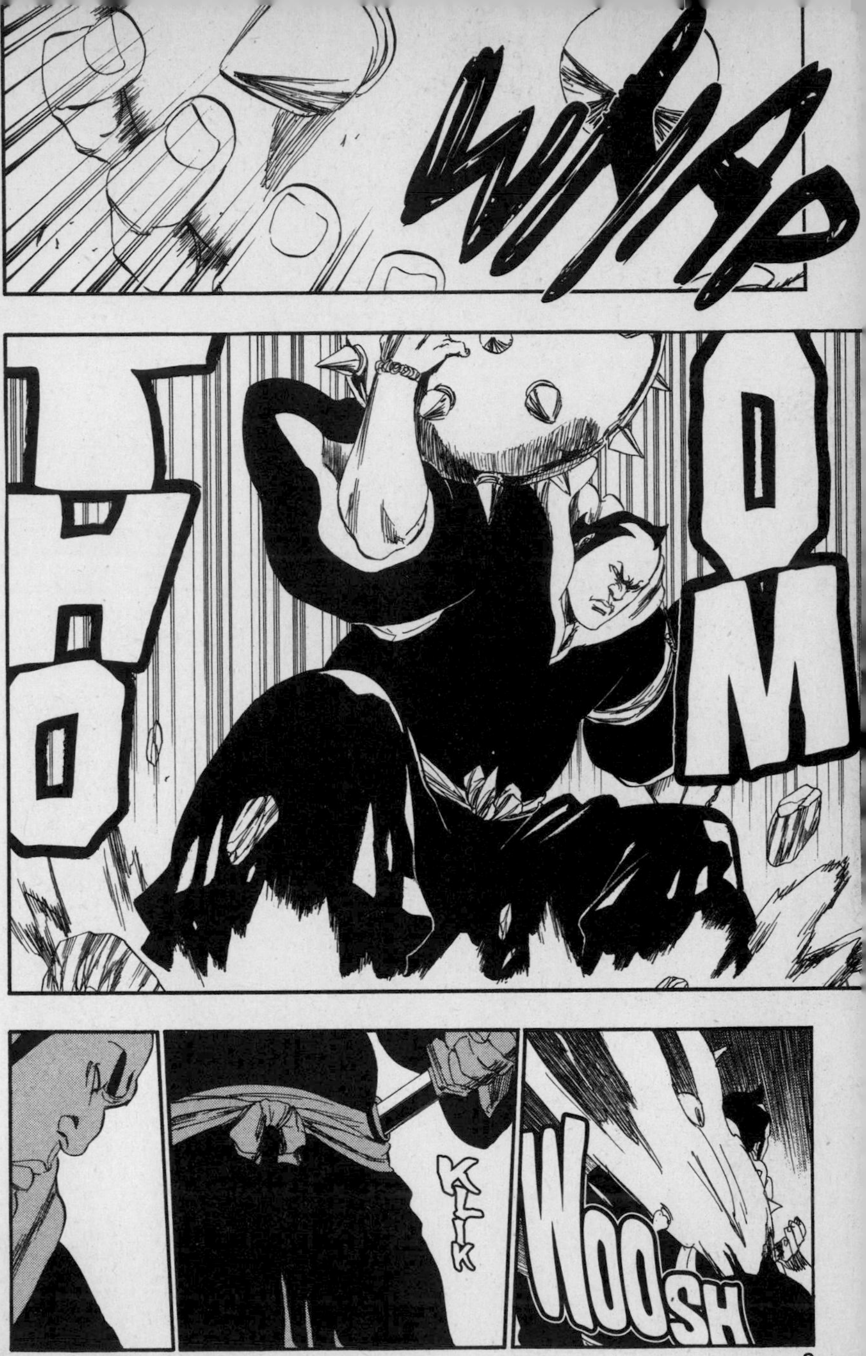
WHAP
KLIK
WOOSH

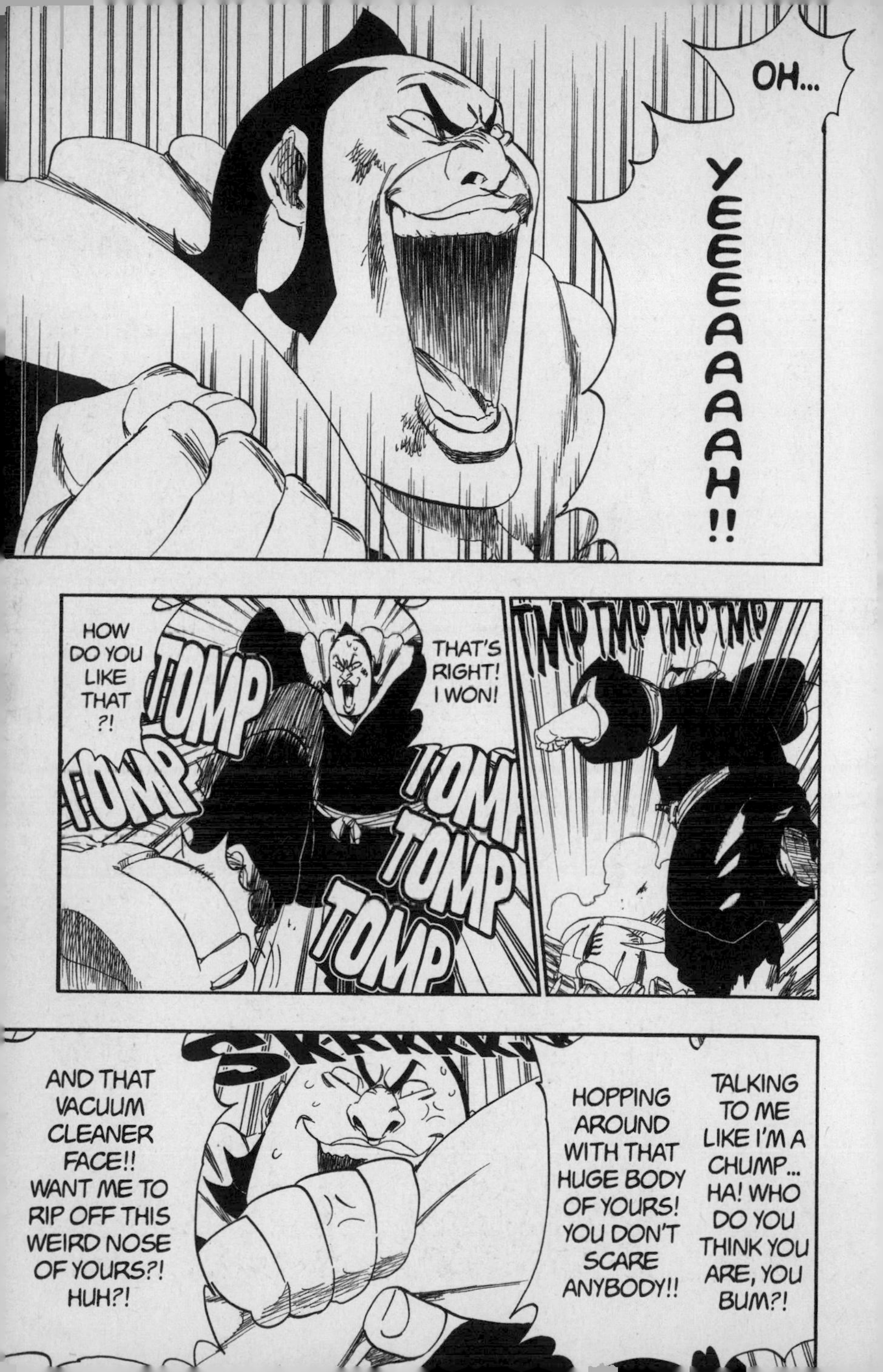
OH... YEEEAAAAAH!!
TMP TMP TMP TMP
THAT'S RIGHT! I WON!
HOW DO YOU LIKE THAT ?!
TOMP
TOMP
TOMP
TOMP
TOMP
TALKING TO ME LIKE I'M A CHUMP... HA! WHO DO YOU THINK YOU ARE, YOU BUM?!
HOPPING AROUND WITH THAT HUGE BODY OF YOURS! YOU DON'T SCARE ANYBODY!!
AND THAT VACUUM CLEANER FACE!! WANT ME TO RIP OFF THIS WEIRD NOSE OF YOURS?! HUH?!

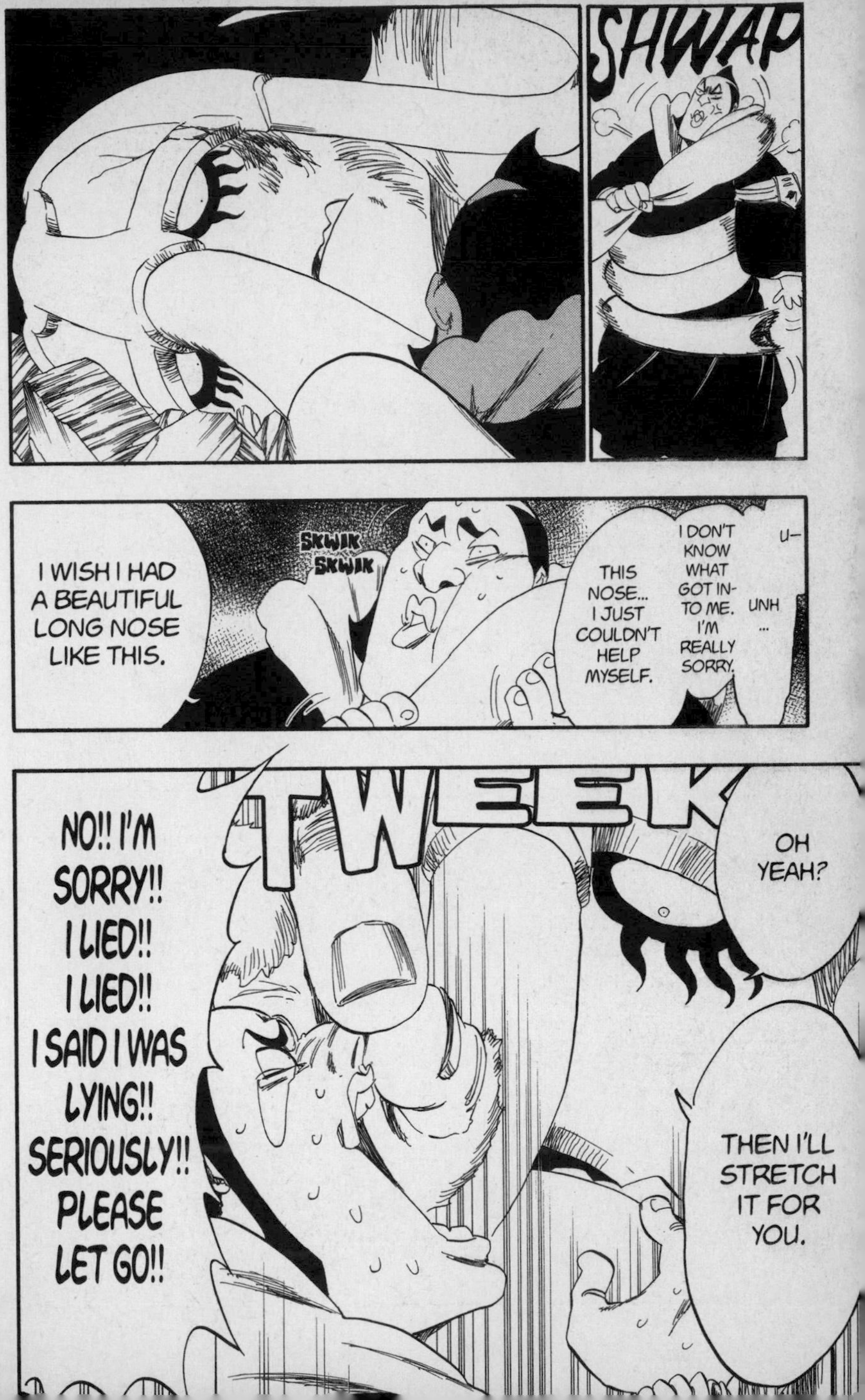
SHWAP
U- UNH ...
I DON'T KNOW WHAT GOT IN- TO ME. I'M REALLY SORRY.
THIS NOSE... I JUST COULDN'T HELP MYSELF.
SKWIK SKWIK
I WISH I HAD A BEAUTIFUL LONG NOSE LIKE THIS.
OH YEAH?
TWEEK
THEN I'LL STRETCH IT FOR YOU.
NO!! I'M SORRY!! I LIED!! I LIED!! I SAID I WAS LYING!! SERIOUSLY!! PLEASE LET GO!!

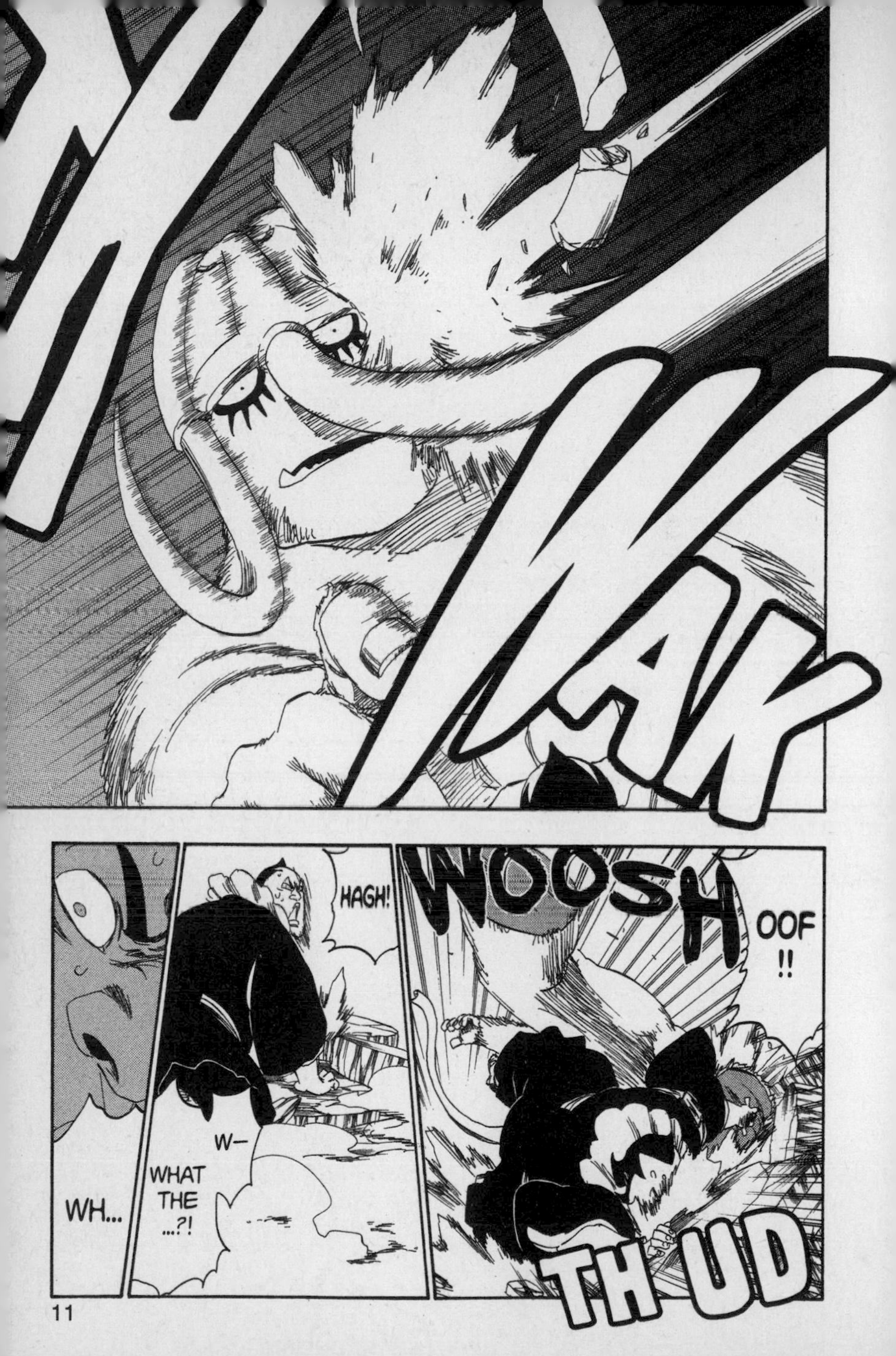
WOOSH
OOF !!
THUD
HAGH!
W—
WHAT THE ...?!
WH...

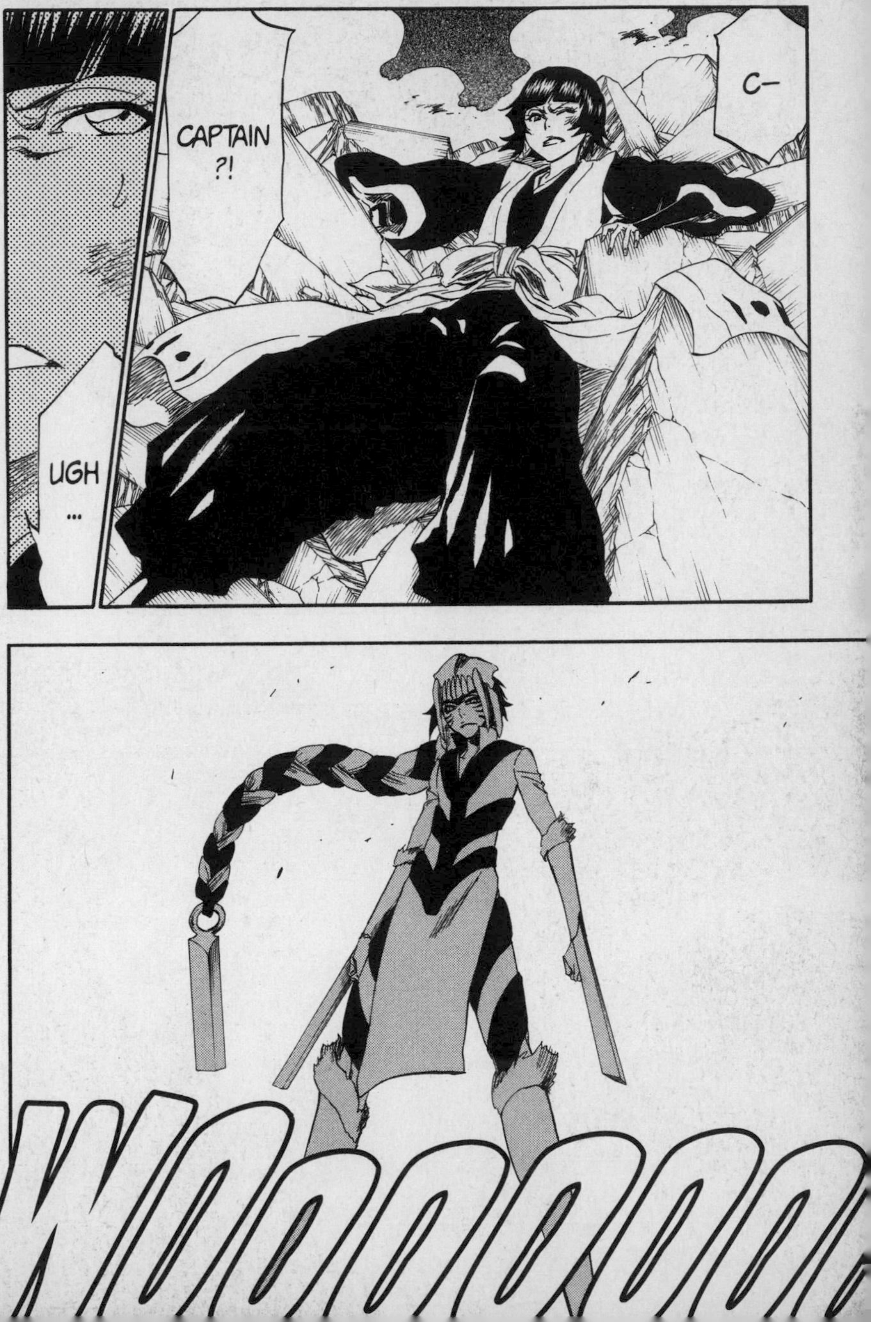
C–
CAPTAIN ?!
UGH ...

BLEACH 332. Stingy Stinger

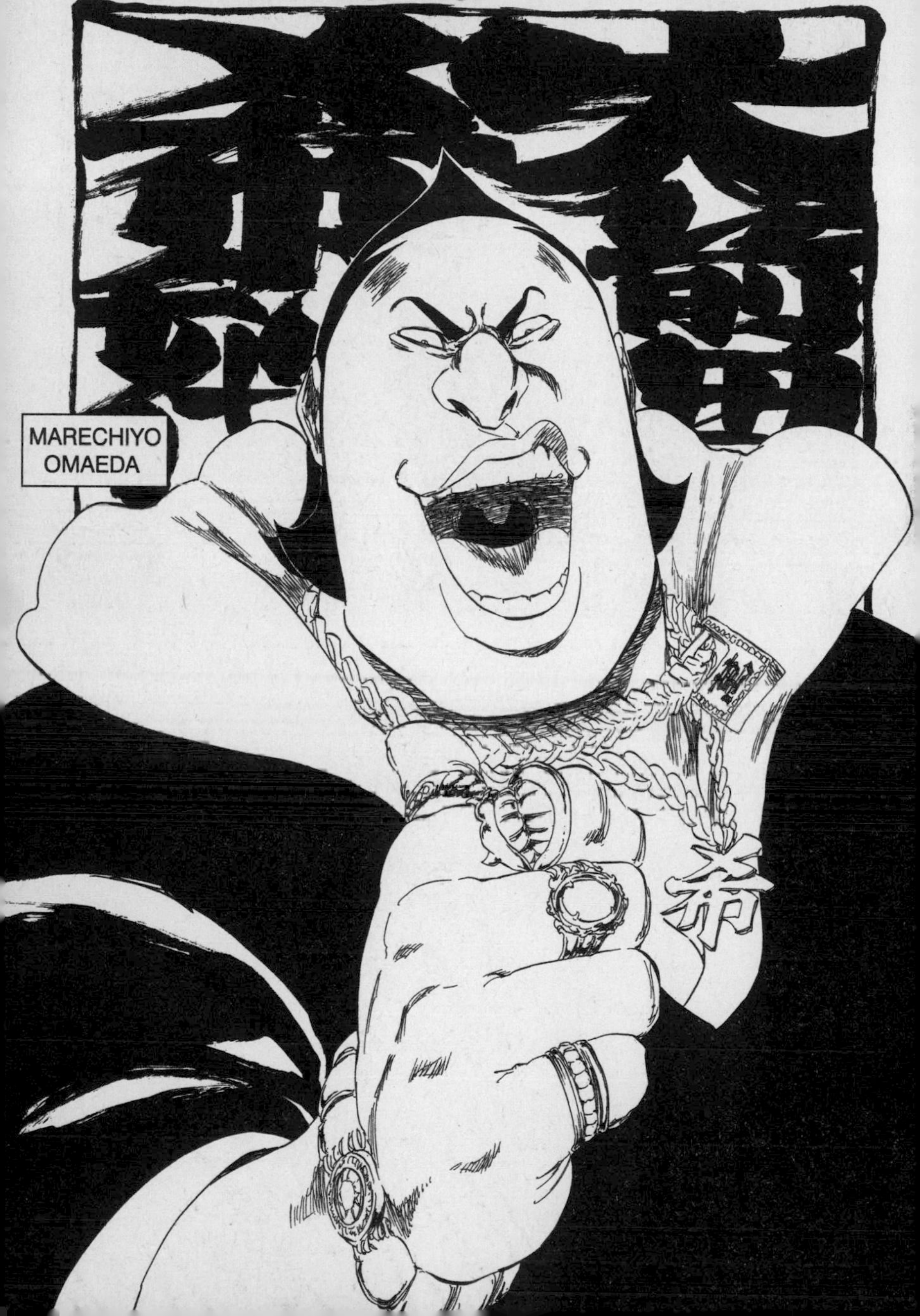
MARECHIYO
OMAEDA

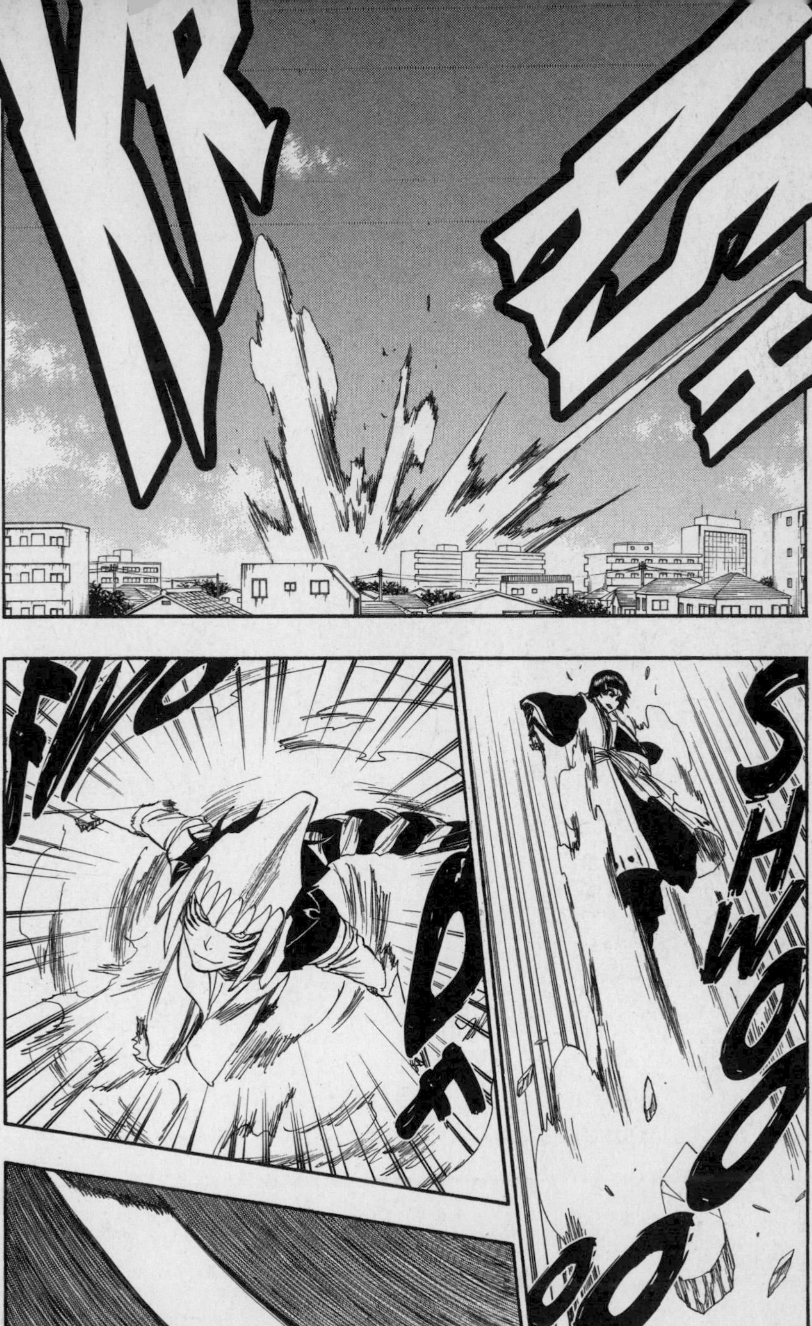

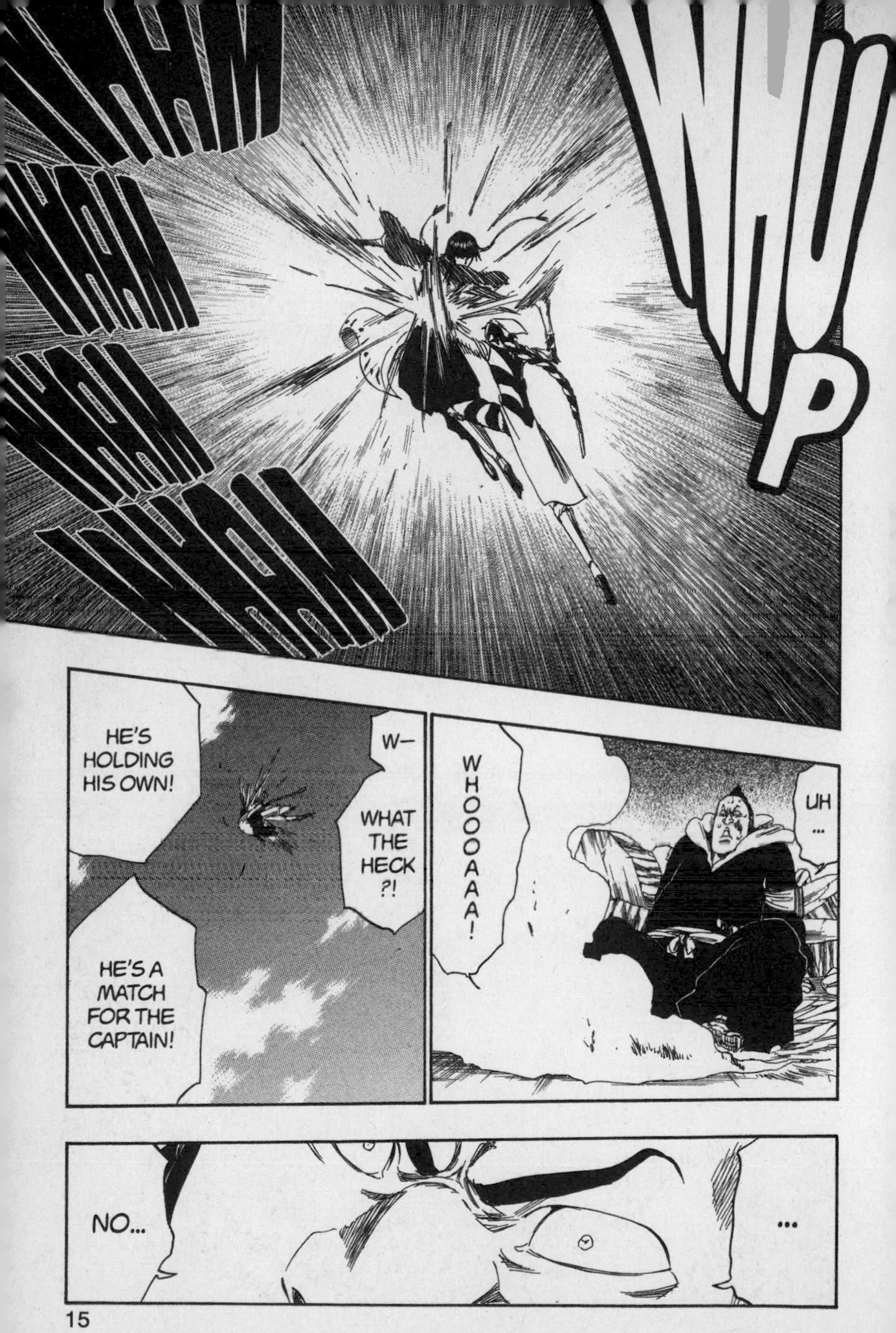
WHOOP
WHAM WHAM WHAM
UH ...
WHOOOAAA!
W—
WHAT THE HECK?!
HE'S HOLDING HIS OWN!
HE'S A MATCH FOR THE CAPTAIN!
...
NO...

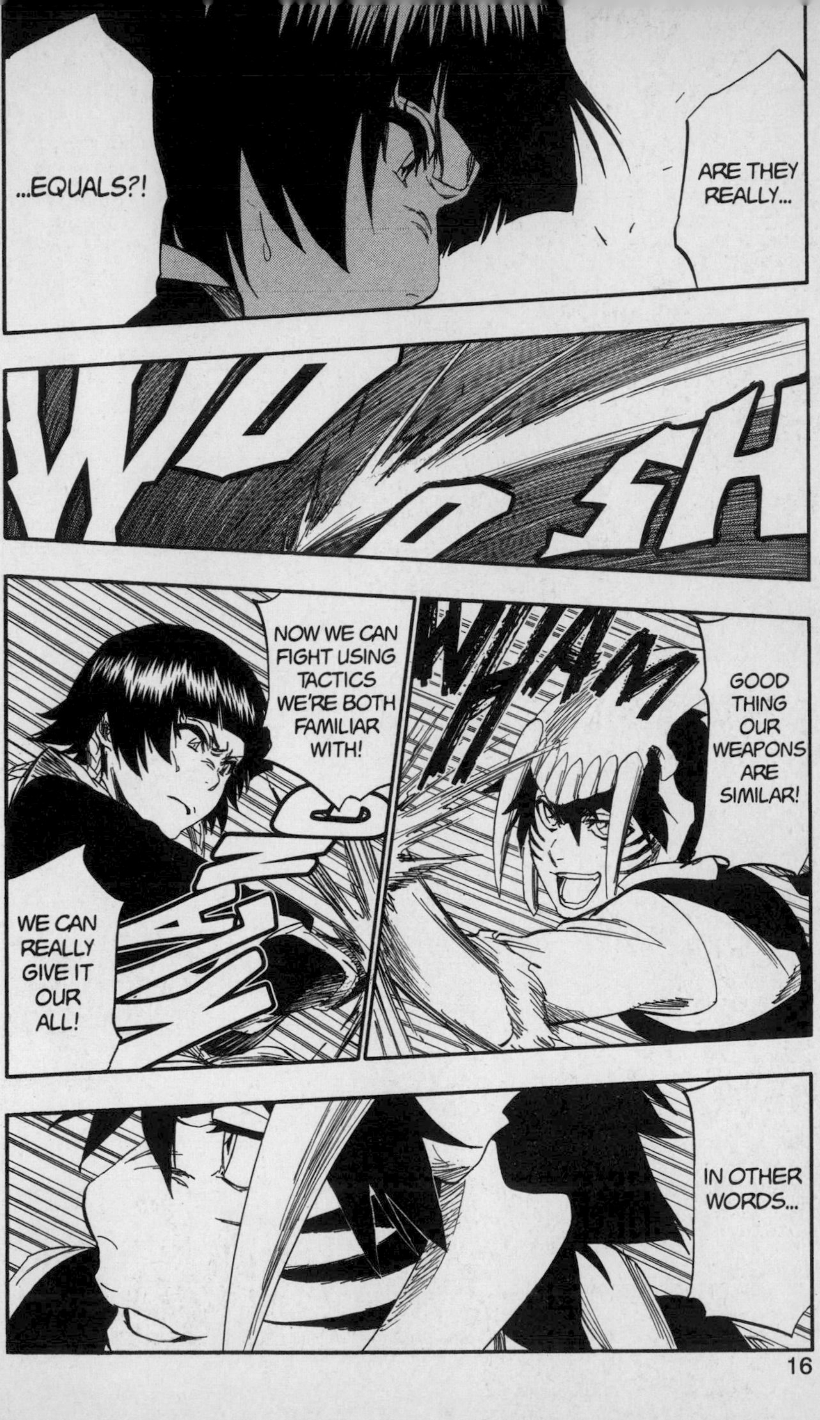
ARE THEY REALLY...
...EQUALS?!
WHAM
GOOD THING OUR WEAPONS ARE SIMILAR!
NOW WE CAN FIGHT USING TACTICS WE'RE BOTH FAMILIAR WITH!
WE CAN REALLY GIVE IT OUR ALL!
IN OTHER WORDS...

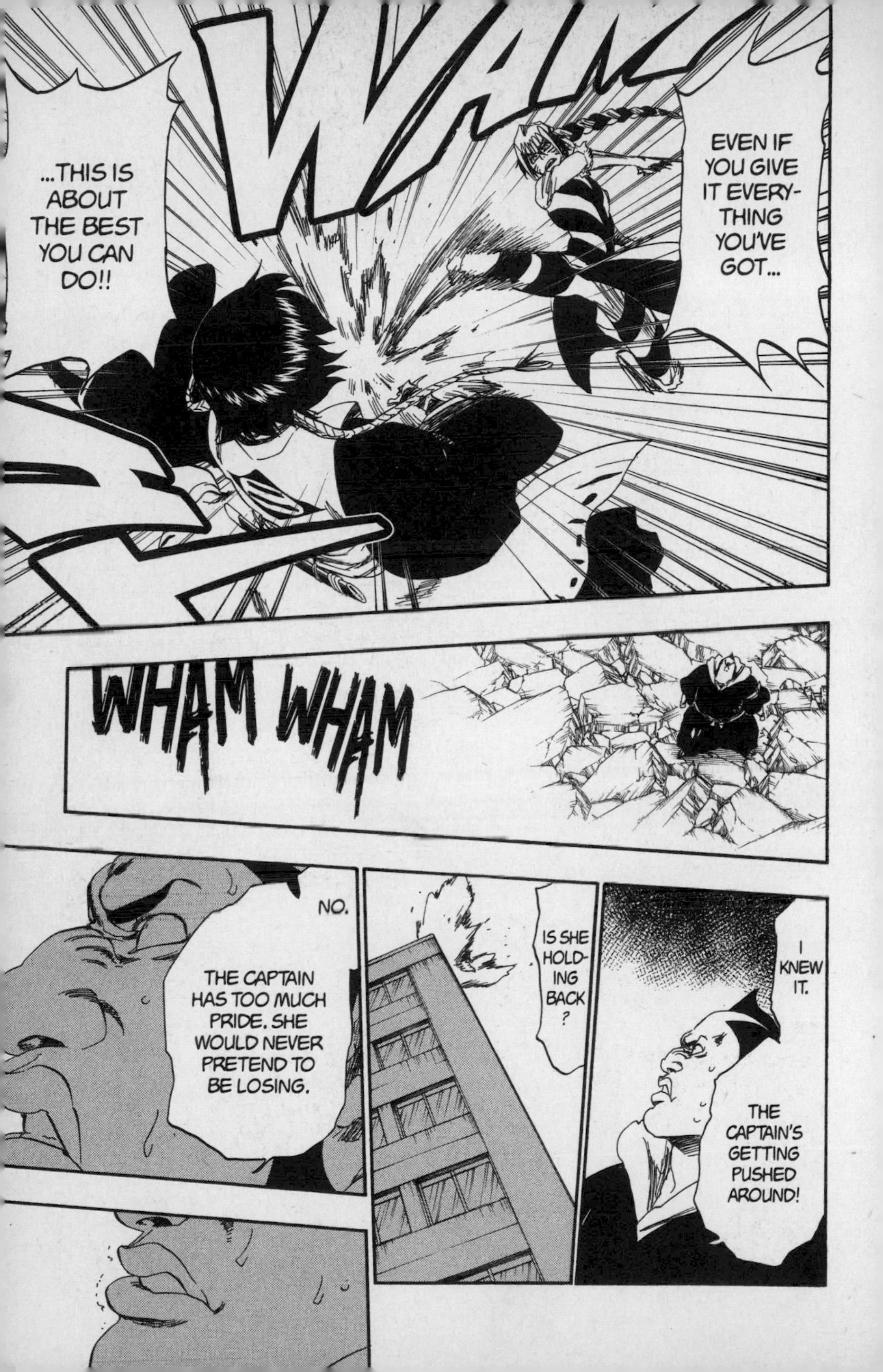
EVEN IF YOU GIVE IT EVERYTHING YOU'VE GOT...
...THIS IS ABOUT THE BEST YOU CAN DO!!
WHAM WHAM
I KNEW IT.
THE CAPTAIN'S GETTING PUSHED AROUND!
IS SHE HOLDING BACK?
NO.
THE CAPTAIN HAS TOO MUCH PRIDE. SHE WOULD NEVER PRETEND TO BE LOSING.

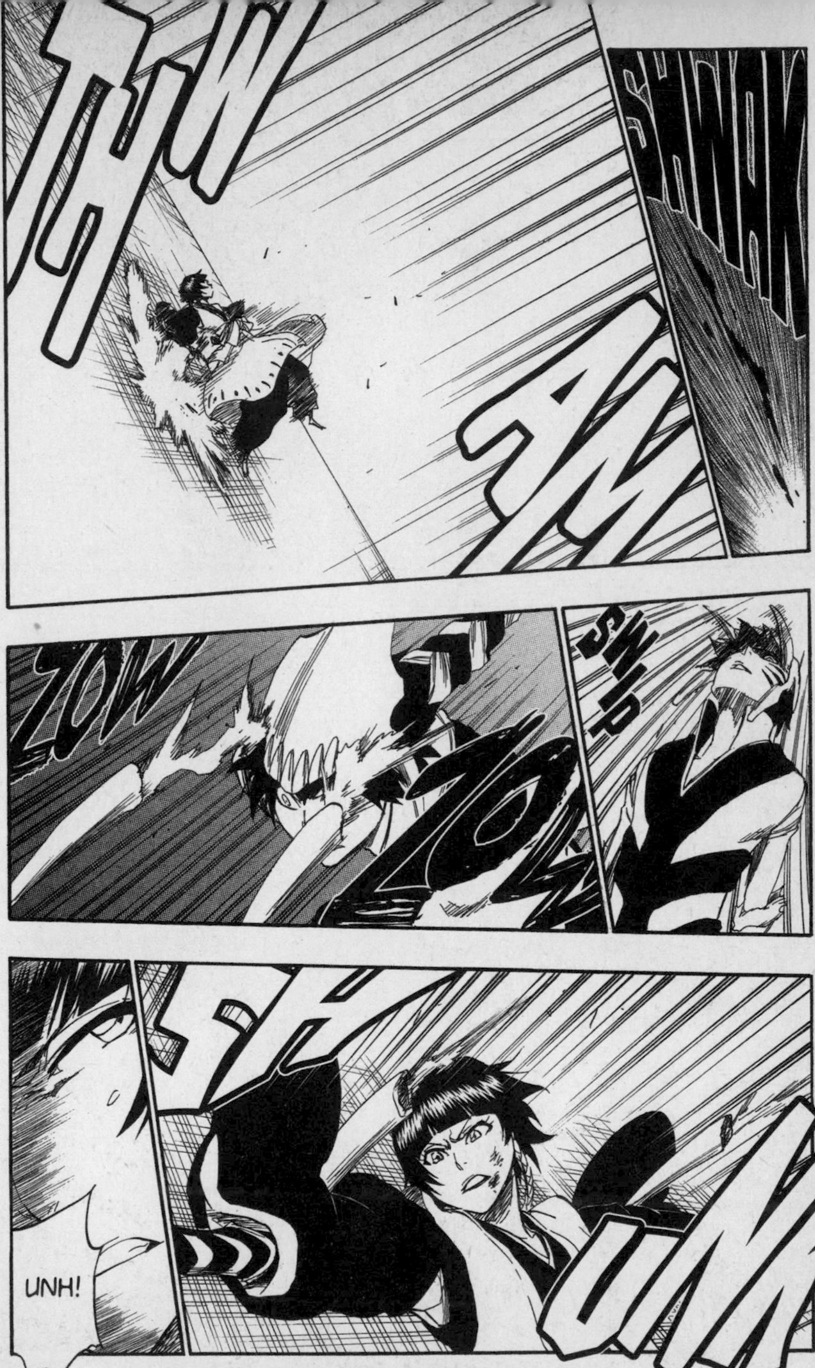
SHUNK
SWIP
ZOW
UNH!

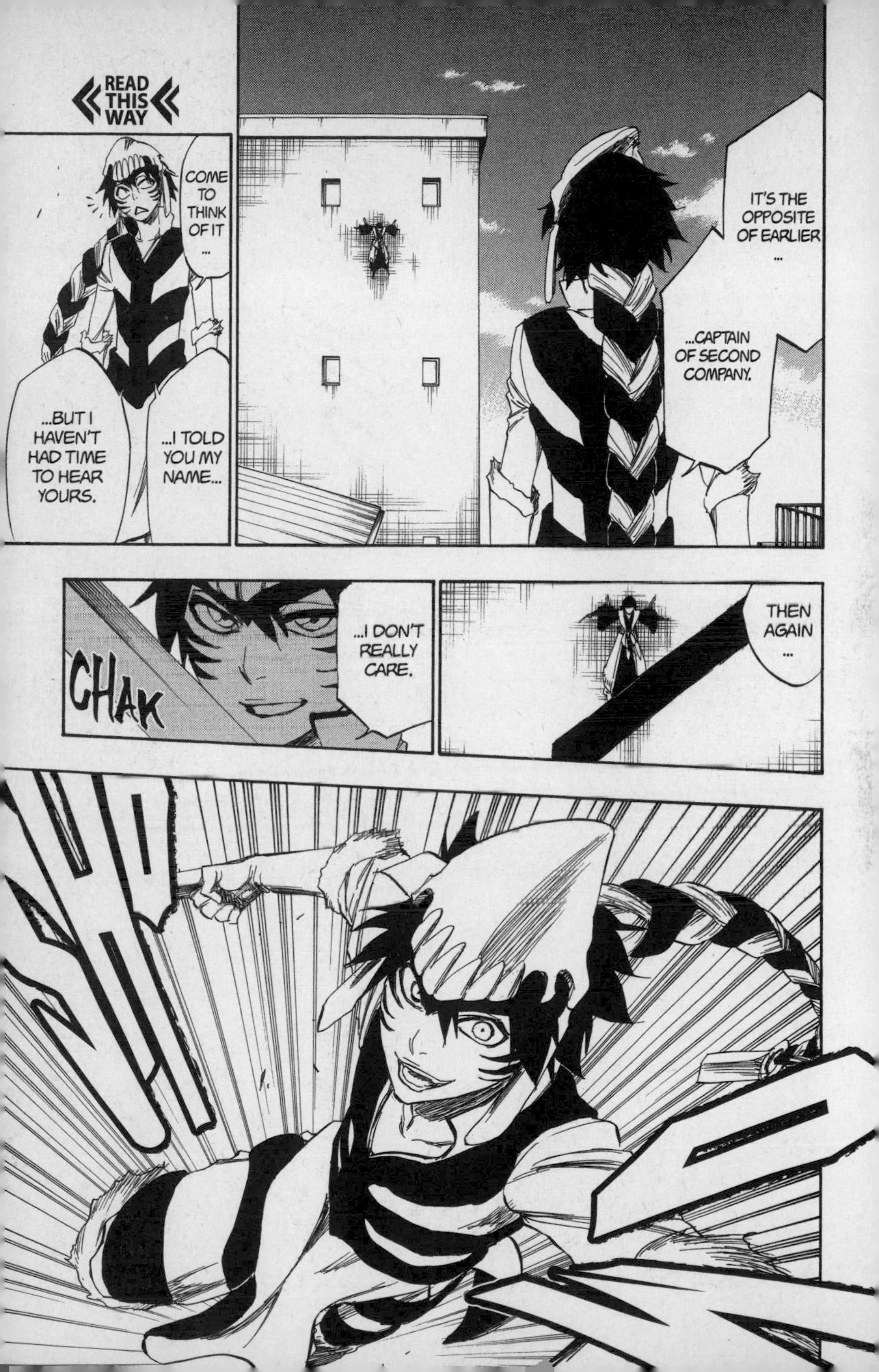
READ THIS WAY
IT'S THE OPPOSITE OF EARLIER ...
...CAPTAIN OF SECOND COMPANY.
COME TO THINK OF IT ...
...I TOLD YOU MY NAME...
...BUT I HAVEN'T HAD TIME TO HEAR YOURS.
THEN AGAIN ...
...I DON'T REALLY CARE.
CHAK

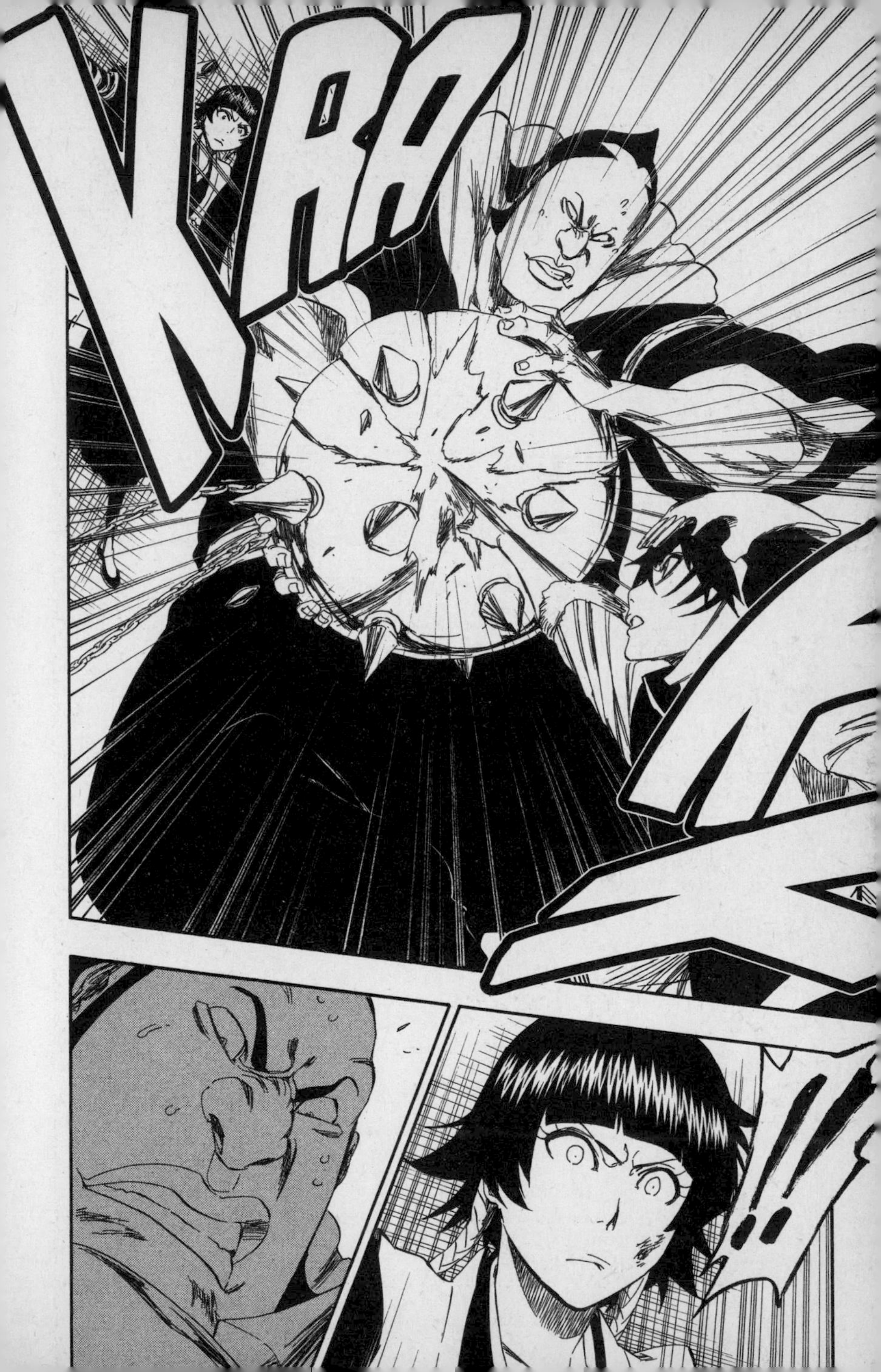
!!

READ THIS WAY

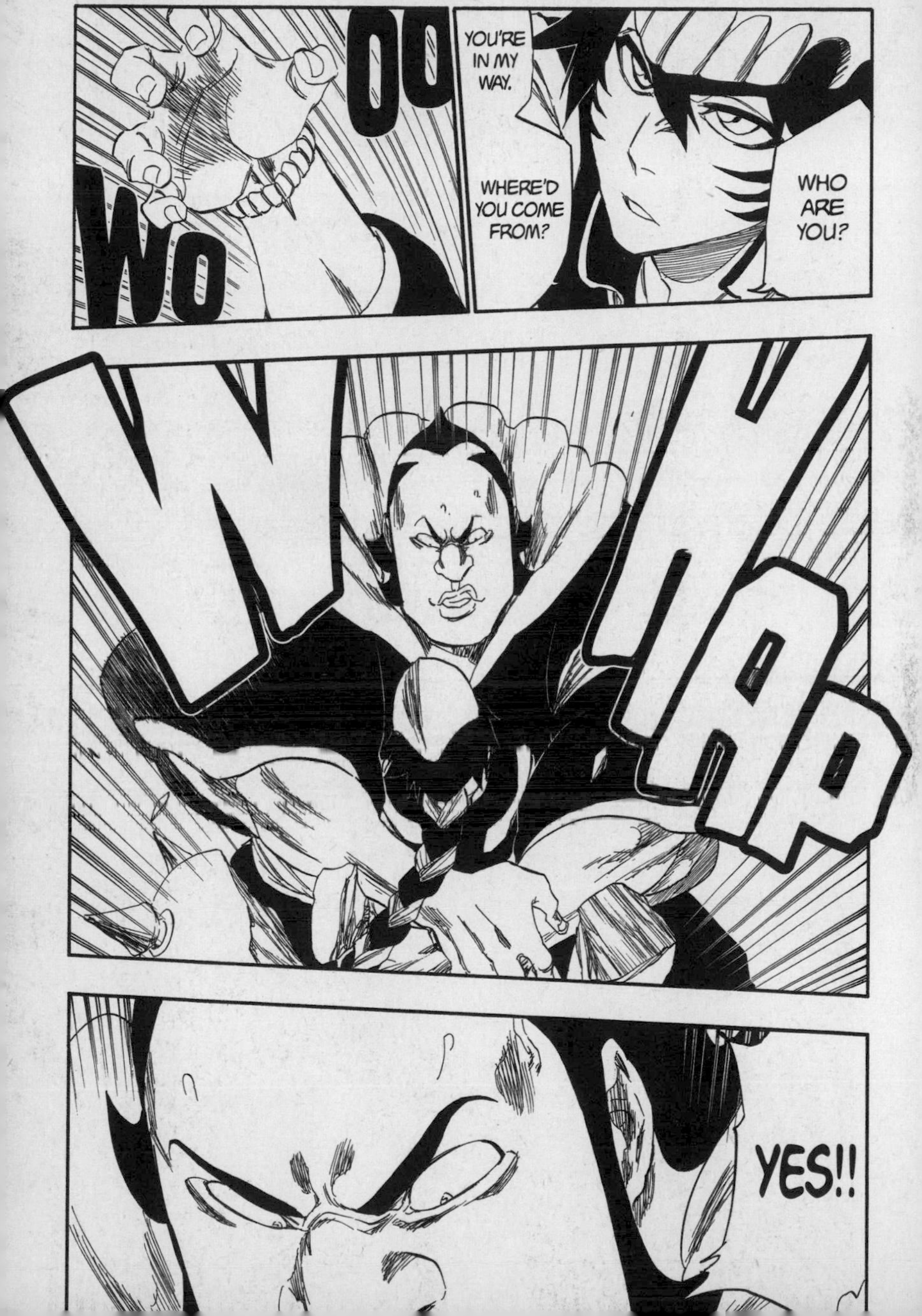
WHO ARE YOU?
WHERE'D YOU COME FROM?
YOU'RE IN MY WAY.
WOOO
WHAP
YES!!

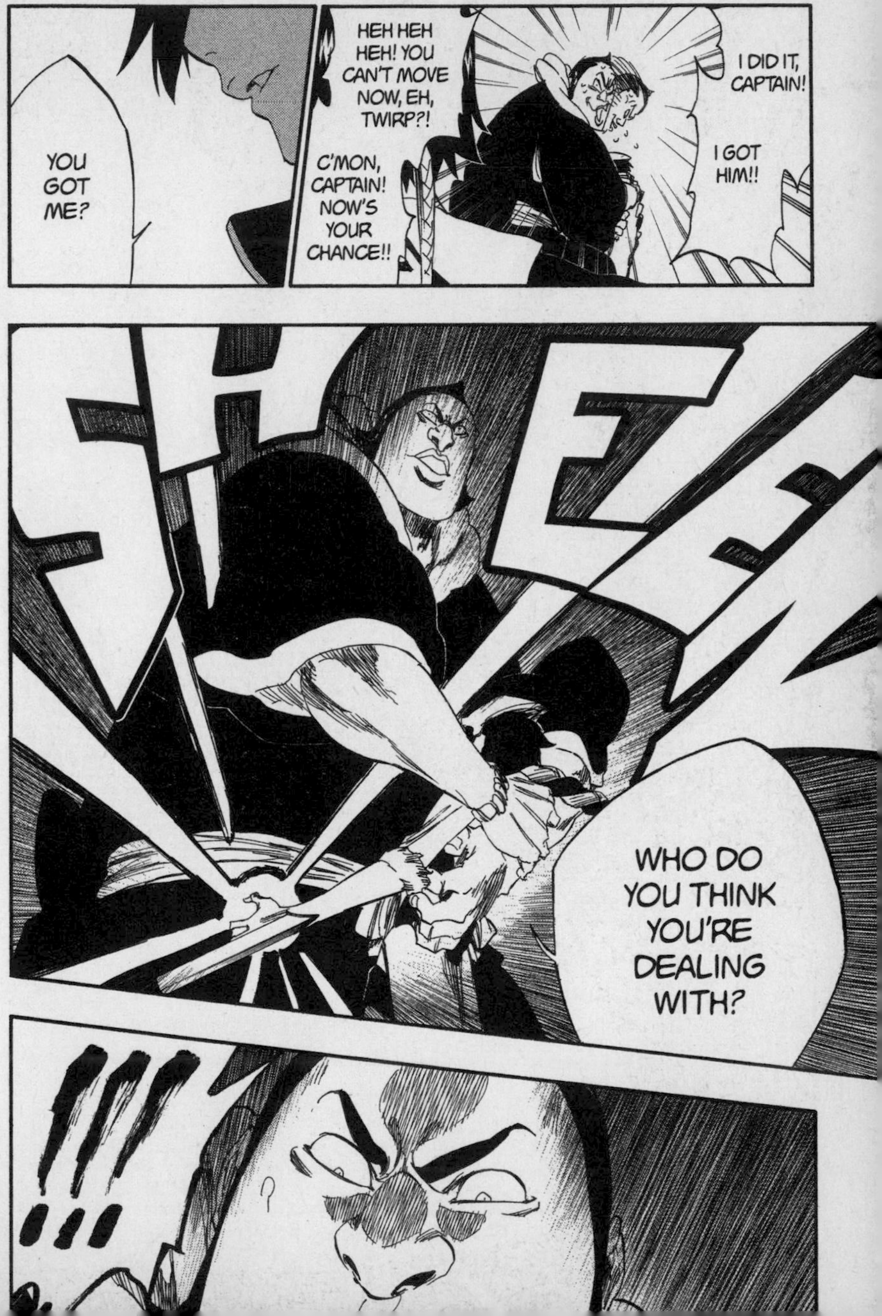
I DID IT, CAPTAIN!
I GOT HIM!!
HEH HEH HEH! YOU CAN'T MOVE NOW, EH, TWIRP?!
C'MON, CAPTAIN! NOW'S YOUR CHANCE!!
YOU GOT ME?
WHO DO YOU THINK YOU'RE DEALING WITH?
!!!
!!!

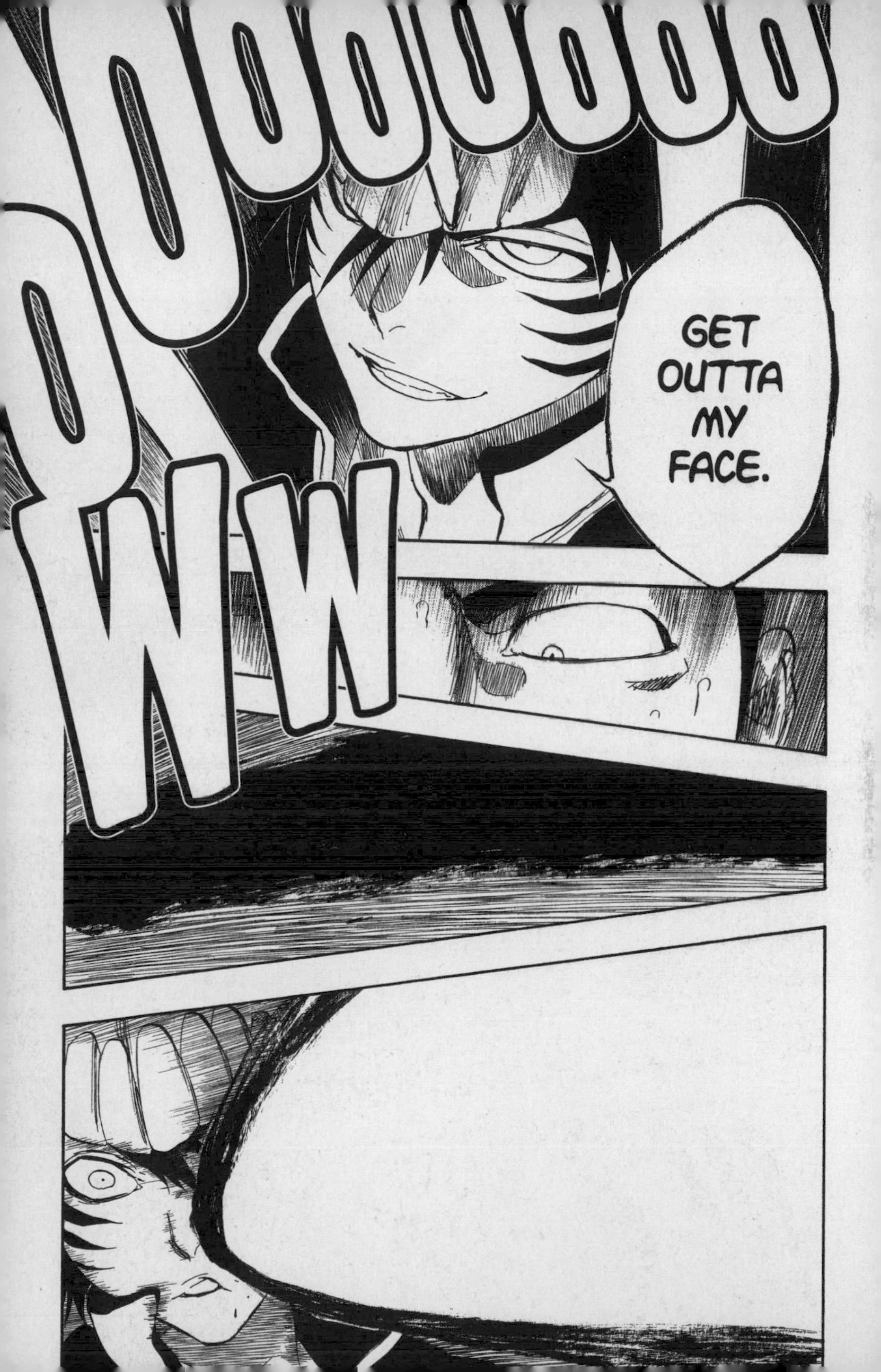
GET OUTTA MY FACE.

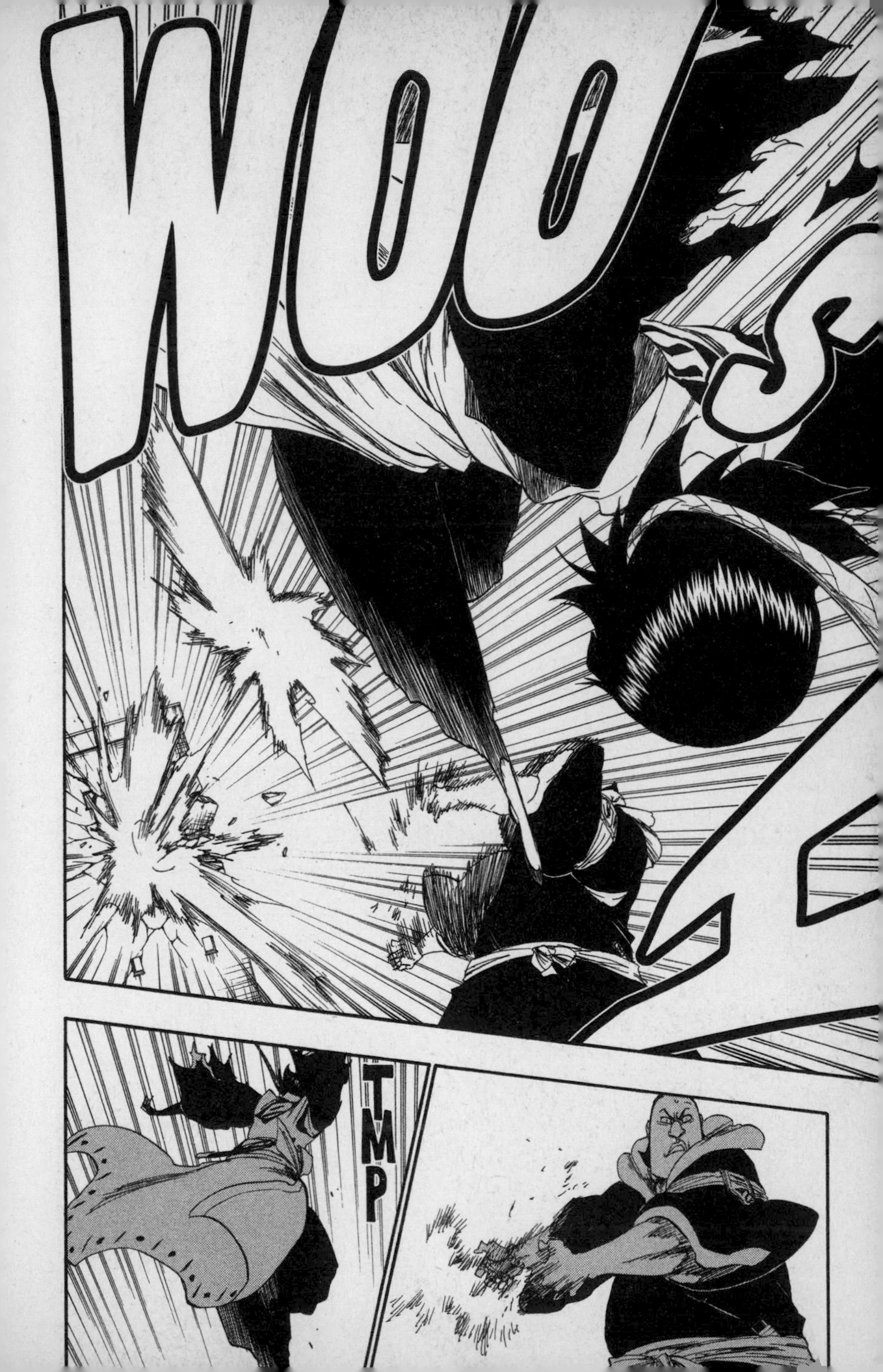
WOOS
TMP

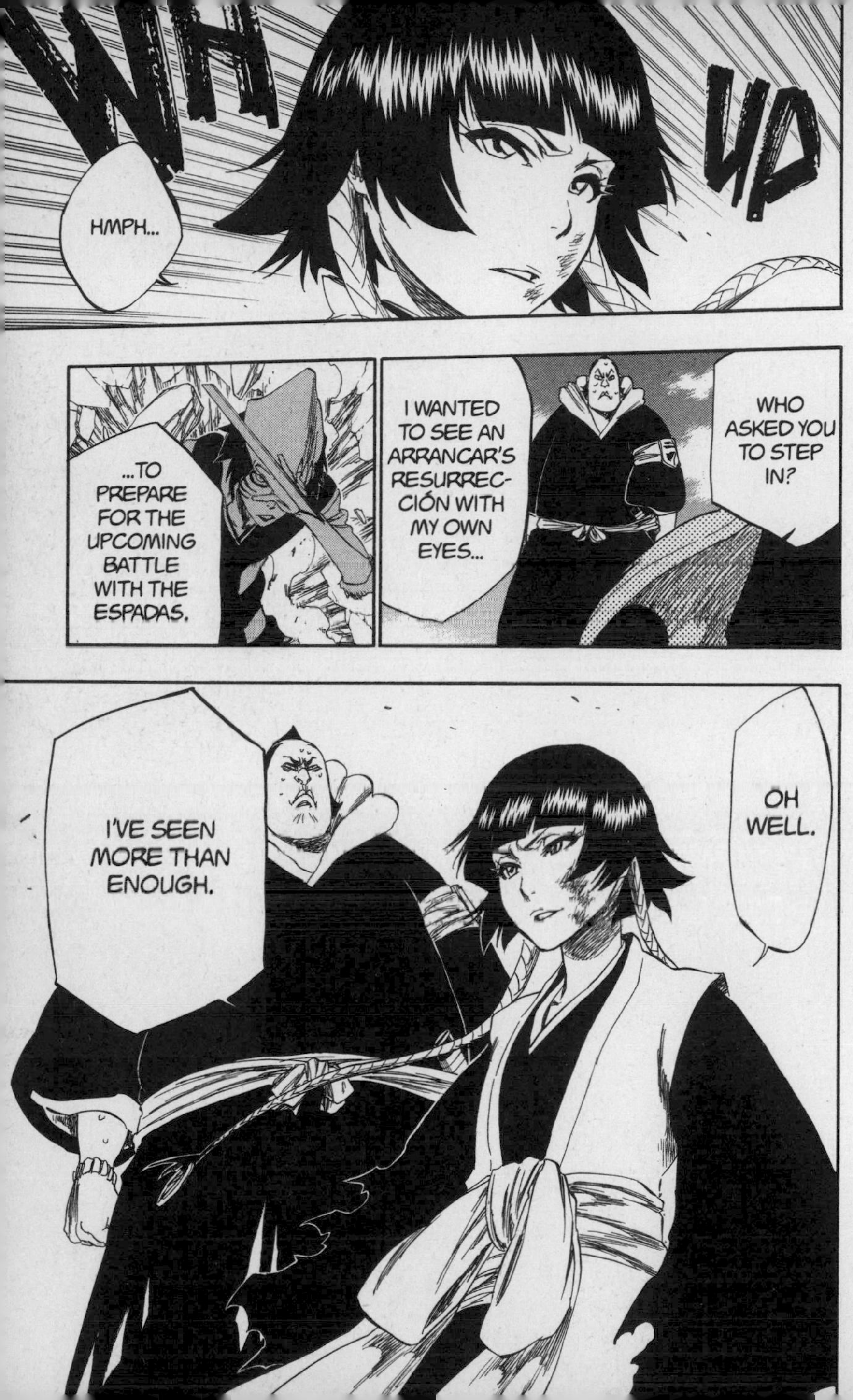
WH UP
HMPH...
WHO ASKED YOU TO STEP IN?
I WANTED TO SEE AN ARRANCAR'S RESURREC-CIÓN WITH MY OWN EYES...
...TO PREPARE FOR THE UPCOMING BATTLE WITH THE ESPADAS.
OH WELL.
I'VE SEEN MORE THAN ENOUGH.

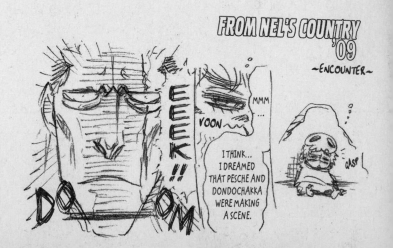

FROM NEL'S COUNTRY
'09
~ENCOUNTER~

EEEK!!

DOOOM

MMM...

VOON

I THINK...
I DREAMED
THAT PESCHE AND
DONDOCHAKKA
WERE MAKING
A SCENE.

GASP

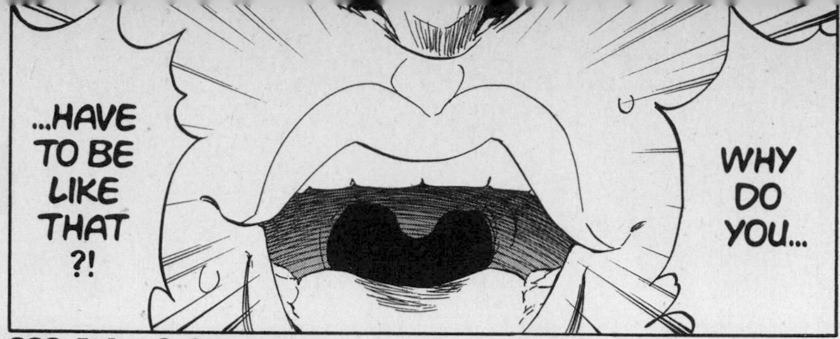
WHY DO YOU...
...HAVE TO BE LIKE THAT?!

333. Ash & Salamander

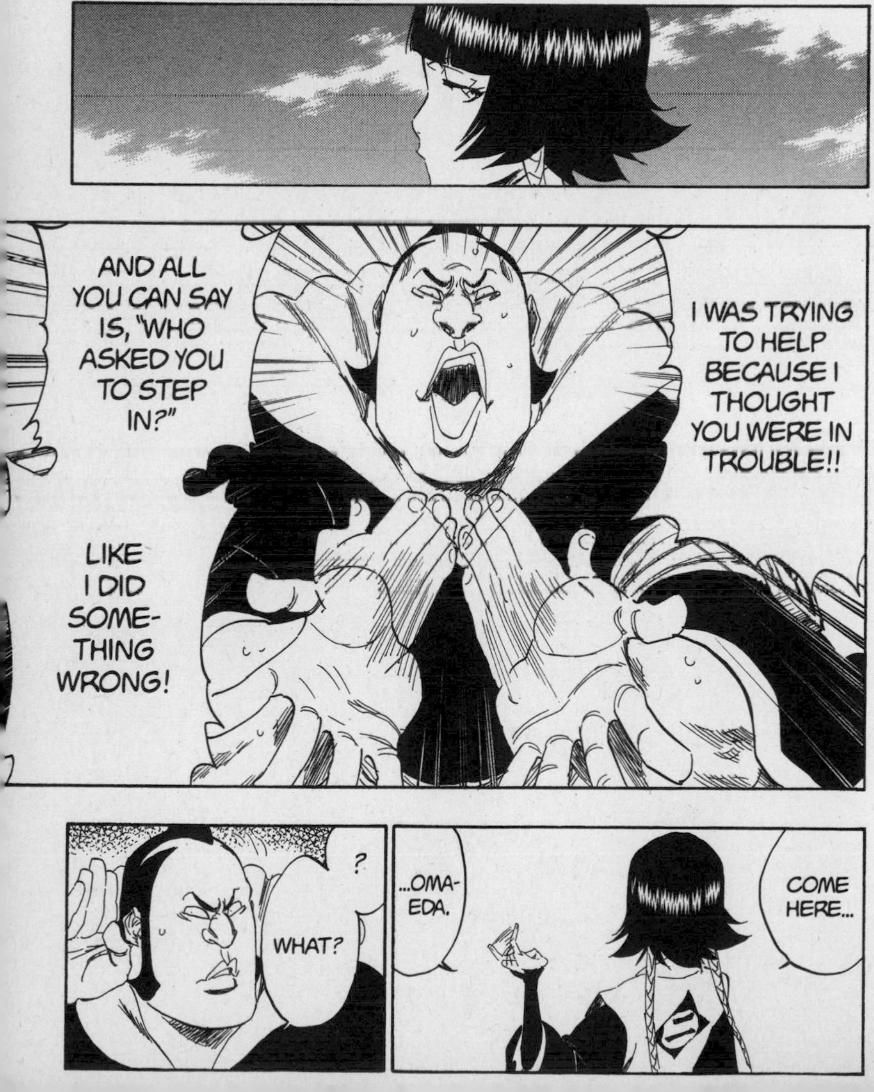
I WAS TRYING TO HELP BECAUSE I THOUGHT YOU WERE IN TROUBLE!!
AND ALL YOU CAN SAY IS, "WHO ASKED YOU TO STEP IN?"
LIKE I DID SOME-THING WRONG!
COME HERE...
...OMA-EDA.
?
WHAT?

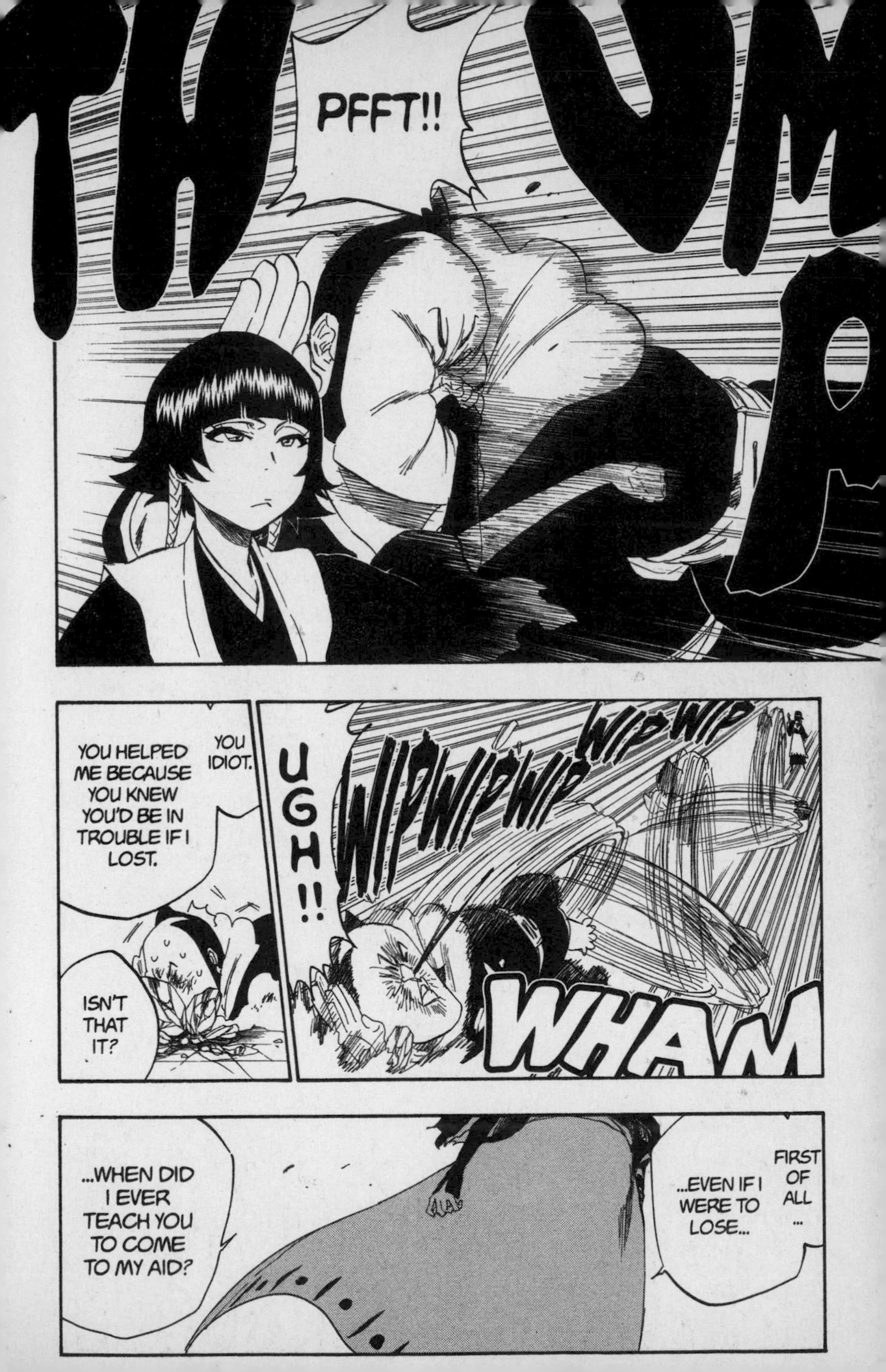
PFFT!!
WIPWIP
WIPWIPWIP
UGH!!
WHAM
YOU IDIOT.
YOU HELPED ME BECAUSE YOU KNEW YOU'D BE IN TROUBLE IF I LOST.
ISN'T THAT IT?
FIRST OF ALL ...
...EVEN IF I WERE TO LOSE...
...WHEN DID I EVER TEACH YOU TO COME TO MY AID?

READ THIS WAY

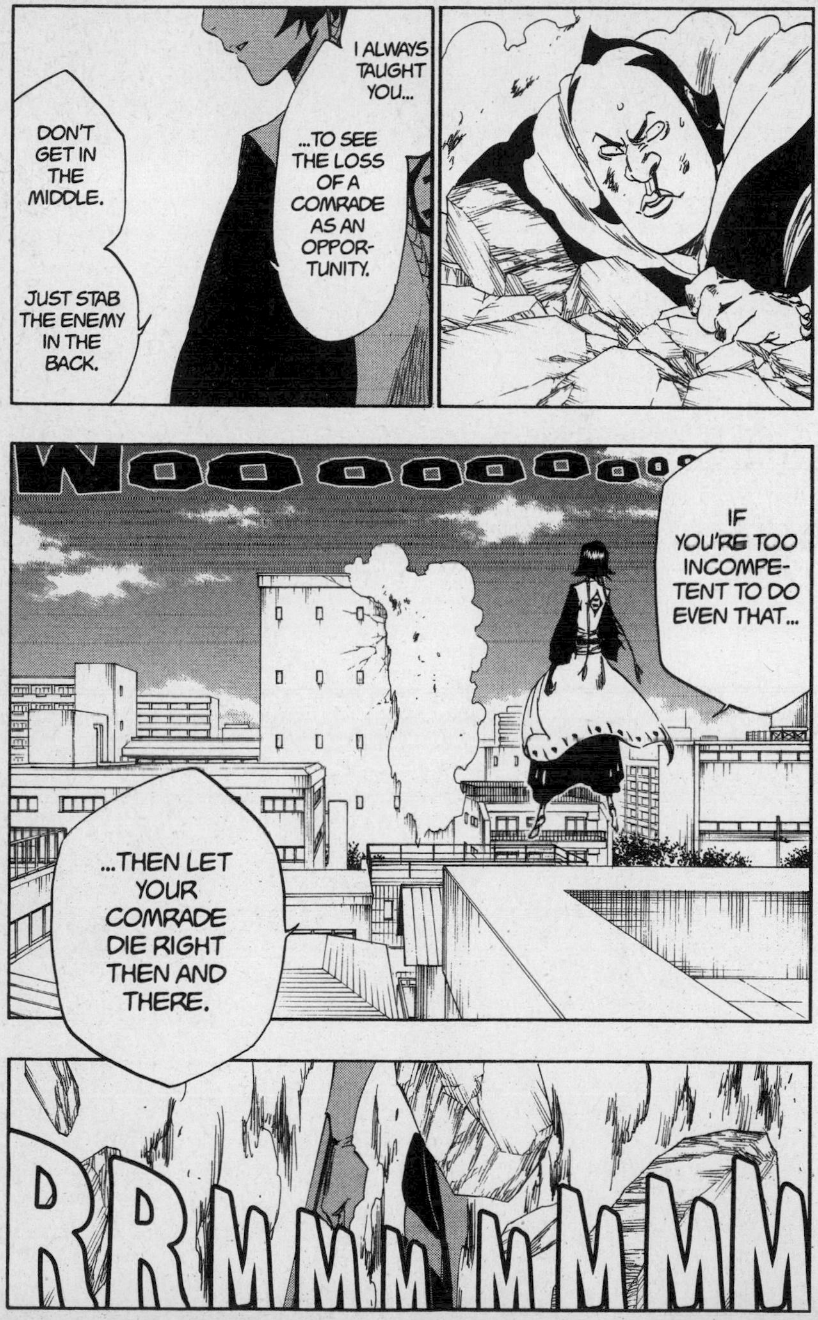
I ALWAYS TAUGHT YOU...
...TO SEE THE LOSS OF A COMRADE AS AN OPPOR-TUNITY.
DON'T GET IN THE MIDDLE.
JUST STAB THE ENEMY IN THE BACK.
WOOOOOOOO
IF YOU'RE TOO INCOMPE-TENT TO DO EVEN THAT...
...THEN LET YOUR COMRADE DIE RIGHT THEN AND THERE.
RRMMMMMMMMM

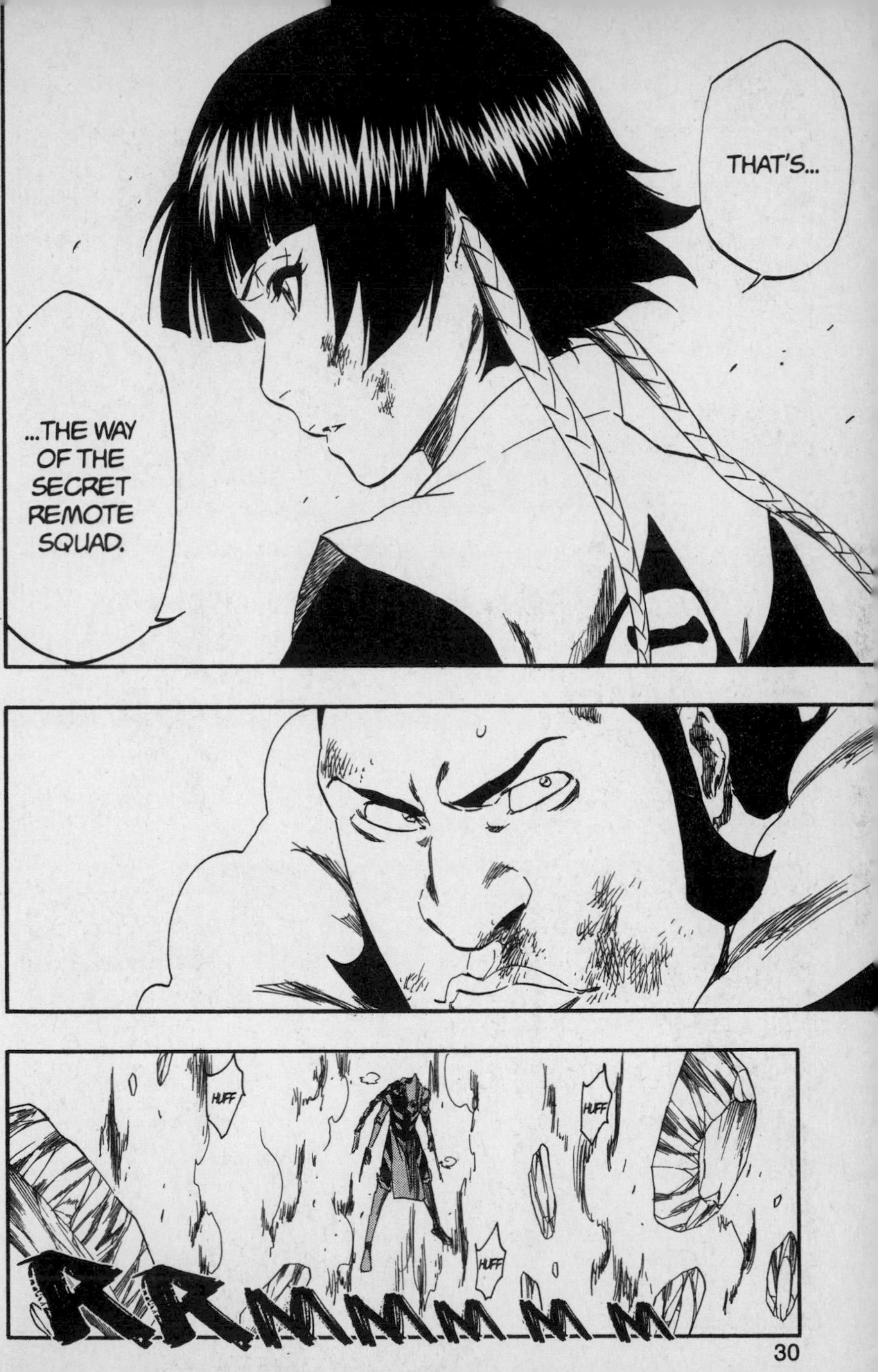
THAT'S...
...THE WAY OF THE SECRET REMOTE SQUAD.
HUFF
HUFF
HUFF
RRMMMMMM

READ THIS WAY

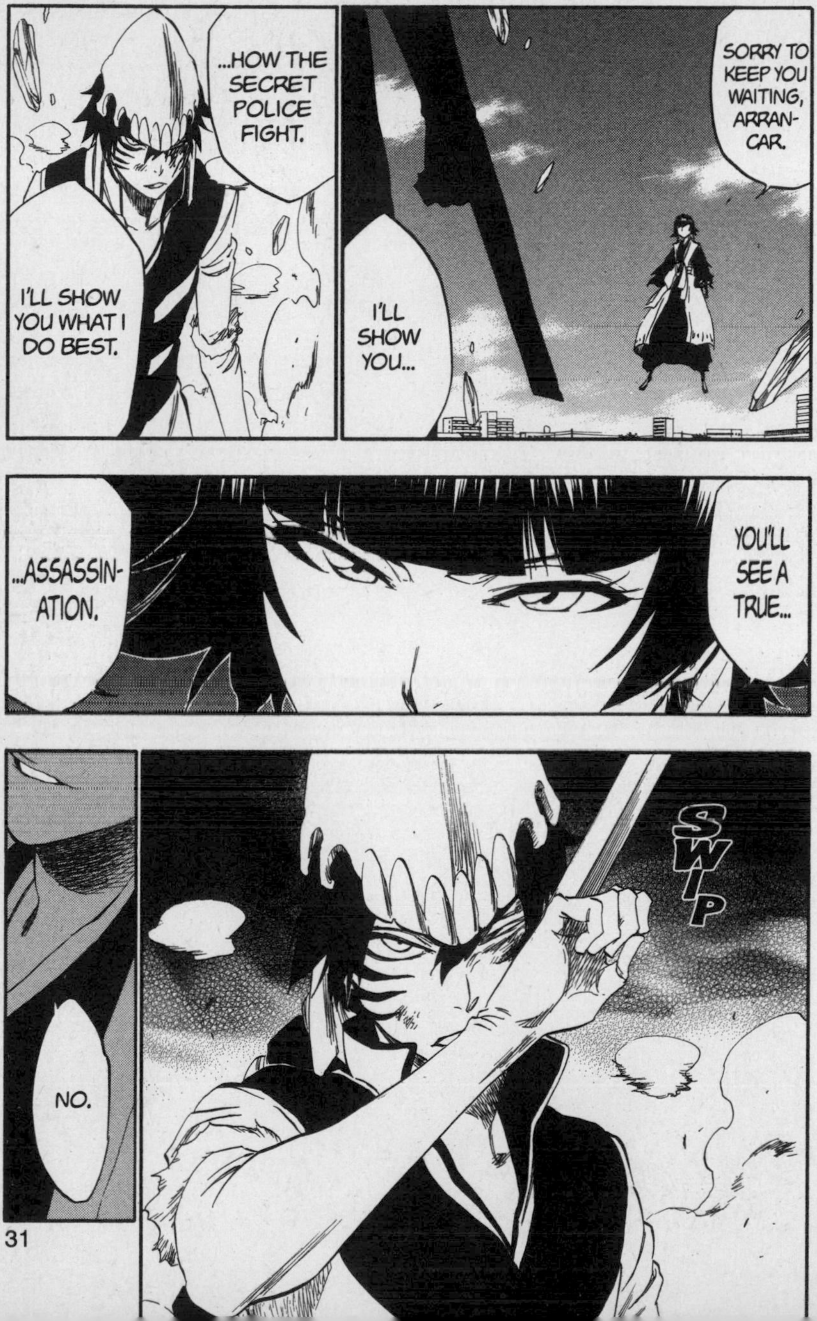

SORRY TO KEEP YOU WAITING, ARRAN-CAR.
I'LL SHOW YOU...
...HOW THE SECRET POLICE FIGHT.
I'LL SHOW YOU WHAT I DO BEST.
YOU'LL SEE A TRUE...
...ASSASSIN-ATION.
SWIP
NO.

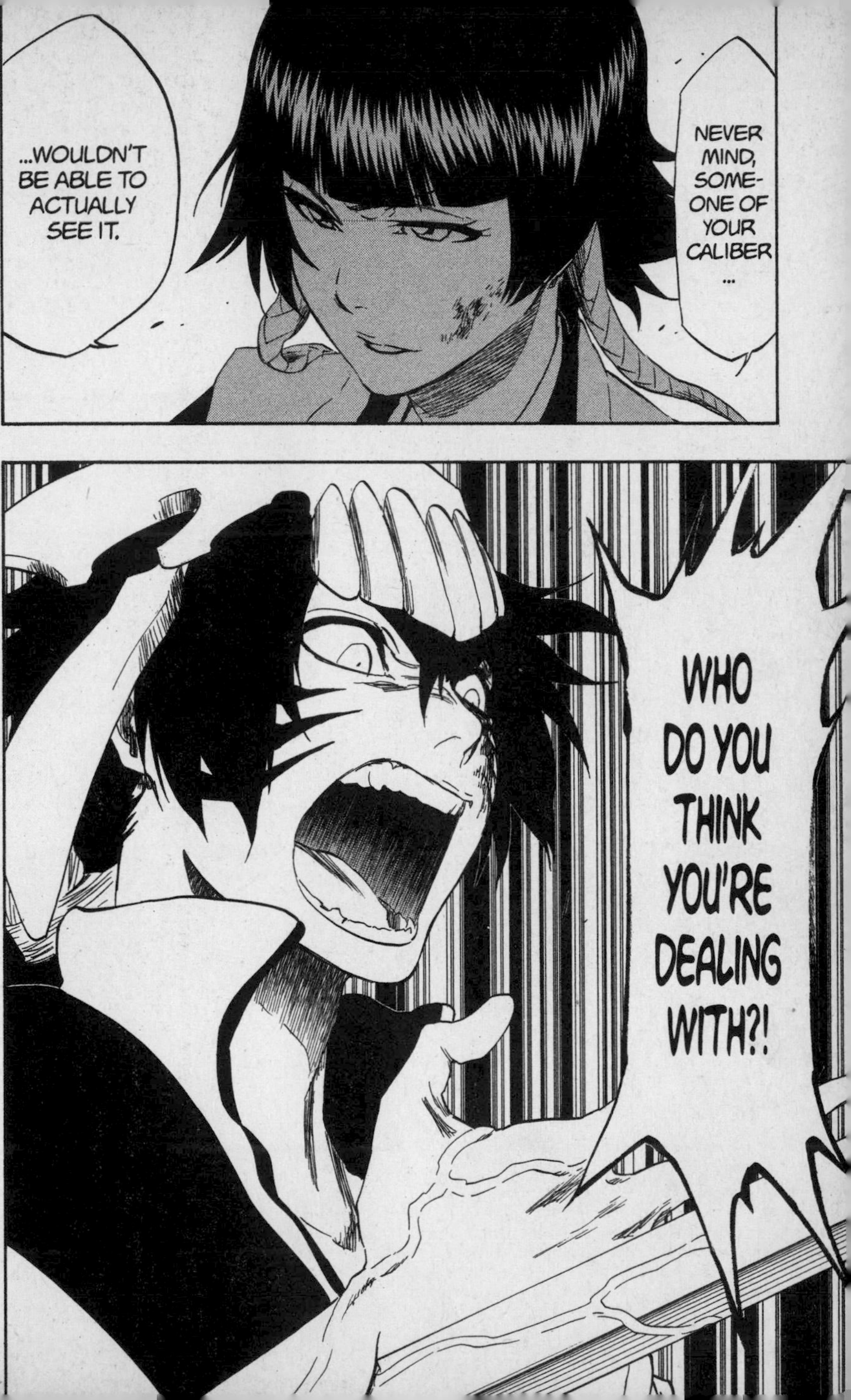
NEVER MIND, SOME-ONE OF YOUR CALIBER...
...WOULDN'T BE ABLE TO ACTUALLY SEE IT.
WHO DO YOU THINK YOU'RE DEALING WITH?!

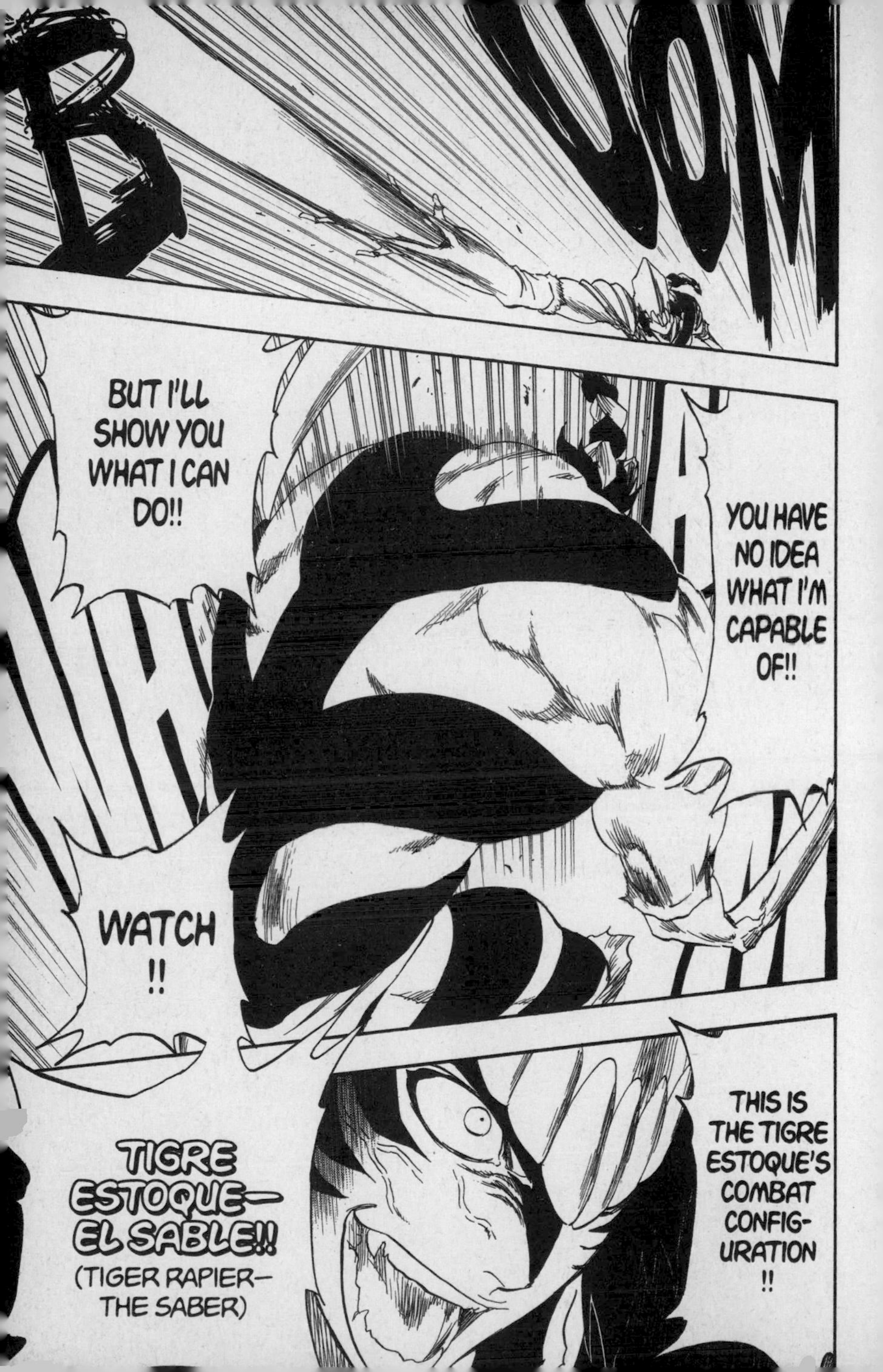
BWOM
YOU HAVE NO IDEA WHAT I'M CAPABLE OF!!
BUT I'LL SHOW YOU WHAT I CAN DO!!
WATCH !!
THIS IS THE TIGRE ESTOQUE'S COMBAT CONFIG-URATION !!
TIGRE ESTOQUE— EL SABLE!!
(TIGER RAPIER— THE SABER)

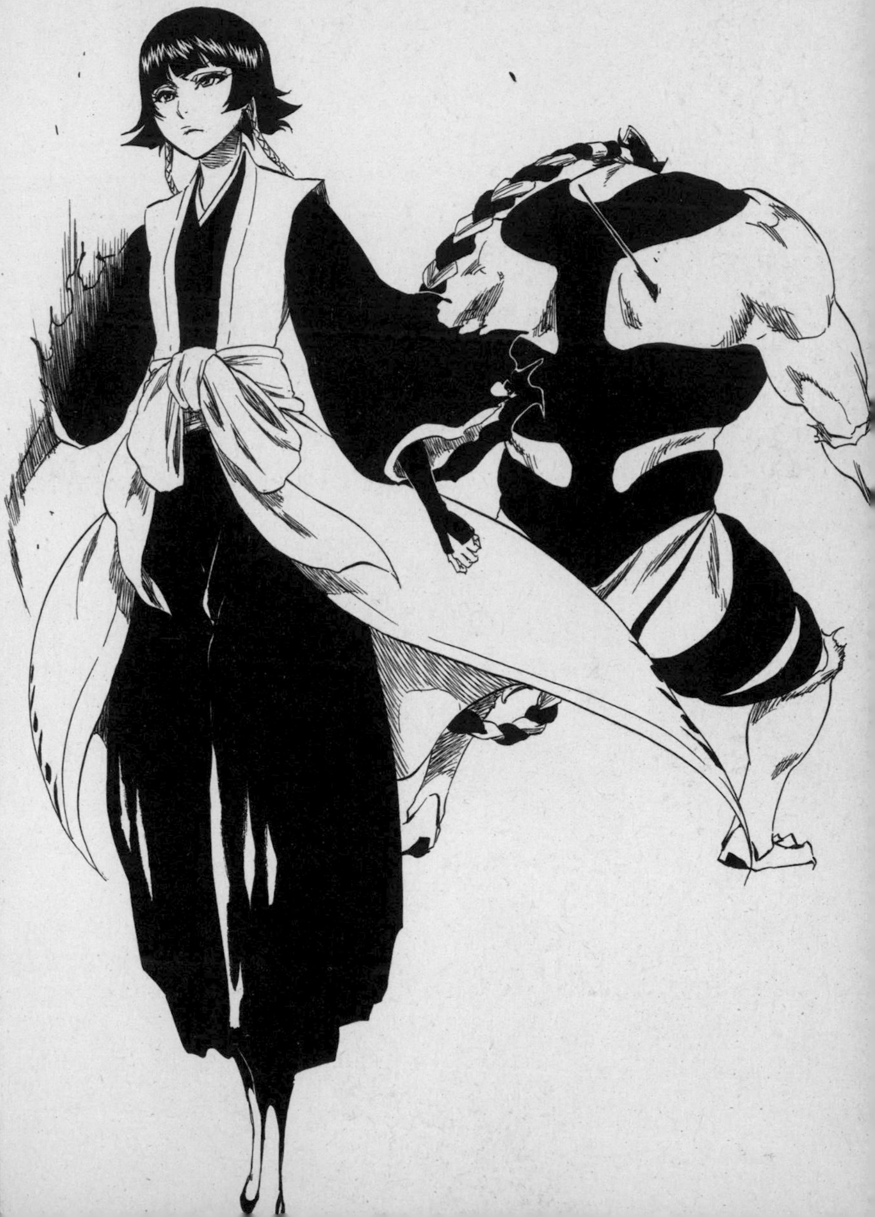

I'M SORRY.

I DID SAY IT WOULD ONLY TAKE TWO STRIKES ...

...ONLY ONE.

BUT IT MAY HAVE FELT LIKE...

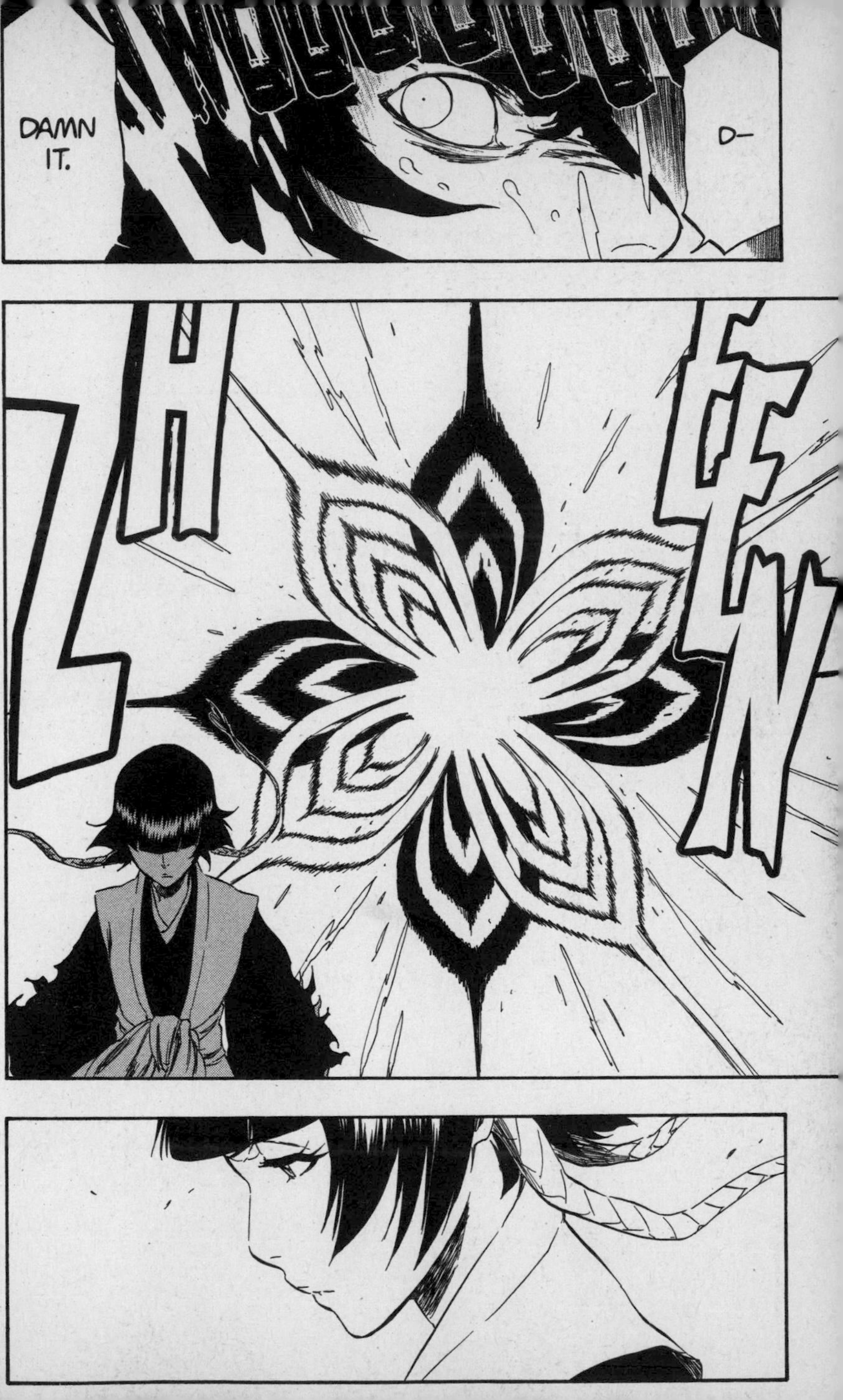
D—
DAMN IT.
ZHEEN

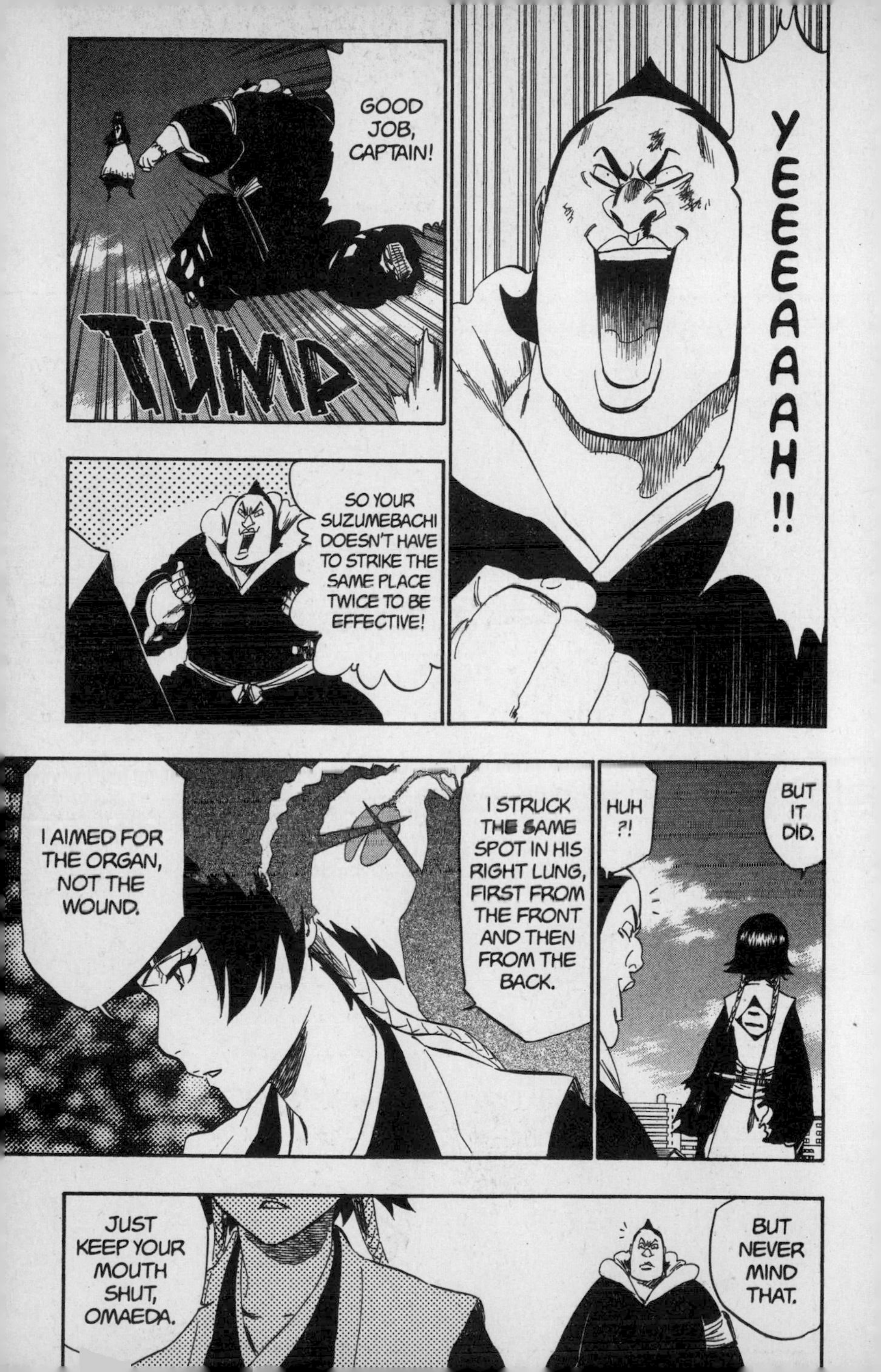
YEEEAAAH!!
GOOD JOB, CAPTAIN!
TUMP
SO YOUR SUZUMEBACHI DOESN'T HAVE TO STRIKE THE SAME PLACE TWICE TO BE EFFECTIVE!
BUT IT DID.
HUH ?!
I STRUCK THE SAME SPOT IN HIS RIGHT LUNG, FIRST FROM THE FRONT AND THEN FROM THE BACK.
I AIMED FOR THE ORGAN, NOT THE WOUND.
BUT NEVER MIND THAT.
JUST KEEP YOUR MOUTH SHUT, OMAEDA.

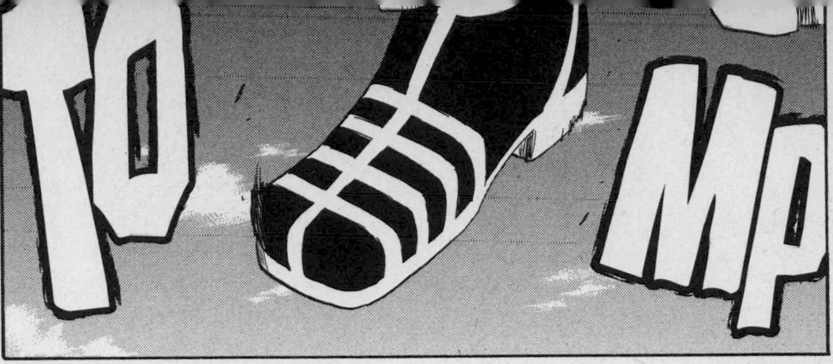
TOMP

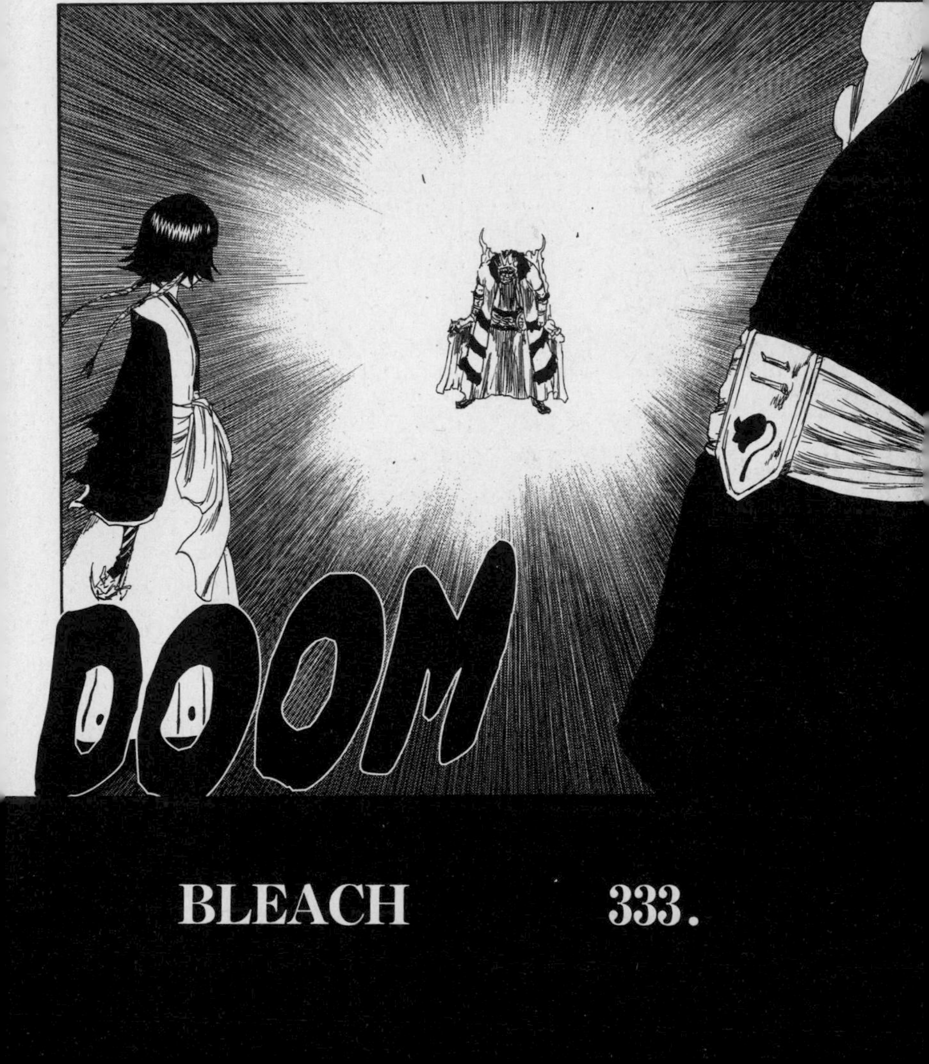
DOOM

BLEACH 333.

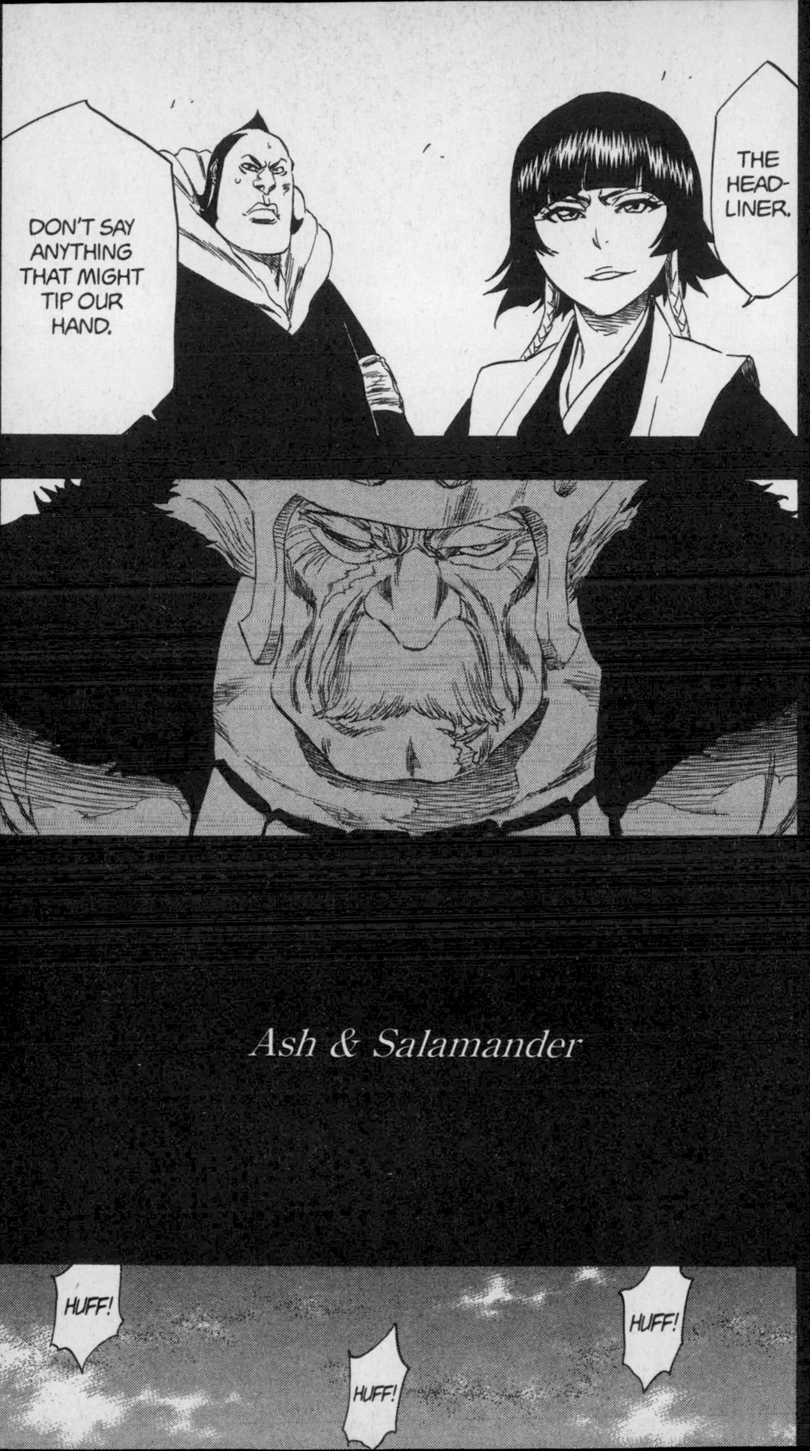
THE HEAD-LINER.
DON'T SAY ANYTHING THAT MIGHT TIP OUR HAND.
Ash & Salamander
HUFF!
HUFF!
HUFF!

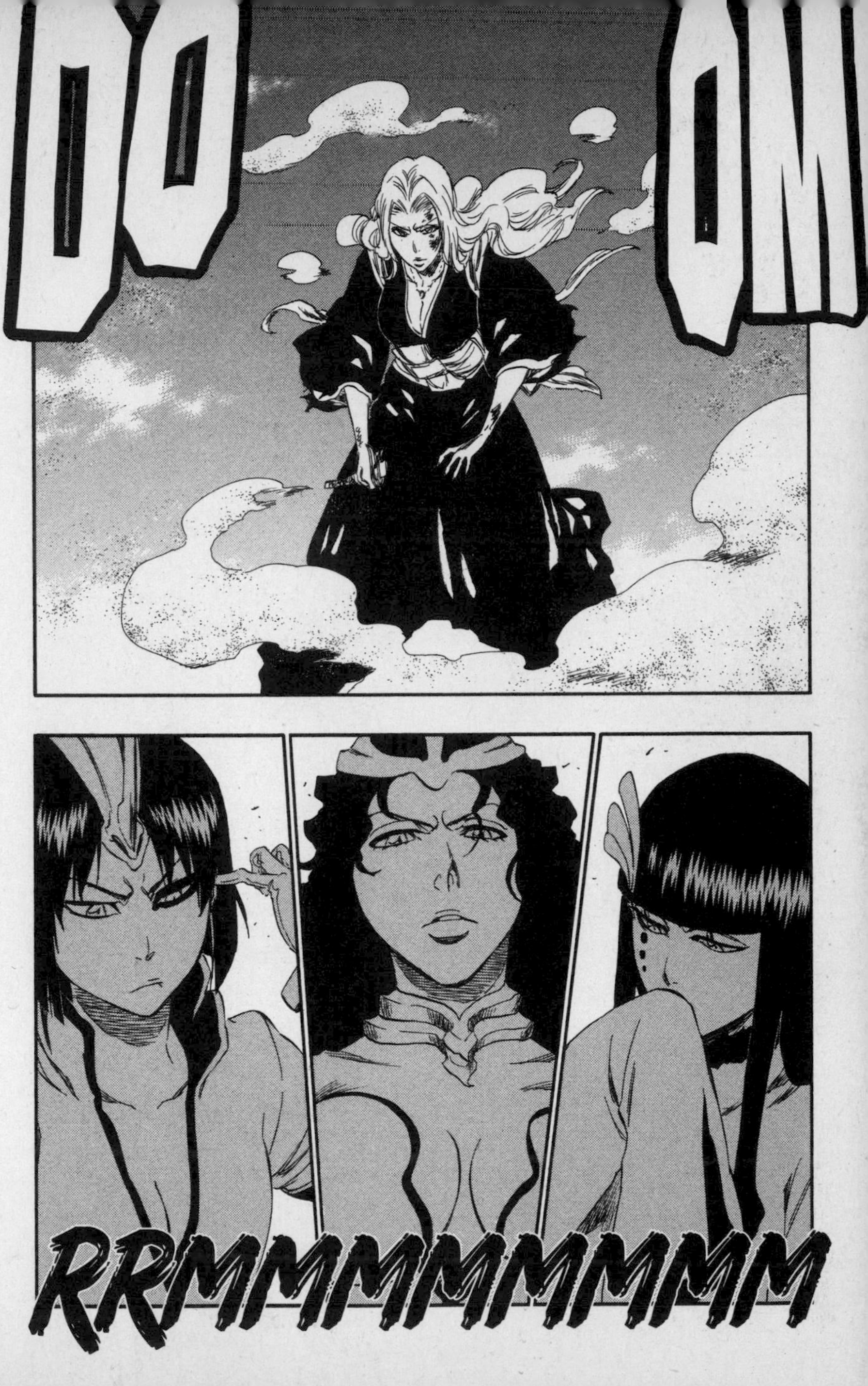
DOOM
RRMMMMMMMM

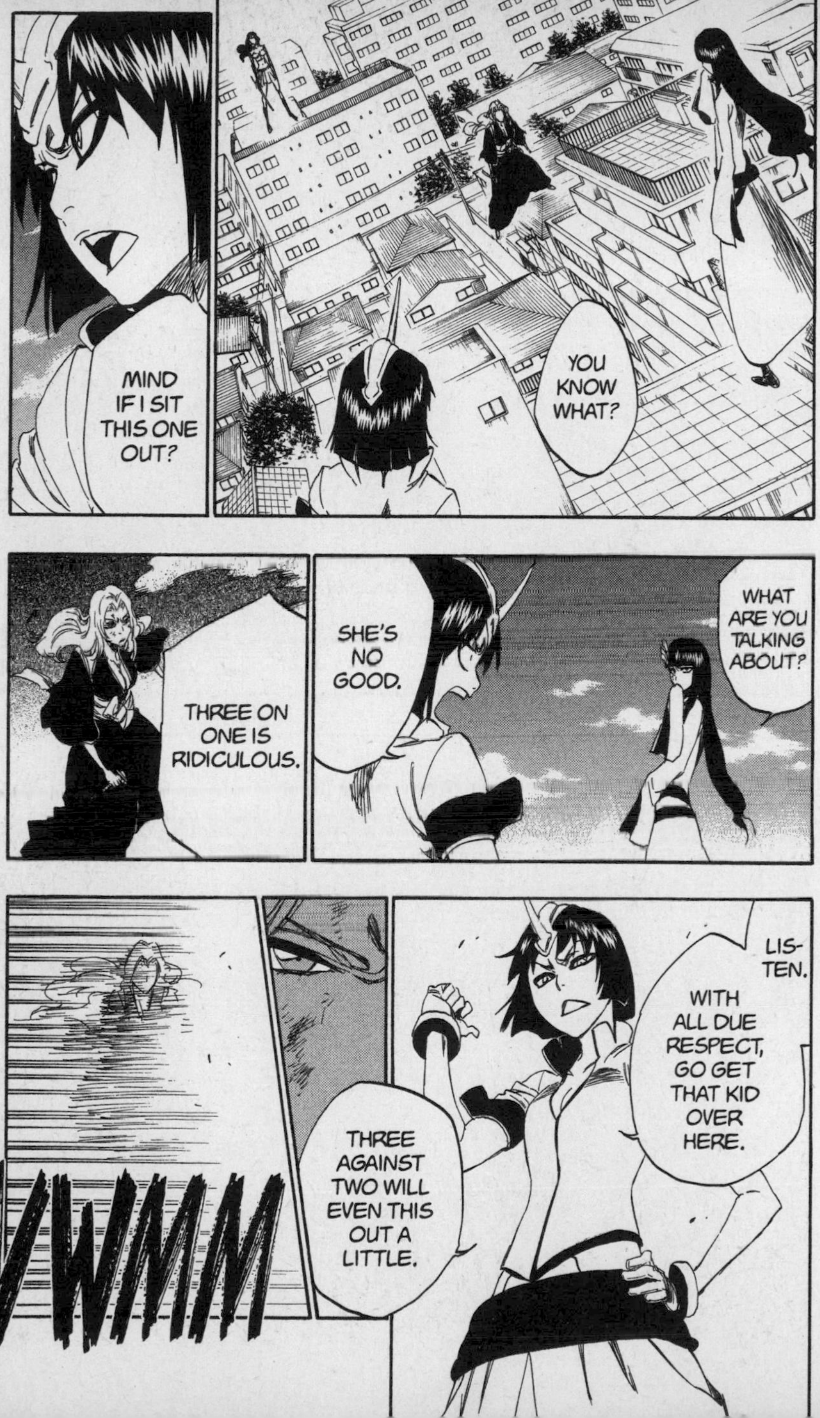
YOU KNOW WHAT?
MIND IF I SIT THIS ONE OUT?
WHAT ARE YOU TALKING ABOUT?
SHE'S NO GOOD.
THREE ON ONE IS RIDICULOUS.
LIS-TEN.
WITH ALL DUE RESPECT, GO GET THAT KID OVER HERE.
THREE AGAINST TWO WILL EVEN THIS OUT A LITTLE.
VWMM

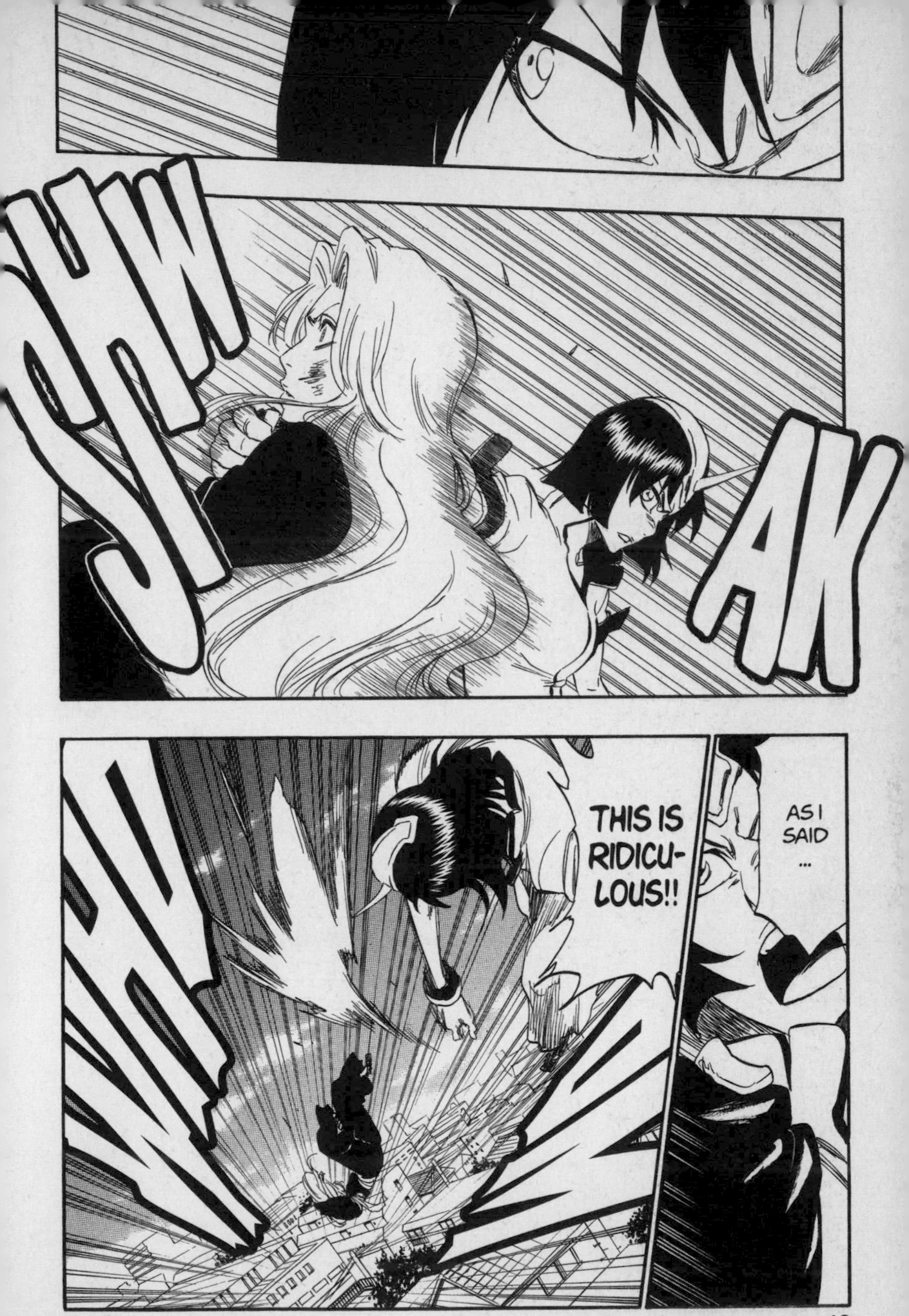
SHW
AK
AS I SAID ...
THIS IS RIDICU-LOUS!!

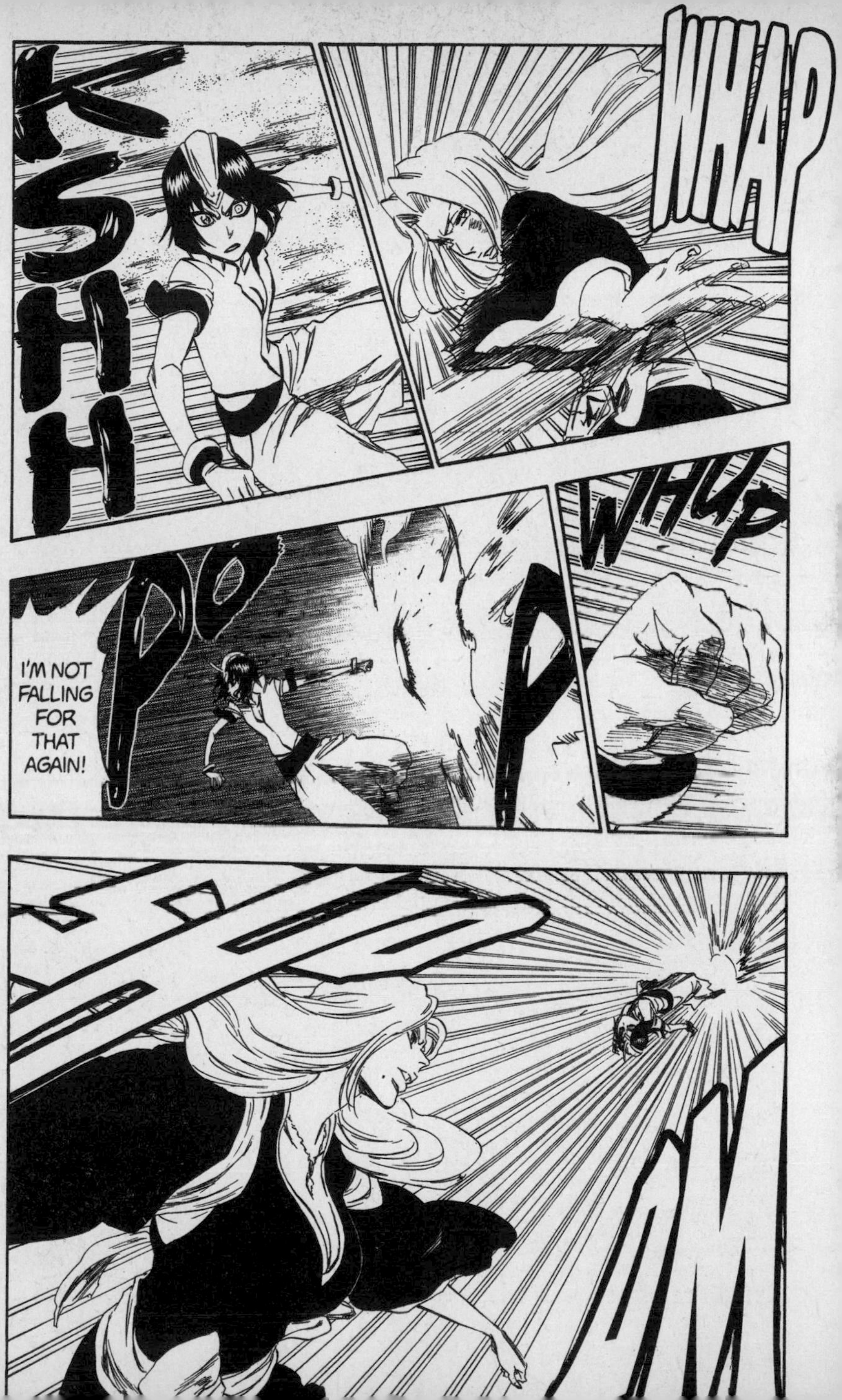
WHAP
KSHH
WHUP
DOP
I'M NOT FALLING FOR THAT AGAIN!

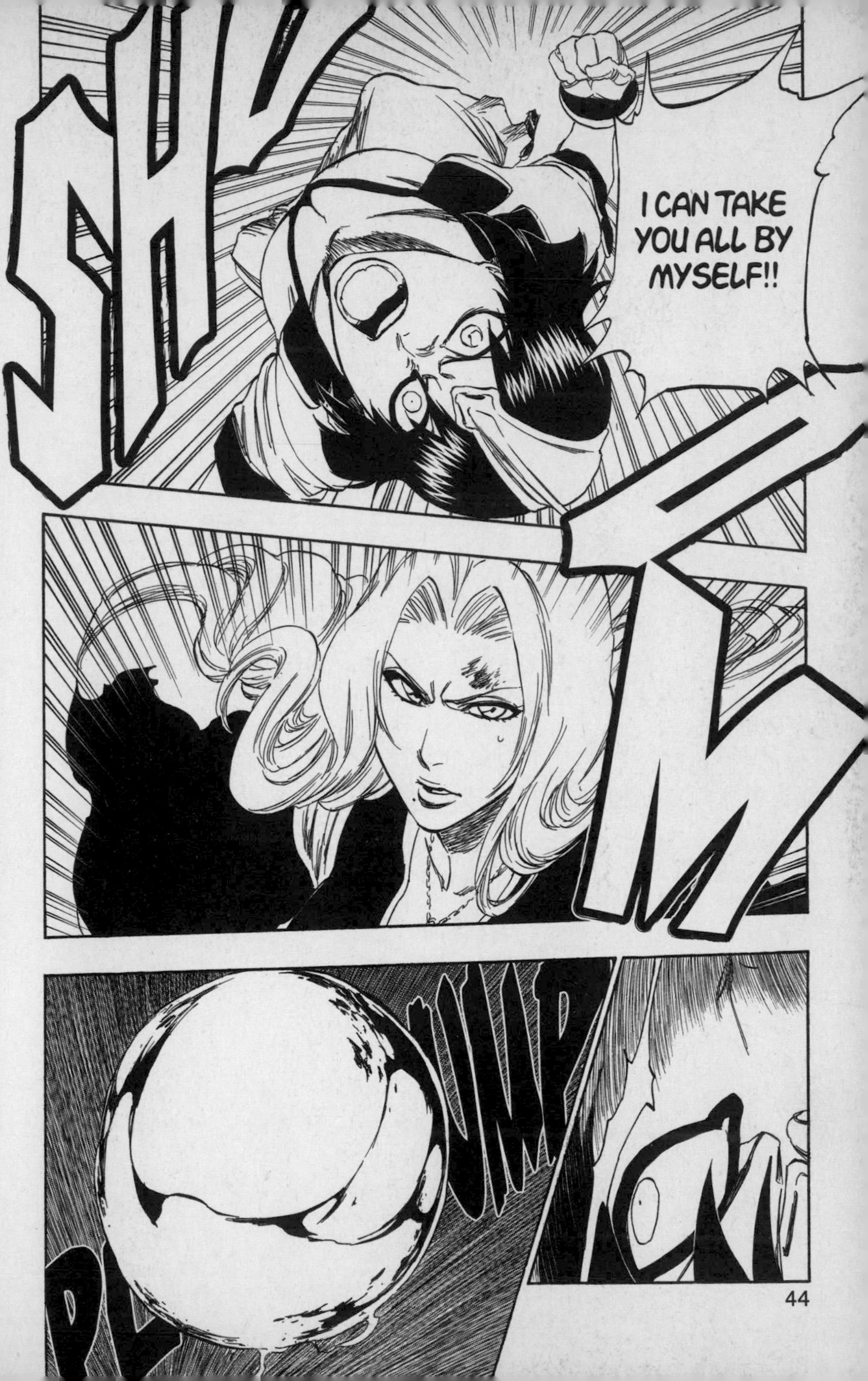
I CAN TAKE YOU ALL BY MYSELF!!

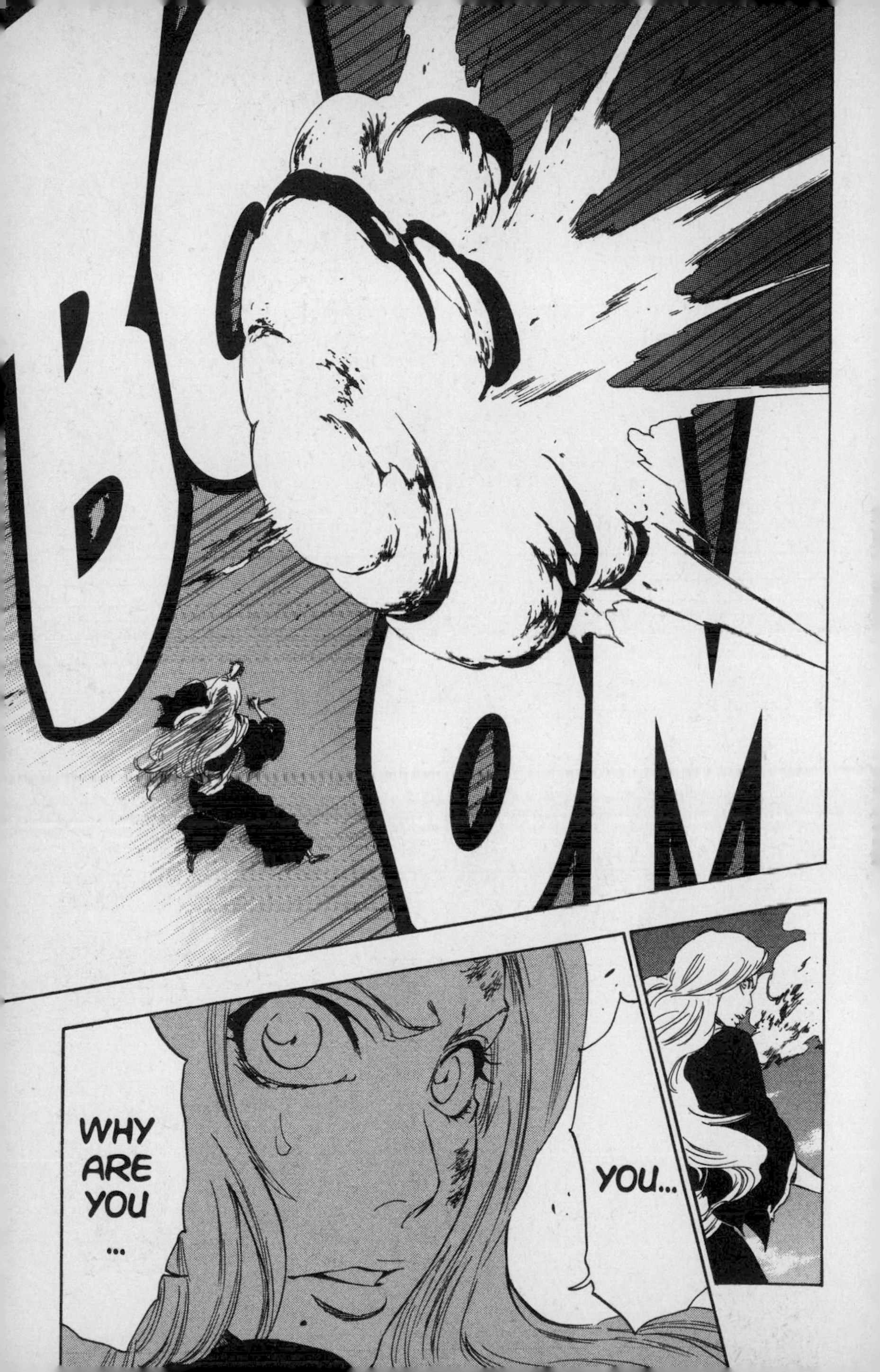
BOOM
YOU...
WHY ARE YOU
...

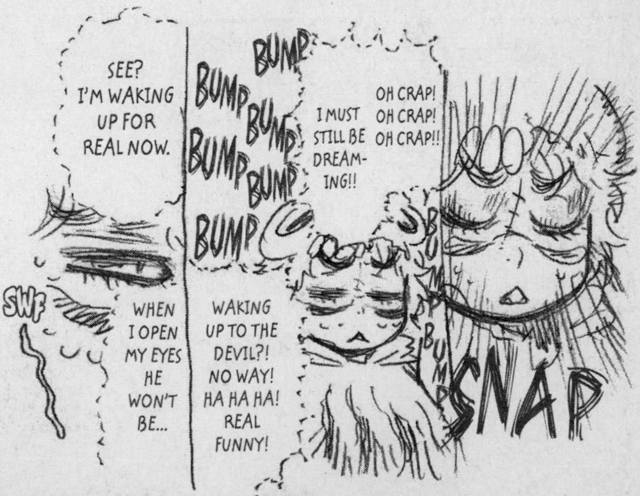
SNAP
BUMP BUMP
OH CRAP! OH CRAP! OH CRAP!!
I MUST STILL BE DREAM-ING!!
BUMP BUMP BUMP BUMP BUMP BUMP
WAKING UP TO THE DEVIL?! NO WAY! HA HA HA! REAL FUNNY!
SEE? I'M WAKING UP FOR REAL NOW.
WHEN I OPEN MY EYES HE WON'T BE...
SWF

334. Dregs of Hypnosis

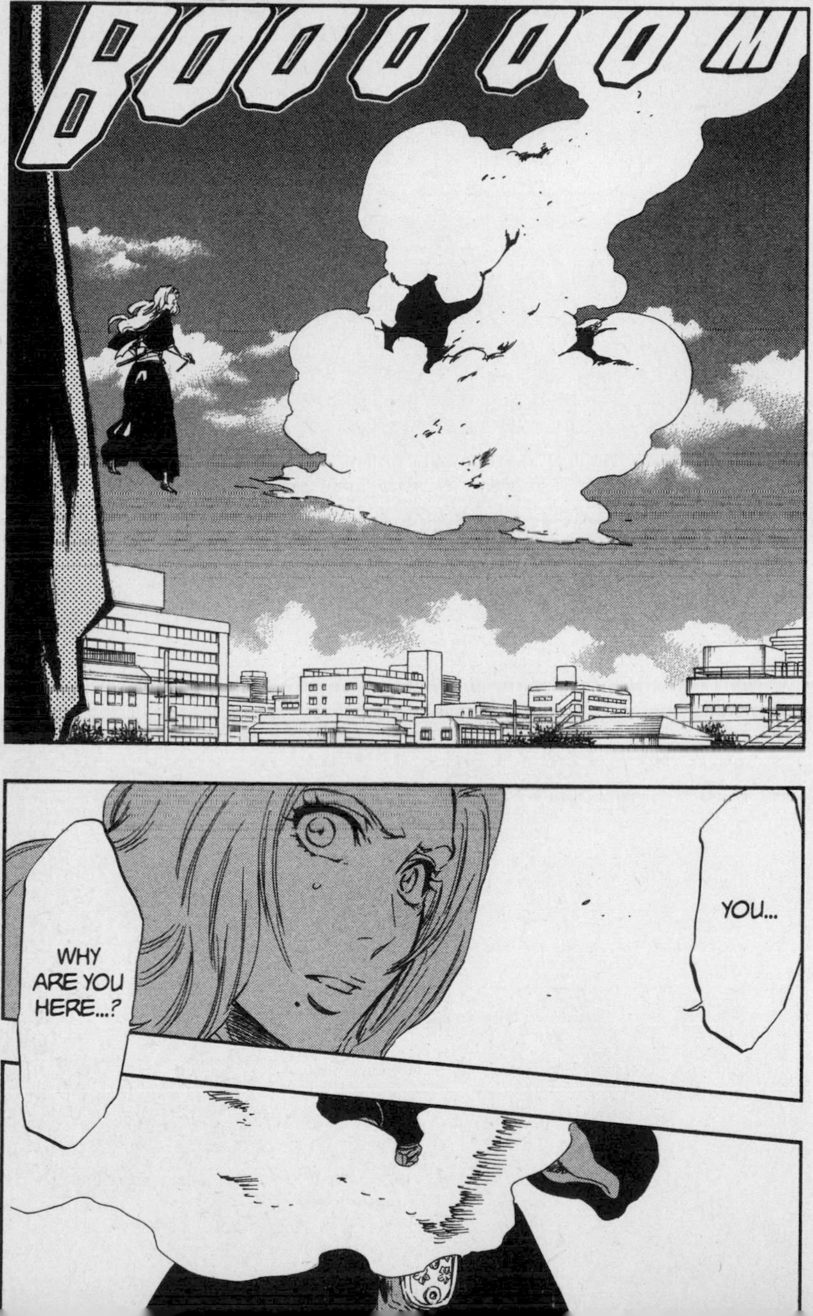
BOOOOOM
YOU...
WHY ARE YOU HERE...?

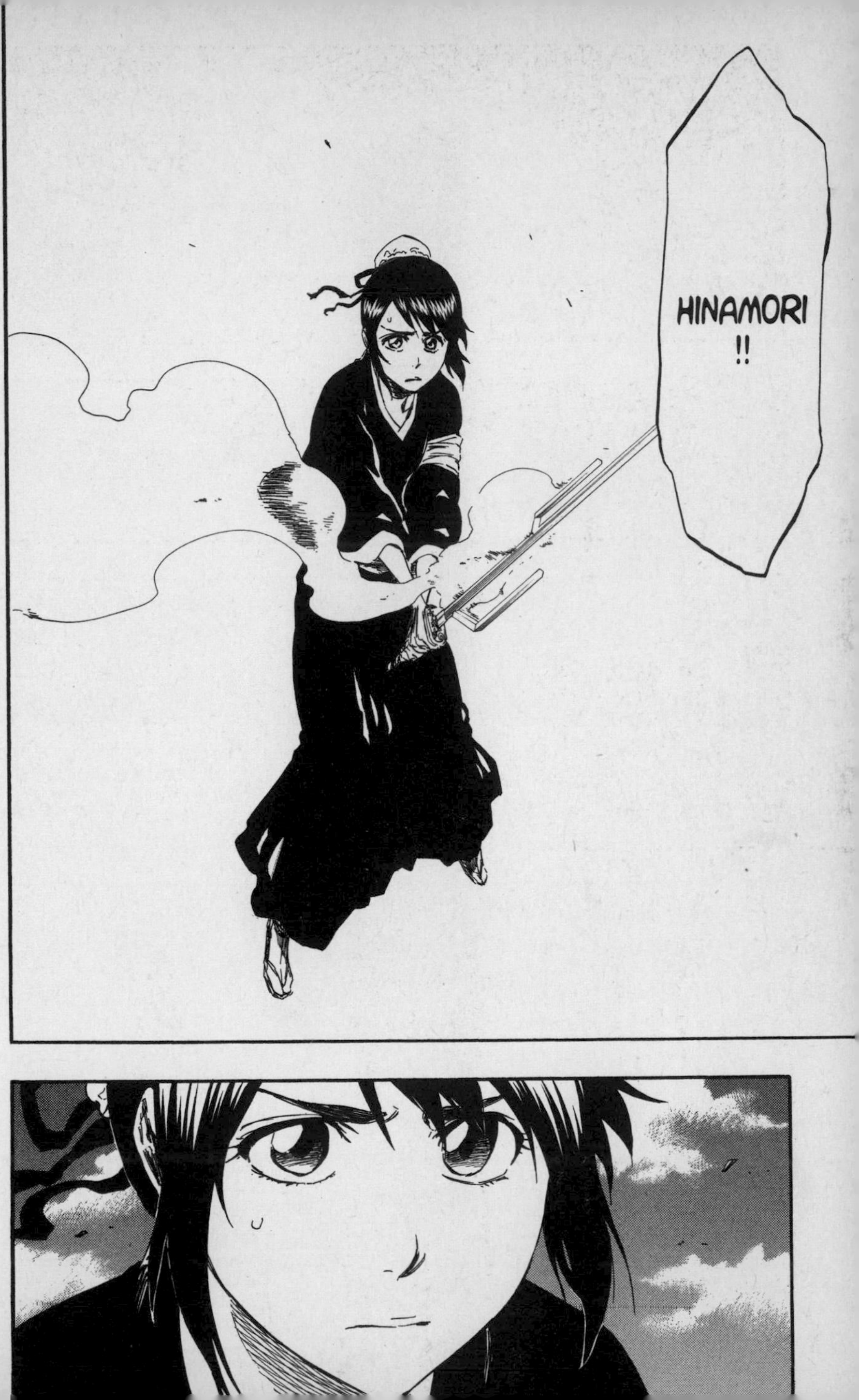
HINAMORI !!

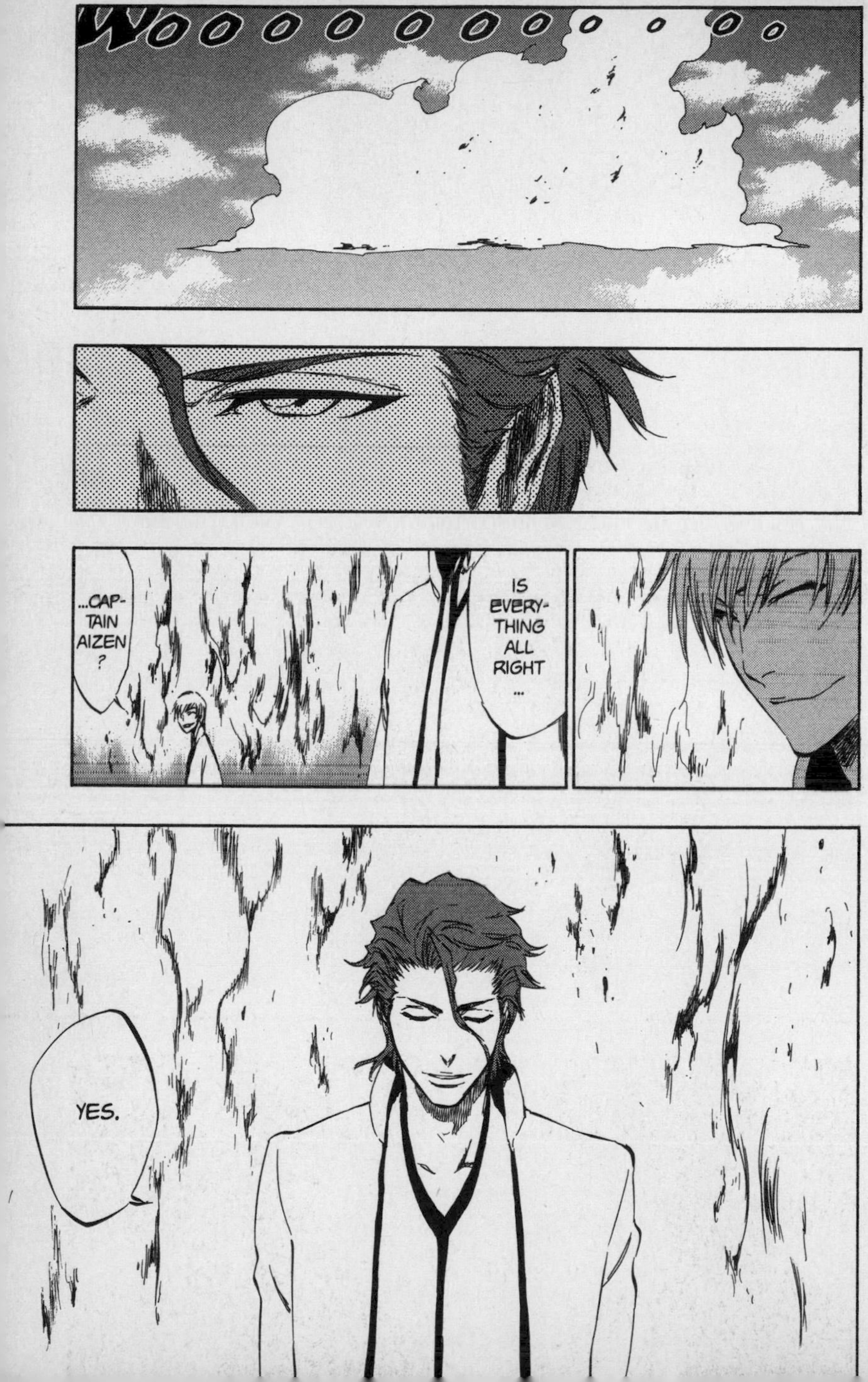
WOOOOOOOOOOO
IS EVERY-THING ALL RIGHT ...
...CAP-TAIN AIZEN ?
YES.

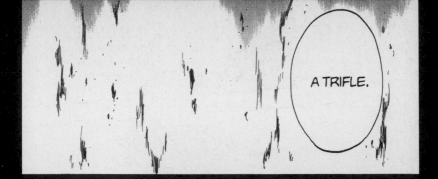

A TRIFLE.

IT'S OF LITTLE
IMPORTANCE.

BLEACH334.

Dregs of Hypnosis

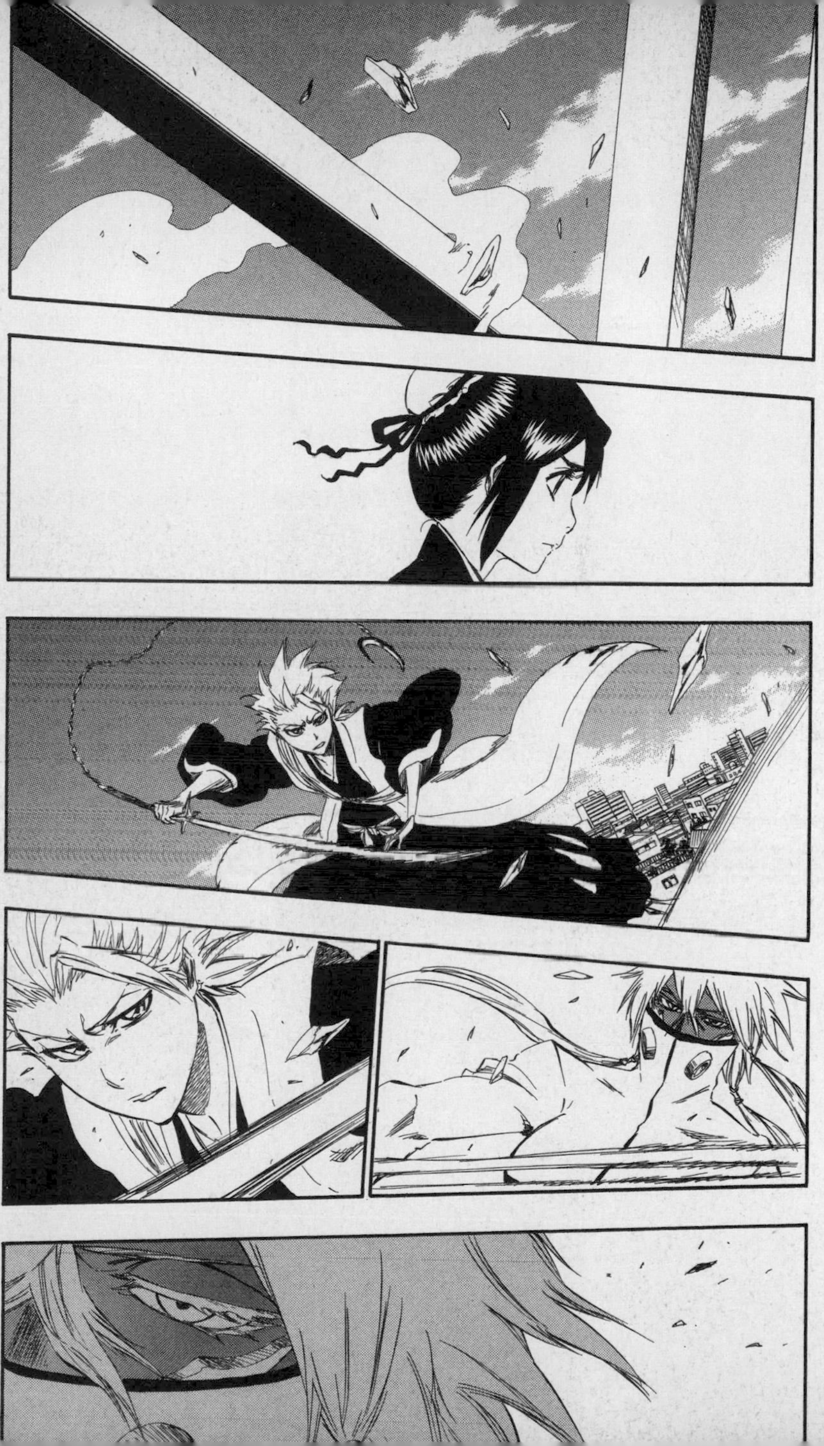

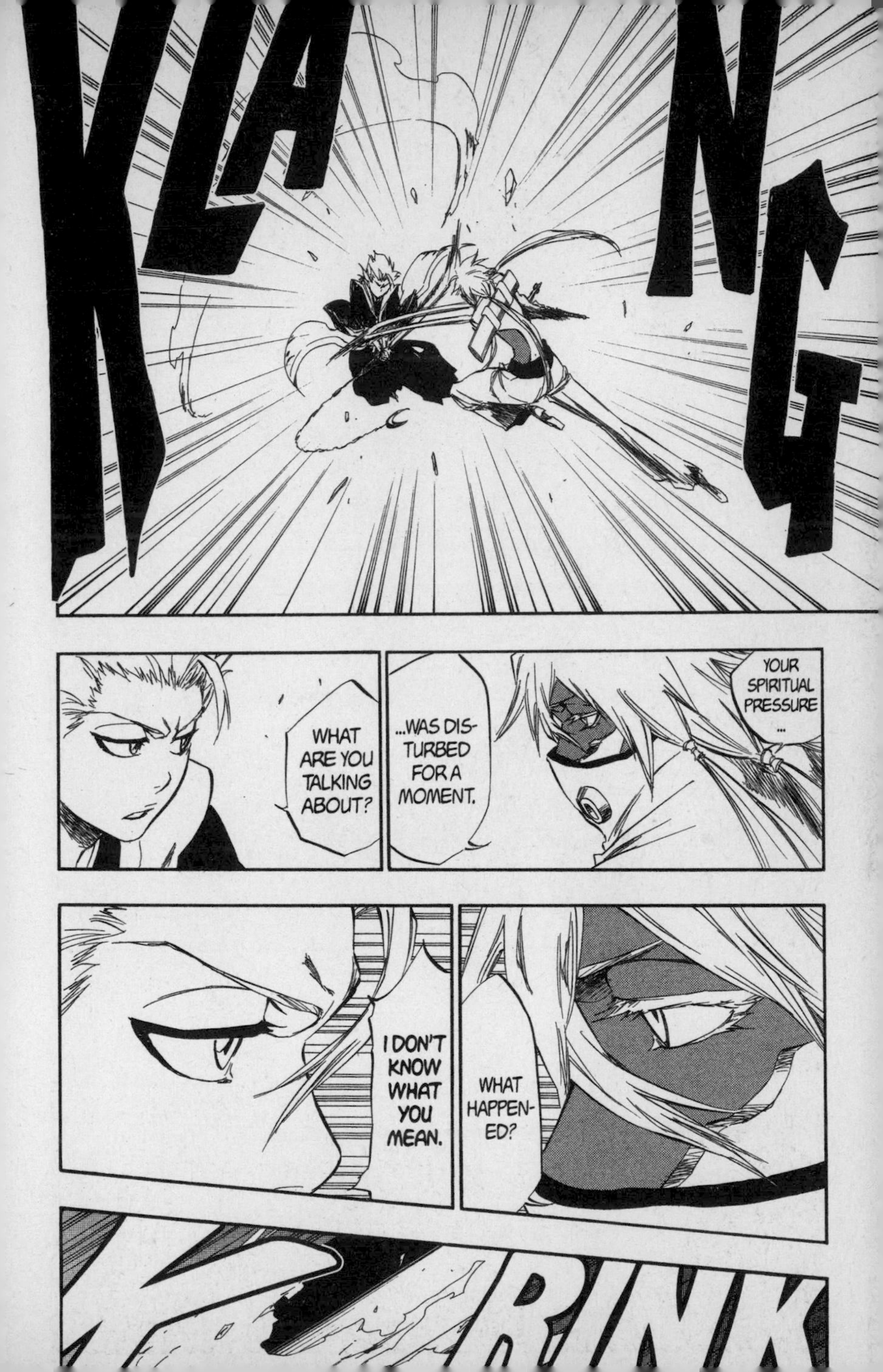
KLANG
YOUR SPIRITUAL PRESSURE ...
...WAS DISTURBED FOR A MOMENT.
WHAT ARE YOU TALKING ABOUT?
WHAT HAPPENED?
I DON'T KNOW WHAT YOU MEAN.
RINK

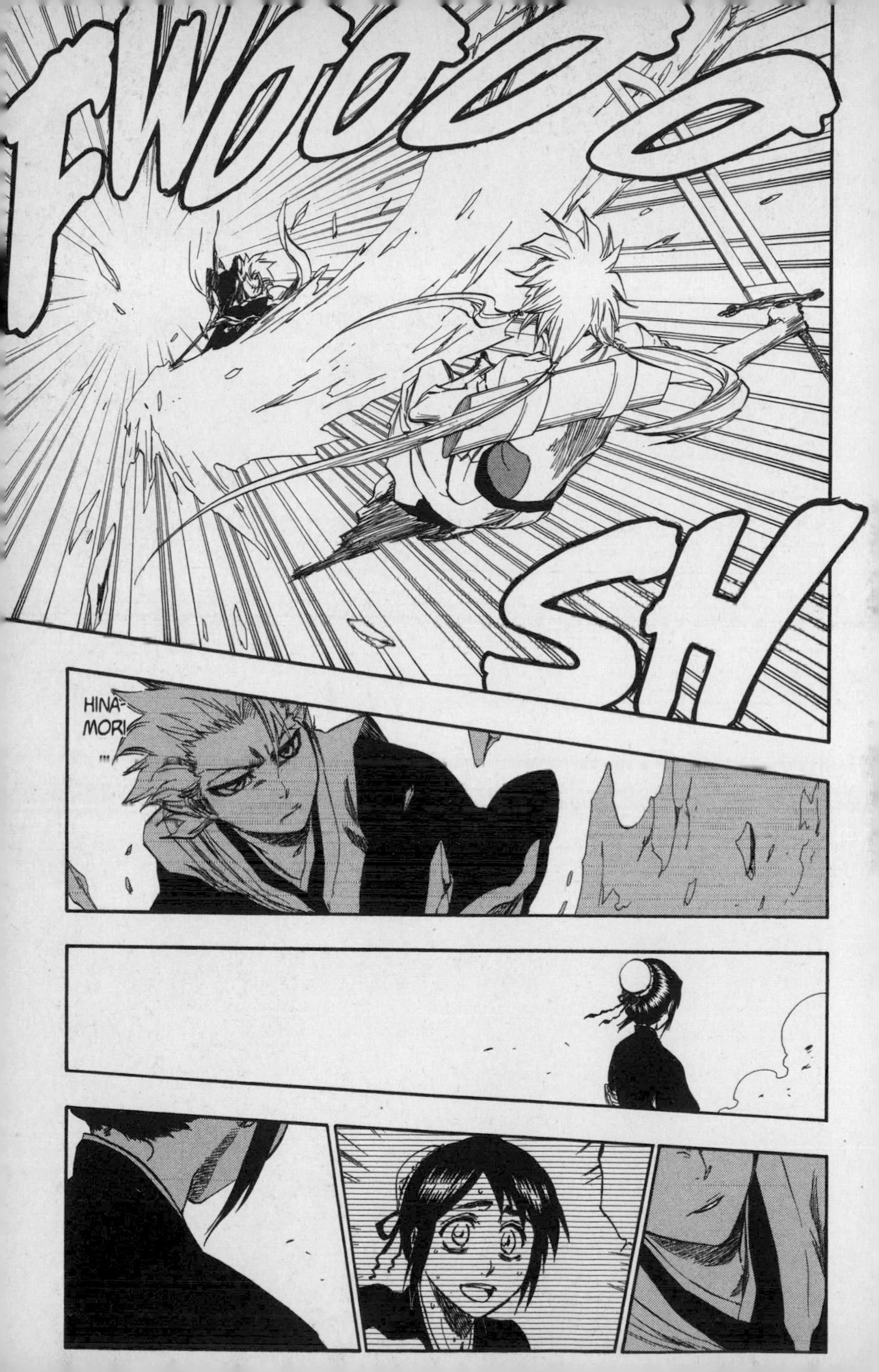
FWOOSH
HINA-
MORI
...

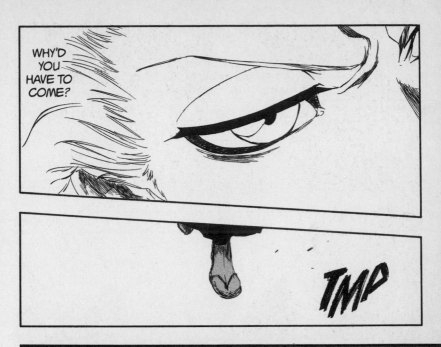

WHY'D YOU HAVE TO COME?

TMP

HINAMORI...

READ THIS WAY

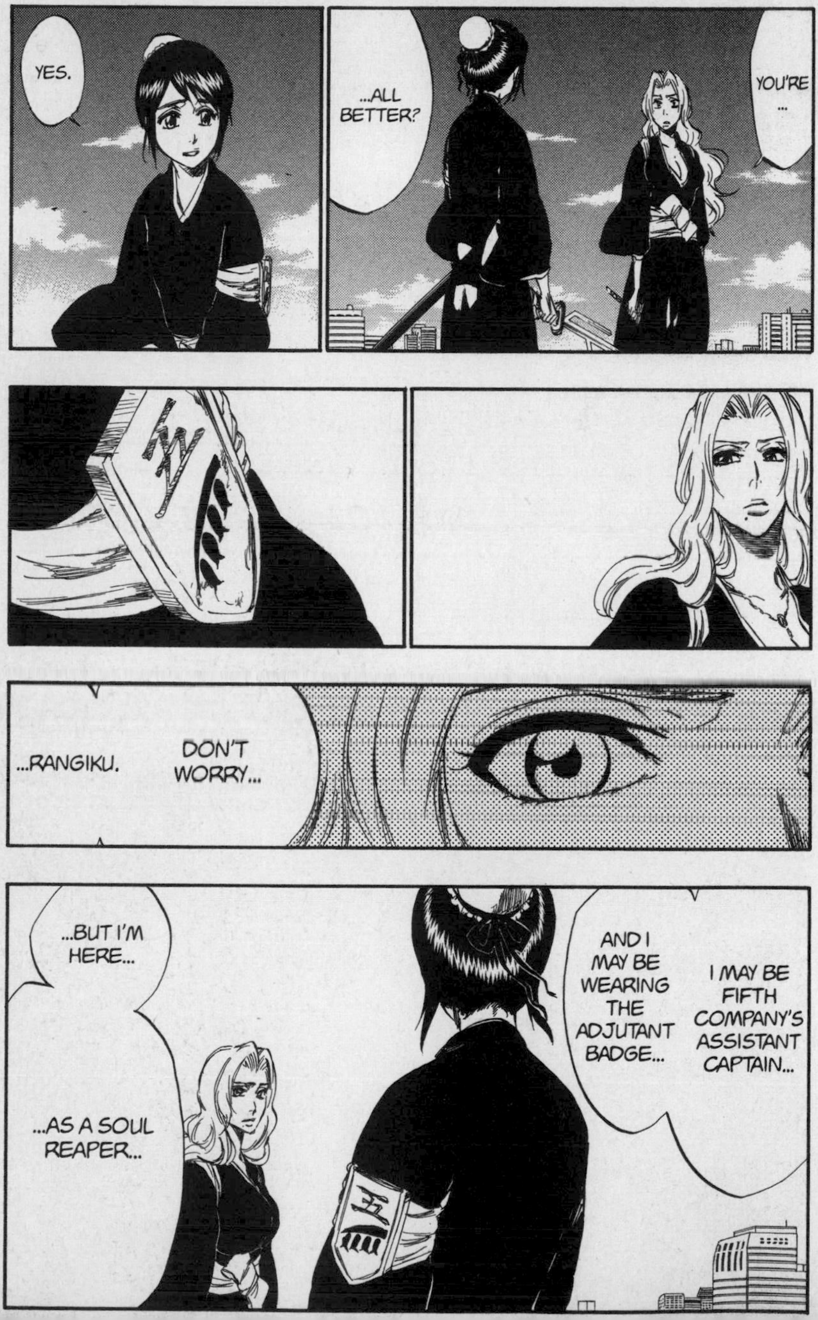
YOU'RE ...
...ALL BETTER?
YES.
DON'T WORRY...
...RANGIKU.
I MAY BE FIFTH COMPANY'S ASSISTANT CAPTAIN...
AND I MAY BE WEARING THE ADJUTANT BADGE...
...BUT I'M HERE...
...AS A SOUL REAPER...

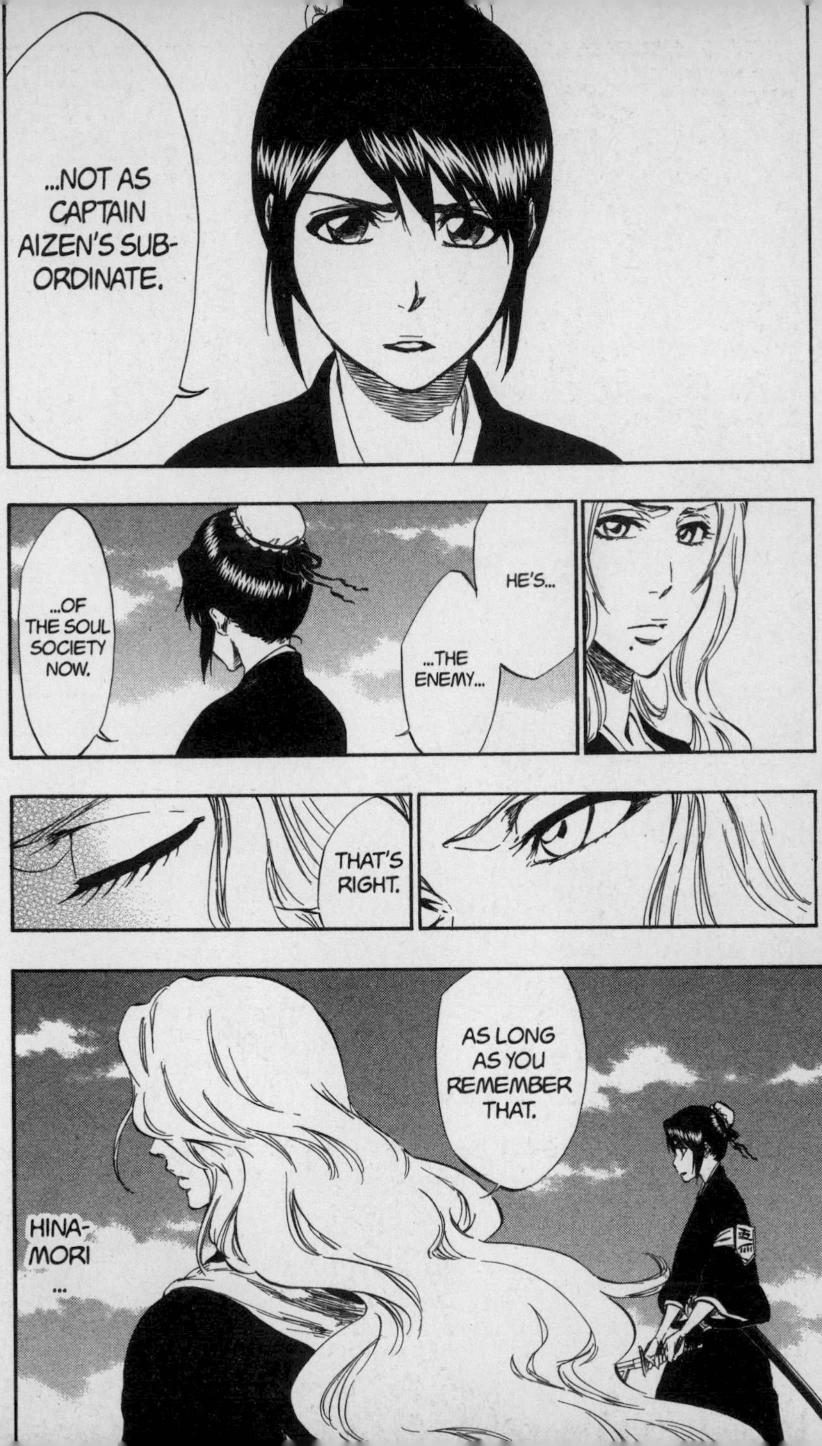
...NOT AS CAPTAIN AIZEN'S SUB-ORDINATE.
HE'S...
...THE ENEMY...
...OF THE SOUL SOCIETY NOW.
THAT'S RIGHT.
AS LONG AS YOU REMEMBER THAT.
HINA-MORI ...

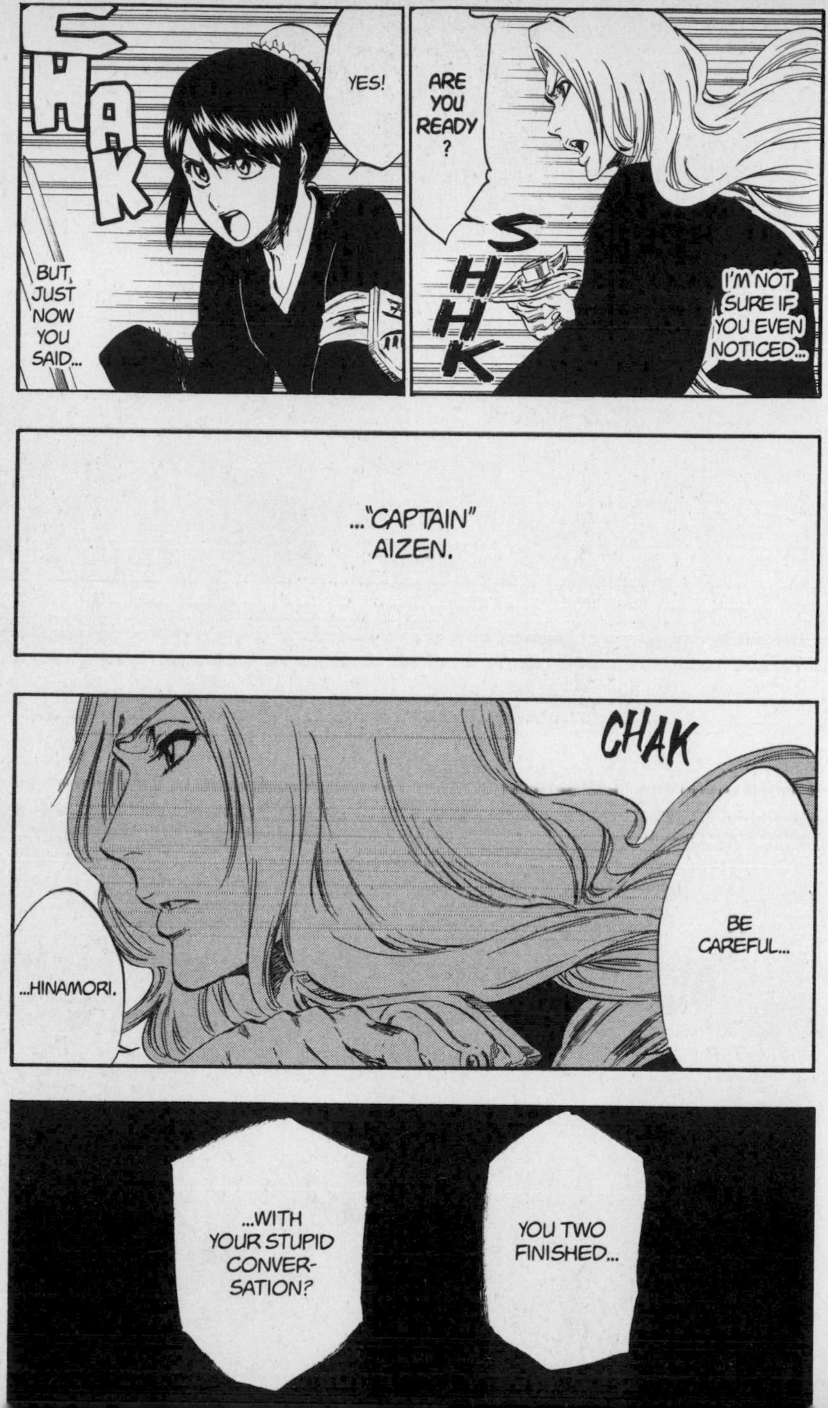
ARE YOU READY?
SHHK
I'M NOT SURE IF YOU EVEN NOTICED...
YES!
CHAK
BUT, JUST NOW YOU SAID...
..."CAPTAIN" AIZEN.
CHAK
BE CAREFUL...
...HINAMORI.
YOU TWO FINISHED...
...WITH YOUR STUPID CONVER-SATION?

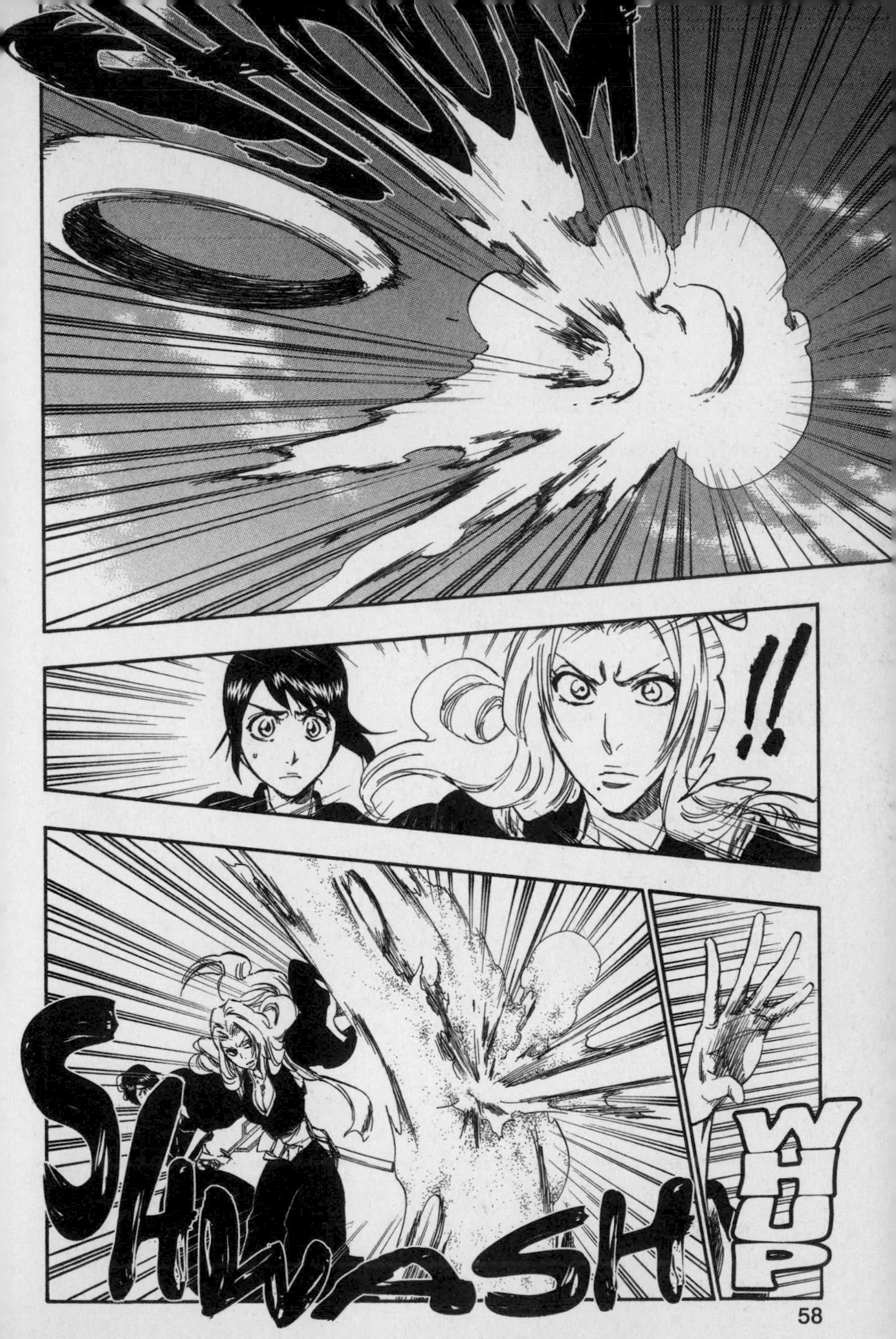
SHOOM
!!
WHUP
SHWASH

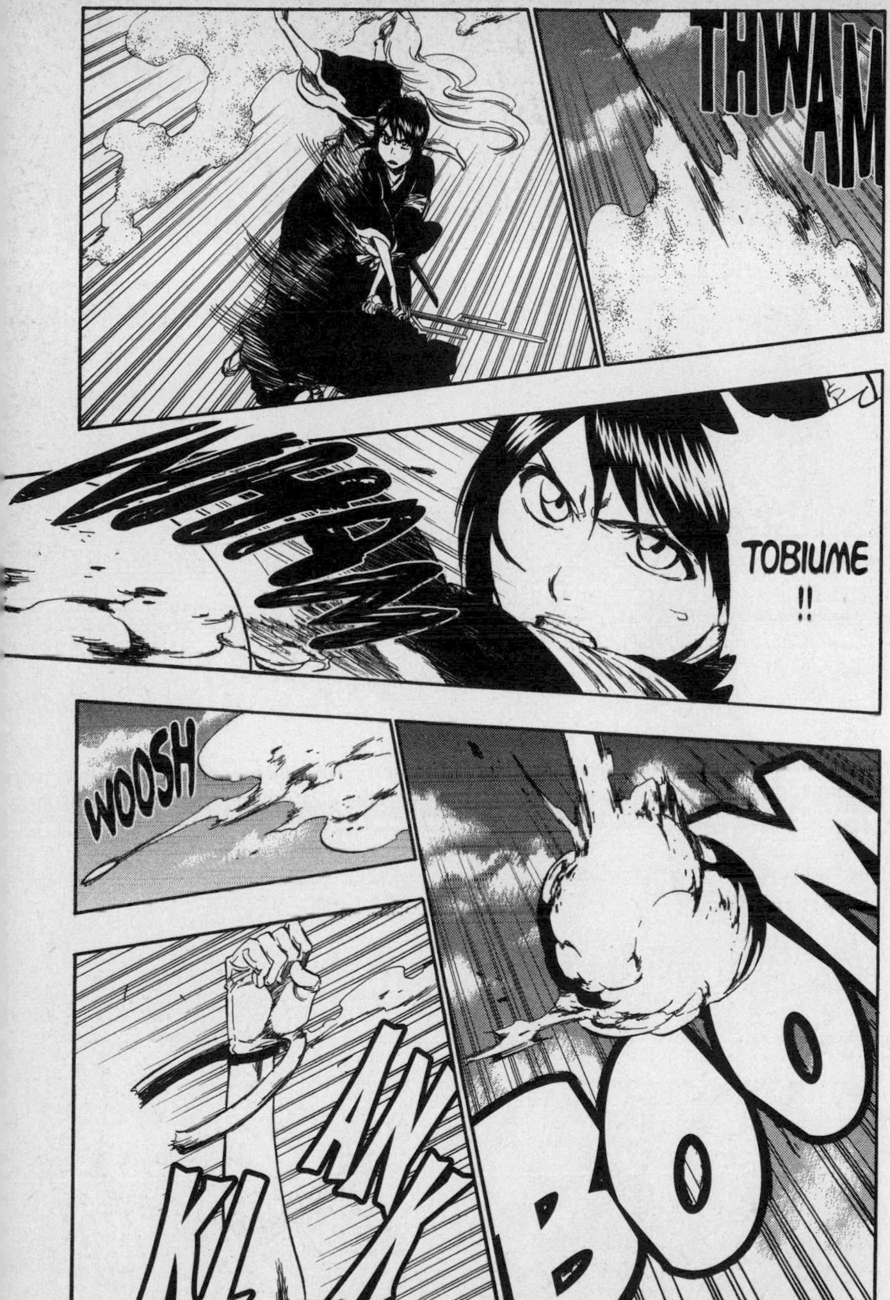
THWAM
TOBIUME !!
BOOM
WOOSH
KLANK

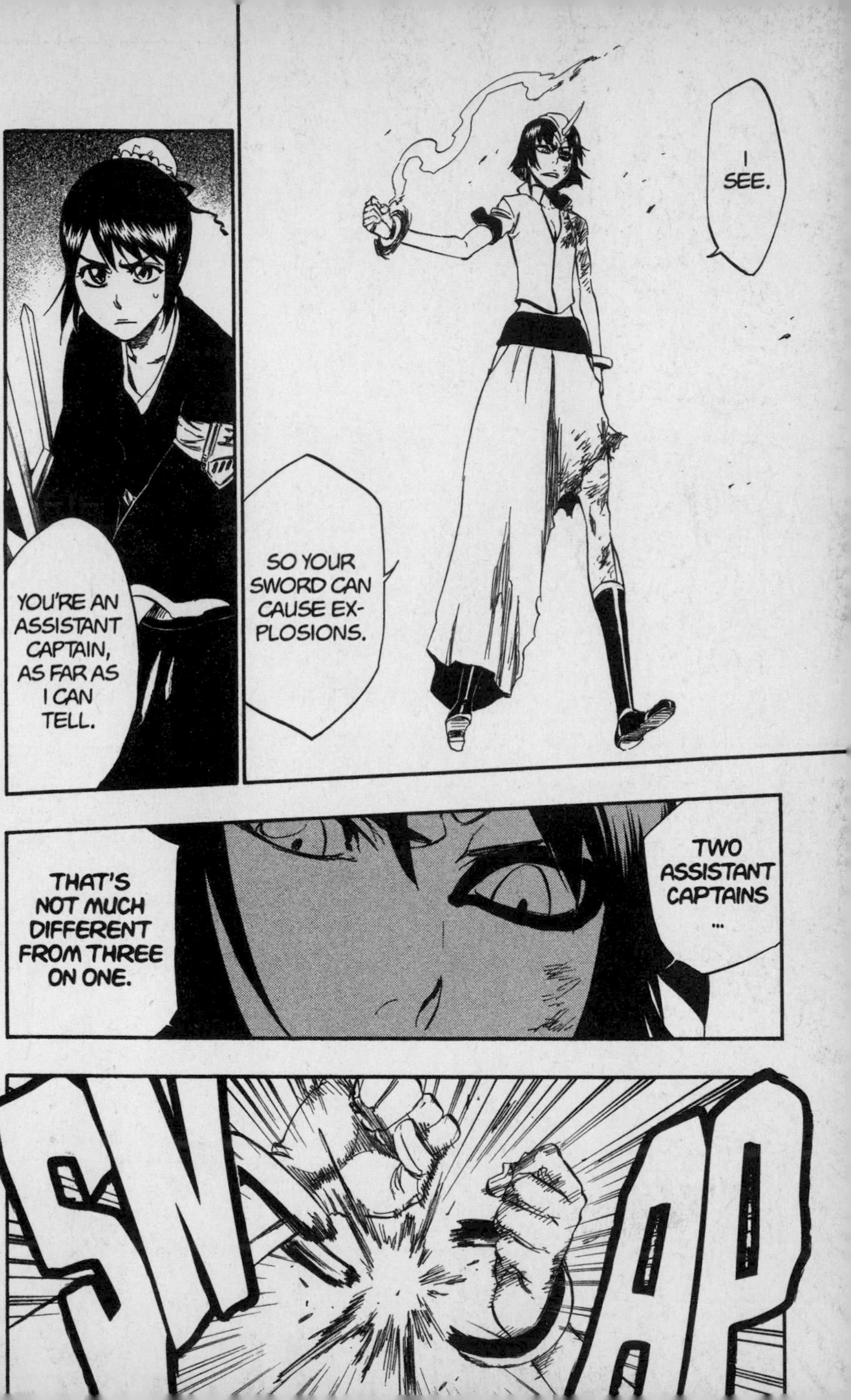
I SEE.
SO YOUR SWORD CAN CAUSE EX-PLOSIONS.
YOU'RE AN ASSISTANT CAPTAIN, AS FAR AS I CAN TELL.
TWO ASSISTANT CAPTAINS ...
THAT'S NOT MUCH DIFFERENT FROM THREE ON ONE.
SNAP

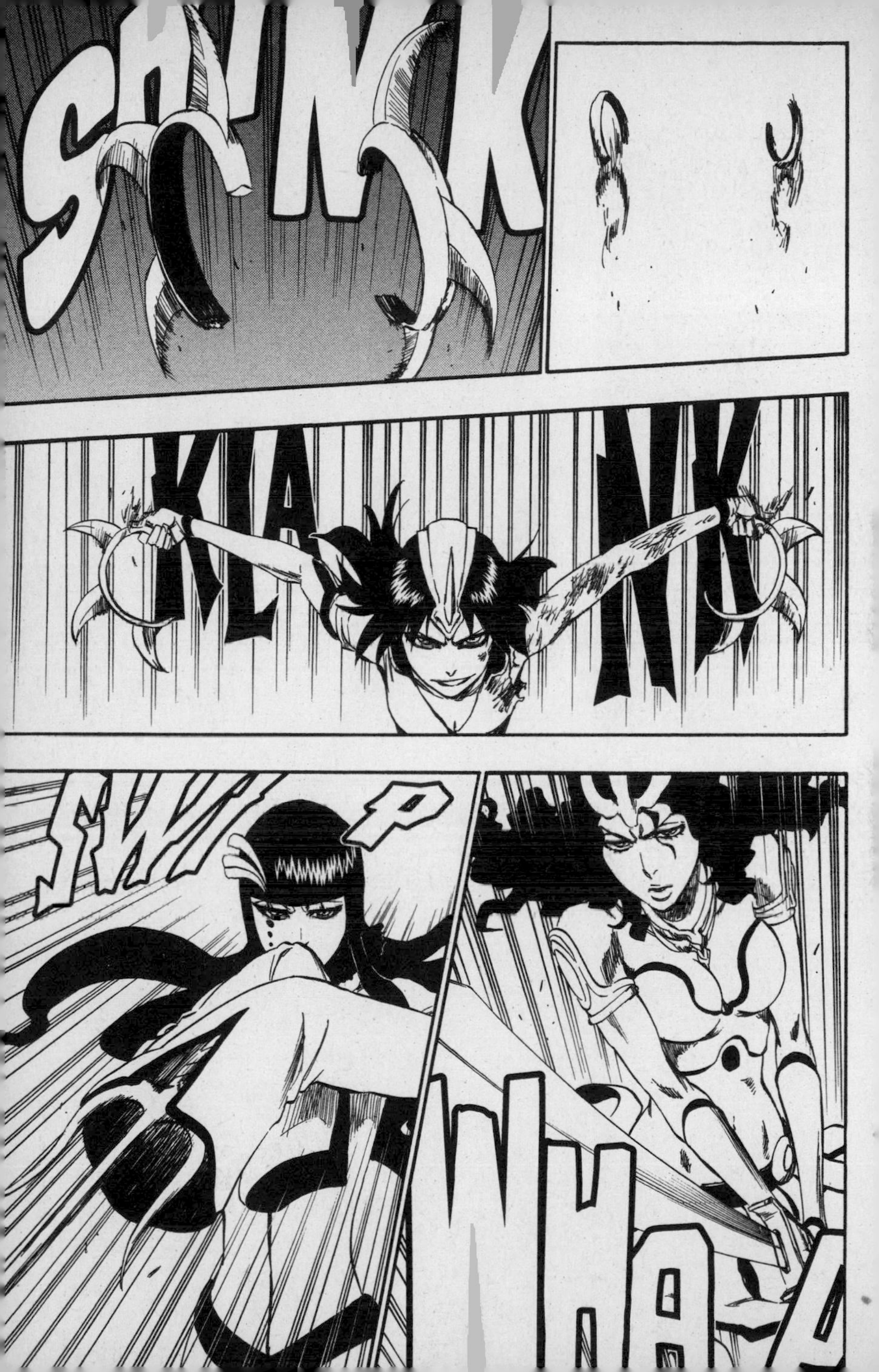
SHNK
KLANK
WHAP
SWP

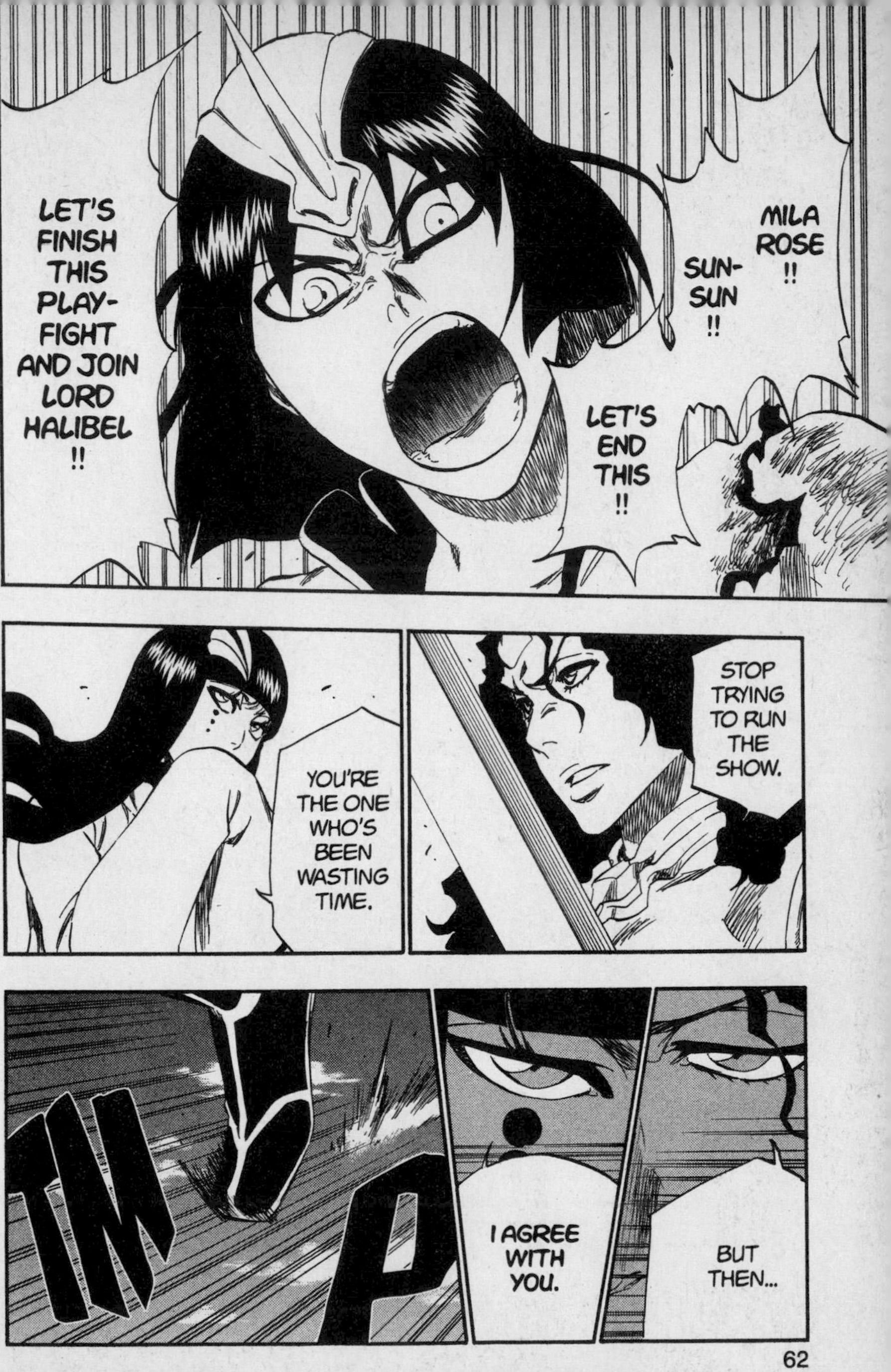
MILA ROSE !!
SUN-SUN !!
LET'S END THIS !!
LET'S FINISH THIS PLAY-FIGHT AND JOIN LORD HALIBEL !!
STOP TRYING TO RUN THE SHOW.
YOU'RE THE ONE WHO'S BEEN WASTING TIME.
BUT THEN...
I AGREE WITH YOU.
TMP

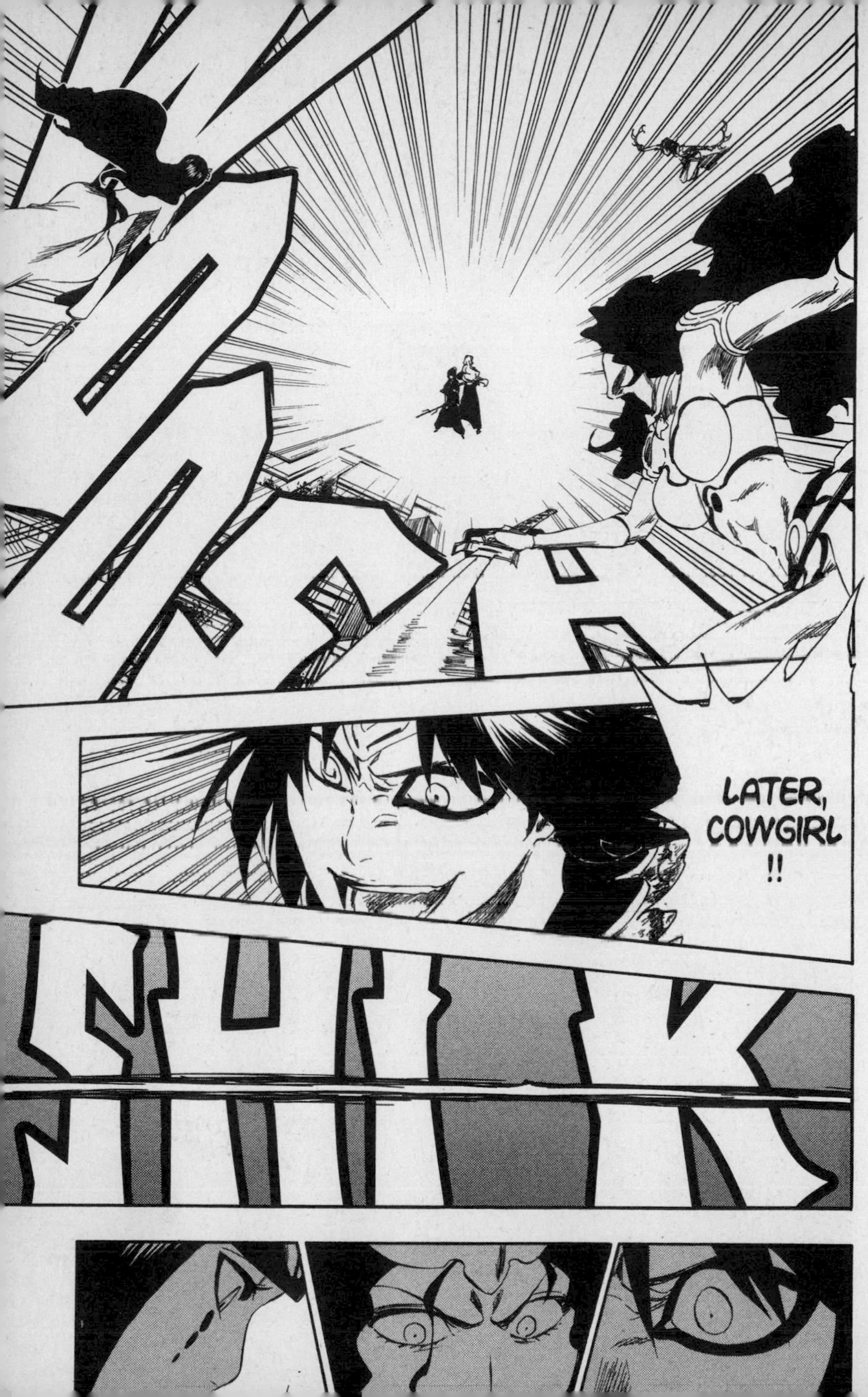
LATER, COWGIRL !!

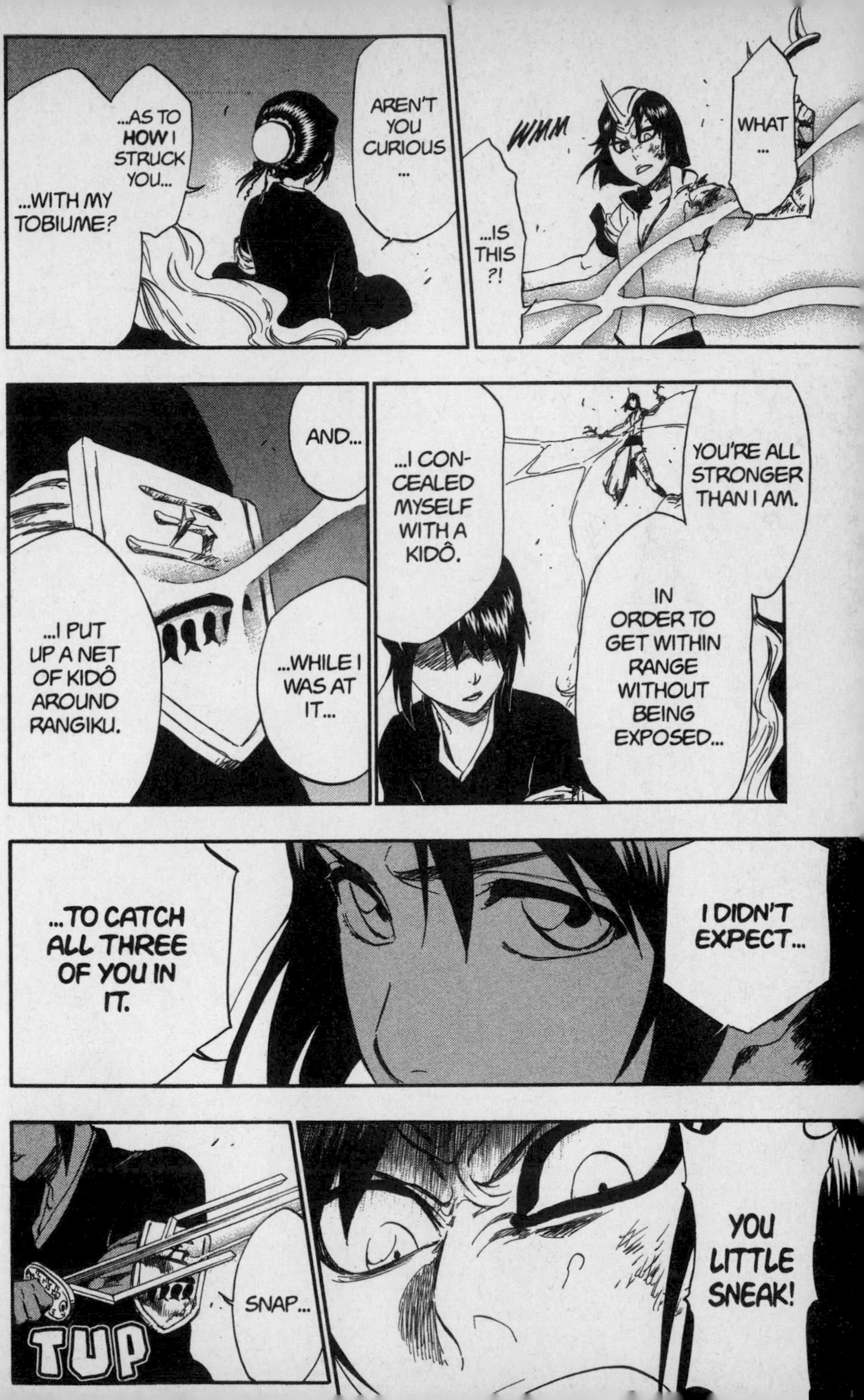
WHAT ...
WMM
...IS THIS ?!
AREN'T YOU CURIOUS ...
...AS TO HOW I STRUCK YOU...
...WITH MY TOBIUME?
YOU'RE ALL STRONGER THAN I AM.
IN ORDER TO GET WITHIN RANGE WITHOUT BEING EXPOSED...
...I CONCEALED MYSELF WITH A KIDÔ.
AND...
...WHILE I WAS AT IT...
...I PUT UP A NET OF KIDÔ AROUND RANGIKU.
I DIDN'T EXPECT...
...TO CATCH ALL THREE OF YOU IN IT.
YOU LITTLE SNEAK!
SNAP...
TUP

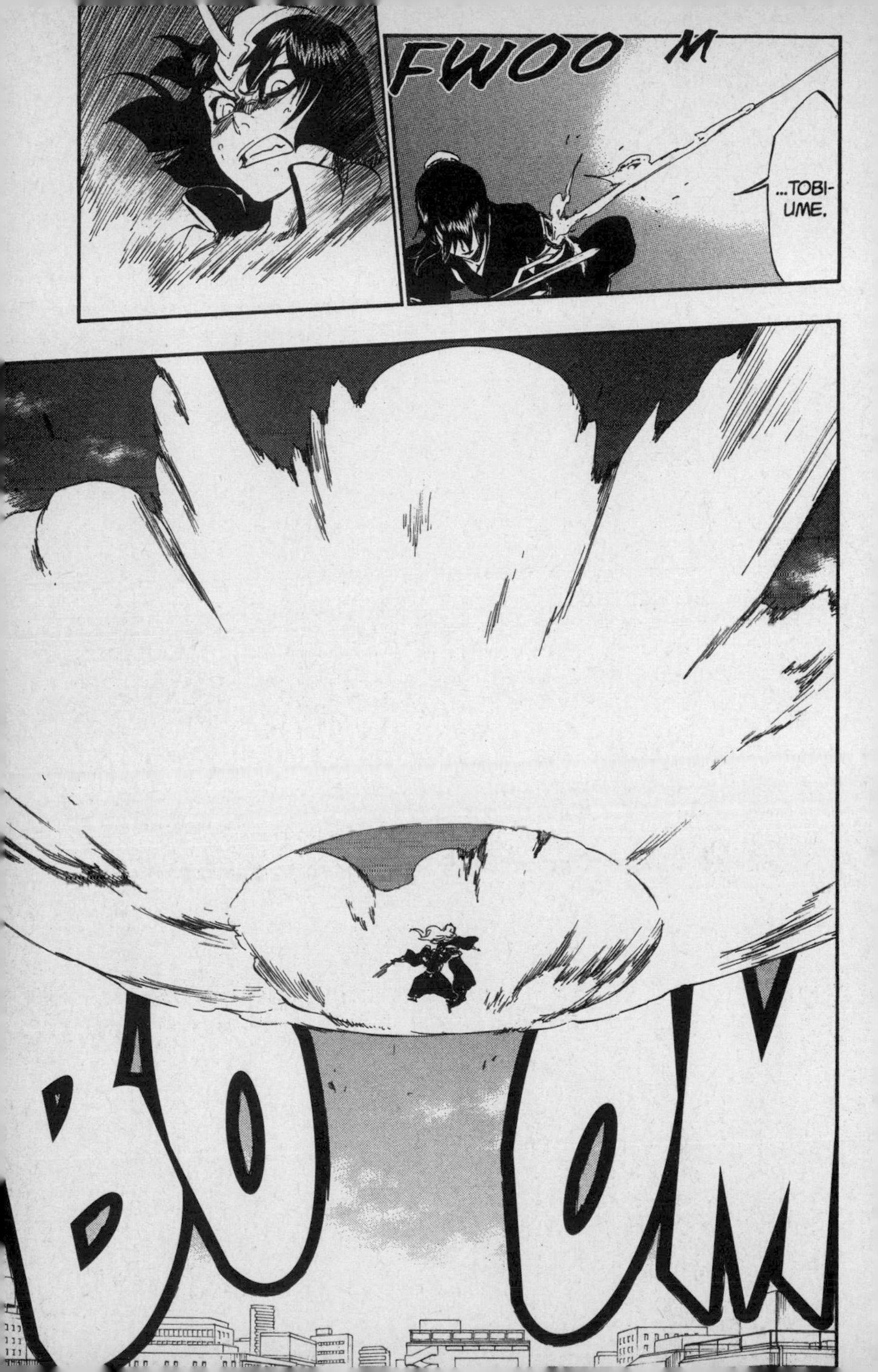
FWOOM
...TOBI-
UME.
BOOM

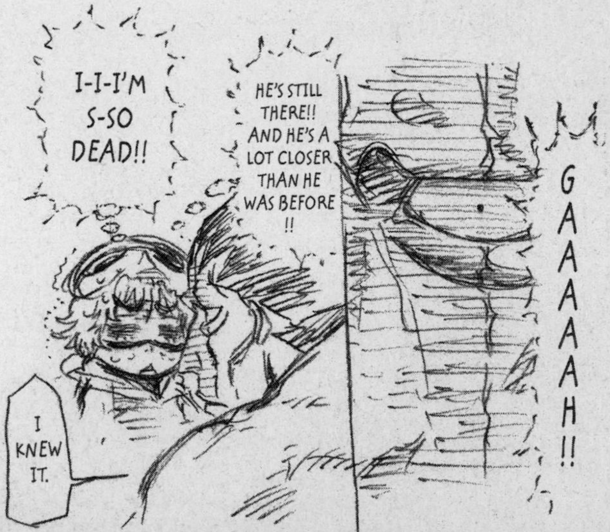
GAAAAAH!!
HE'S STILL THERE!! AND HE'S A LOT CLOSER THAN HE WAS BEFORE !!
I-I-I'M S-SO DEAD!!
I KNEW IT.

335. chimaera chord

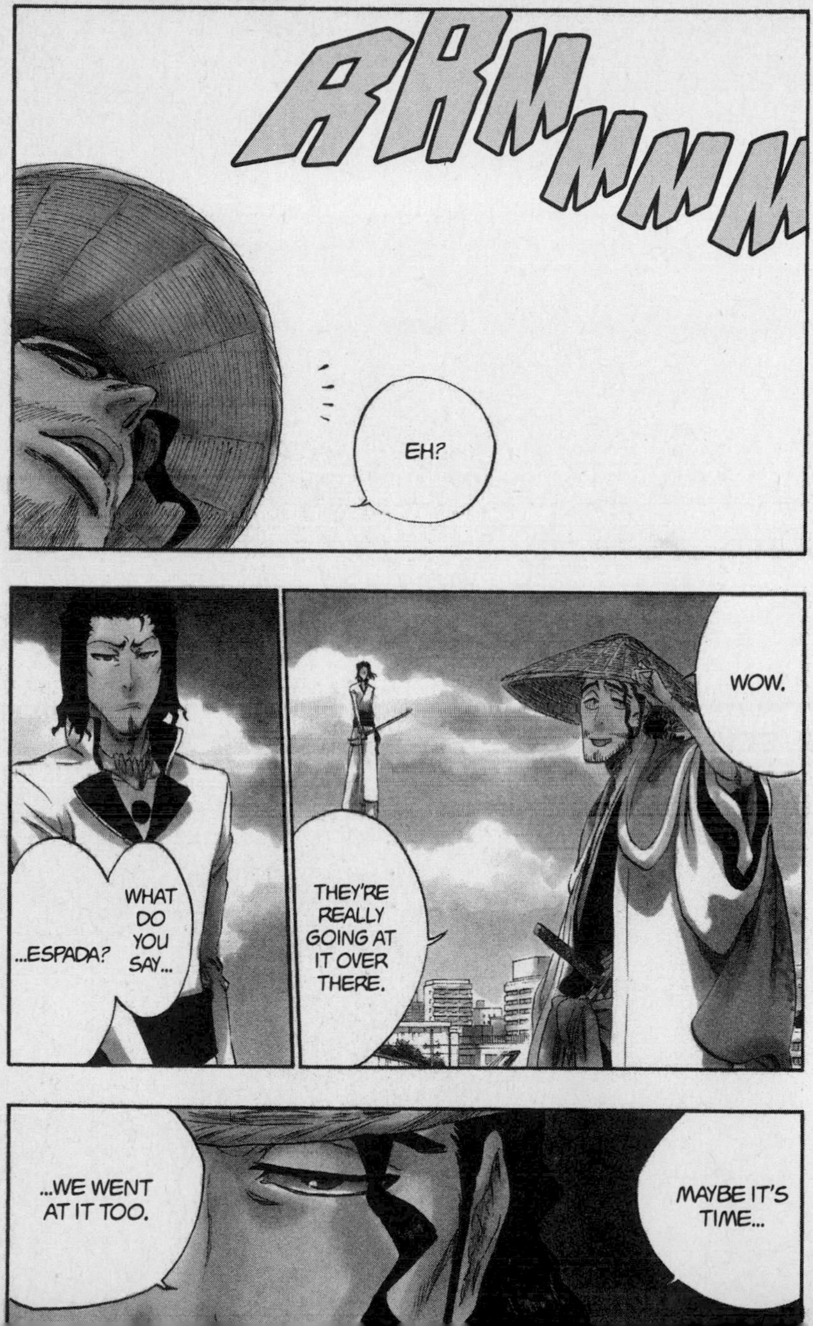
RRMMMMM
EH?
WOW.
THEY'RE REALLY GOING AT IT OVER THERE.
WHAT DO YOU SAY...
...ESPADA?
MAYBE IT'S TIME...
...WE WENT AT IT TOO.

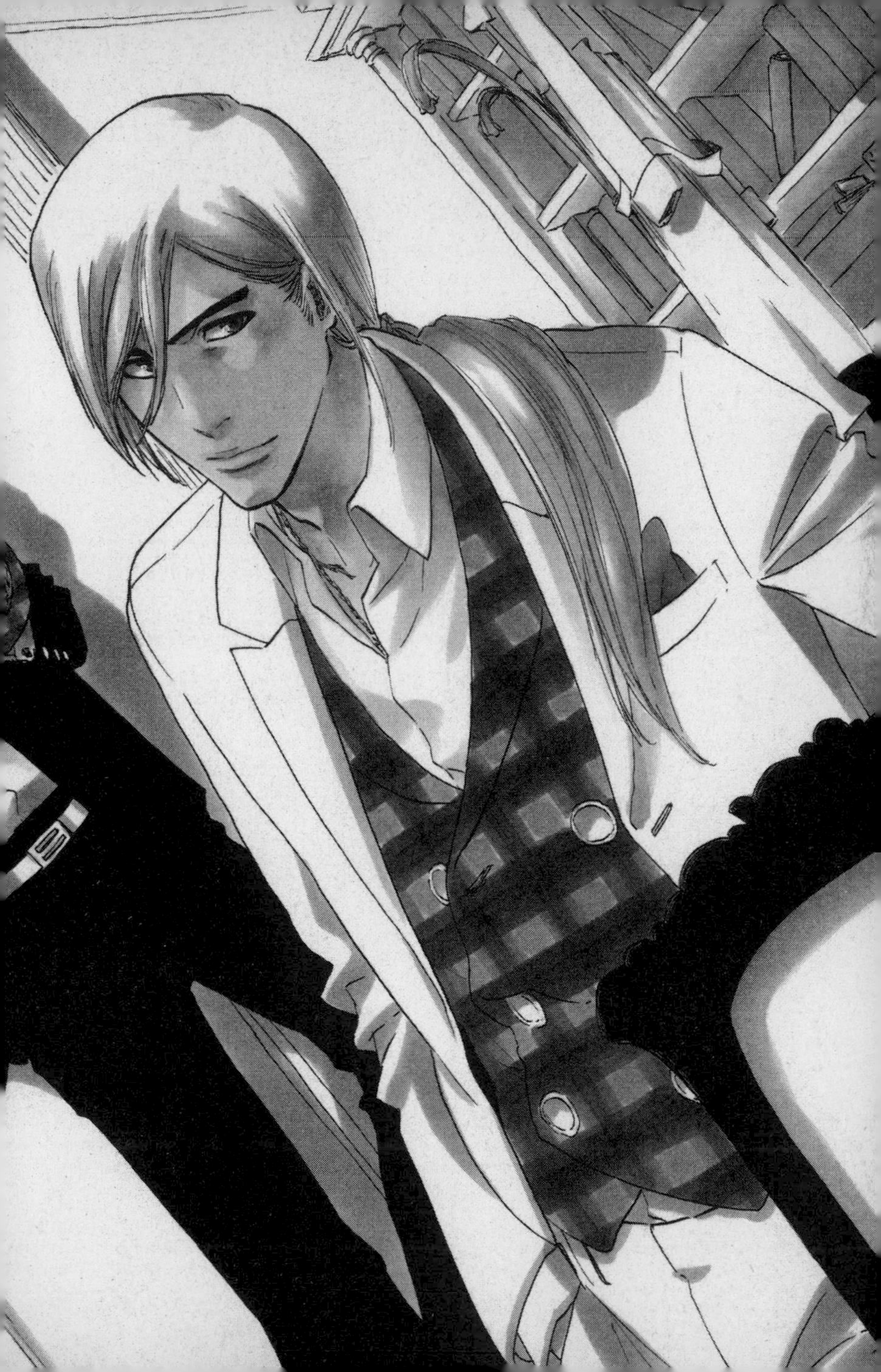

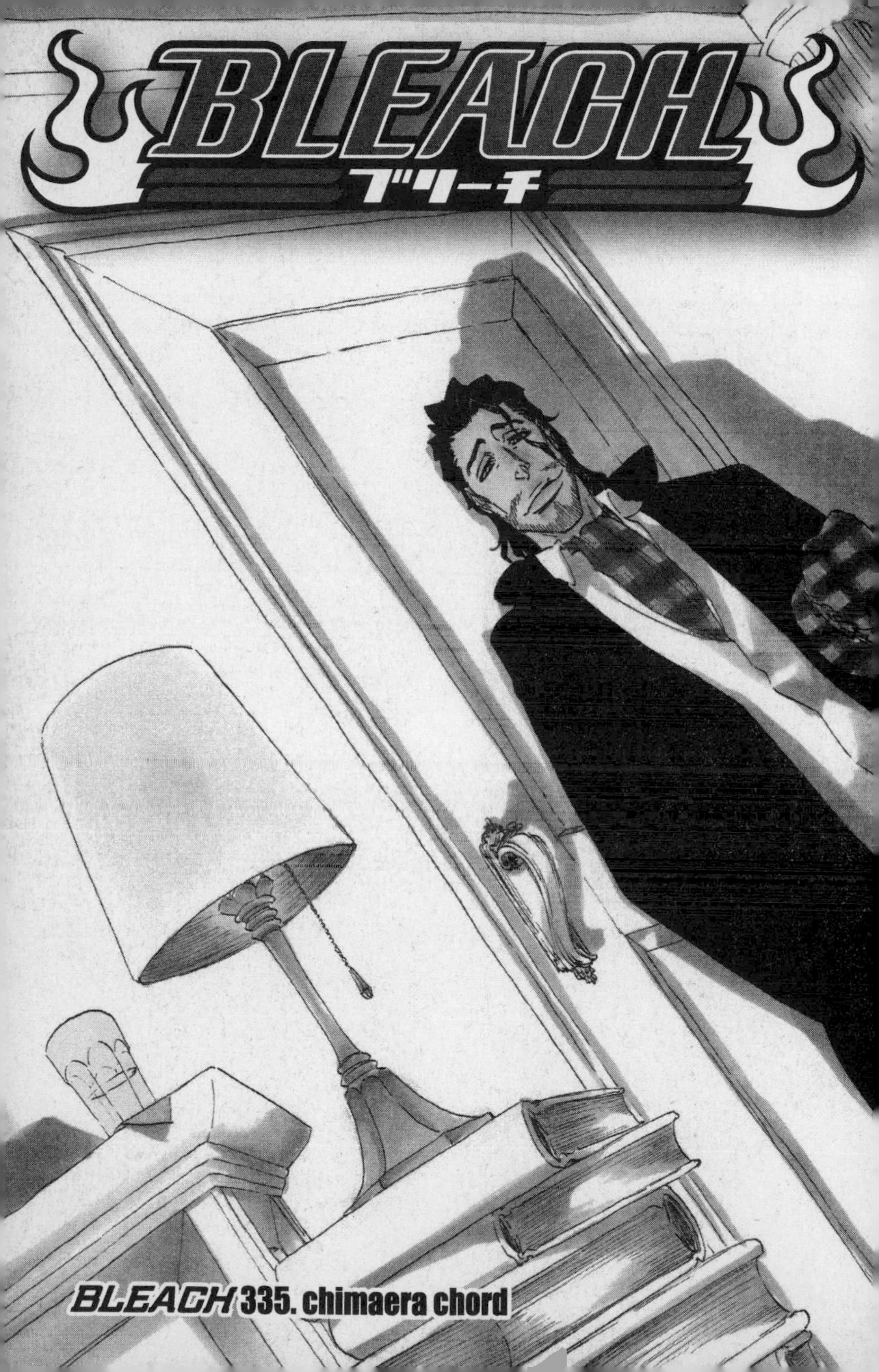
BLEACH
ブリーチ
BLEACH 335. chimaera chord

BLEACH
ブリーチ

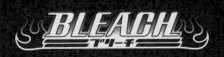

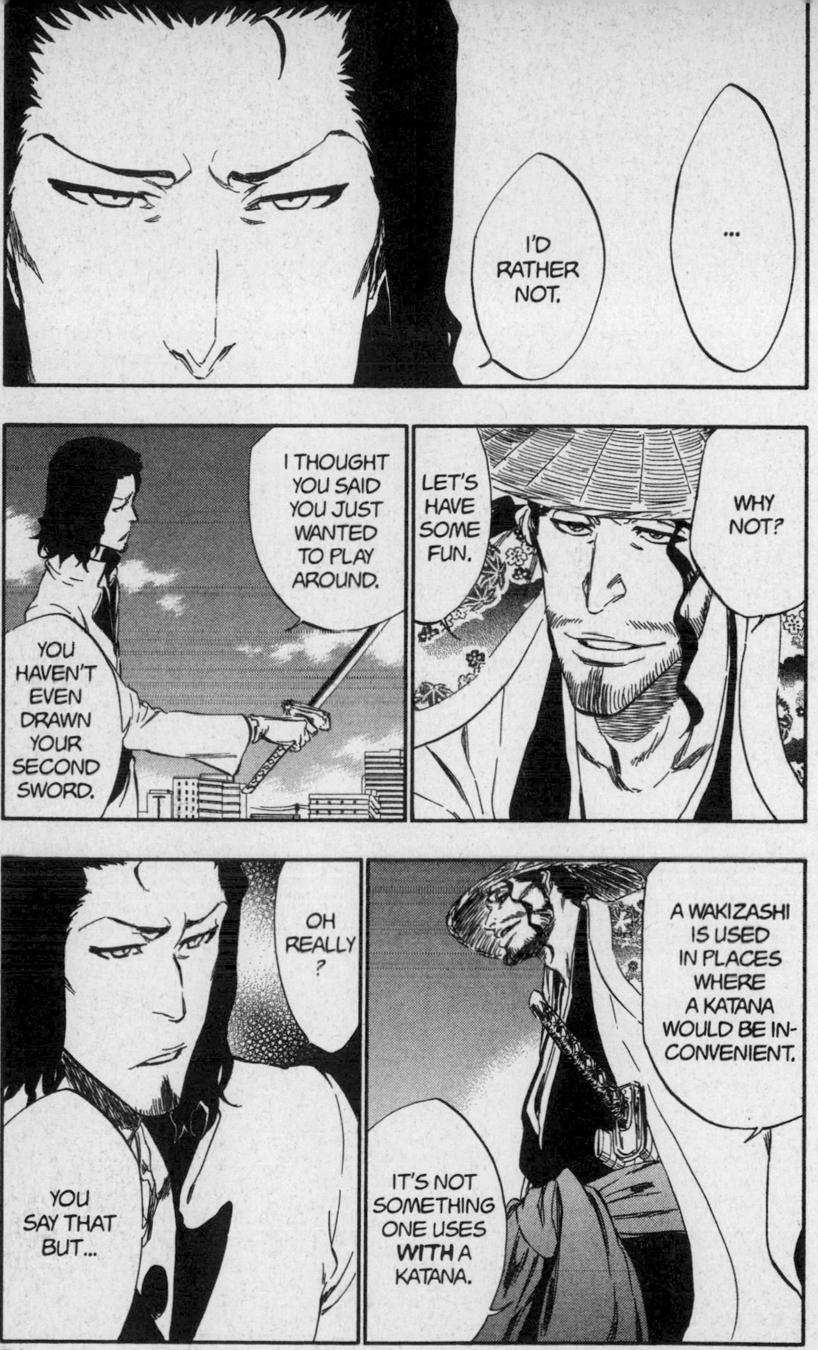
...
I'D RATHER NOT.
WHY NOT?
LET'S HAVE SOME FUN.
I THOUGHT YOU SAID YOU JUST WANTED TO PLAY AROUND.
YOU HAVEN'T EVEN DRAWN YOUR SECOND SWORD.
A WAKIZASHI IS USED IN PLACES WHERE A KATANA WOULD BE IN-CONVENIENT.
IT'S NOT SOMETHING ONE USES **WITH** A KATANA.
OH REALLY?
YOU SAY THAT BUT...

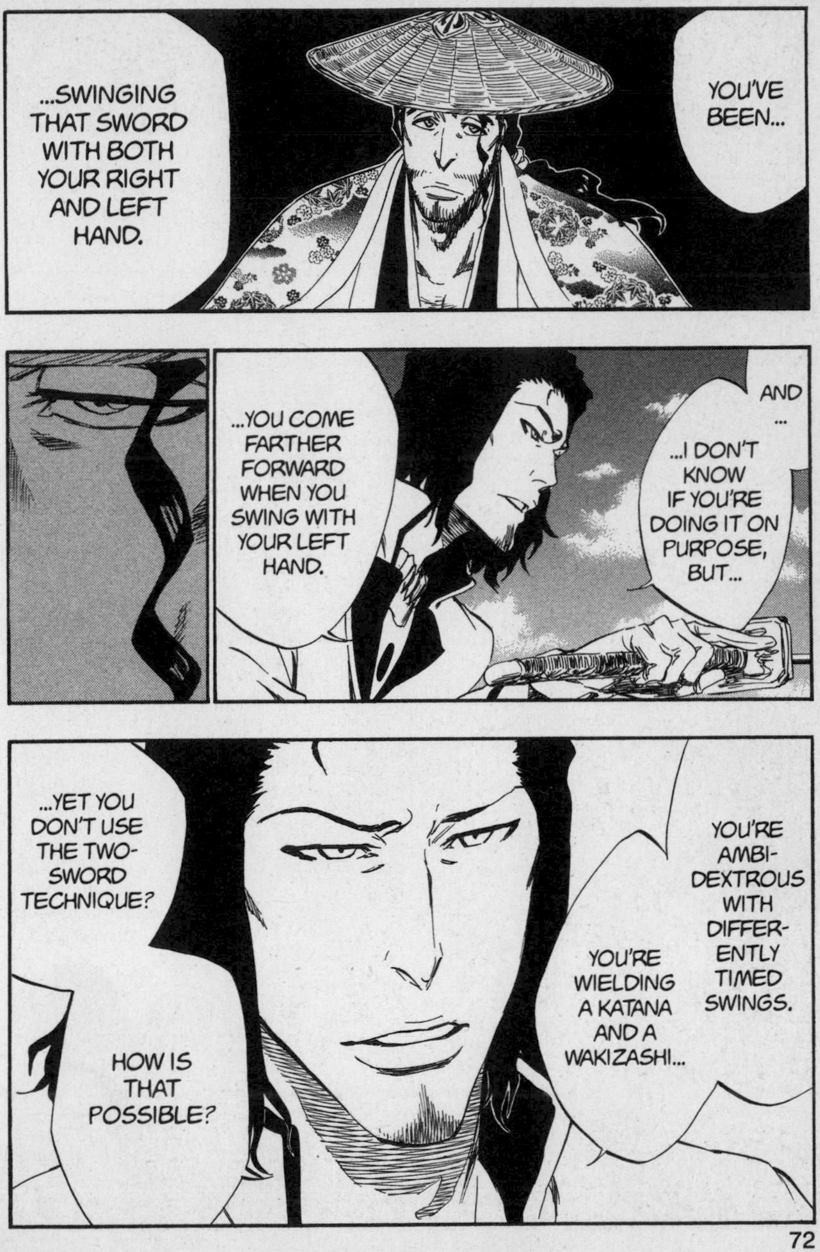
YOU'VE BEEN...
...SWINGING THAT SWORD WITH BOTH YOUR RIGHT AND LEFT HAND.
AND ...
...I DON'T KNOW IF YOU'RE DOING IT ON PURPOSE, BUT...
...YOU COME FARTHER FORWARD WHEN YOU SWING WITH YOUR LEFT HAND.
YOU'RE AMBI-DEXTROUS WITH DIFFER-ENTLY TIMED SWINGS.
YOU'RE WIELDING A KATANA AND A WAKIZASHI...
...YET YOU DON'T USE THE TWO-SWORD TECHNIQUE?
HOW IS THAT POSSIBLE?

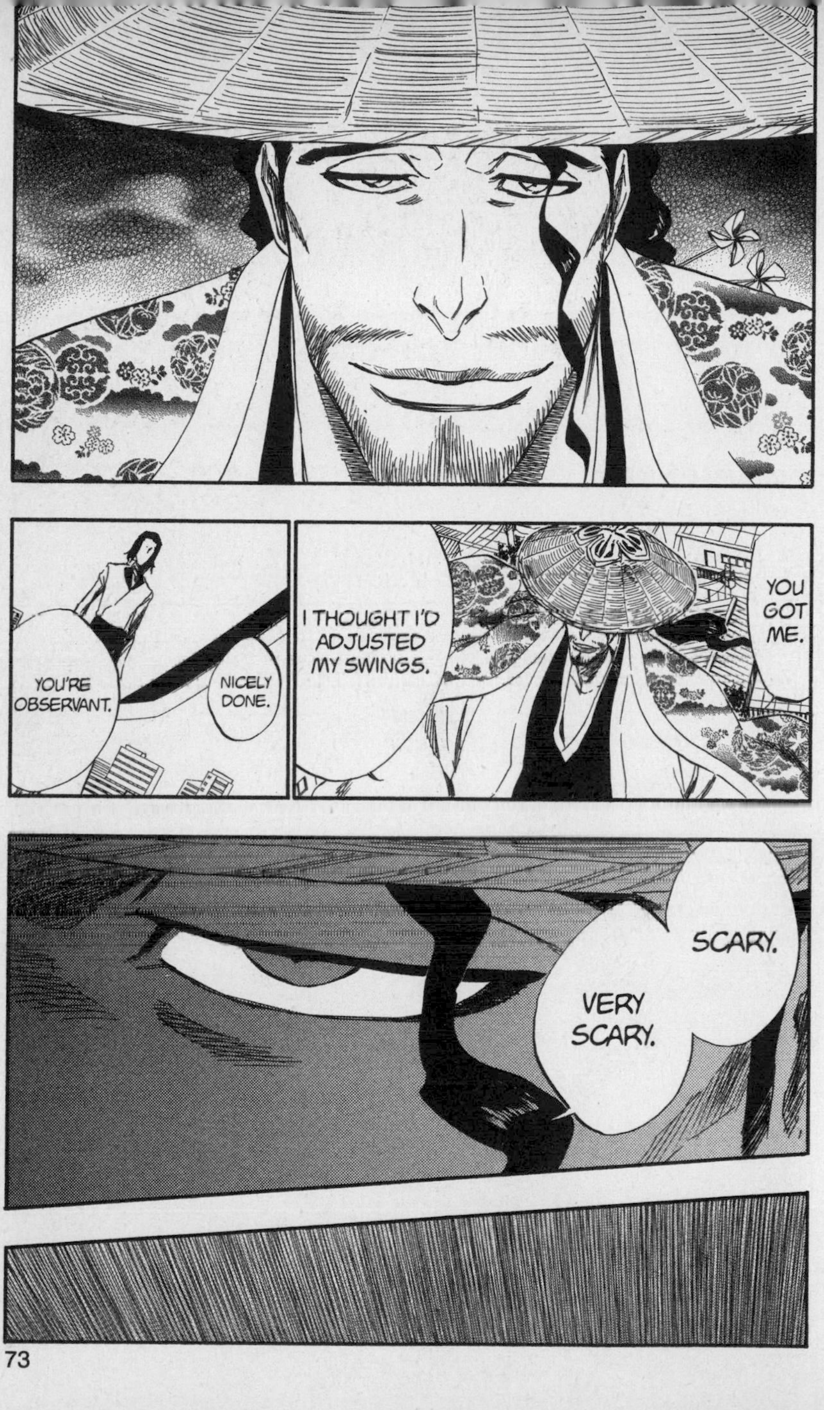
YOU GOT ME.
I THOUGHT I'D ADJUSTED MY SWINGS.
NICELY DONE.
YOU'RE OBSERVANT.
SCARY.
VERY SCARY.

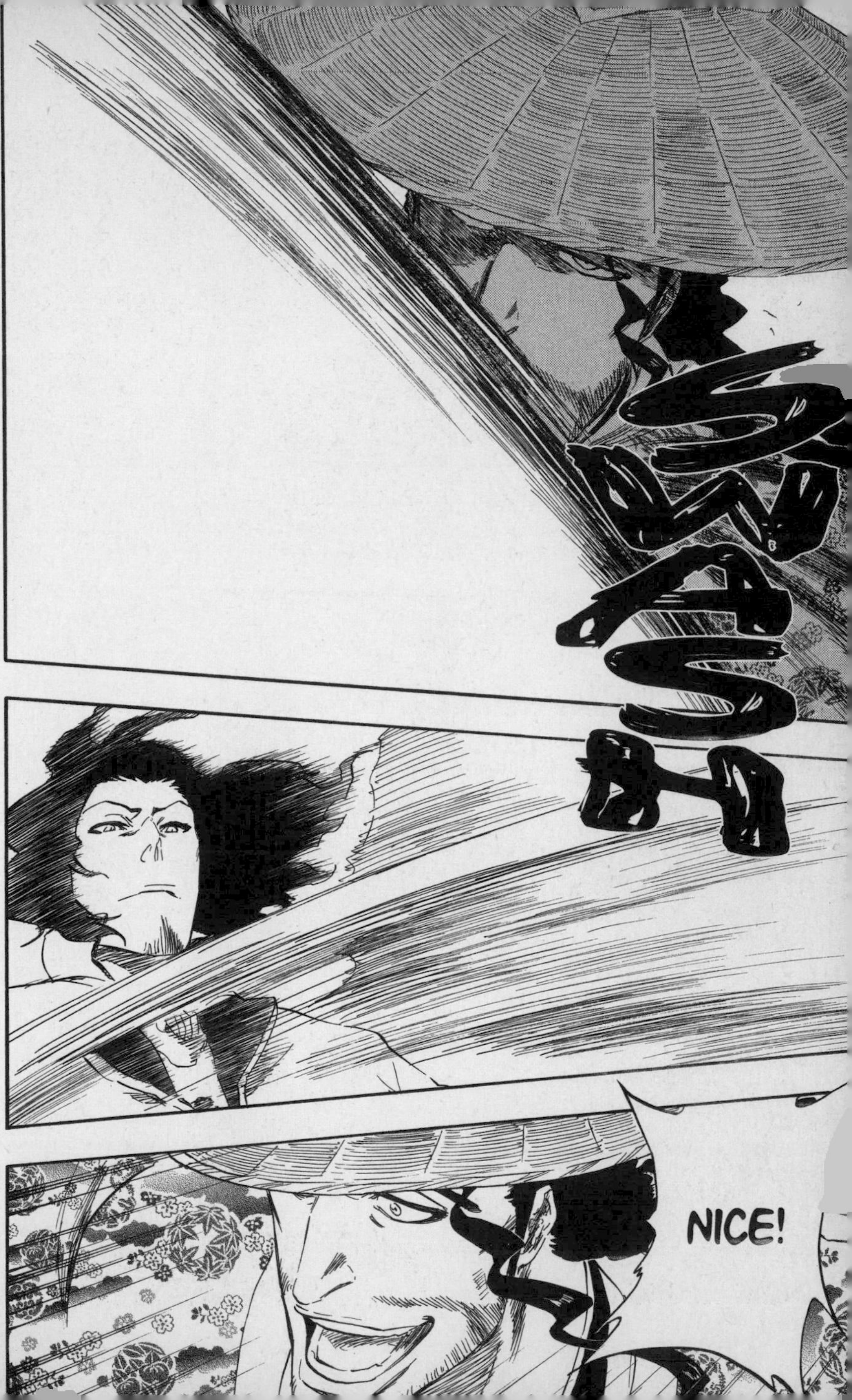
SWASH
NICE!

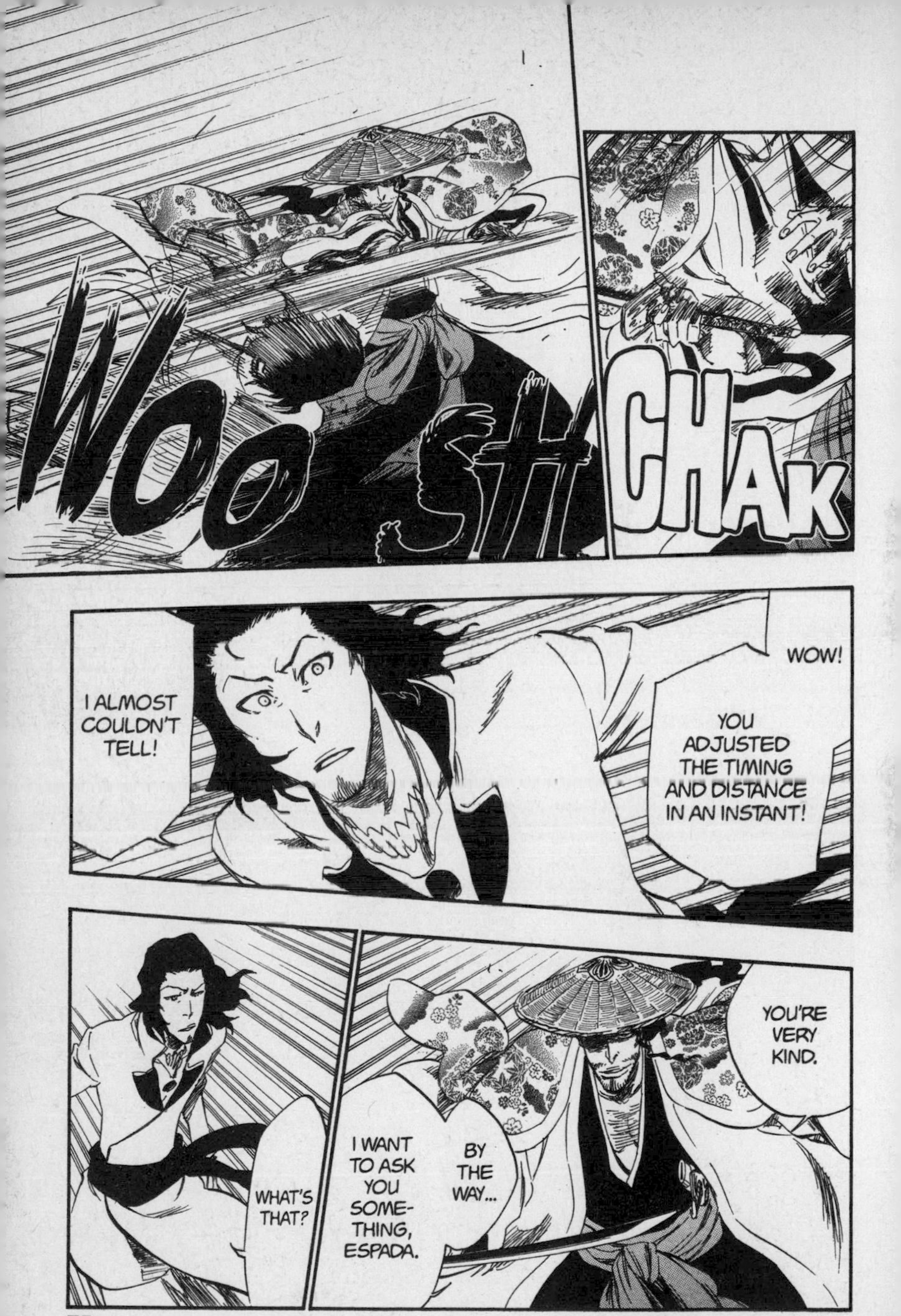
CHAK
WOOSH
WOW!
YOU ADJUSTED THE TIMING AND DISTANCE IN AN INSTANT!
I ALMOST COULDN'T TELL!
YOU'RE VERY KIND.
BY THE WAY...
I WANT TO ASK YOU SOMETHING, ESPADA.
WHAT'S THAT?

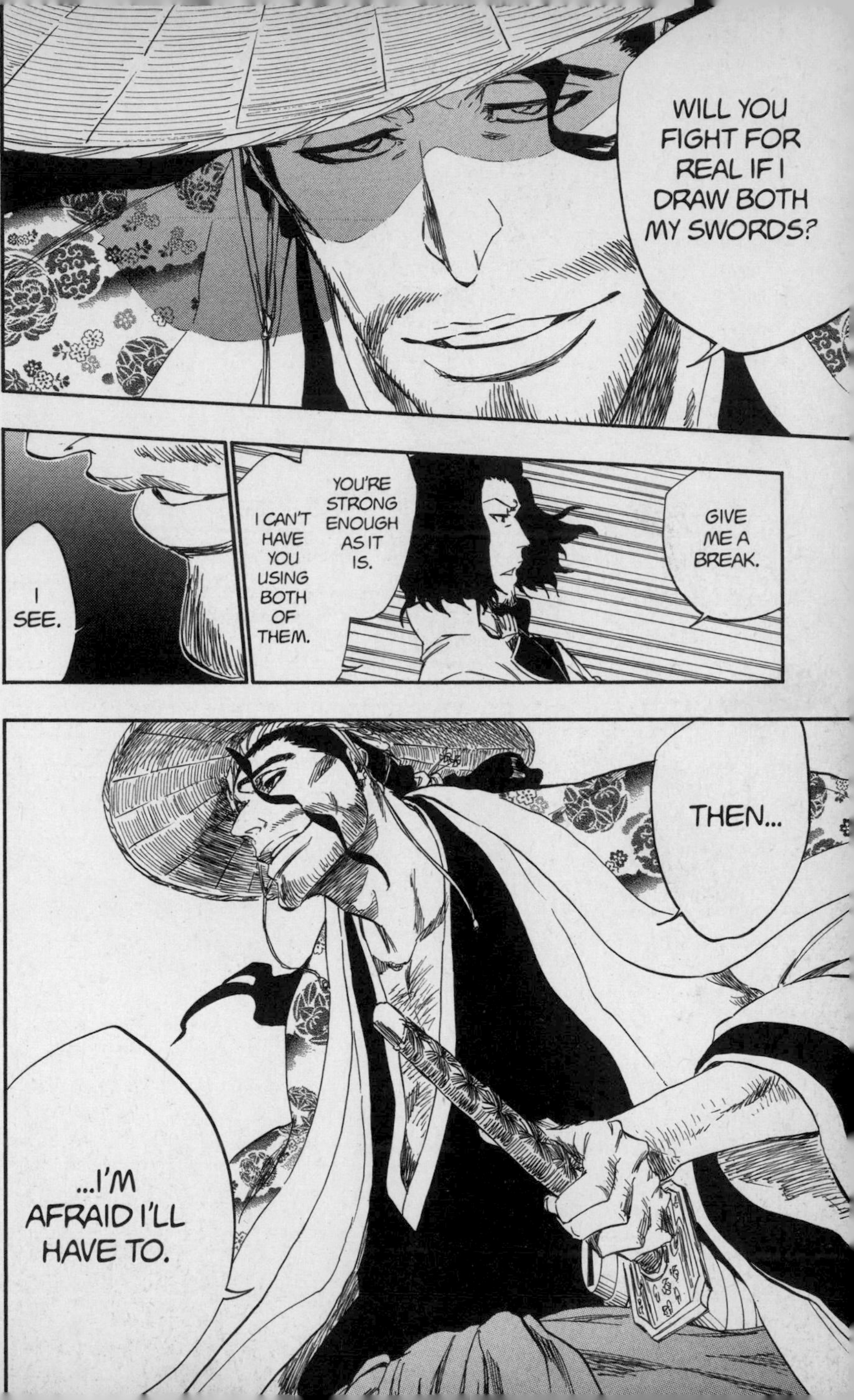
WILL YOU FIGHT FOR REAL IF I DRAW BOTH MY SWORDS?
GIVE ME A BREAK.
YOU'RE STRONG ENOUGH AS IT IS.
I CAN'T HAVE YOU USING BOTH OF THEM.
I SEE.
THEN...
...I'M AFRAID I'LL HAVE TO.

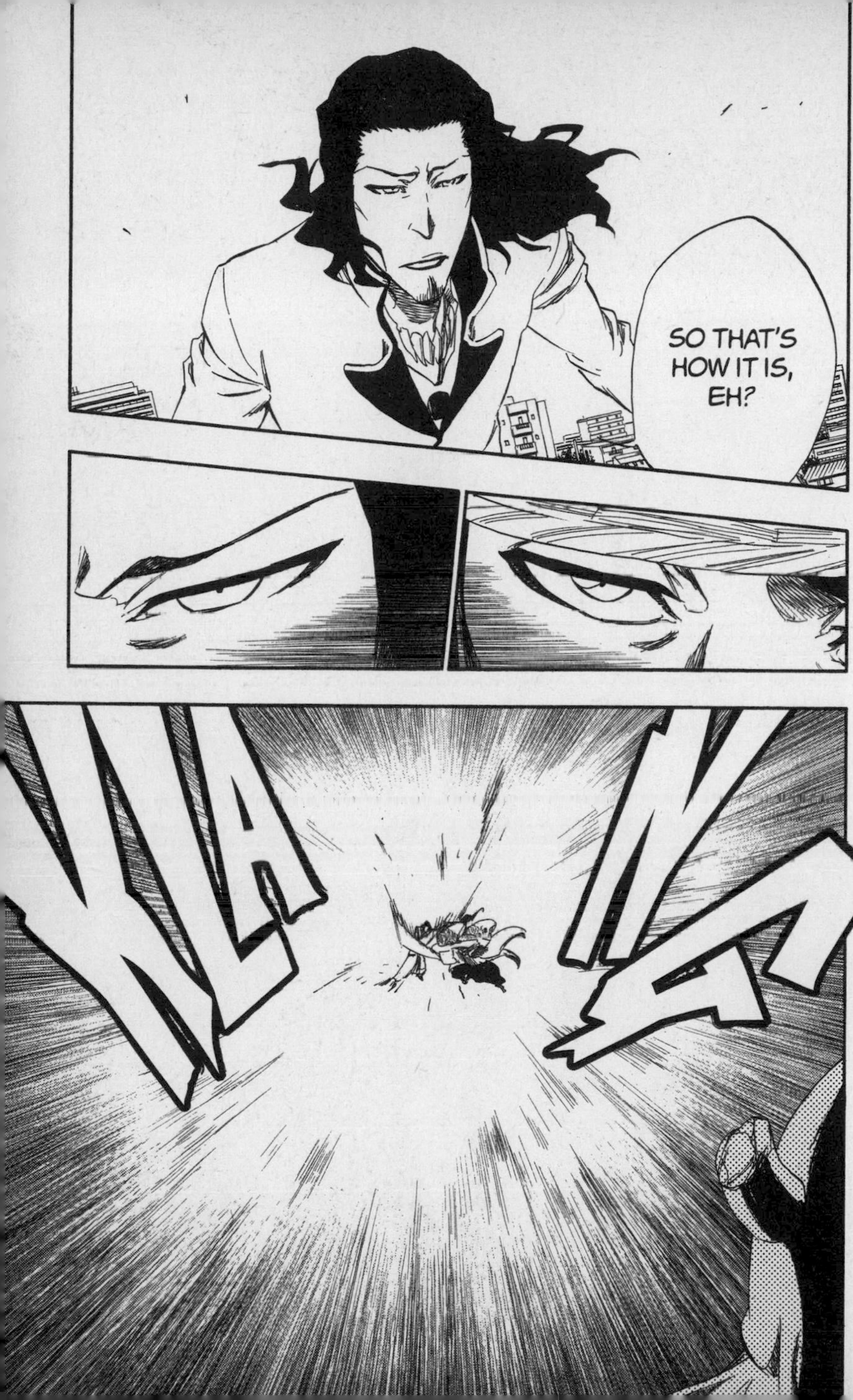
SO THAT'S HOW IT IS, EH?

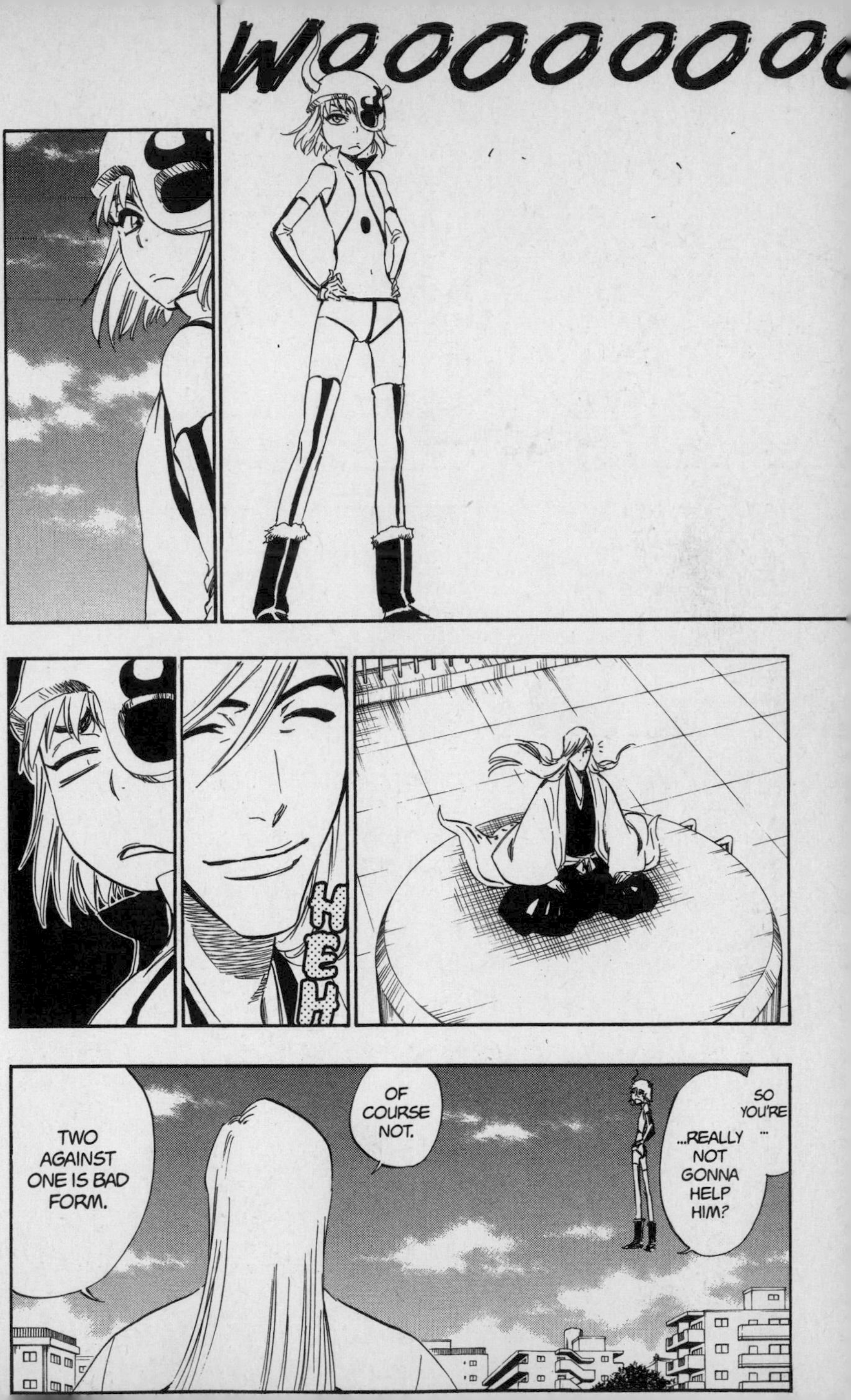
WOOOOOOOO
HEH
SO YOU'RE ... ...REALLY NOT GONNA HELP HIM?
OF COURSE NOT.
TWO AGAINST ONE IS BAD FORM.

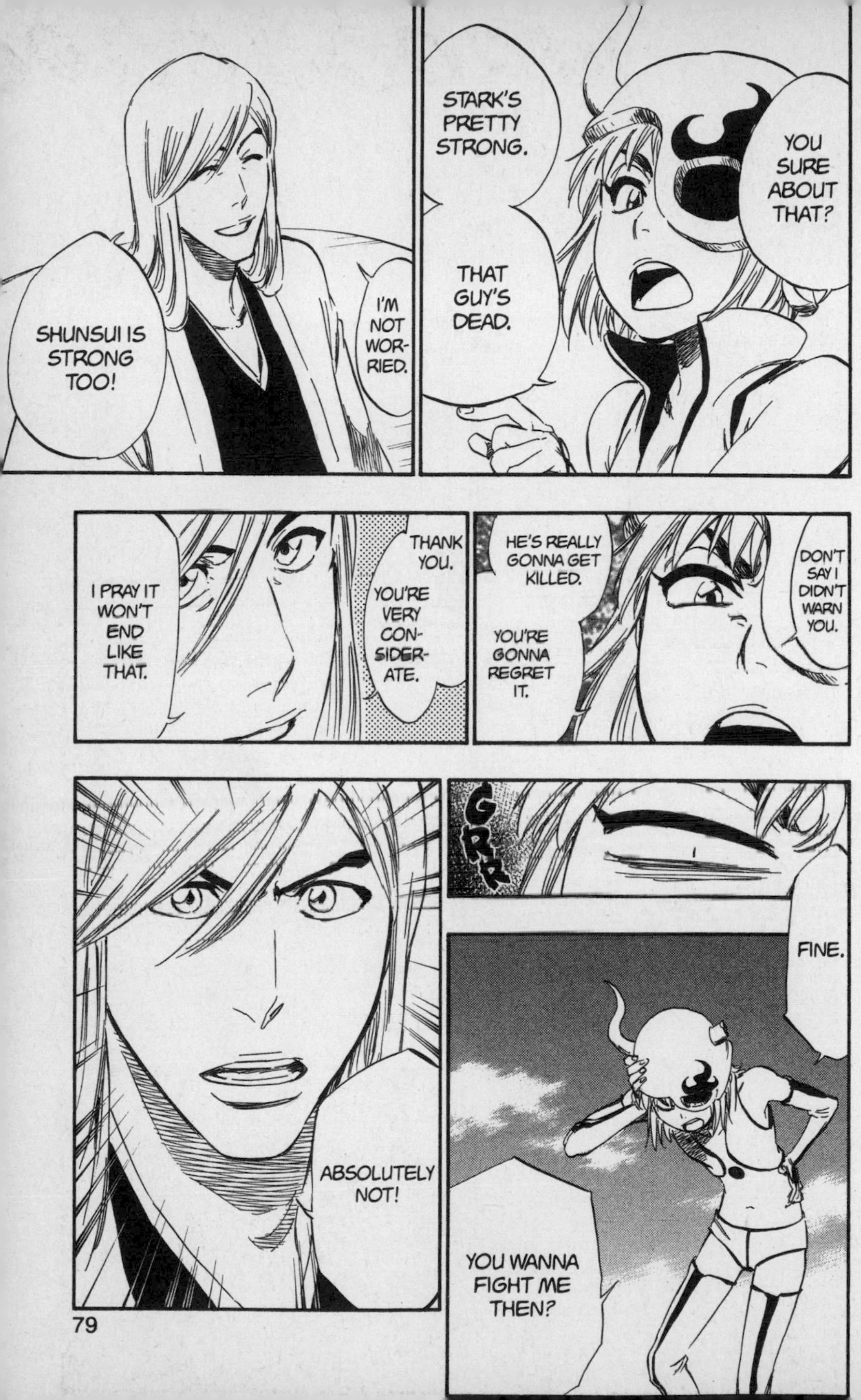
YOU SURE ABOUT THAT?
STARK'S PRETTY STRONG.
THAT GUY'S DEAD.
I'M NOT WORRIED.
SHUNSUI IS STRONG TOO!
DON'T SAY I DIDN'T WARN YOU.
HE'S REALLY GONNA GET KILLED.
YOU'RE GONNA REGRET IT.
THANK YOU.
YOU'RE VERY CONSIDERATE.
I PRAY IT WON'T END LIKE THAT.
GRRR
FINE.
YOU WANNA FIGHT ME THEN?
ABSOLUTELY NOT!

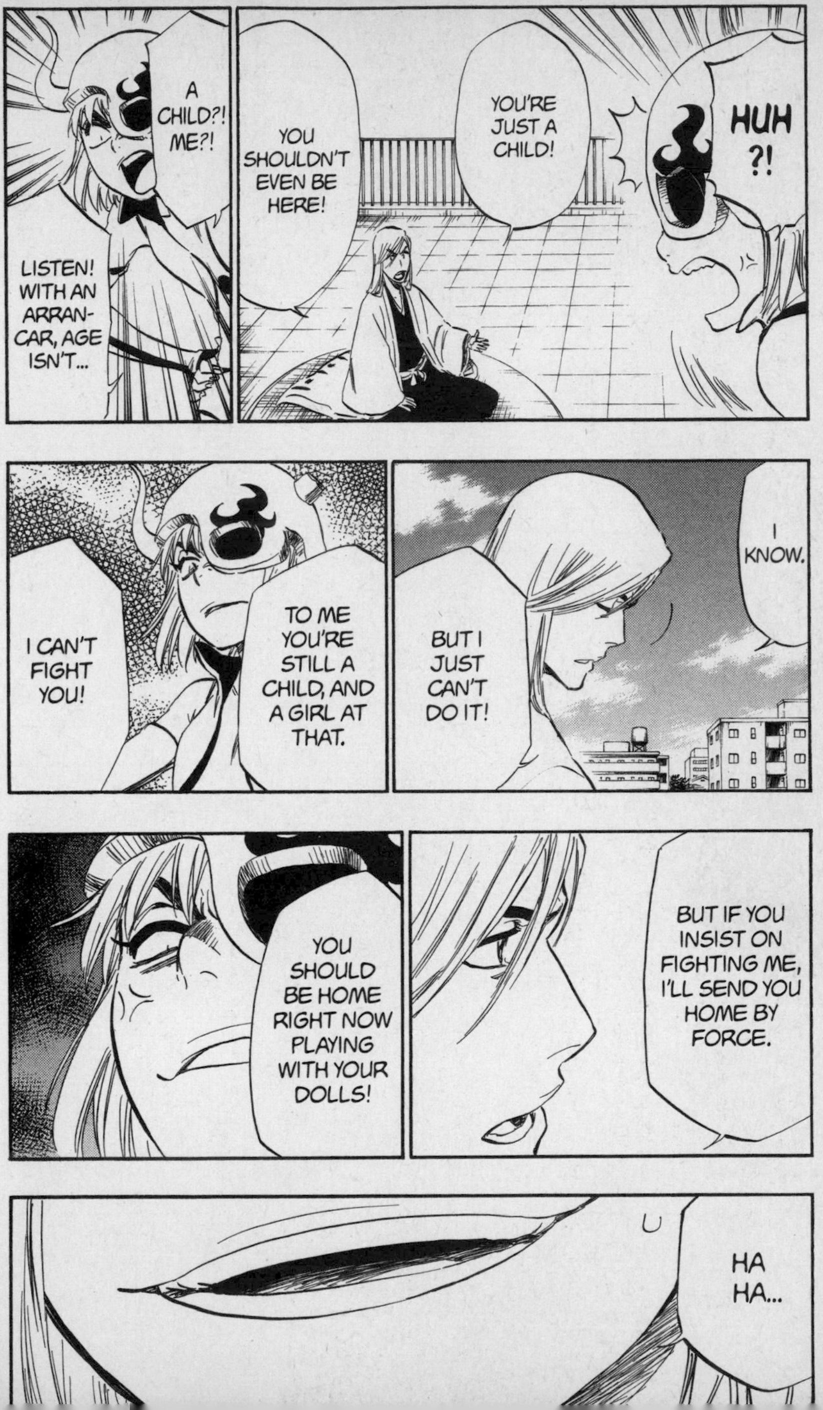
HUH?!
YOU'RE JUST A CHILD!
YOU SHOULDN'T EVEN BE HERE!
A CHILD?! ME?!
LISTEN! WITH AN ARRAN-CAR, AGE ISN'T...
I KNOW.
BUT I JUST CAN'T DO IT!
TO ME YOU'RE STILL A CHILD, AND A GIRL AT THAT.
I CAN'T FIGHT YOU!
BUT IF YOU INSIST ON FIGHTING ME, I'LL SEND YOU HOME BY FORCE.
YOU SHOULD BE HOME RIGHT NOW PLAYING WITH YOUR DOLLS!
HA HA...

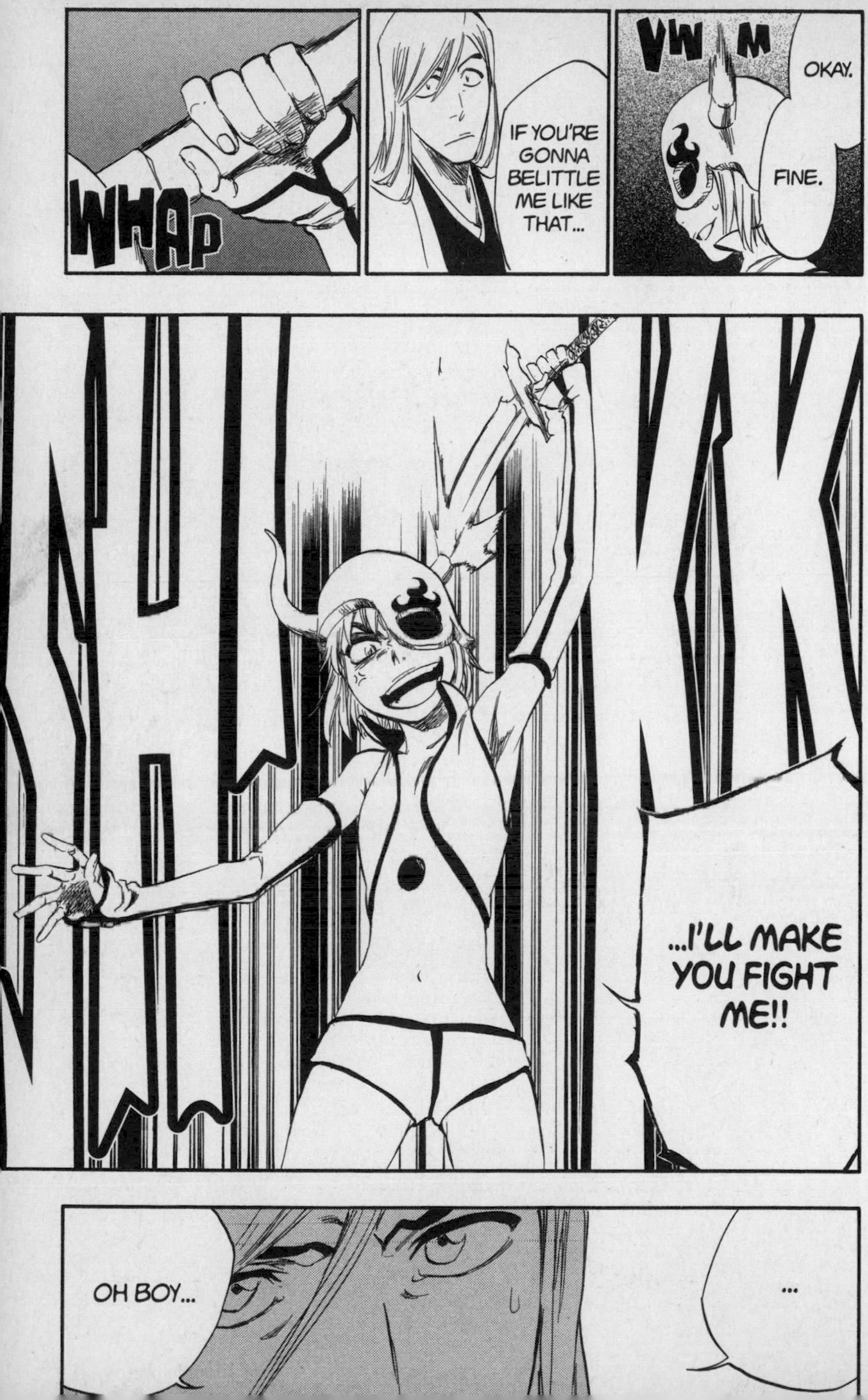
VWM
OKAY.
FINE.
IF YOU'RE GONNA BELITTLE ME LIKE THAT...
WHAP
...I'LL MAKE YOU FIGHT ME!!
...
OH BOY...

RRMMMMMMM

haff

haff

haff

I'M SORRY.

THAT'S THE FIRST TIME I'VE EVER USED THAT COMBINATION.

YES.

ARE YOU ALL RIGHT, HINAMORI?

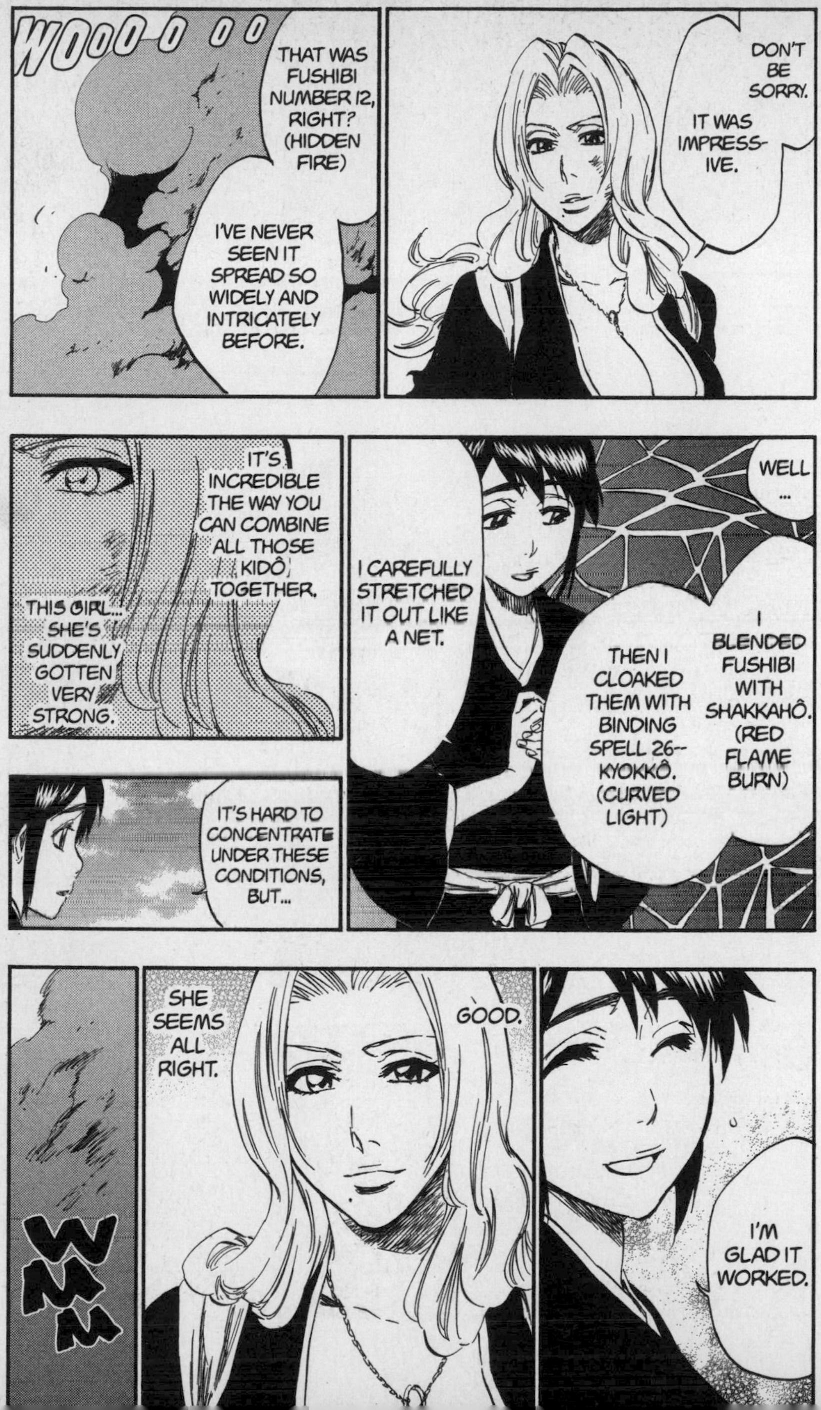
DON'T BE SORRY.
IT WAS IMPRESS-IVE.
WOOOOOO
THAT WAS FUSHIBI NUMBER 12, RIGHT? (HIDDEN FIRE)
I'VE NEVER SEEN IT SPREAD SO WIDELY AND INTRICATELY BEFORE.
WELL...
I BLENDED FUSHIBI WITH SHAKKAHÔ. (RED FLAME BURN)
THEN I CLOAKED THEM WITH BINDING SPELL 26--KYOKKÔ. (CURVED LIGHT)
I CAREFULLY STRETCHED IT OUT LIKE A NET.
IT'S INCREDIBLE THE WAY YOU CAN COMBINE ALL THOSE KIDÔ TOGETHER.
THIS GIRL... SHE'S SUDDENLY GOTTEN VERY STRONG.
IT'S HARD TO CONCENTRATE UNDER THESE CONDITIONS, BUT...
I'M GLAD IT WORKED.
GOOD.
SHE SEEMS ALL RIGHT.
WMM

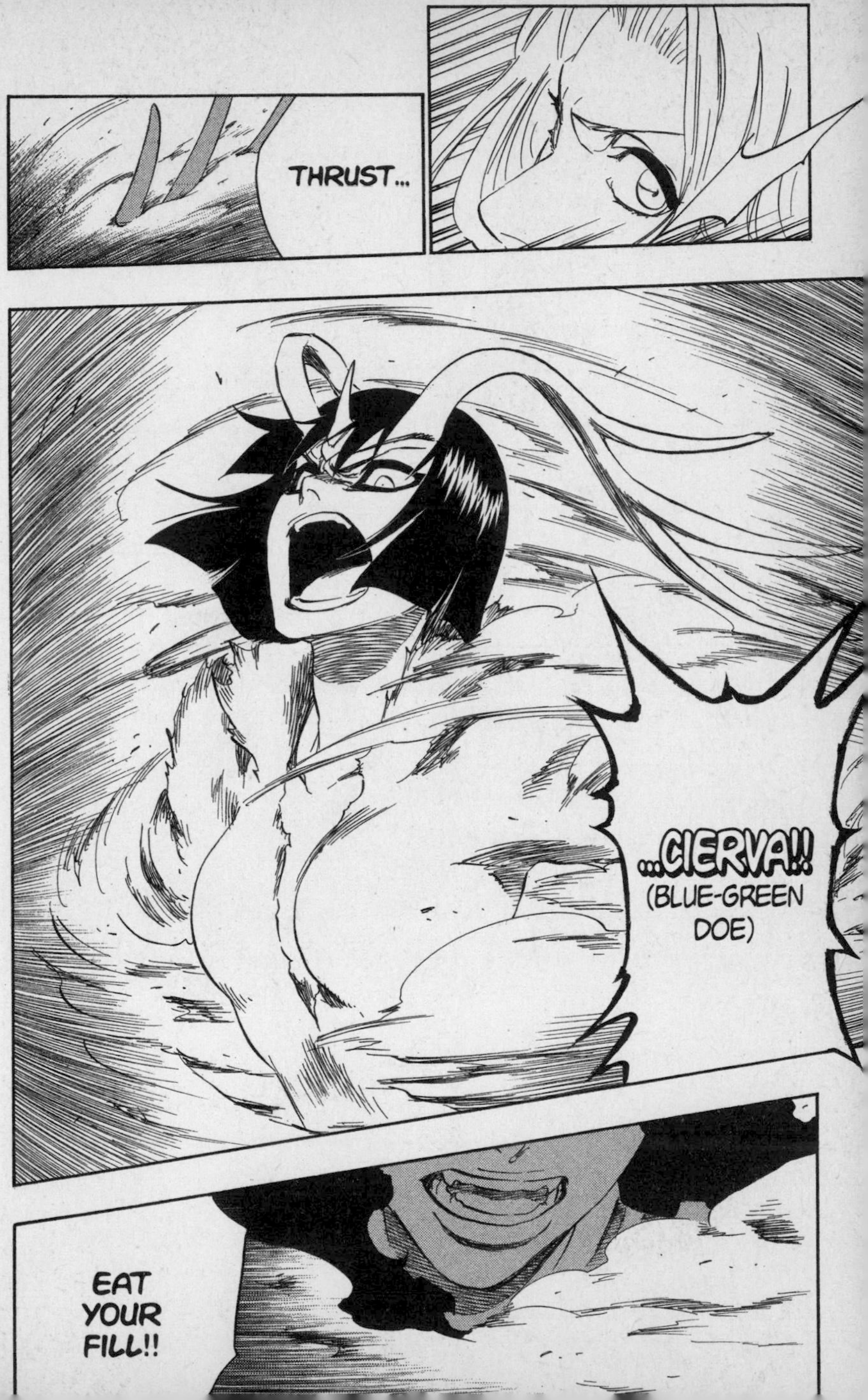
THRUST...
...CIERVA!!
(BLUE-GREEN DOE)
EAT YOUR FILL!!

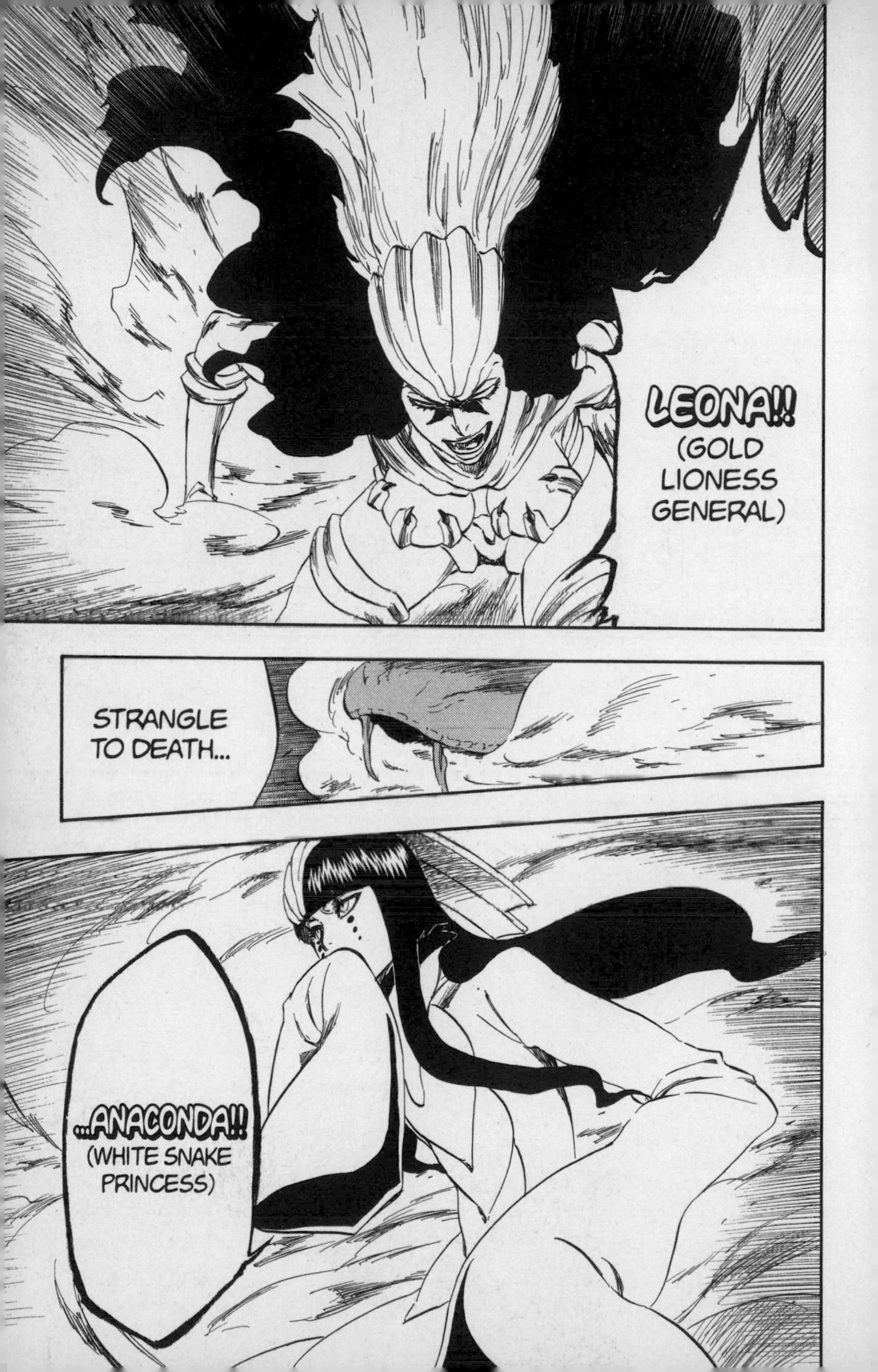
LEONA!!
(GOLD LIONESS GENERAL)
STRANGLE TO DEATH...
...ANACONDA!!
(WHITE SNAKE PRINCESS)

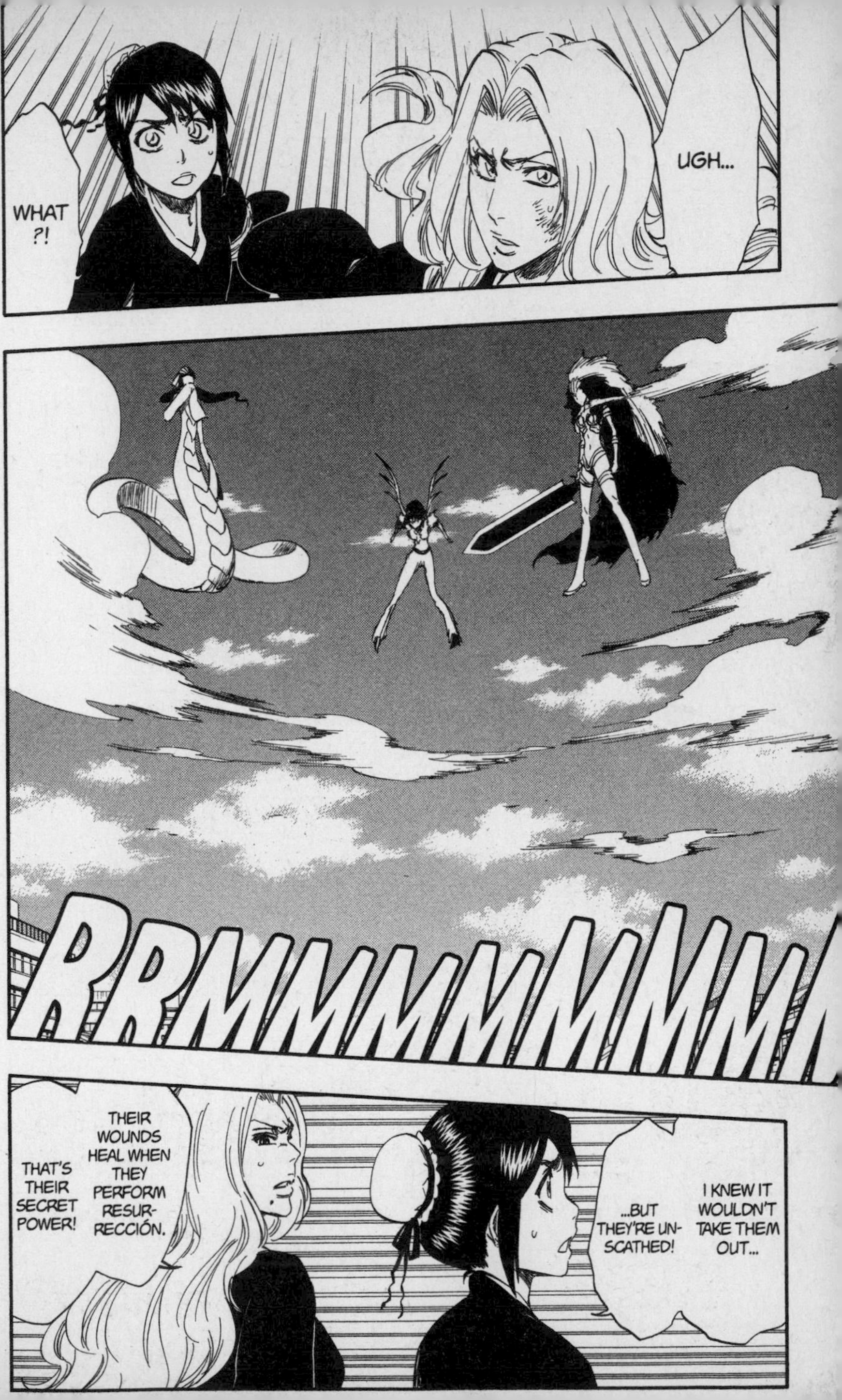
UGH...
WHAT ?!
RRMMMMMMMMM
I KNEW IT WOULDN'T TAKE THEM OUT...
...BUT THEY'RE UN-SCATHED!
THEIR WOUNDS HEAL WHEN THEY PERFORM RESUR-RECCIÓN.
THAT'S THEIR SECRET POWER!

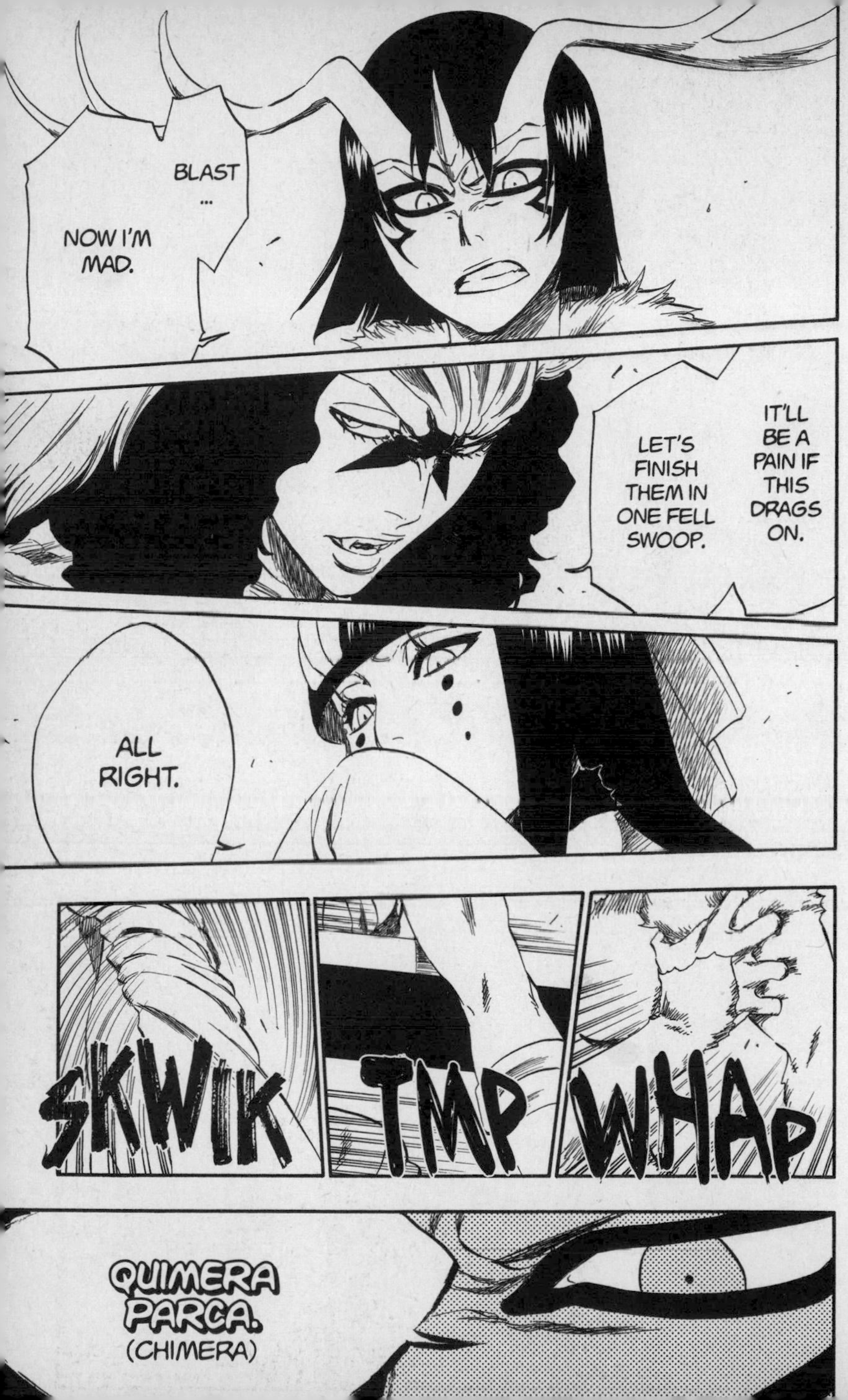
BLAST ... NOW I'M MAD.
IT'LL BE A PAIN IF THIS DRAGS ON.
LET'S FINISH THEM IN ONE FELL SWOOP.
ALL RIGHT.
WHAP
TMP
SKWIK
QUIMERA PARCA. (CHIMERA)

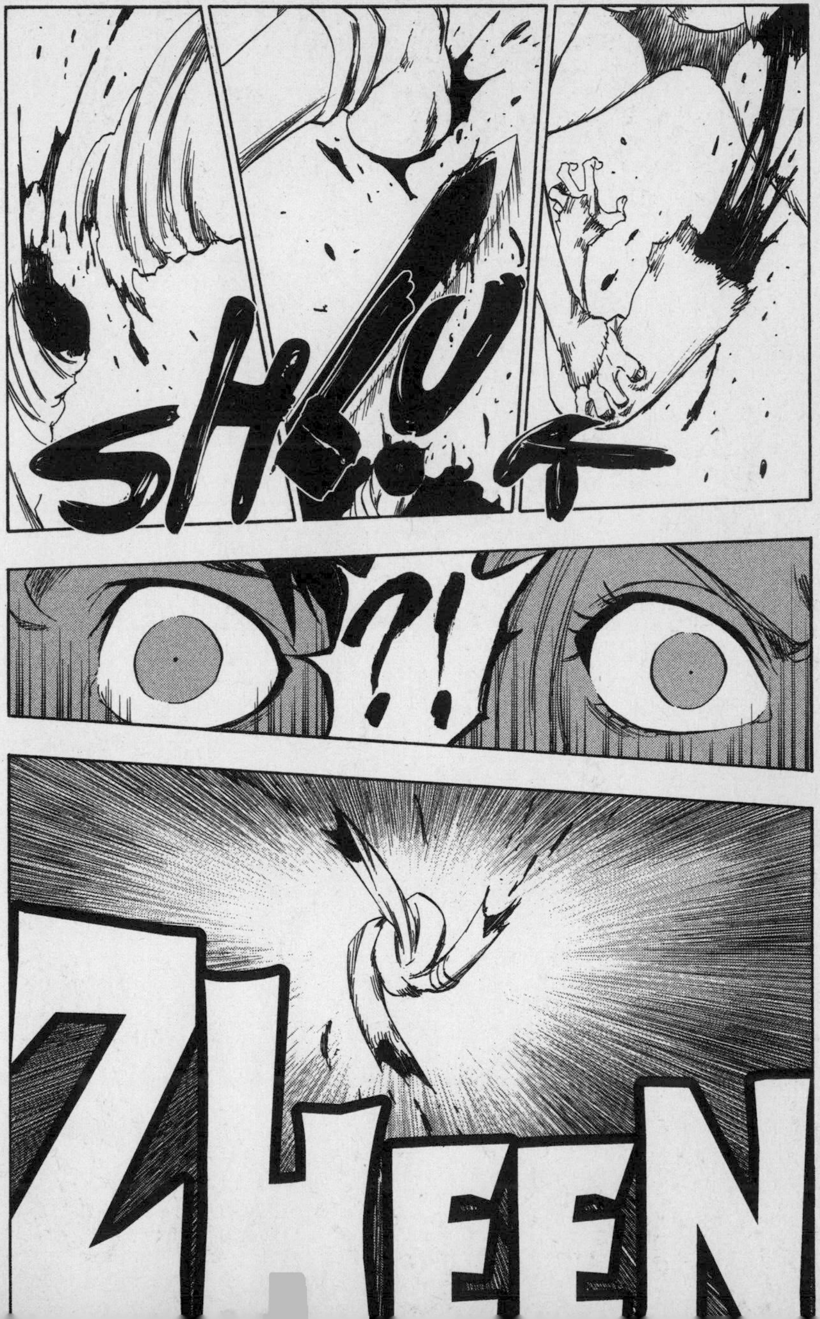
SHUT
?!
ZHEEN

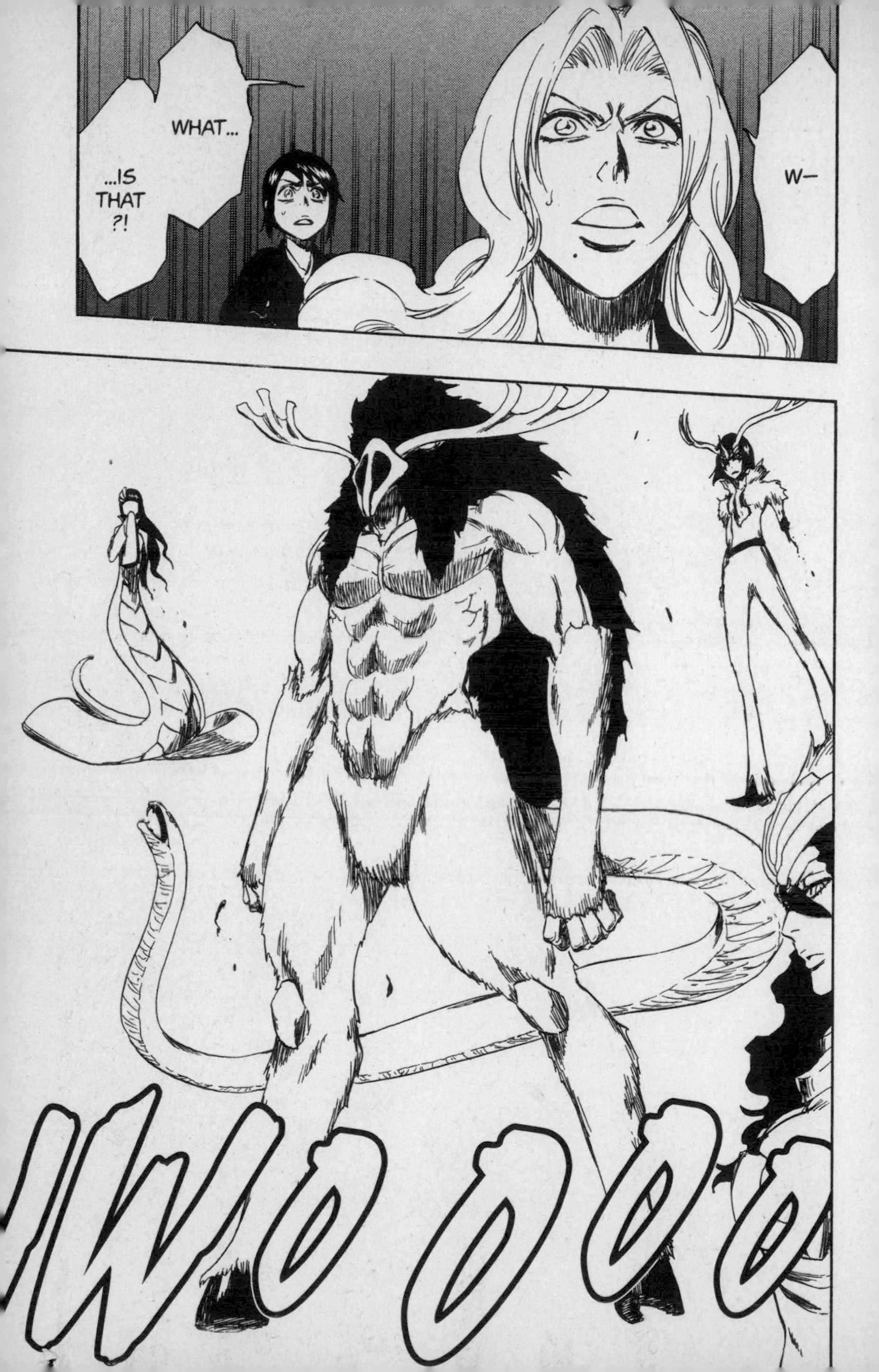
W—
WHAT...
...IS THAT?!
WOOOO

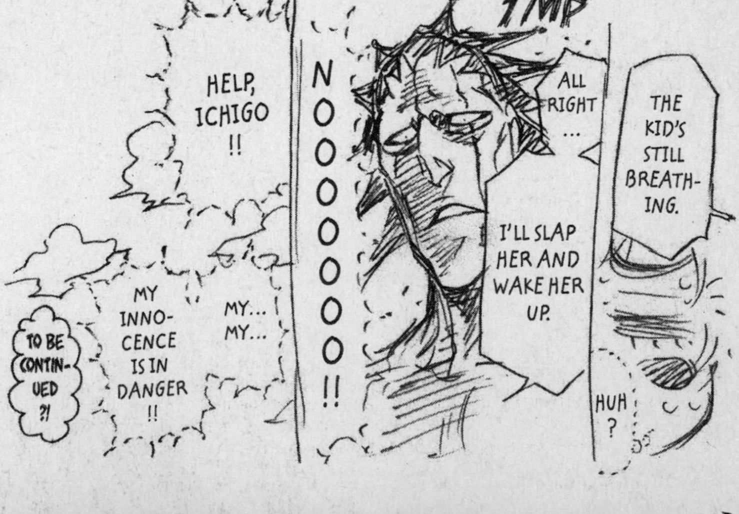
THE KID'S STILL BREATHING.
HUH?
TMP
ALL RIGHT ...
I'LL SLAP HER AND WAKE HER UP.
NOOOOOOO!!
HELP, ICHIGO !!
MY... MY...
MY INNOCENCE IS IN DANGER !!
TO BE CONTINUED ?!

336 El Verdugo

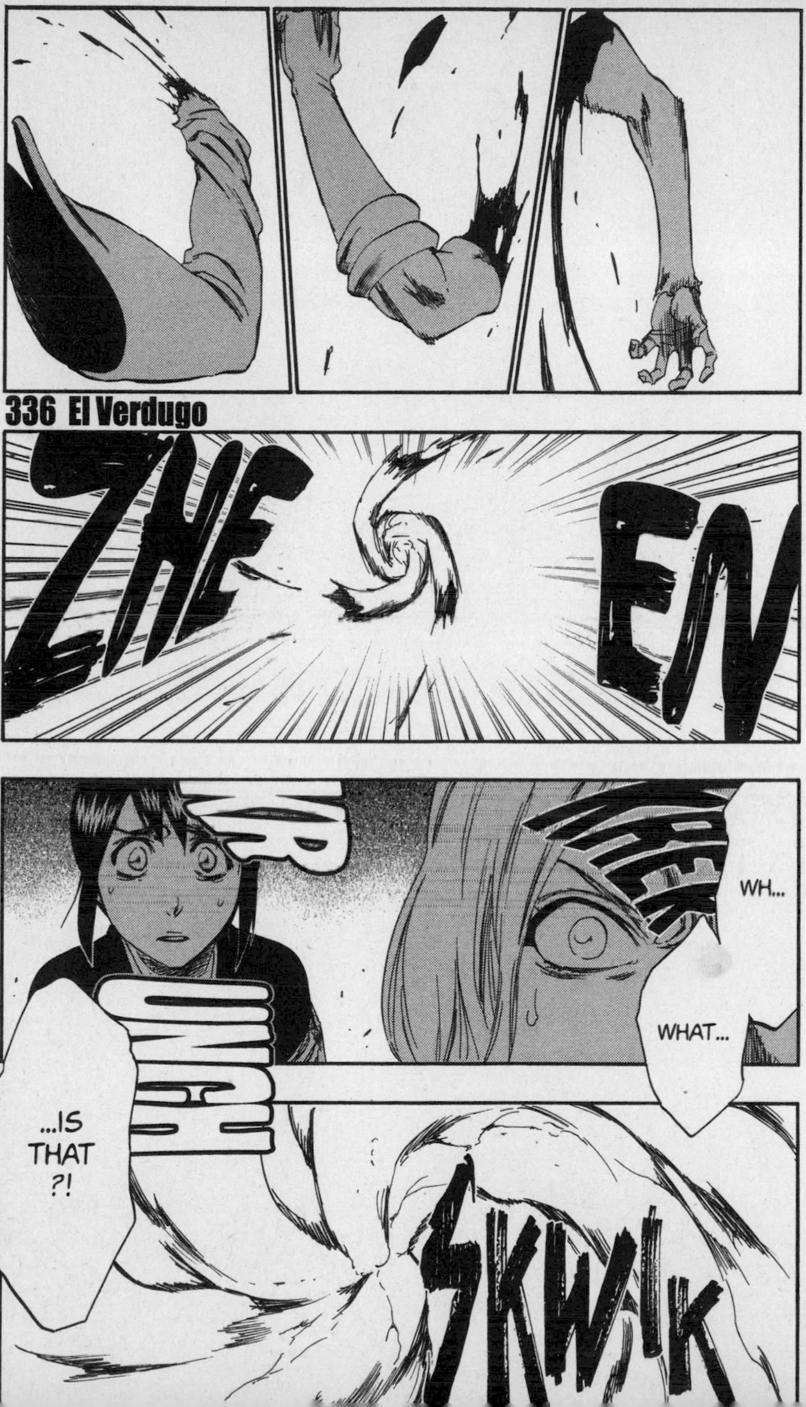
ZHE
EN
WH...
WHAT...
...IS THAT ?!

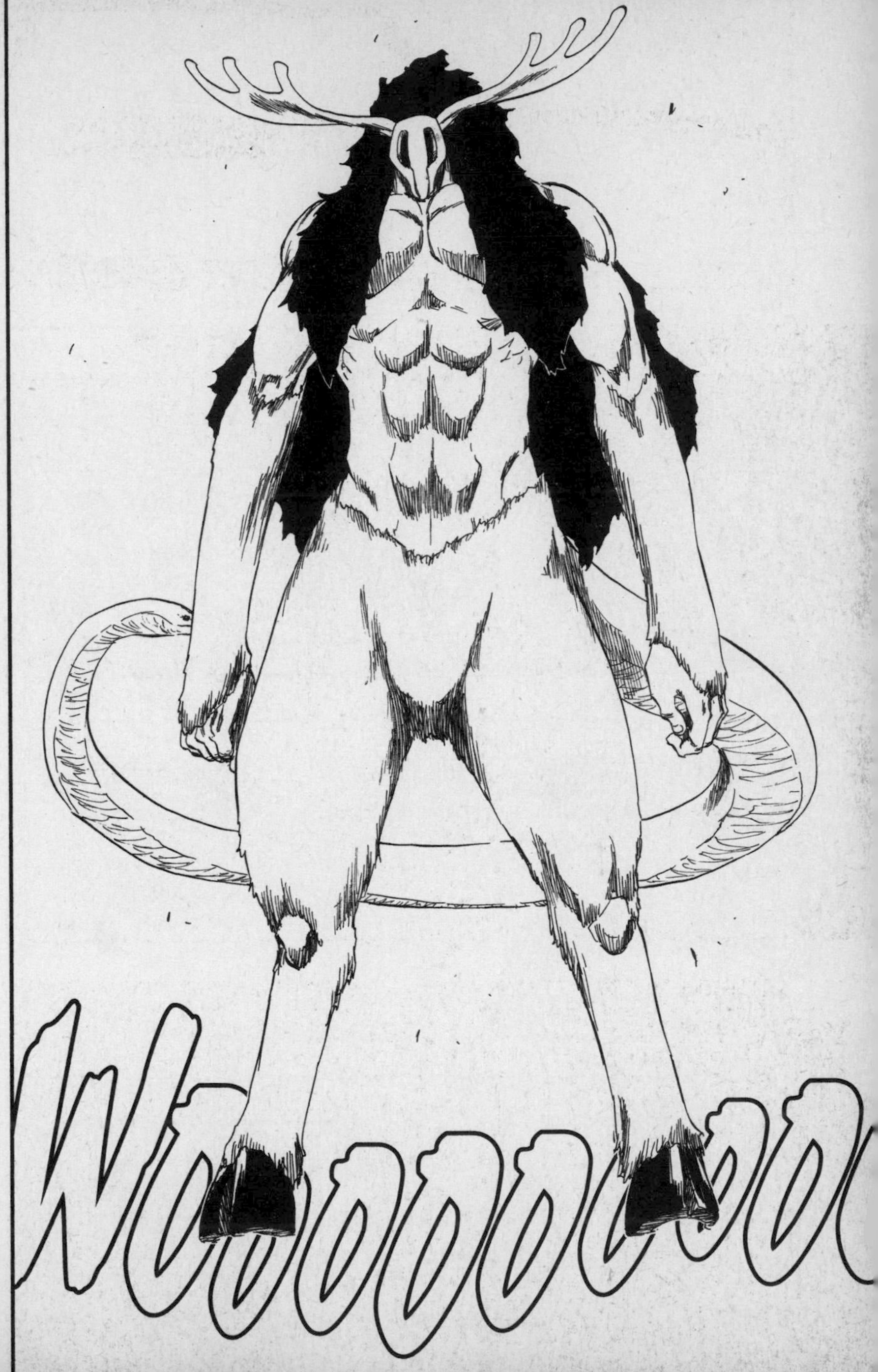
Wooooooooo

QUIMERA PARCA.

THIS IS THE CREATION OF OUR THREE FREED LEFT ARMS.

MEET OUR PET.

ITS NAME IS AYON.

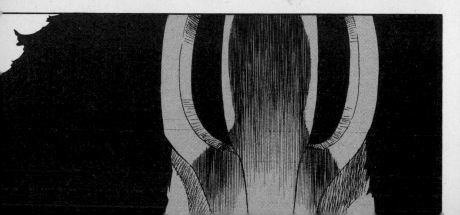

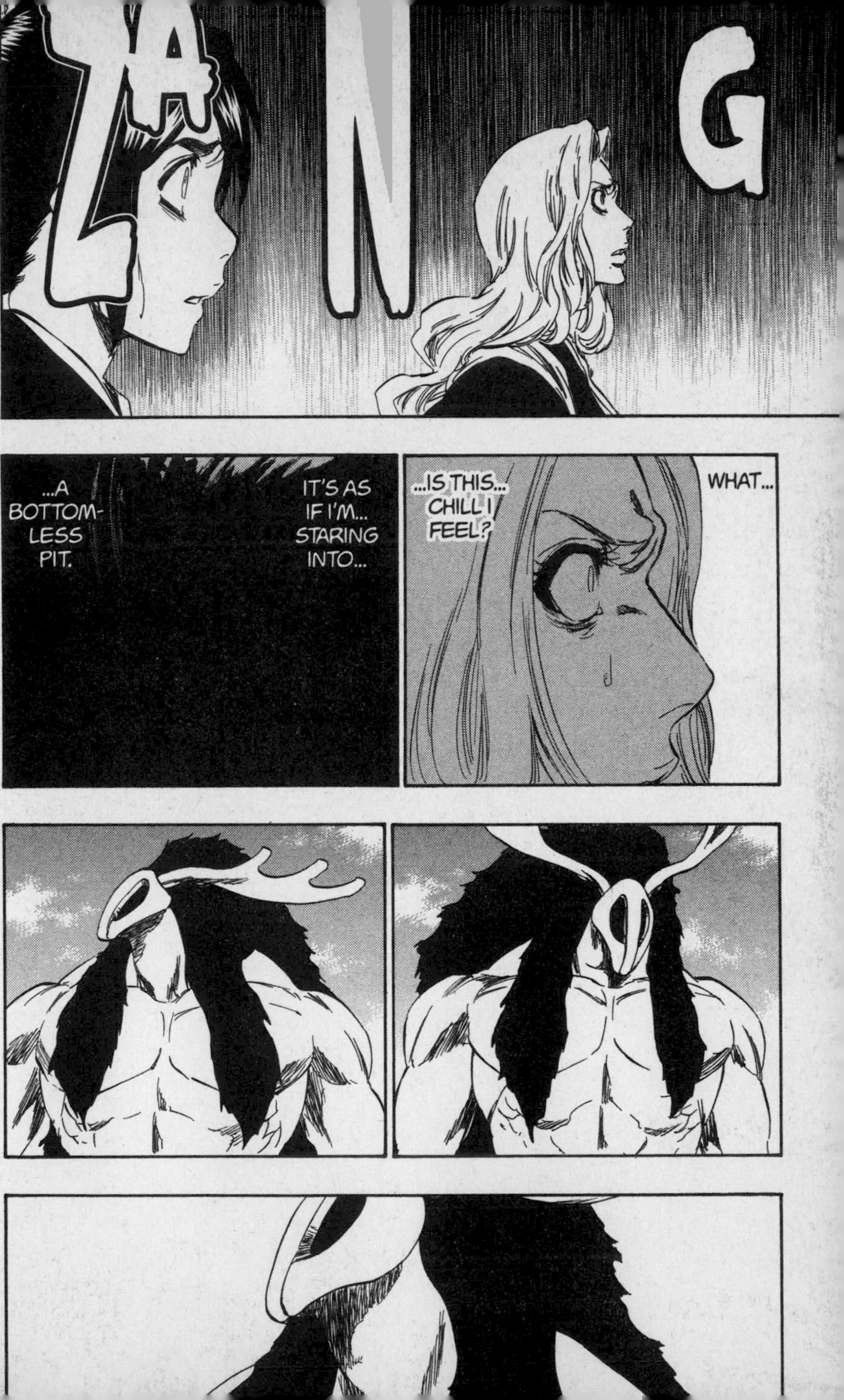
ZANG
WHAT...
...IS THIS... CHILL I FEEL?
IT'S AS IF I'M... STARING INTO...
...A BOTTOM-LESS PIT.

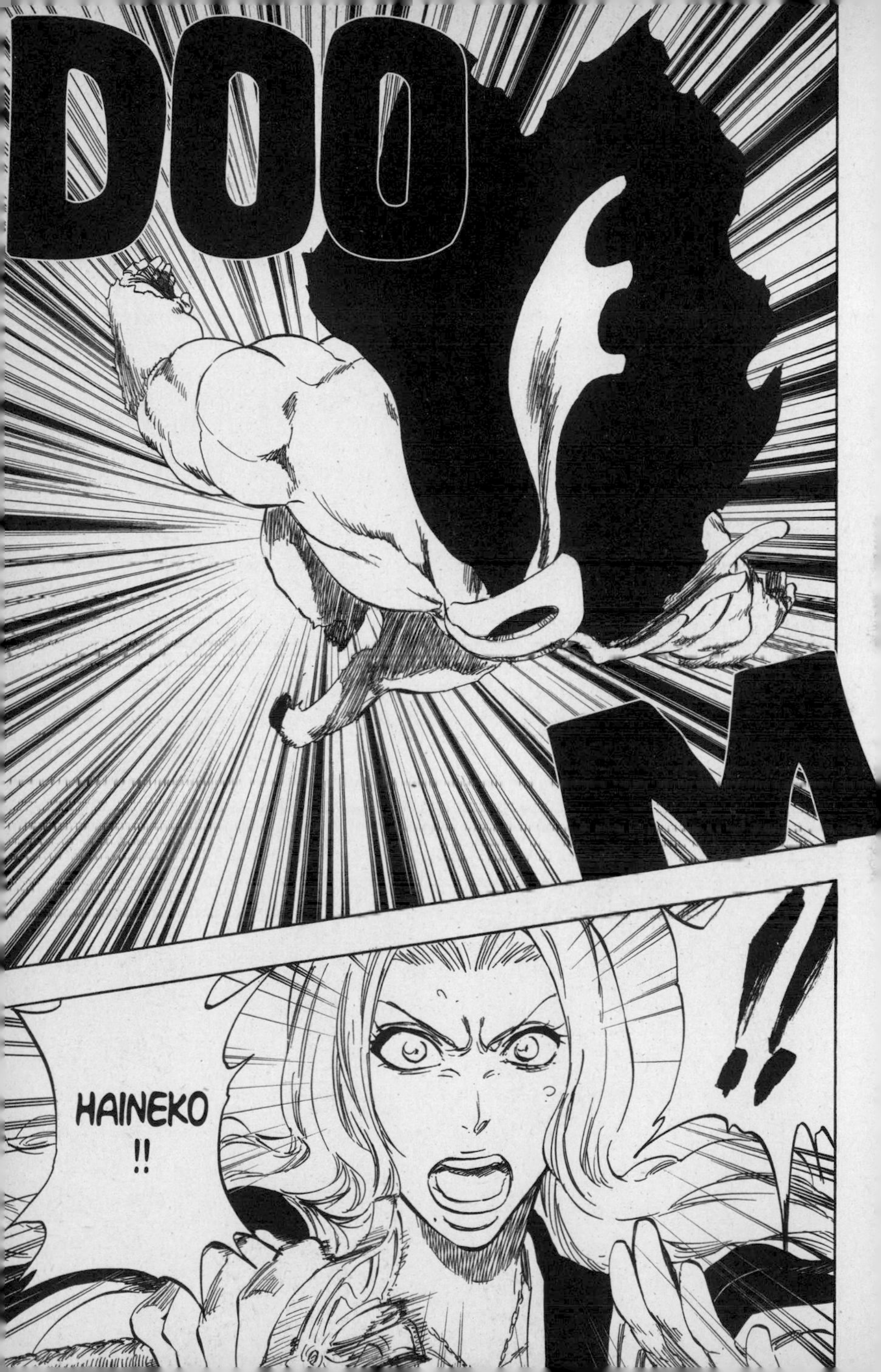
DOOM!!
HAINEKO !!

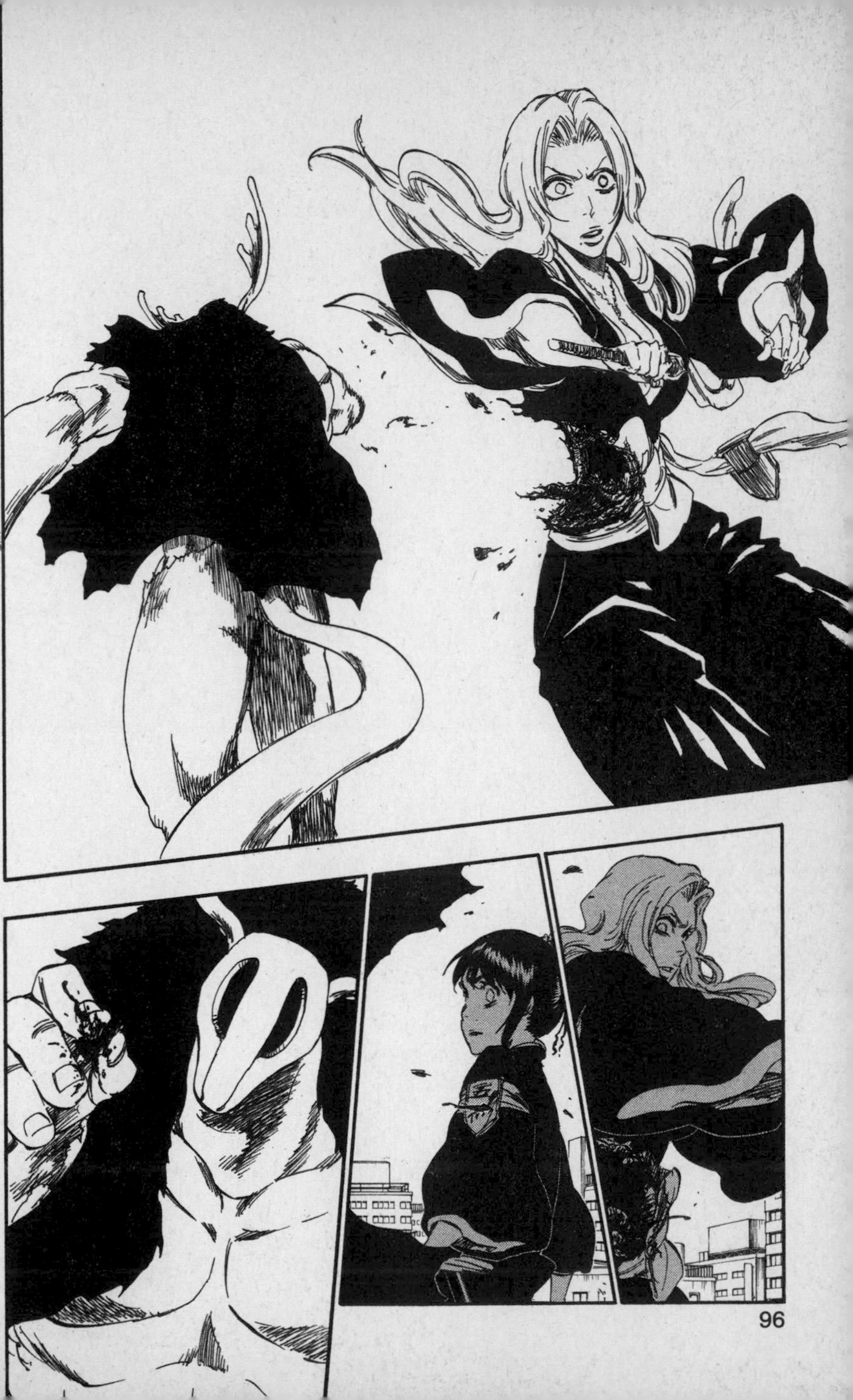

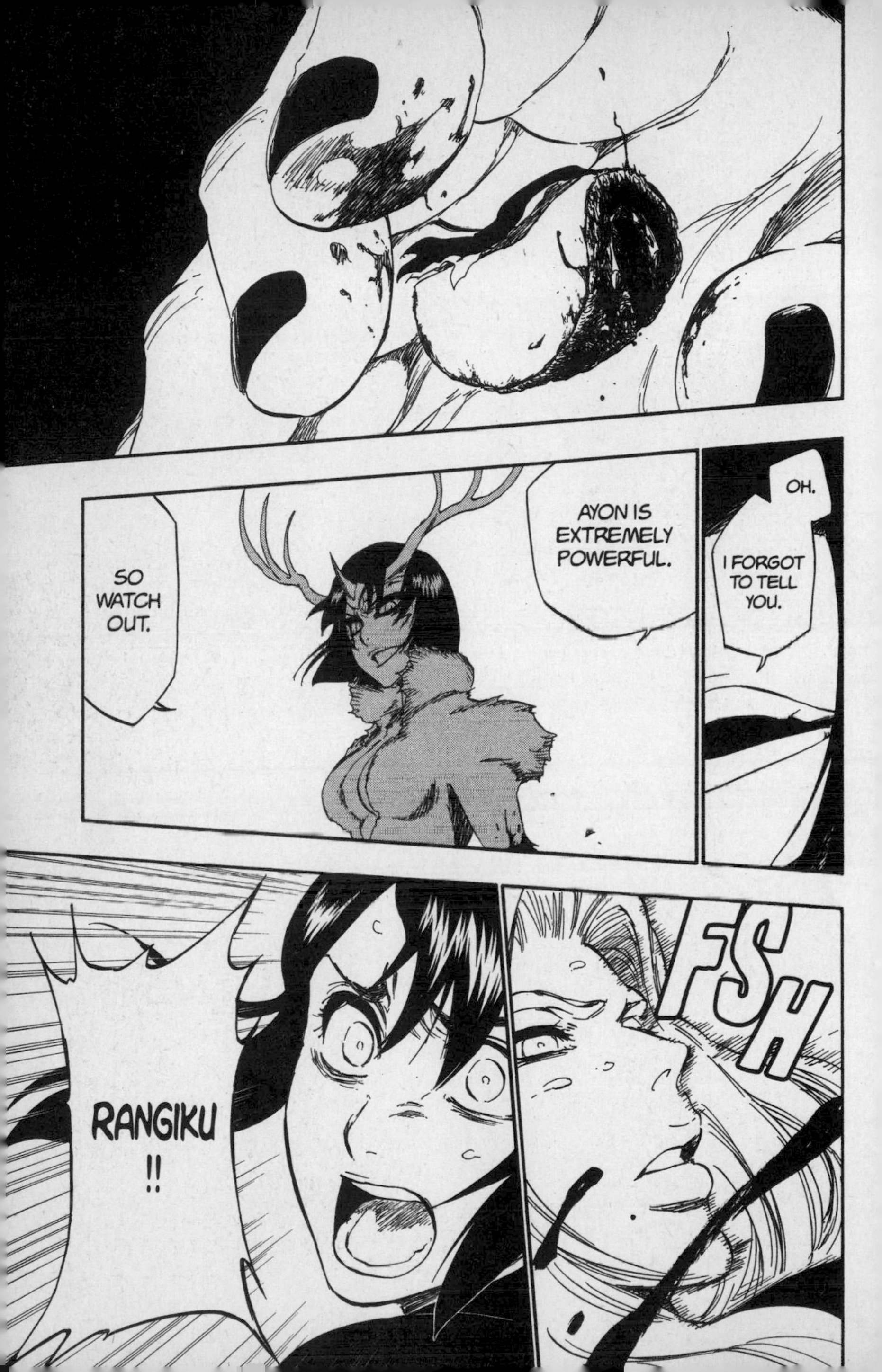
OH.
I FORGOT TO TELL YOU.
AYON IS EXTREMELY POWERFUL.
SO WATCH OUT.
FSH
RANGIKU !!

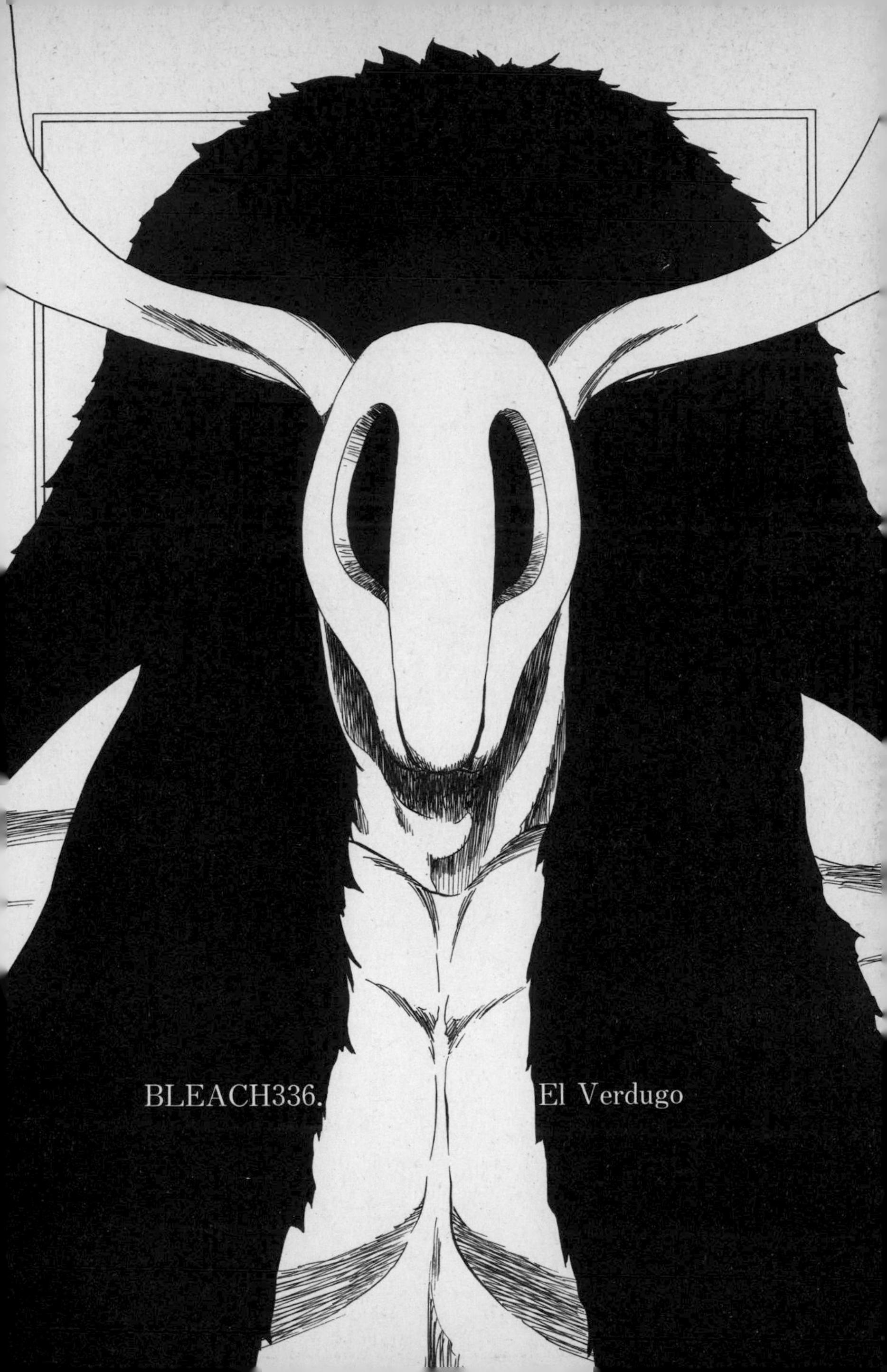
BLEACH336.
El Verdugo

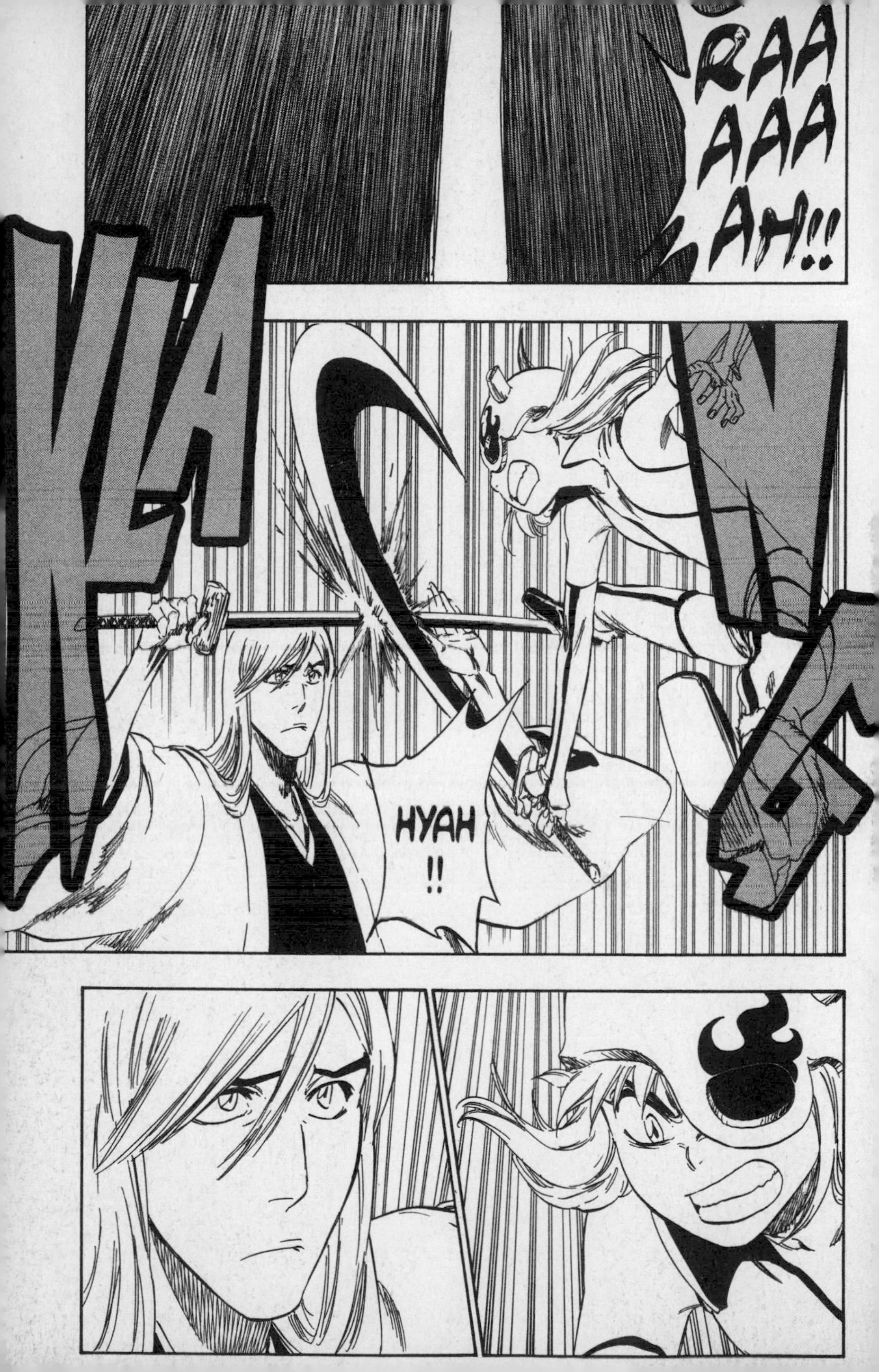
RAAAAAAAH!!
HYAH !!

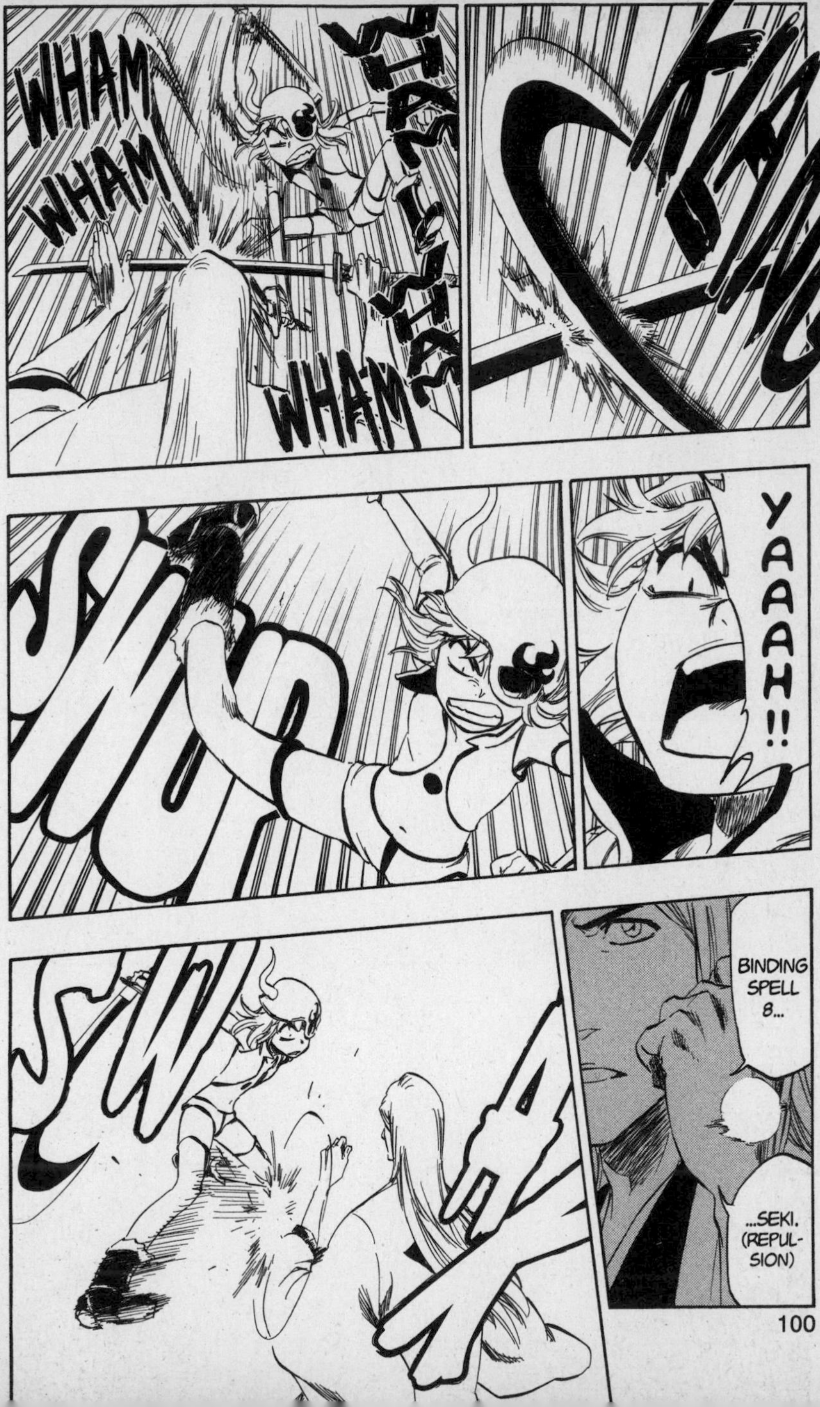
KLANG
WHAM
WHAM
WHAM
WHAM
YAAAAH!!
BINDING SPELL 8...
...SEKI. (REPULSION)

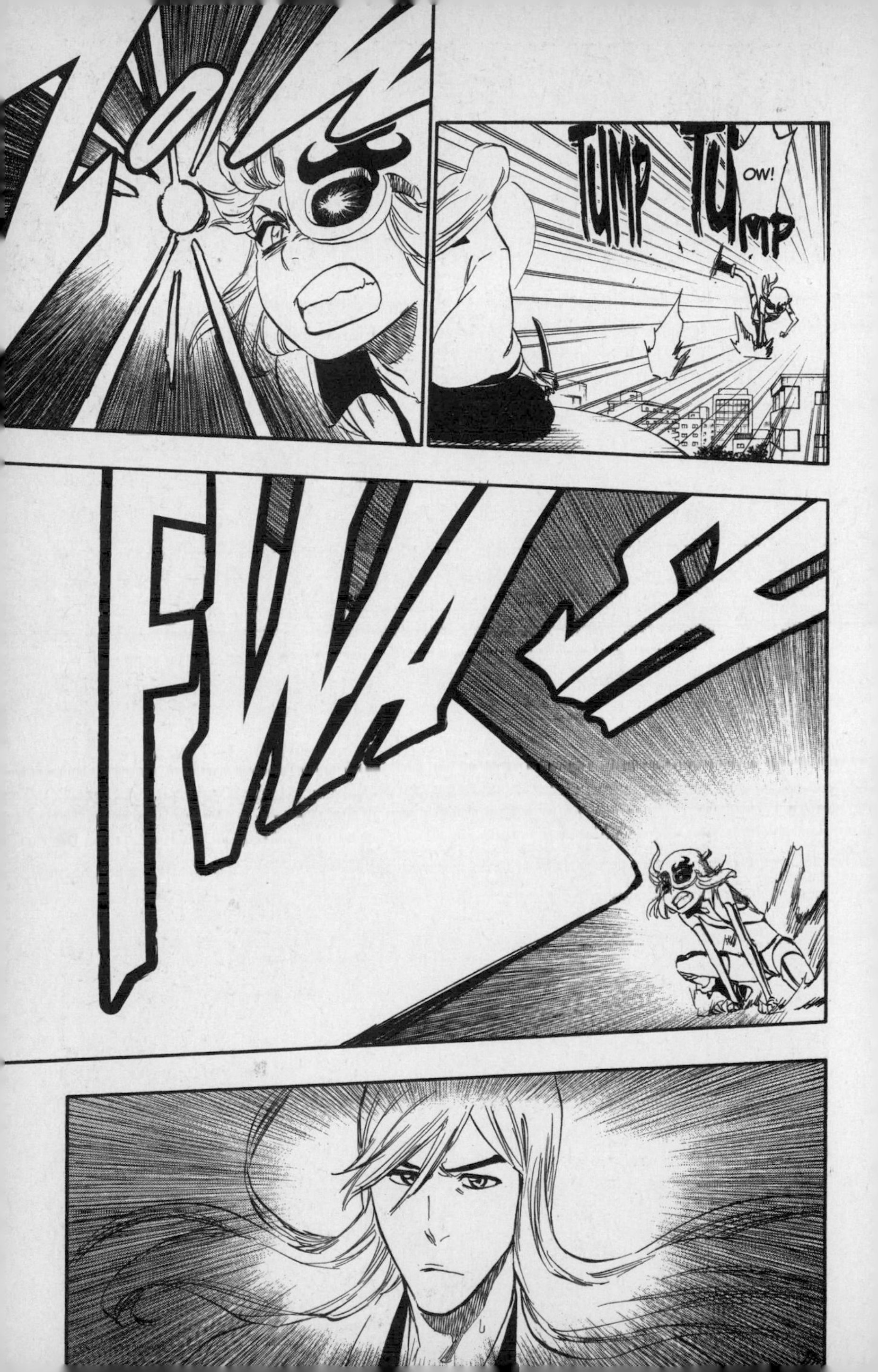
TUMP TUMP
OW!

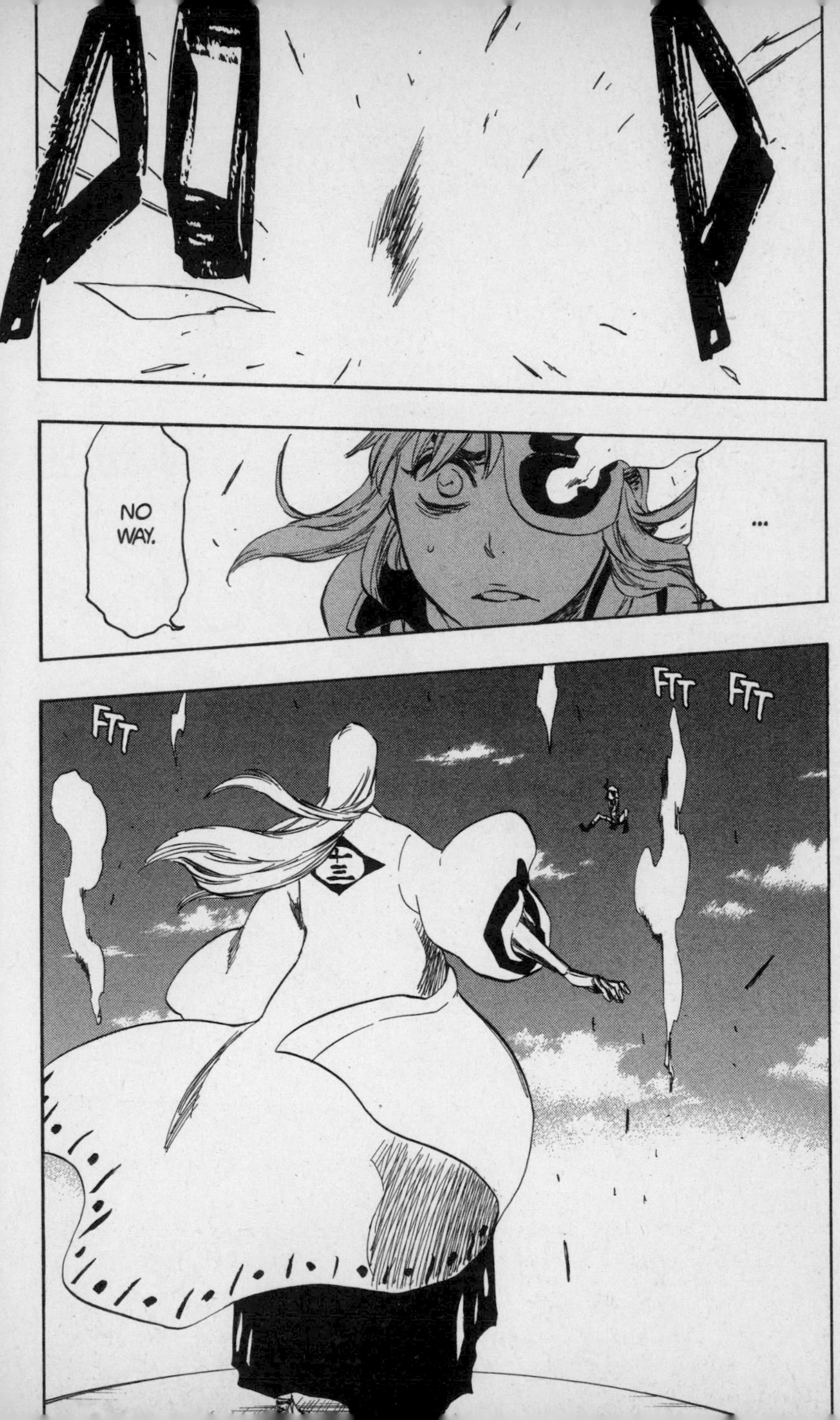
...
NO WAY.
FTT
FTT
FTT

READ THIS WAY

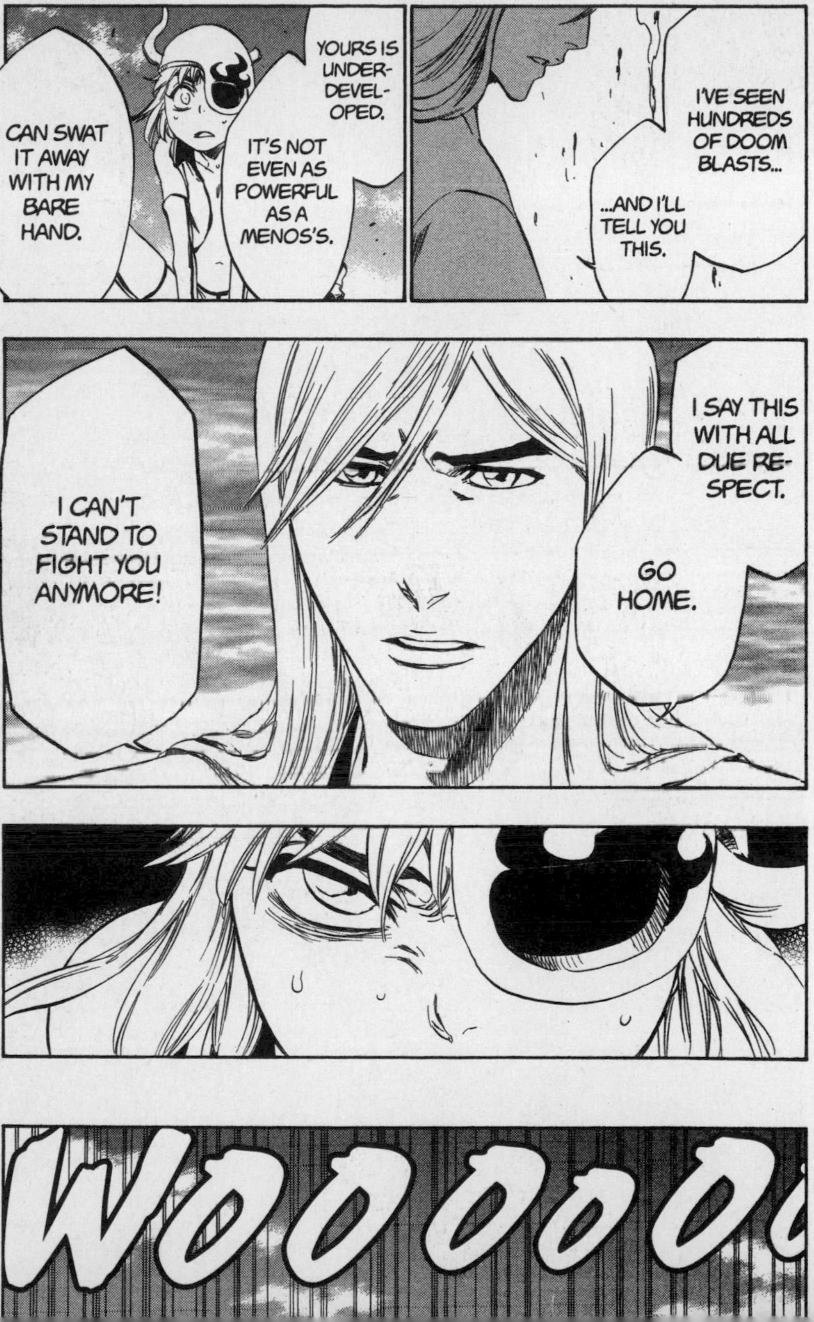
I'VE SEEN HUNDREDS OF DOOM BLASTS...
...AND I'LL TELL YOU THIS.
YOURS IS UNDER-DEVEL-OPED.
IT'S NOT EVEN AS POWERFUL AS A MENOS'S.
I CAN SWAT IT AWAY WITH MY BARE HAND.
I SAY THIS WITH ALL DUE RE-SPECT.
GO HOME.
I CAN'T STAND TO FIGHT YOU ANYMORE!
WOOOOO

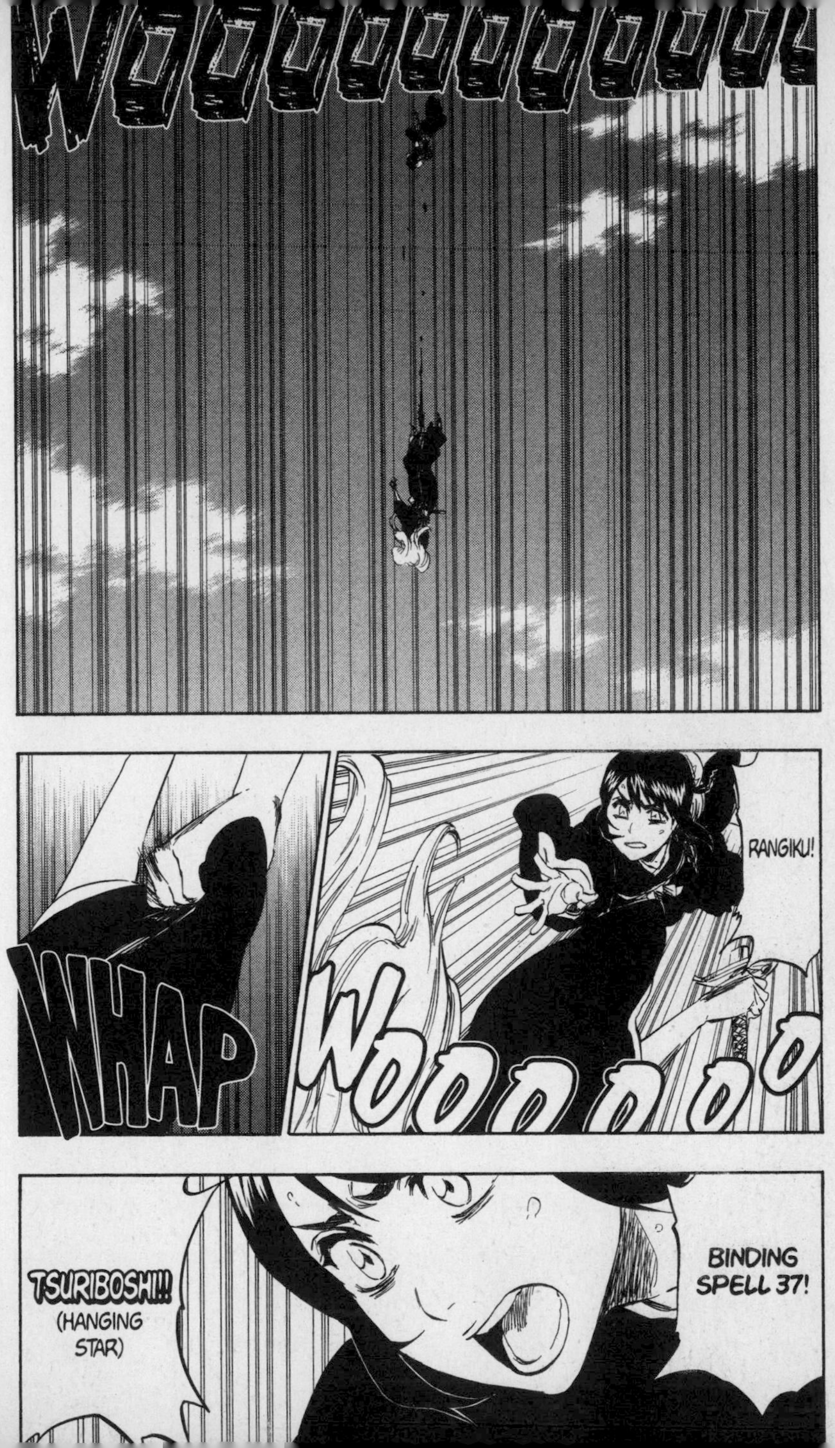
WOOOOOOOOOOO
RANGIKU!
WOOOOOOOO
WHAP
BINDING SPELL 37!
TSURIBOSHI!!!
(HANGING STAR)

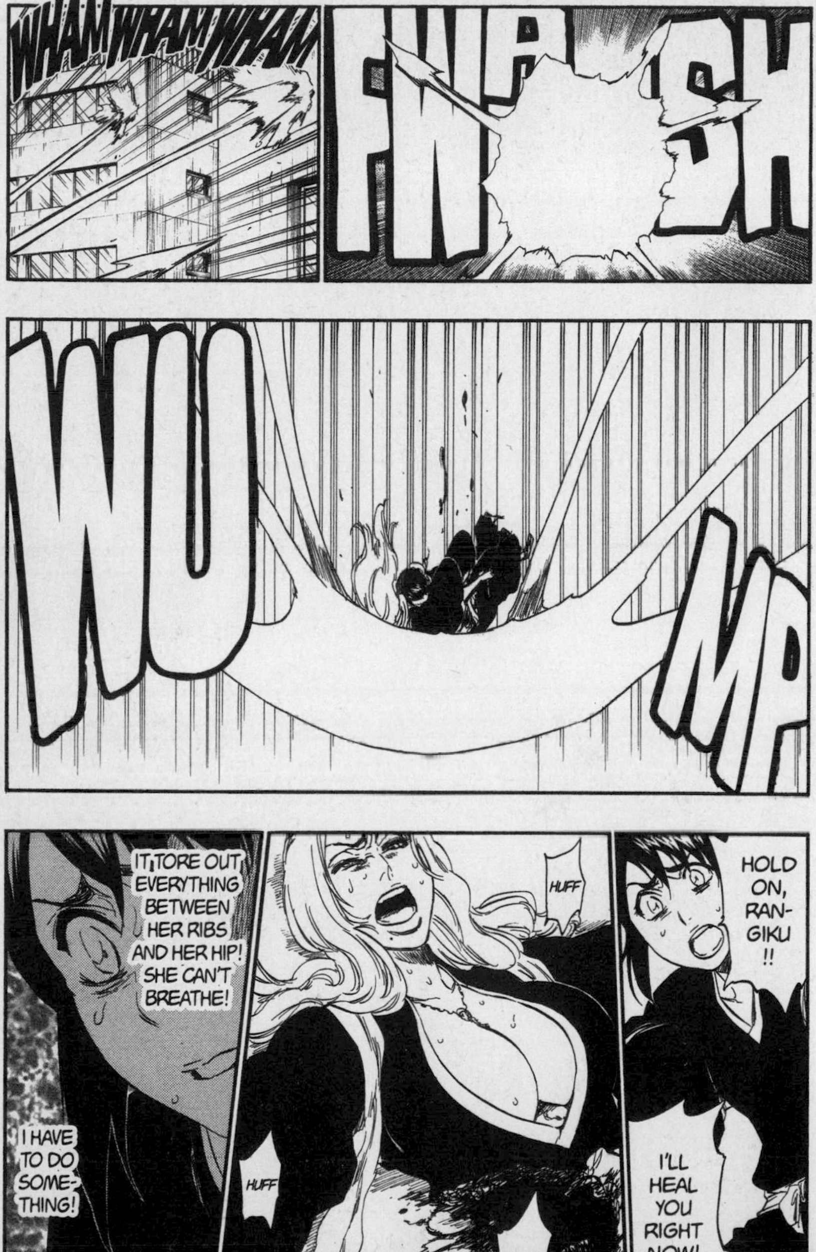
FWASH
WHAM WHAM WHAM
WUMP
HOLD ON, RAN-GIKU!!
I'LL HEAL YOU RIGHT NOW!
HUFF
HUFF
HUFF
IT TORE OUT EVERYTHING BETWEEN HER RIBS AND HER HIP! SHE CAN'T BREATHE!
I HAVE TO DO SOME-THING!

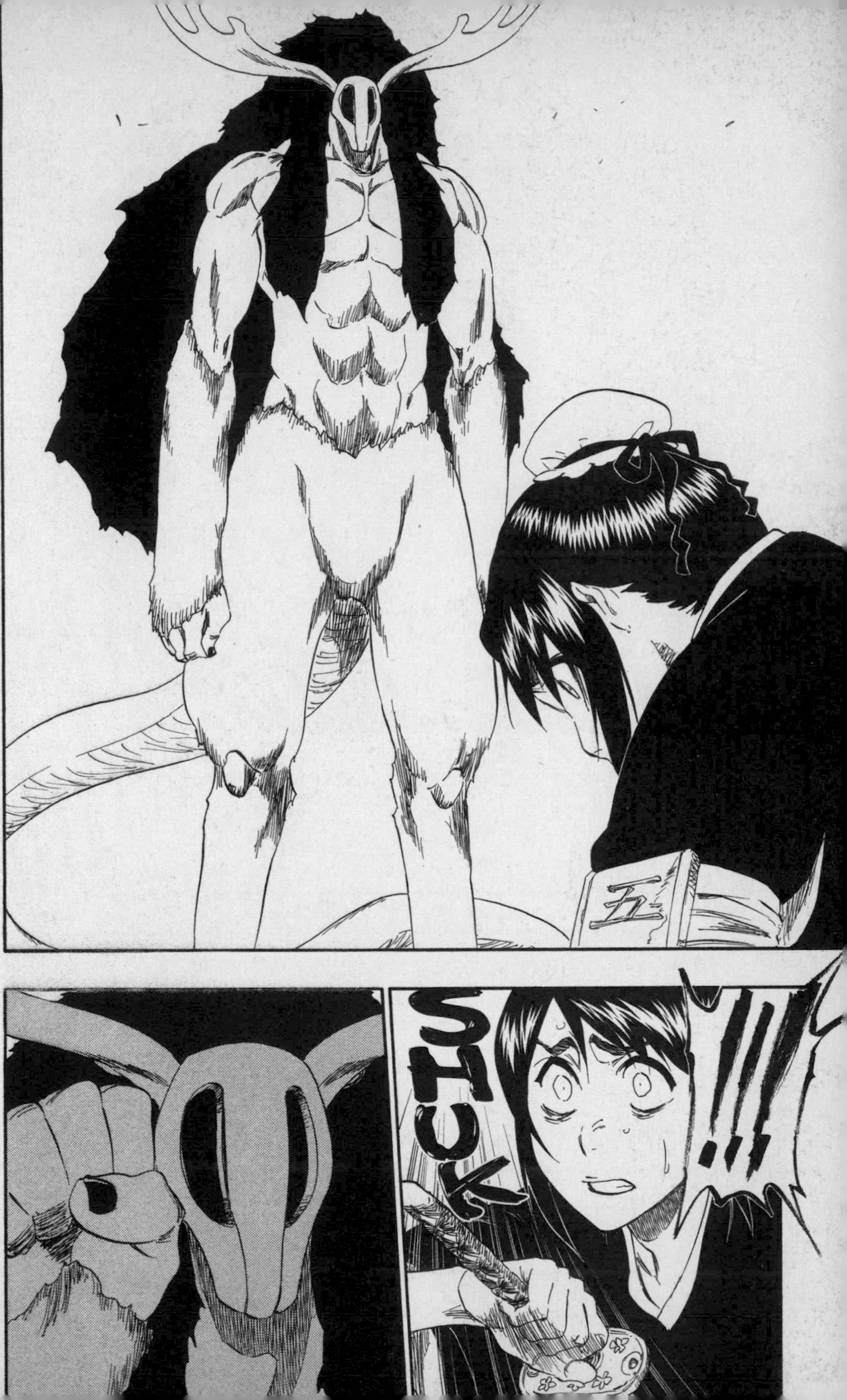
SHUK
!!!

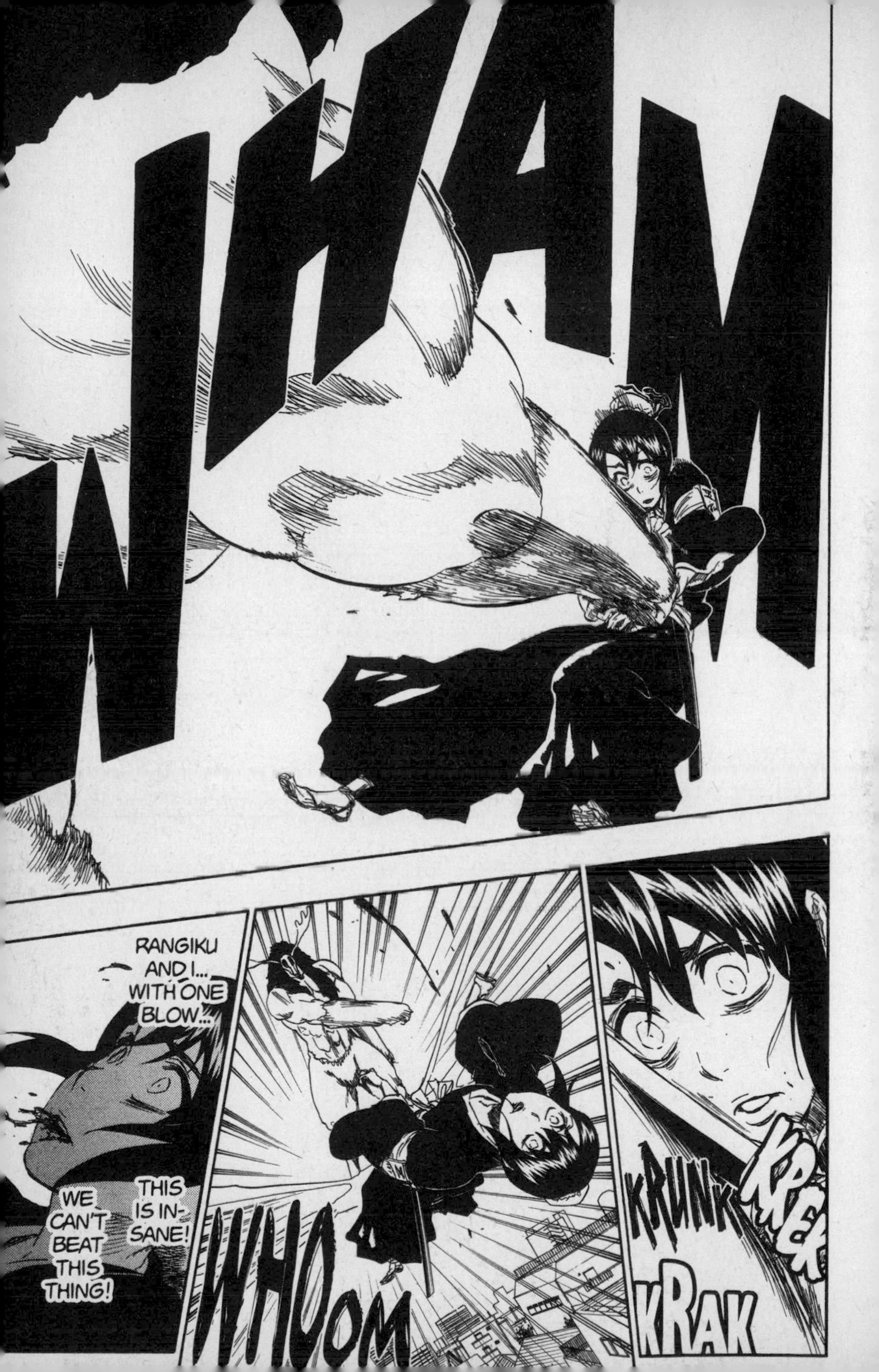
WHAM
KREK
KRUNK
KRAK
WHOOM
RANGIKU AND I... WITH ONE BLOW...
THIS IS IN-SANE!
WE CAN'T BEAT THIS THING!

BINDING SPELL 37...

...TSURI-BOSHI!!

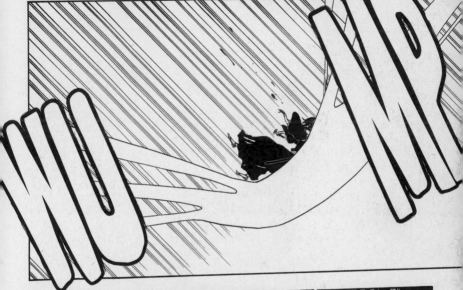

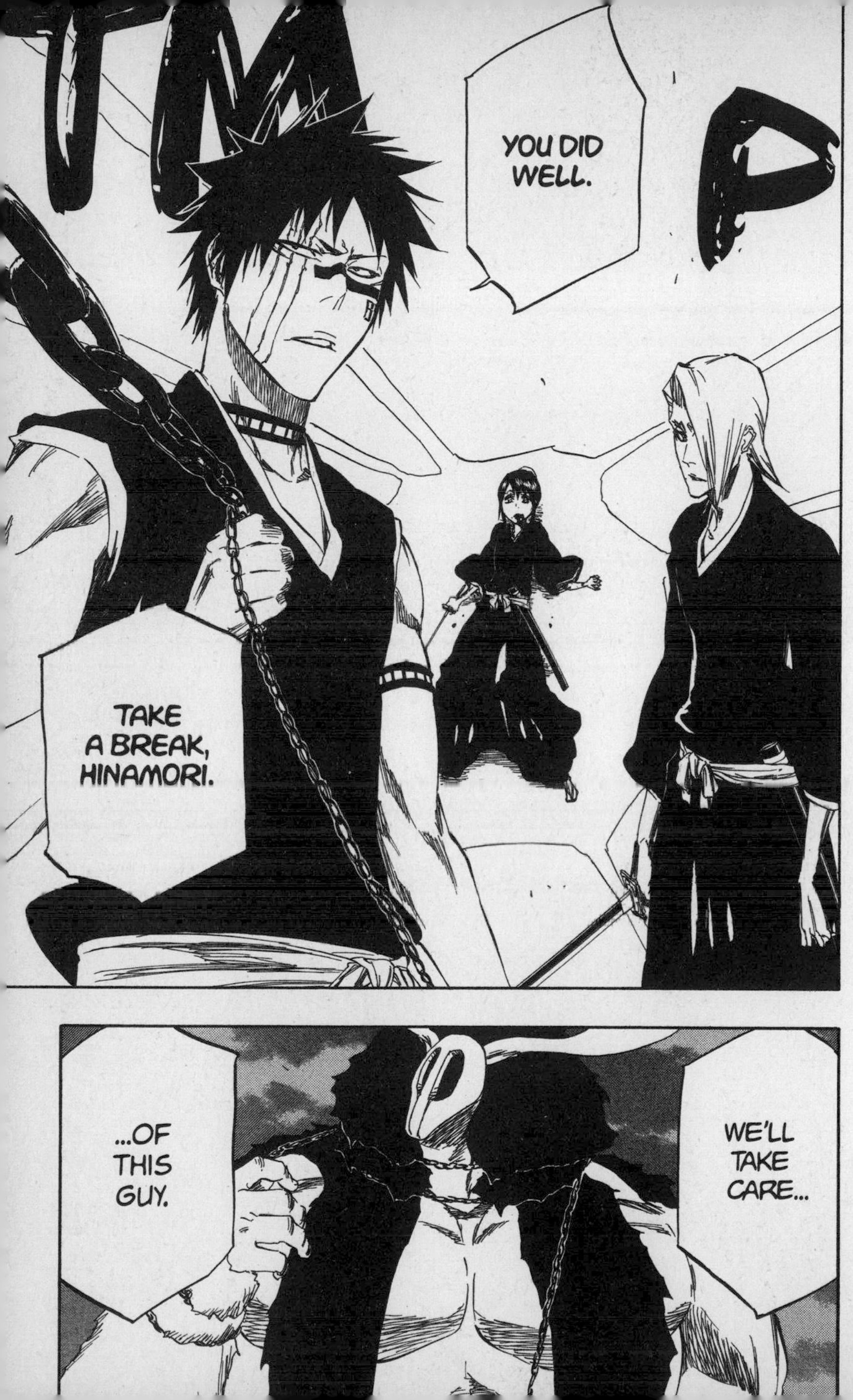
YOU DID WELL.
TAKE A BREAK, HINAMORI.
WE'LL TAKE CARE...
...OF THIS GUY.

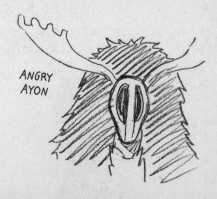

ANGRY
AYON

337. Hall In Your Inferno

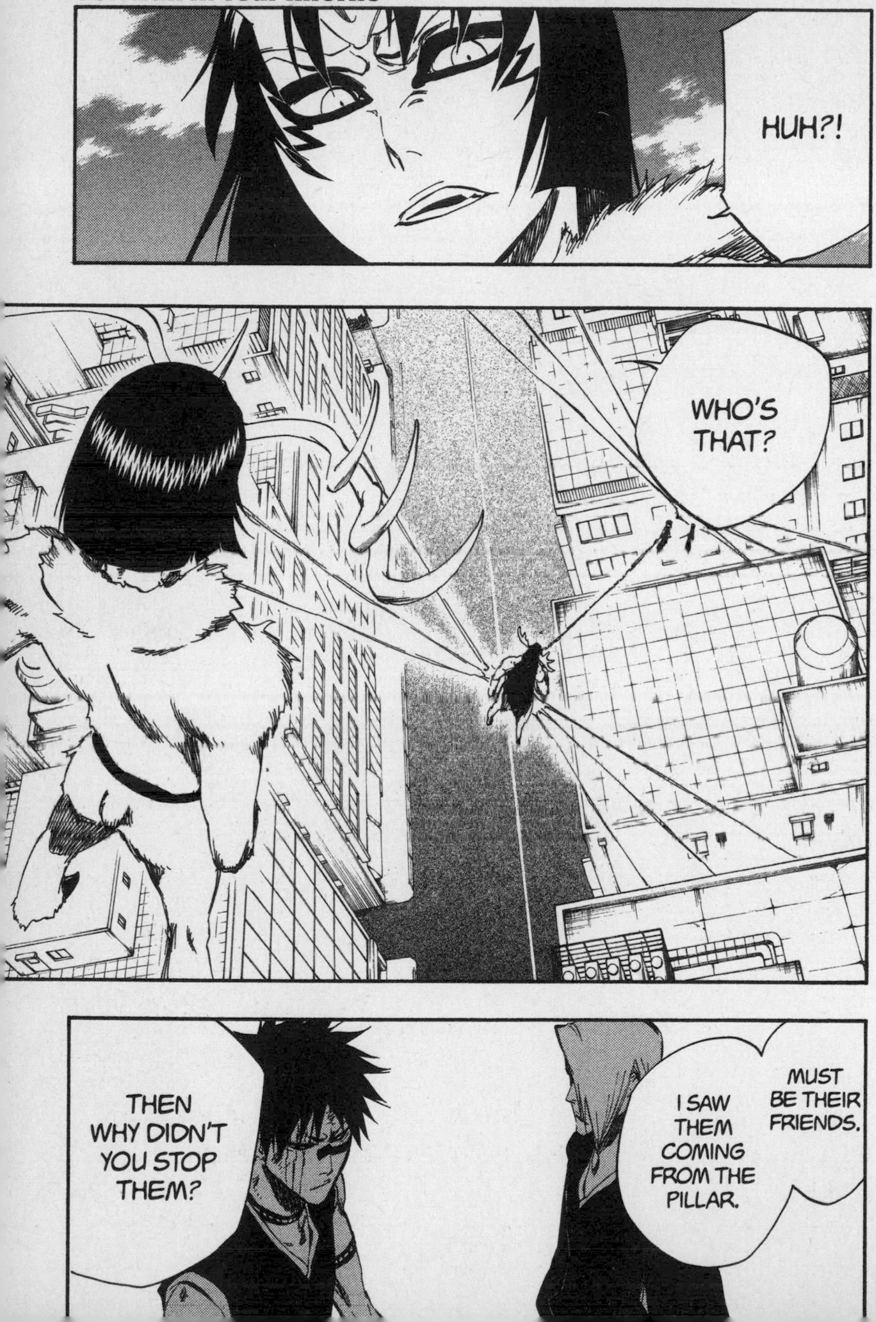
HUH?!
WHO'S THAT?
MUST BE THEIR FRIENDS.
I SAW THEM COMING FROM THE PILLAR.
THEN WHY DIDN'T YOU STOP THEM?

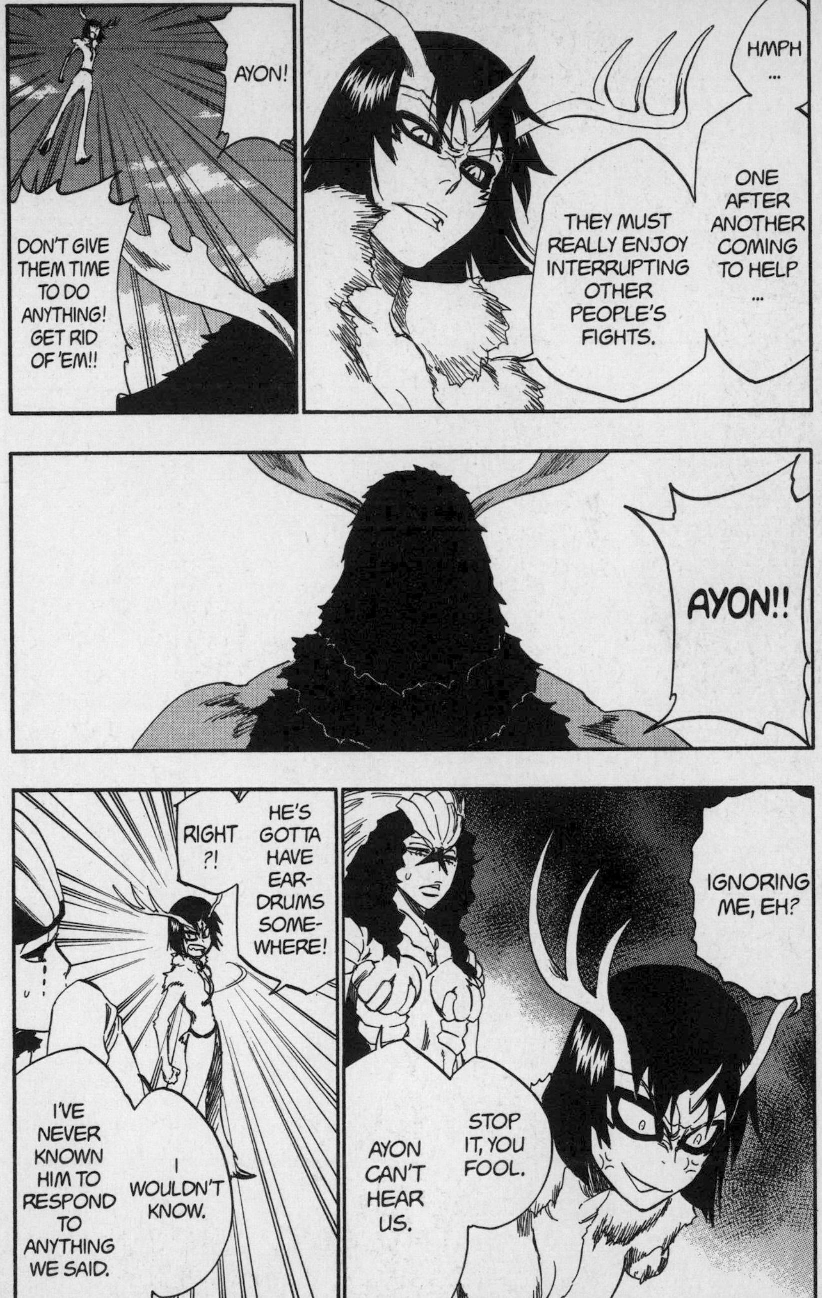
HMPH ...
ONE AFTER ANOTHER COMING TO HELP ...
THEY MUST REALLY ENJOY INTERRUPTING OTHER PEOPLE'S FIGHTS.
AYON!
DON'T GIVE THEM TIME TO DO ANYTHING! GET RID OF 'EM!!
AYON!!
IGNORING ME, EH?
STOP IT, YOU FOOL.
AYON CAN'T HEAR US.
HE'S GOTTA HAVE EAR-DRUMS SOME-WHERE!
RIGHT ?!
I WOULDN'T KNOW.
I'VE NEVER KNOWN HIM TO RESPOND TO ANYTHING WE SAID.

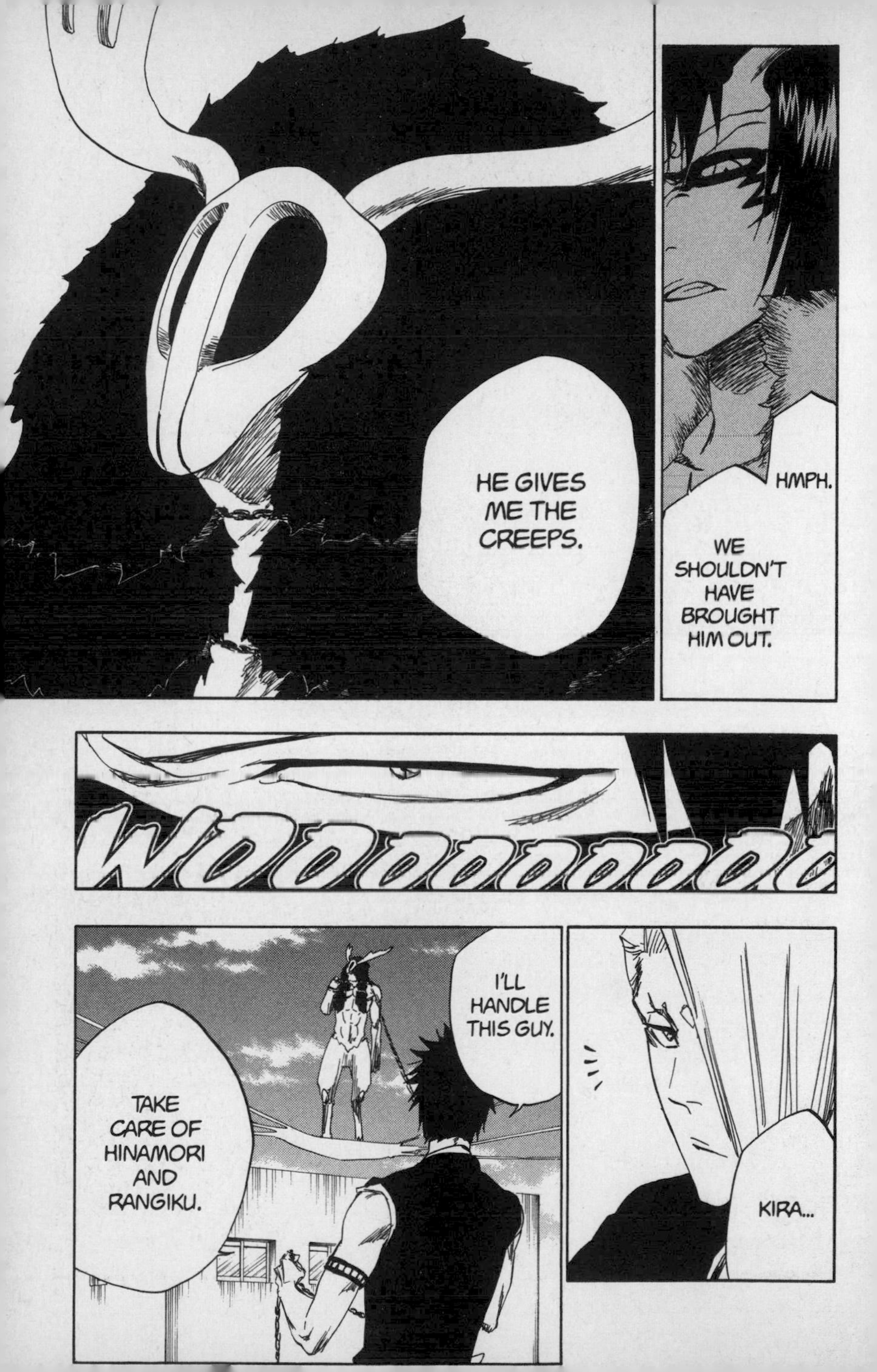
HMPH.
WE SHOULDN'T HAVE BROUGHT HIM OUT.
HE GIVES ME THE CREEPS.
WOOOOOOOOOOOO
KIRA...
I'LL HANDLE THIS GUY.
TAKE CARE OF HINAMORI AND RANGIKU.

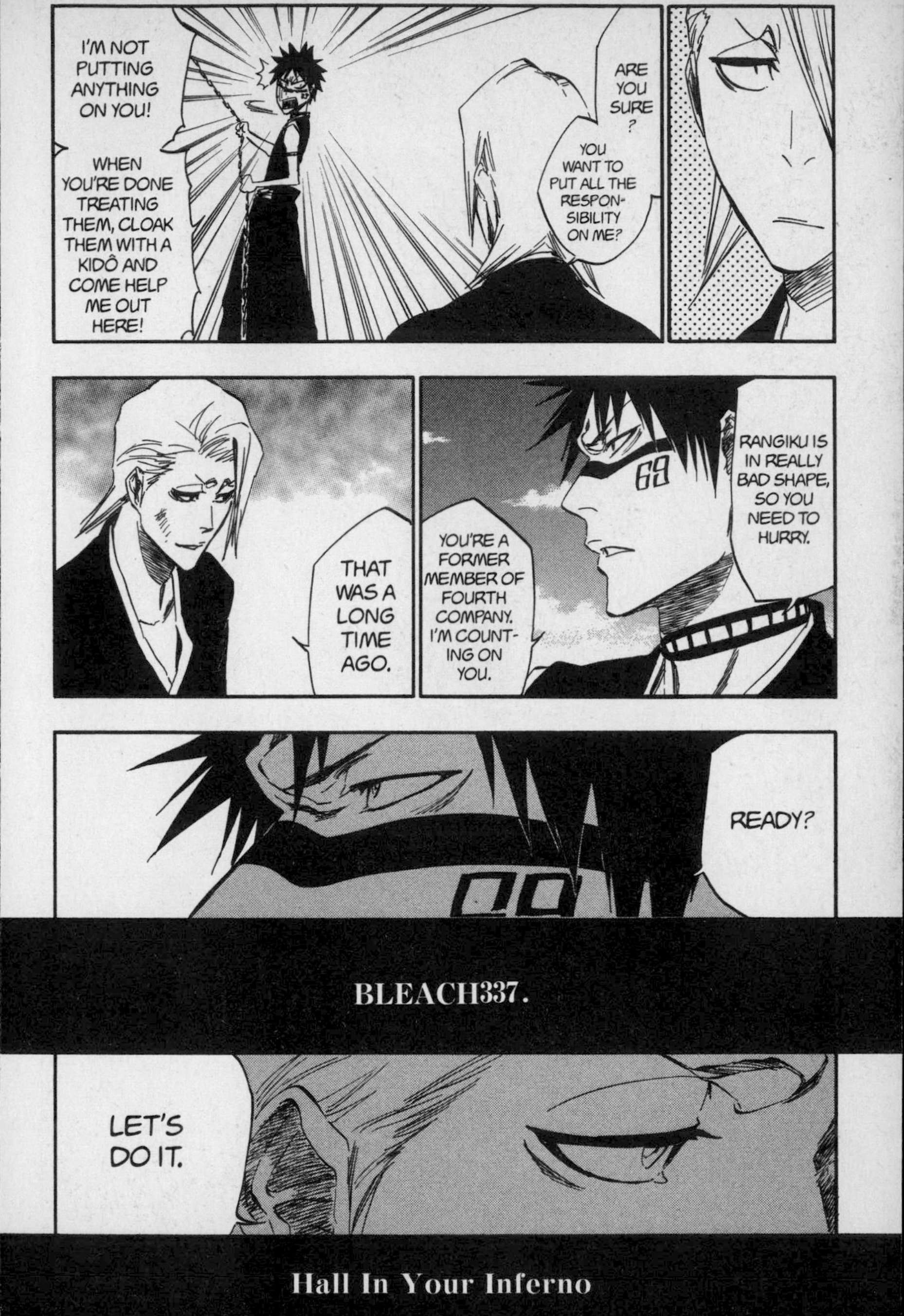
ARE YOU SURE ?
YOU WANT TO PUT ALL THE RESPONSIBILITY ON ME?
I'M NOT PUTTING ANYTHING ON YOU!
WHEN YOU'RE DONE TREATING THEM, CLOAK THEM WITH A KIDÔ AND COME HELP ME OUT HERE!
RANGIKU IS IN REALLY BAD SHAPE, SO YOU NEED TO HURRY.
YOU'RE A FORMER MEMBER OF FOURTH COMPANY. I'M COUNTING ON YOU.
THAT WAS A LONG TIME AGO.
READY?
BLEACH337.
LET'S DO IT.
Hall In Your Inferno

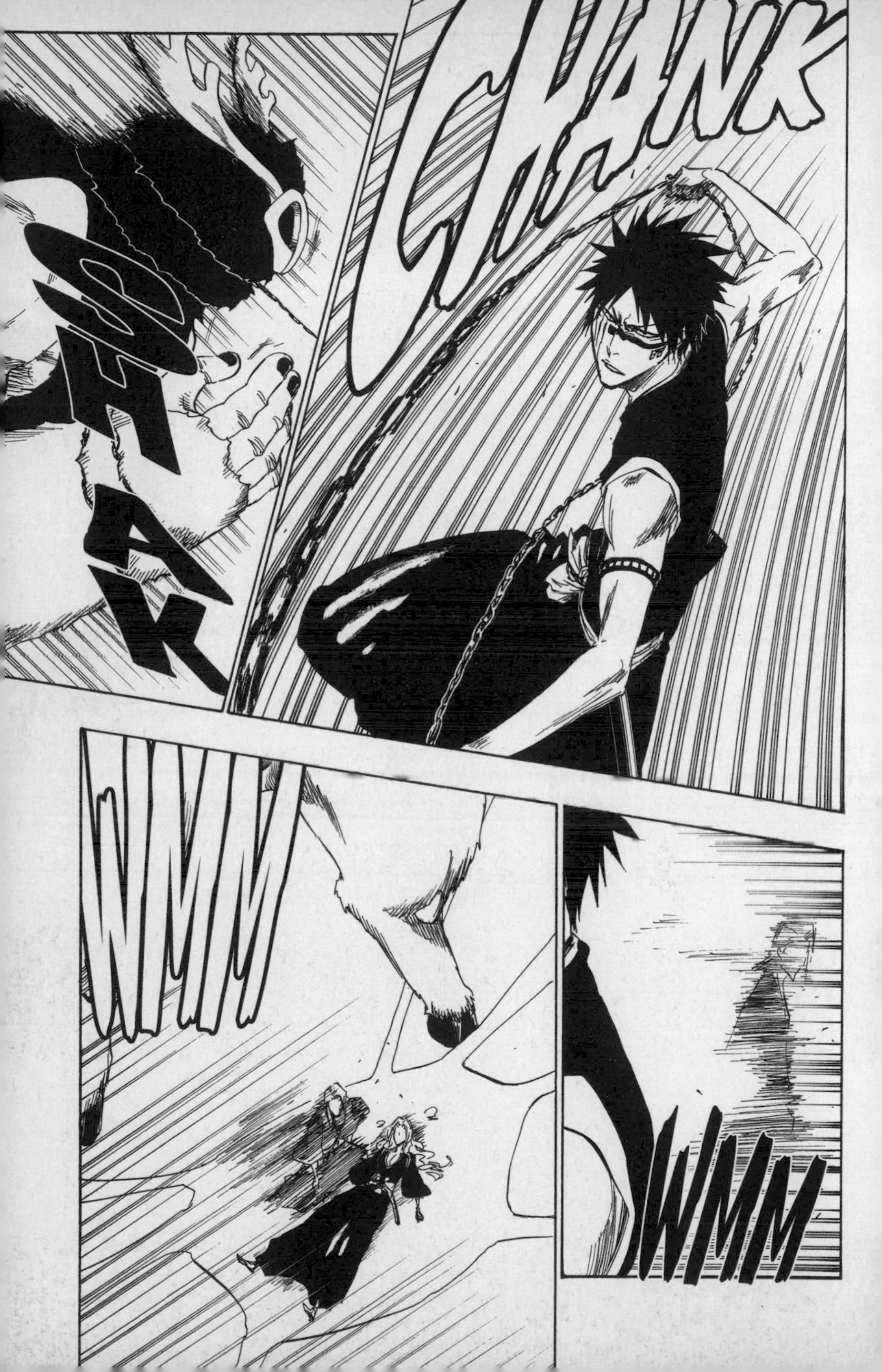
CHANK
CHAK
WMM
WMMM

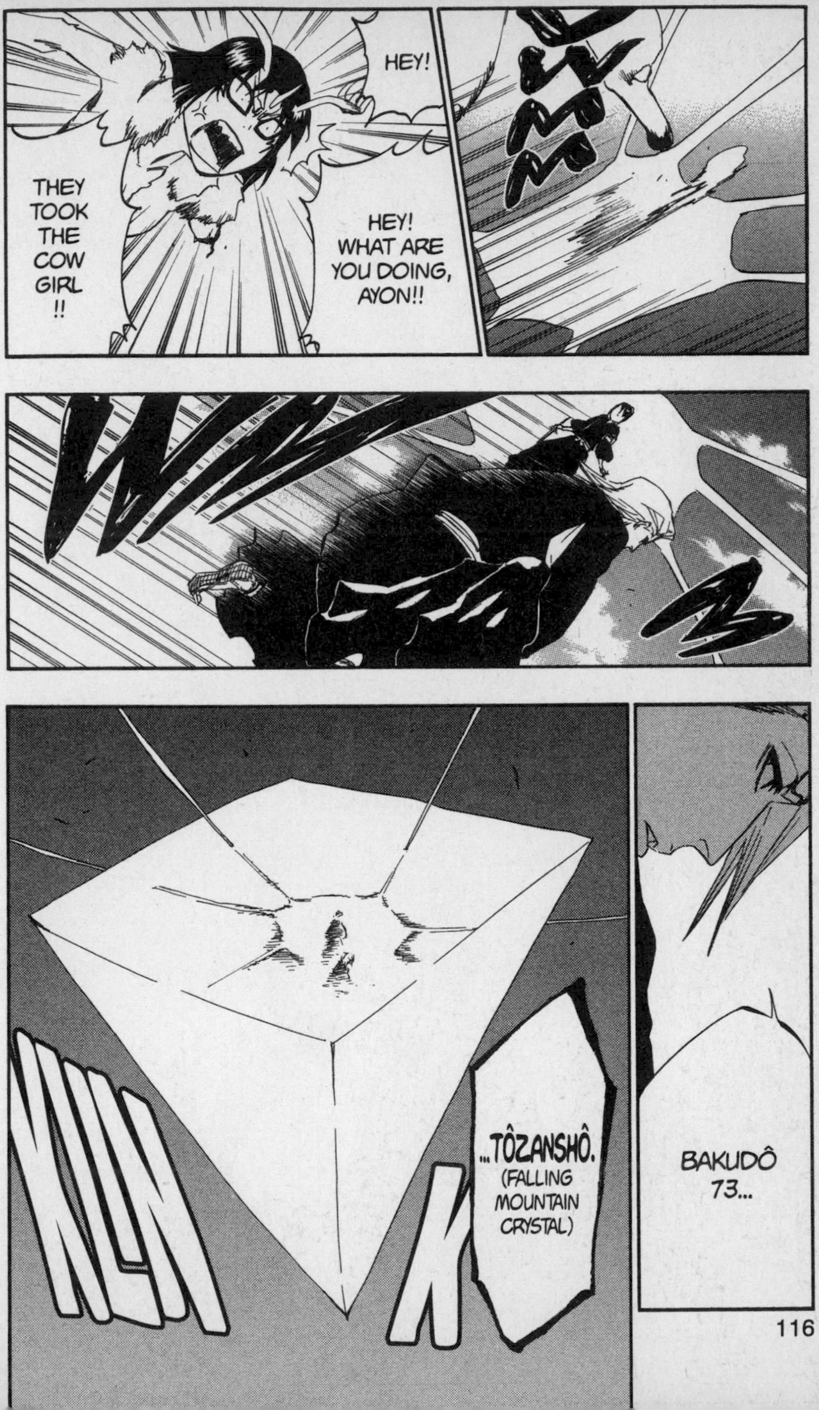

HEY!
HEY! WHAT ARE YOU DOING, AYON!!
THEY TOOK THE COW GIRL !!
BAKUDÔ 73...
...TÔZANSHÔ. (FALLING MOUNTAIN CRYSTAL)

READ THIS WAY

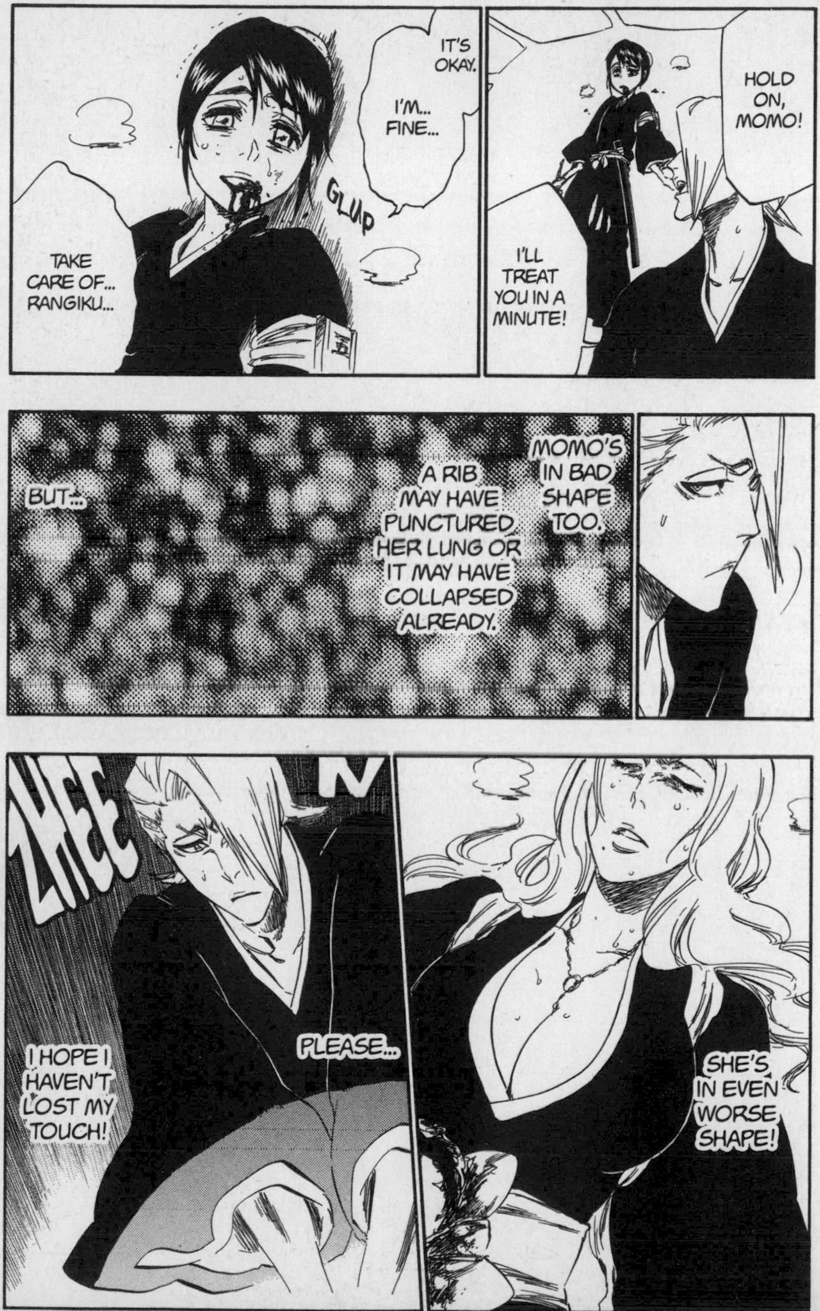
HOLD ON, MOMO!
I'LL TREAT YOU IN A MINUTE!
IT'S OKAY.
I'M... FINE...
GLUP
TAKE CARE OF... RANGIKU...
MOMO'S IN BAD SHAPE TOO.
A RIB MAY HAVE PUNCTURED HER LUNG OR IT MAY HAVE COLLAPSED ALREADY.
BUT...
SHE'S IN EVEN WORSE SHAPE!
ZHEEN
PLEASE...
I HOPE I HAVEN'T LOST MY TOUCH!

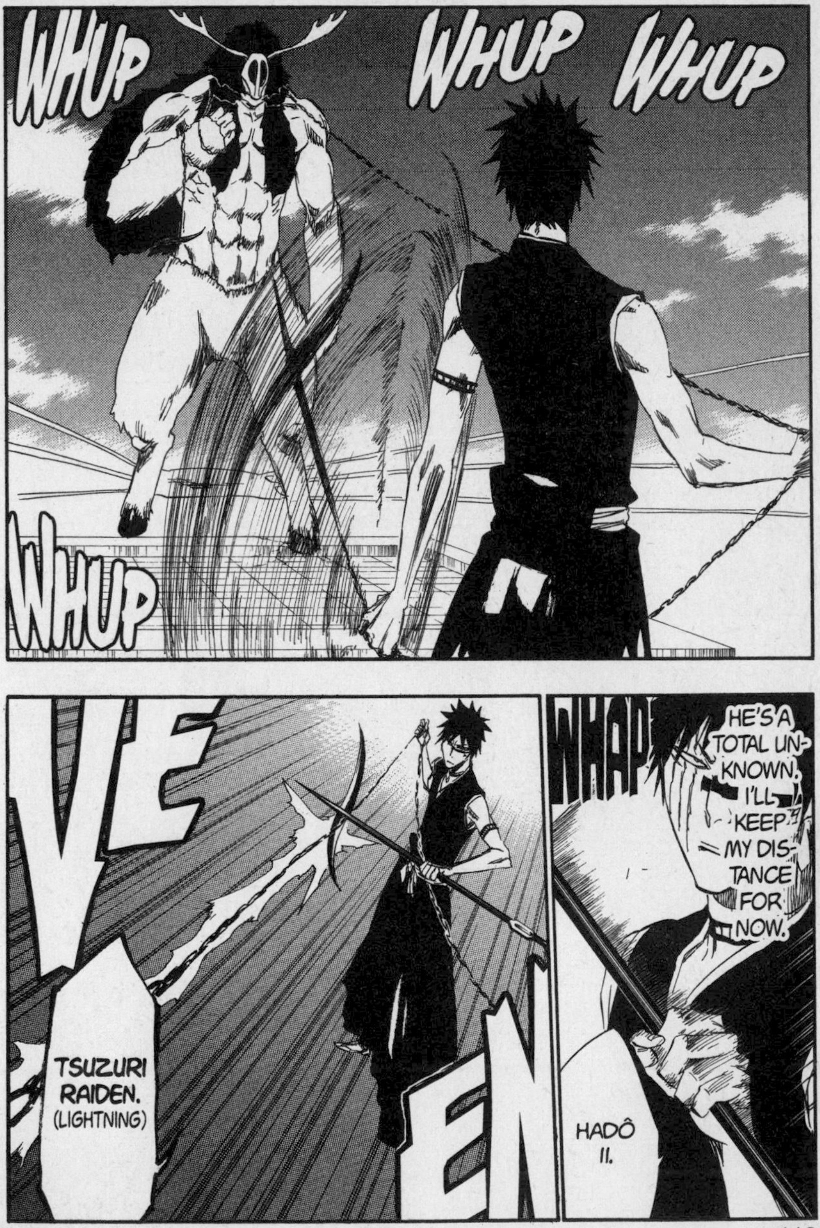
WHUP
WHUP
WHUP
WHUP
WHAP
HE'S A TOTAL UNKNOWN. I'LL KEEP MY DISTANCE FOR NOW.
HADÔ 11.
VE
EN
TSUZURI RAIDEN. (LIGHTNING)

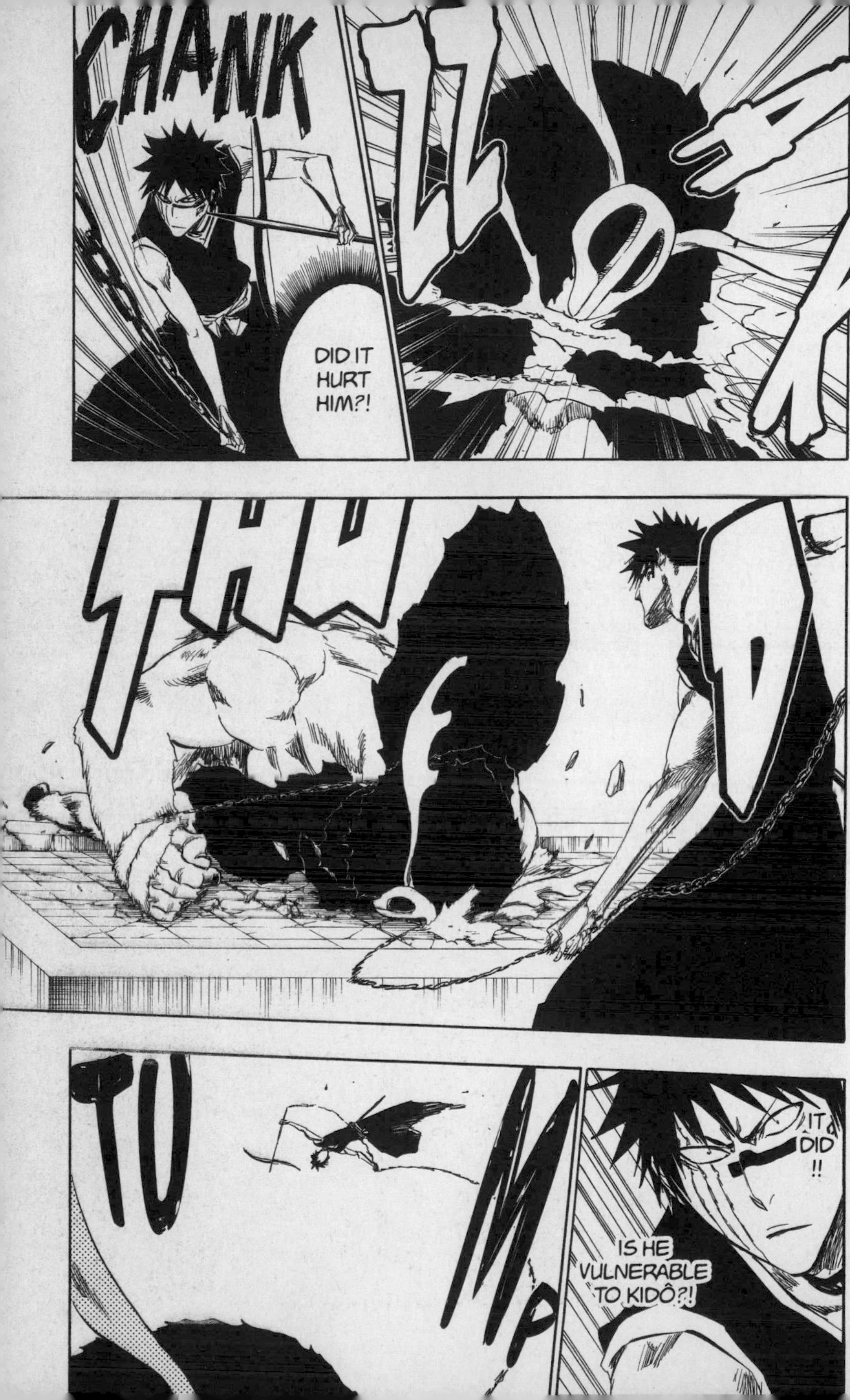
CHANK
DID IT HURT HIM?!
IT DID!!
IS HE VULNERABLE TO KIDÔ?!

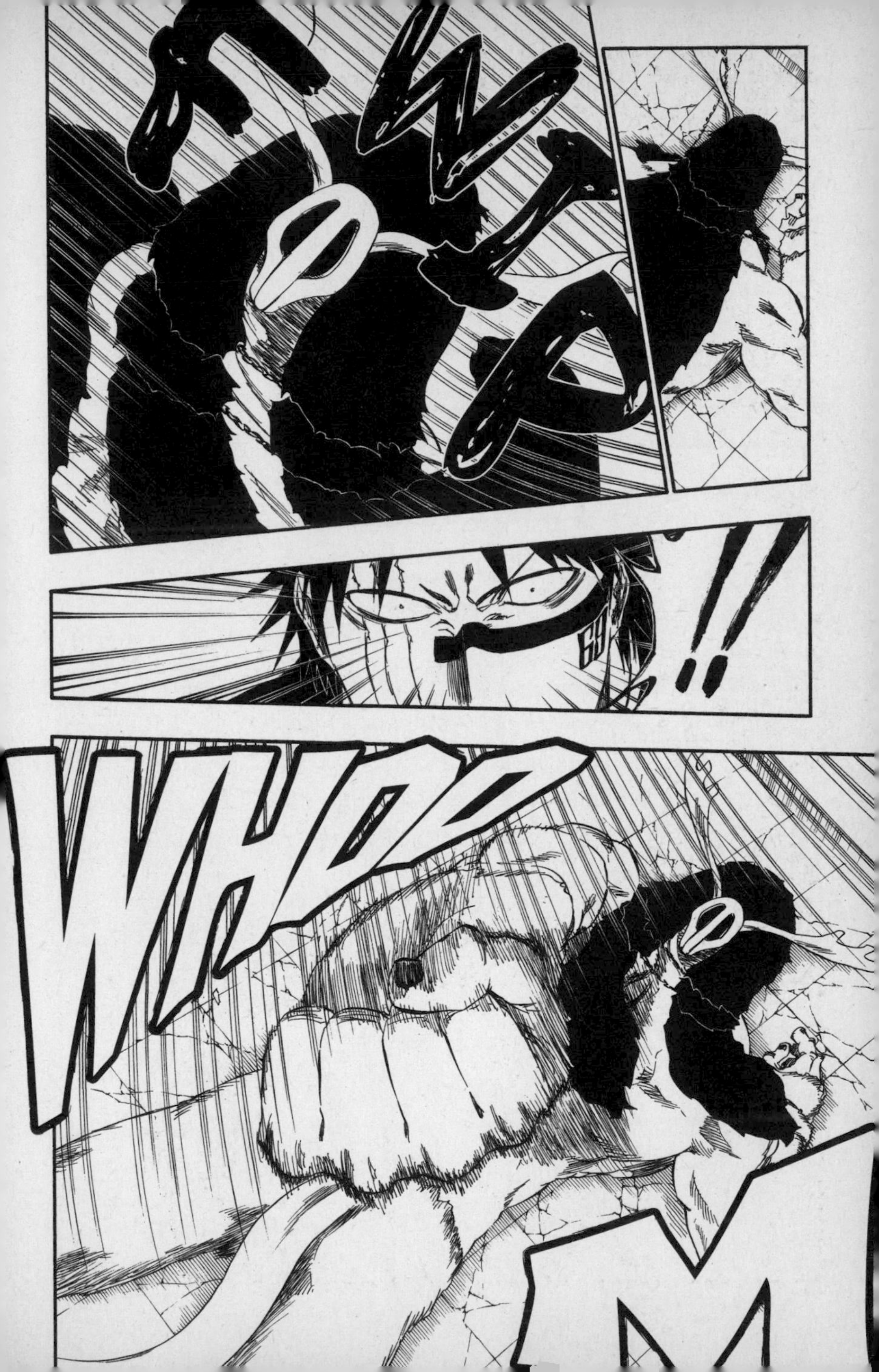

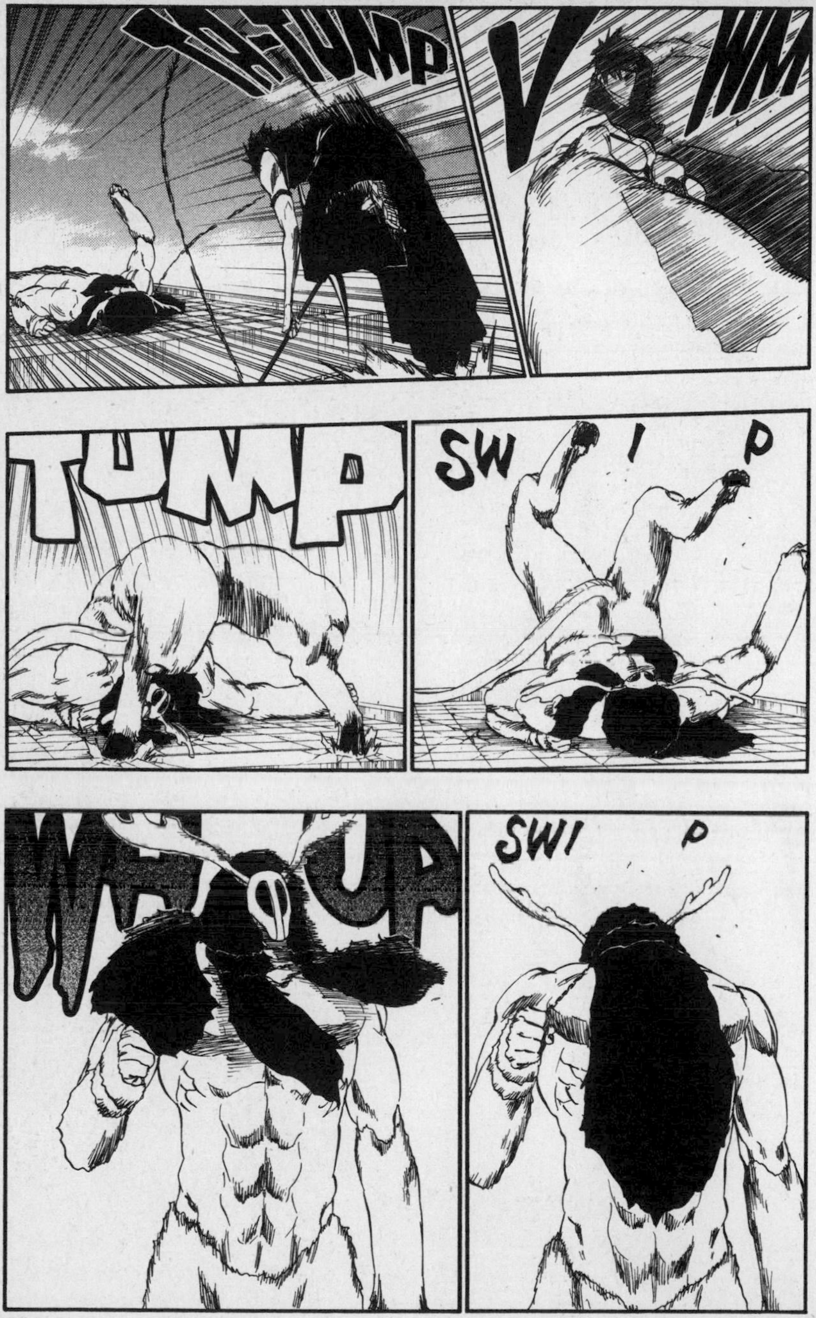
V WM
TUMP
SWIP
TUMP
SWIP

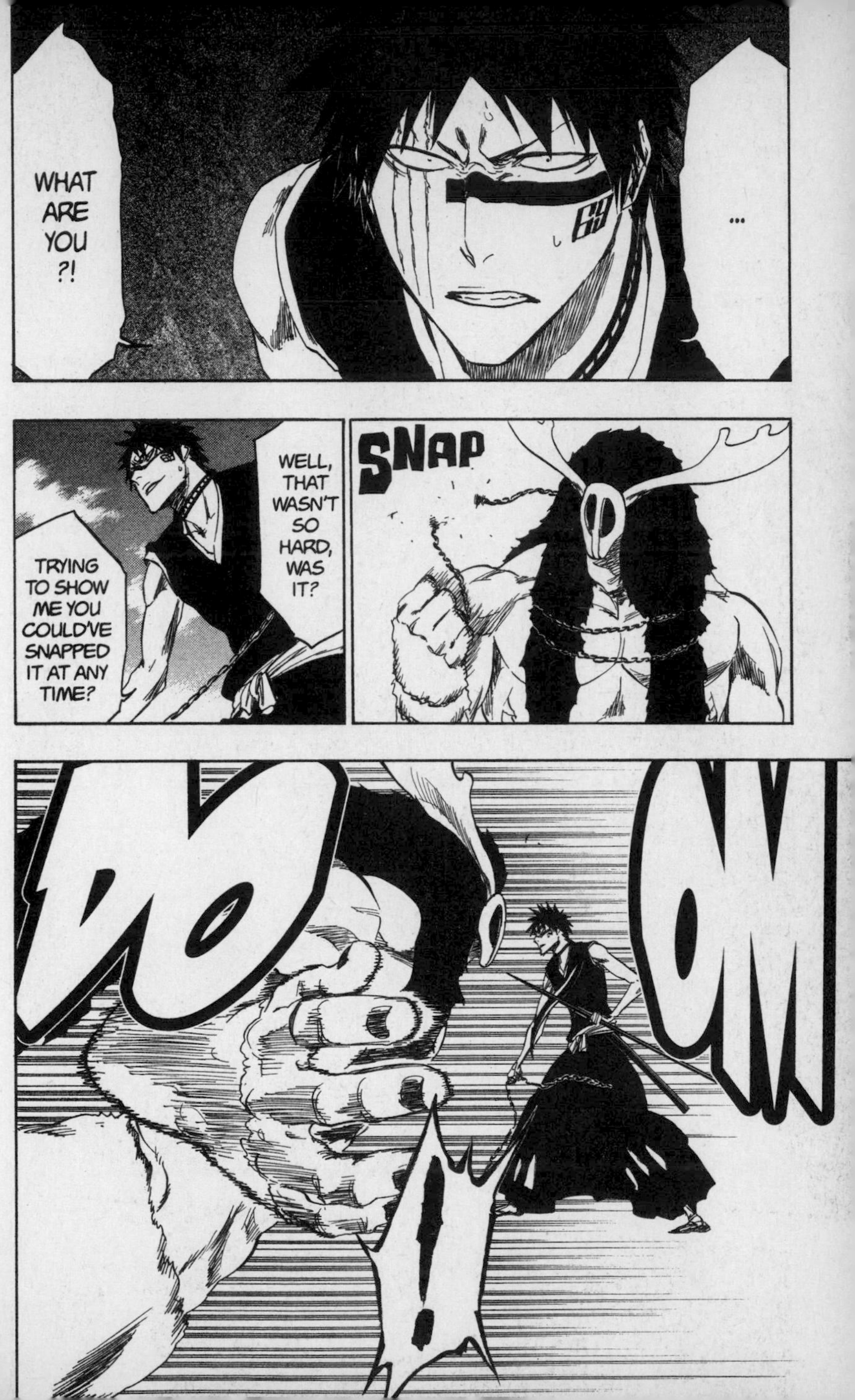
...
WHAT ARE YOU ?!
SNAP
WELL, THAT WASN'T SO HARD, WAS IT?
TRYING TO SHOW ME YOU COULD'VE SNAPPED IT AT ANY TIME?
DOOM
!

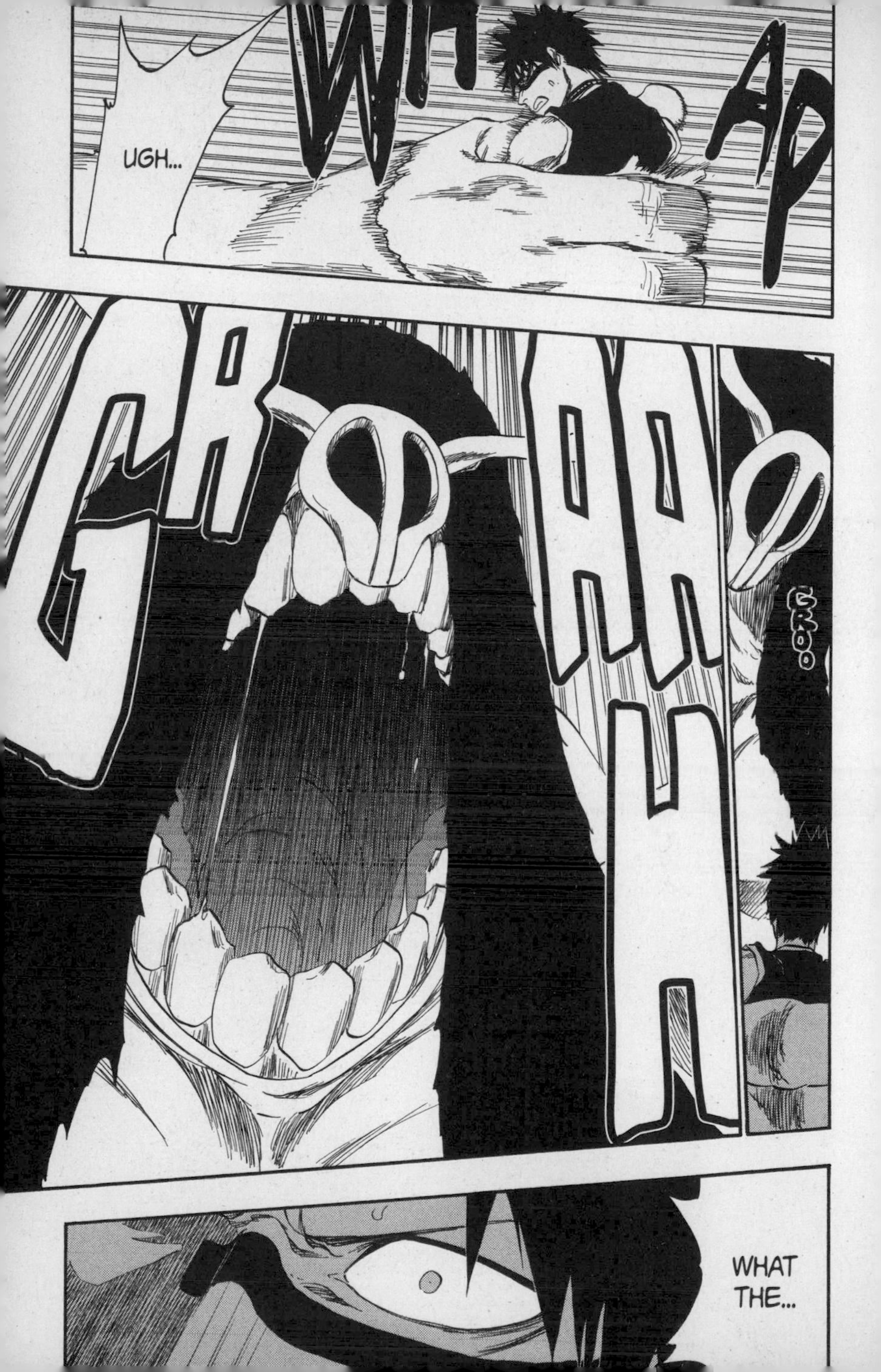
WHAP
UGH...
CRAAASH
GROO
WHAT THE...

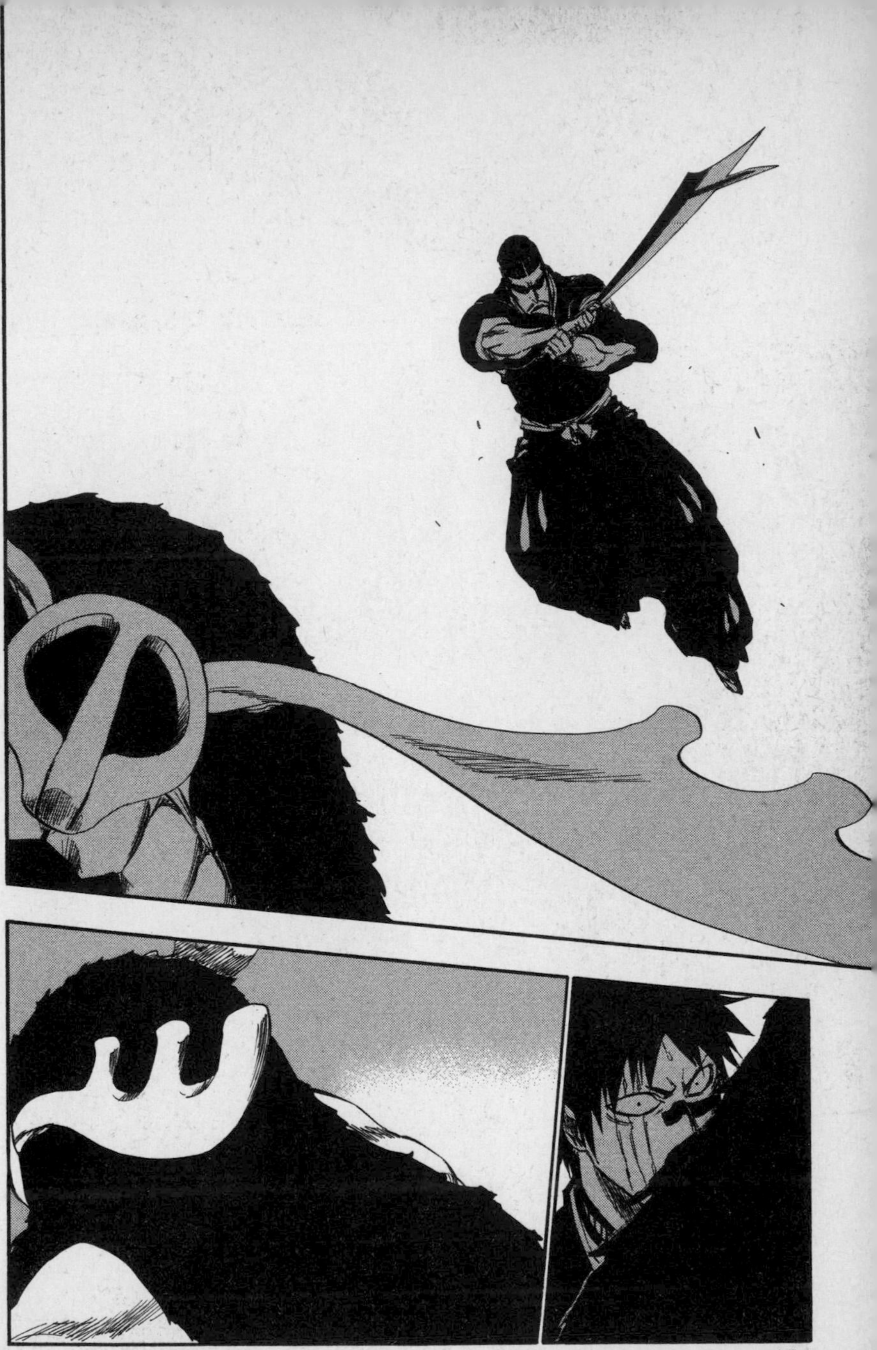

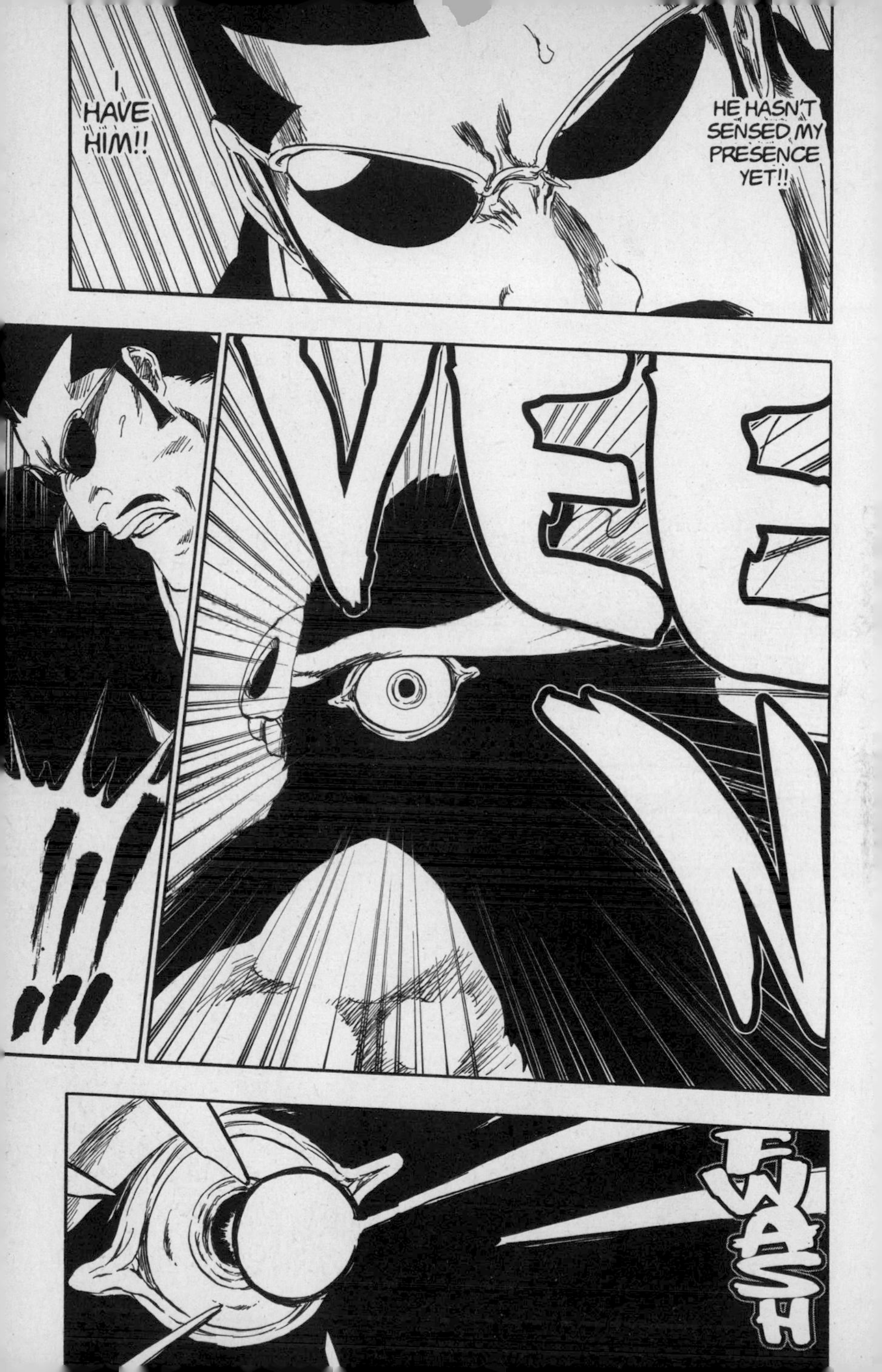
HE HASN'T SENSED MY PRESENCE YET!!
I HAVE HIM!!
VEEN
!!
FWASH

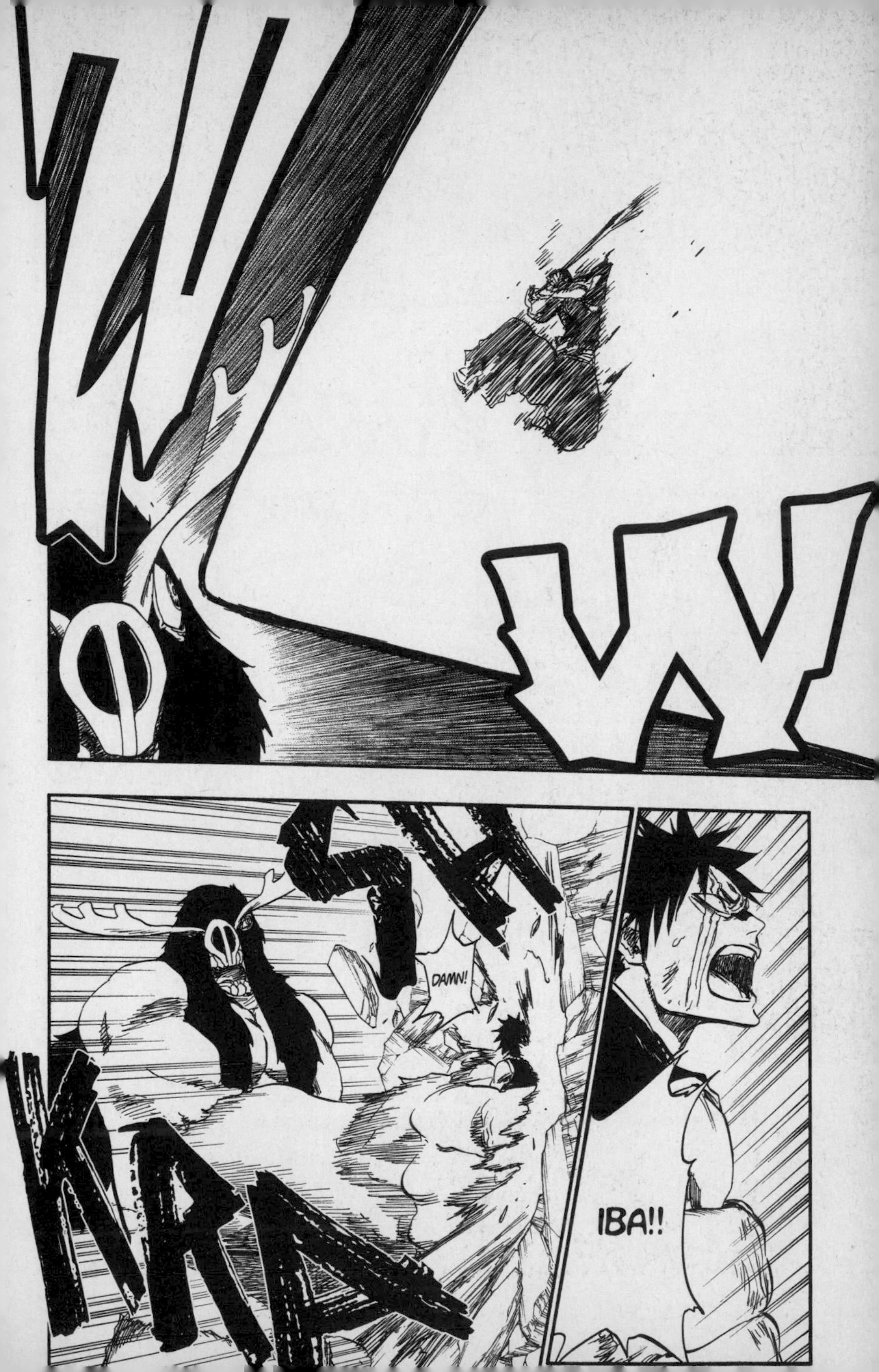
IBA!!
DAMN!

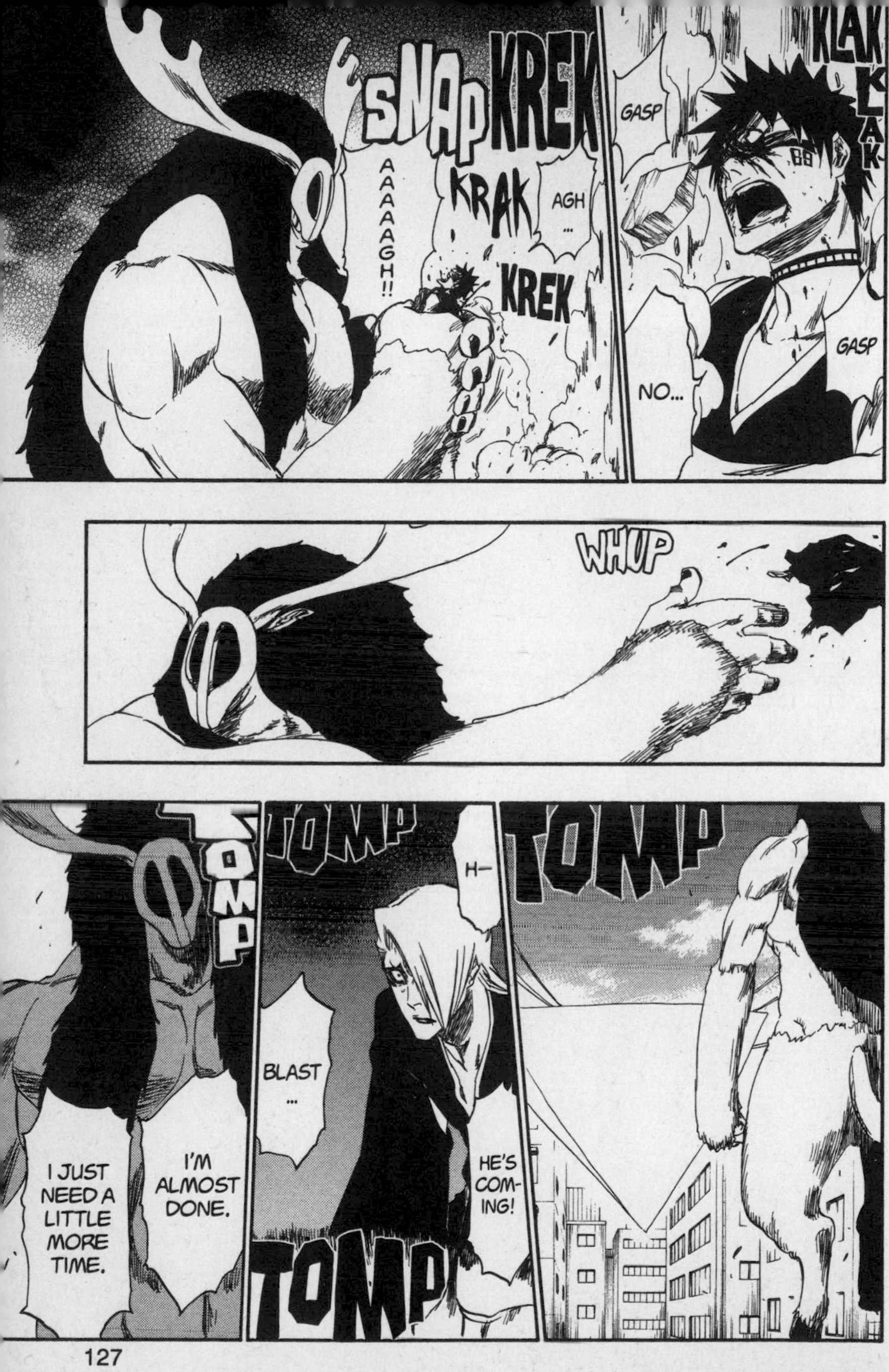

KLAK
KLAK
GASP
GASP
NO...
SNAP
KREK
AAAAAAGH!!
KRAK
AGH ...
KREK
WHUP
TOMP
H—
TOMP
BLAST ...
HE'S COMING!
TOMP
TOMP
I'M ALMOST DONE.
I JUST NEED A LITTLE MORE TIME.

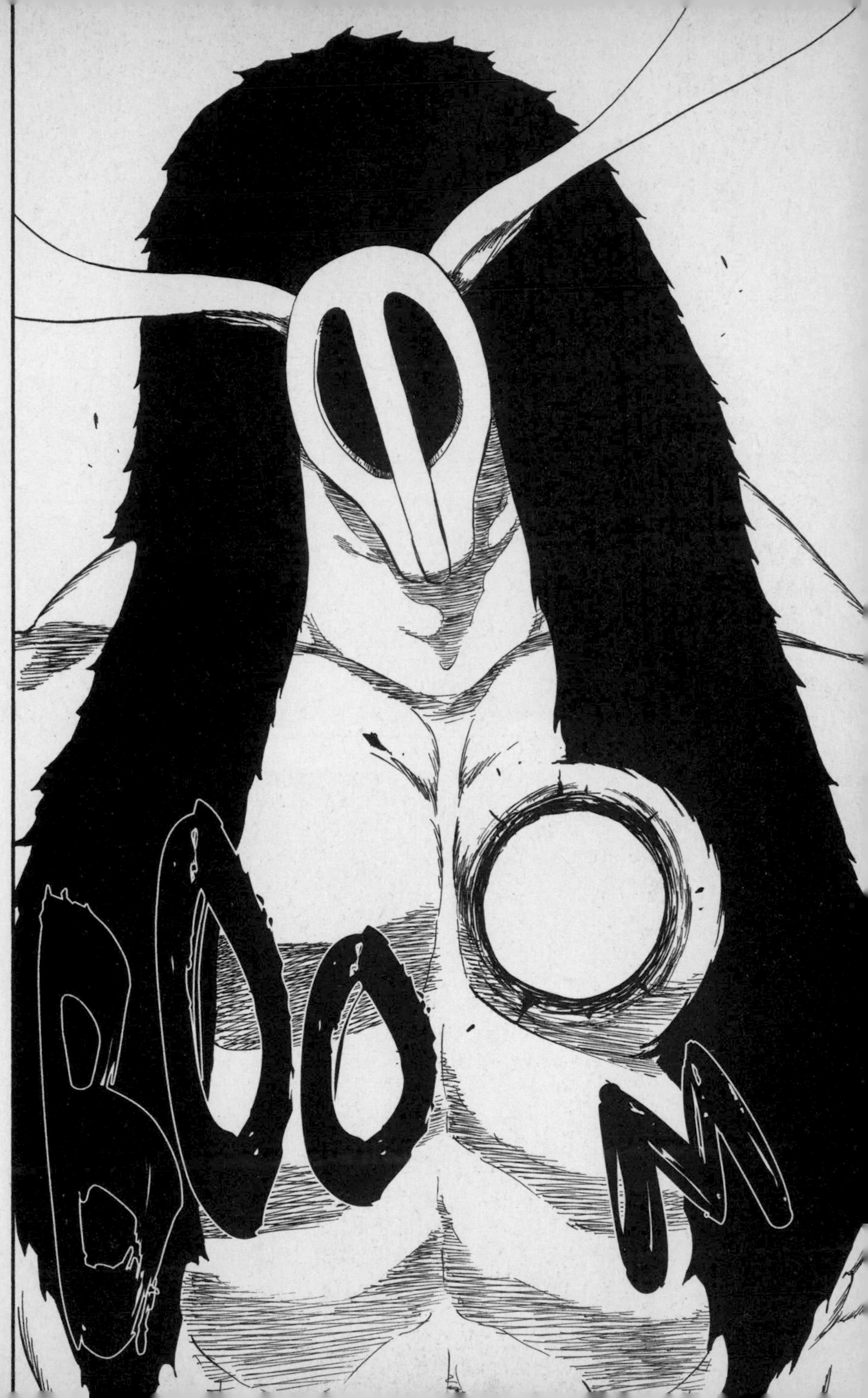
BOOOM

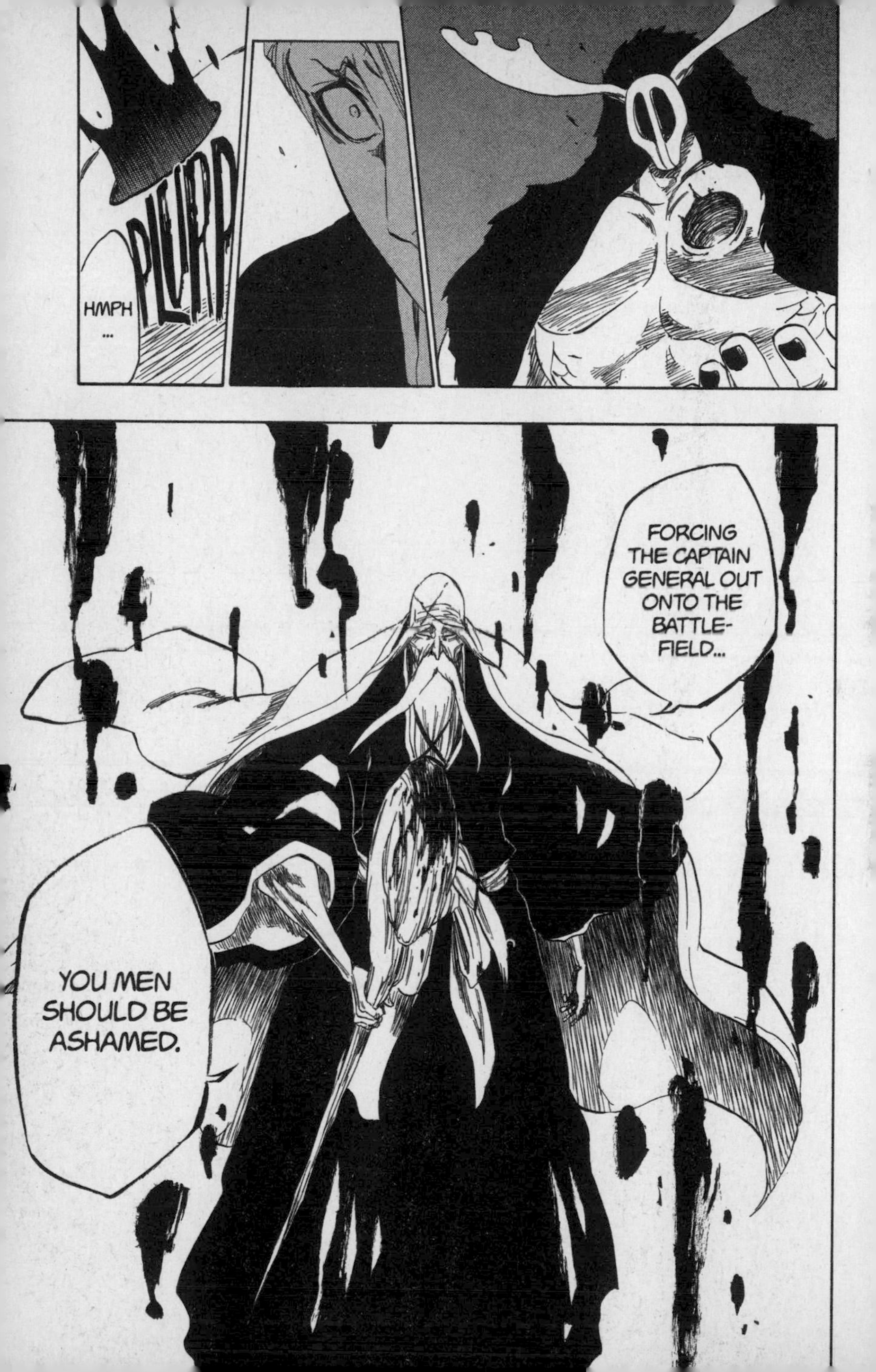
PLURP
HMPH ...
FORCING THE CAPTAIN GENERAL OUT ONTO THE BATTLE-FIELD...
YOU MEN SHOULD BE ASHAMED.

LAUGHING
AYON

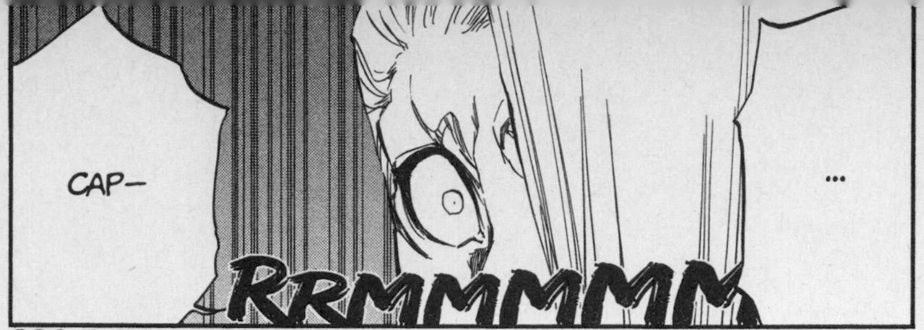
...
CAP—
RRMMMMMM

338. Fall Into My Inferno

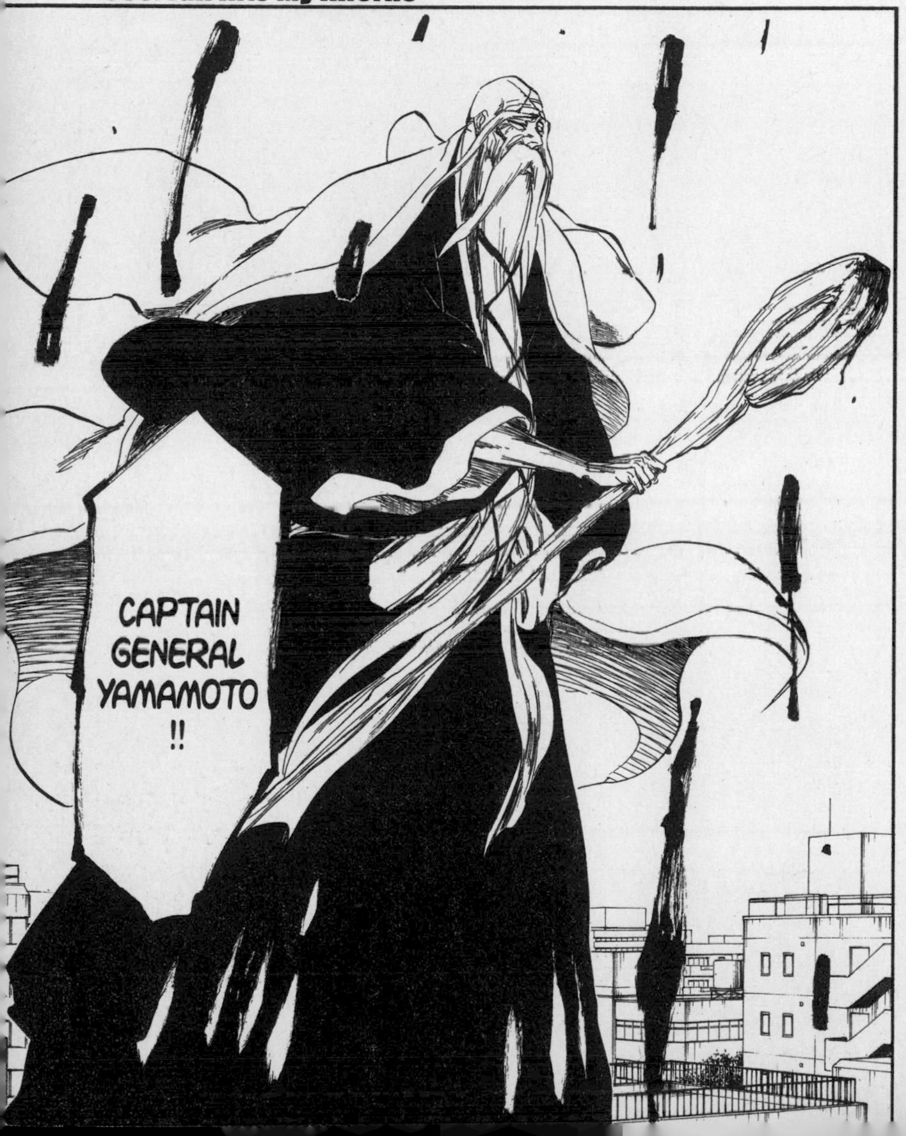
CAPTAIN GENERAL YAMAMOTO !!

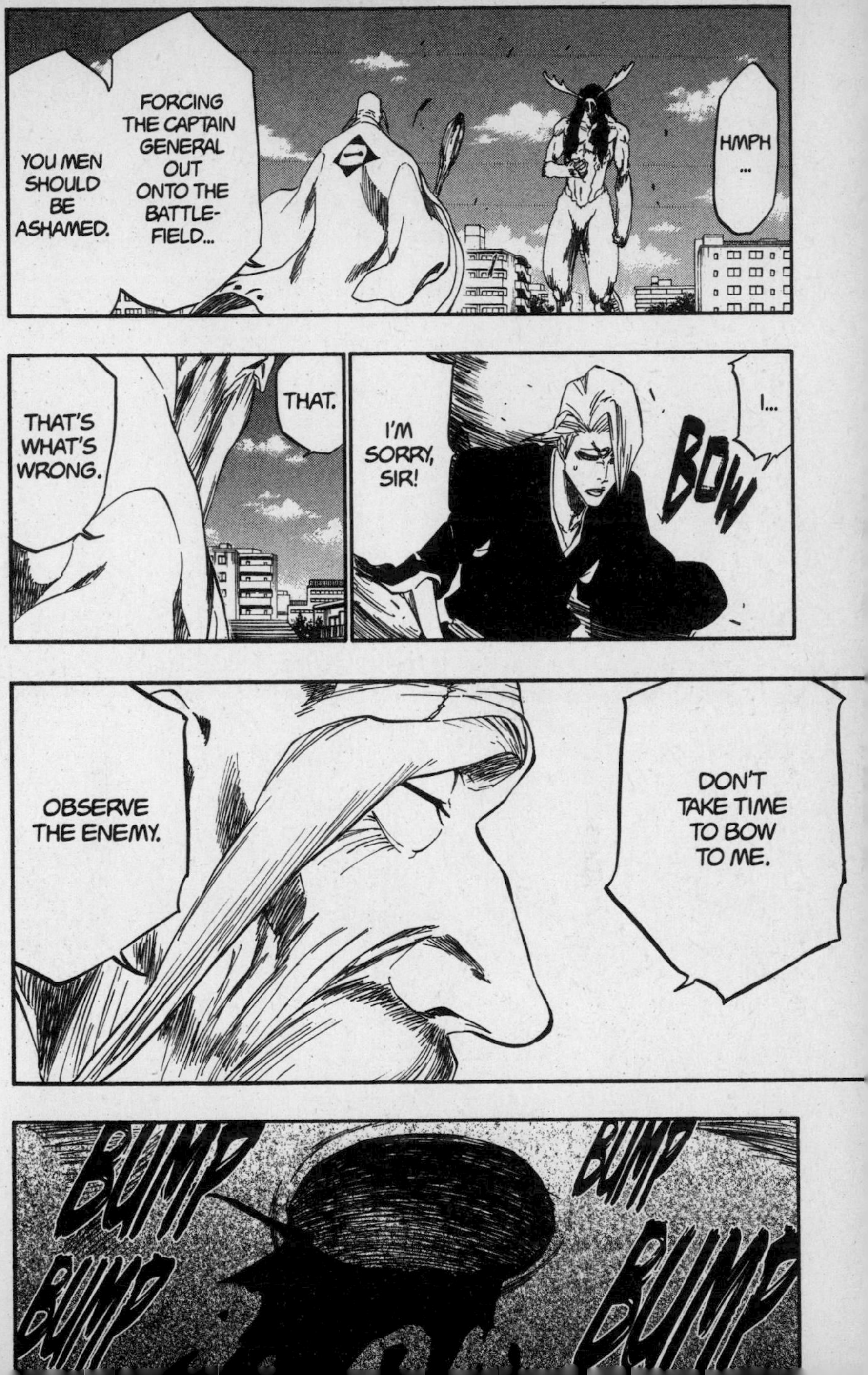
HMPH ...
FORCING THE CAPTAIN GENERAL OUT ONTO THE BATTLE-FIELD...
YOU MEN SHOULD BE ASHAMED.
I...
BOW
I'M SORRY, SIR!
THAT.
THAT'S WHAT'S WRONG.
DON'T TAKE TIME TO BOW TO ME.
OBSERVE THE ENEMY.
BUMP
BUMP
BUMP
BUMP

READ THIS WAY

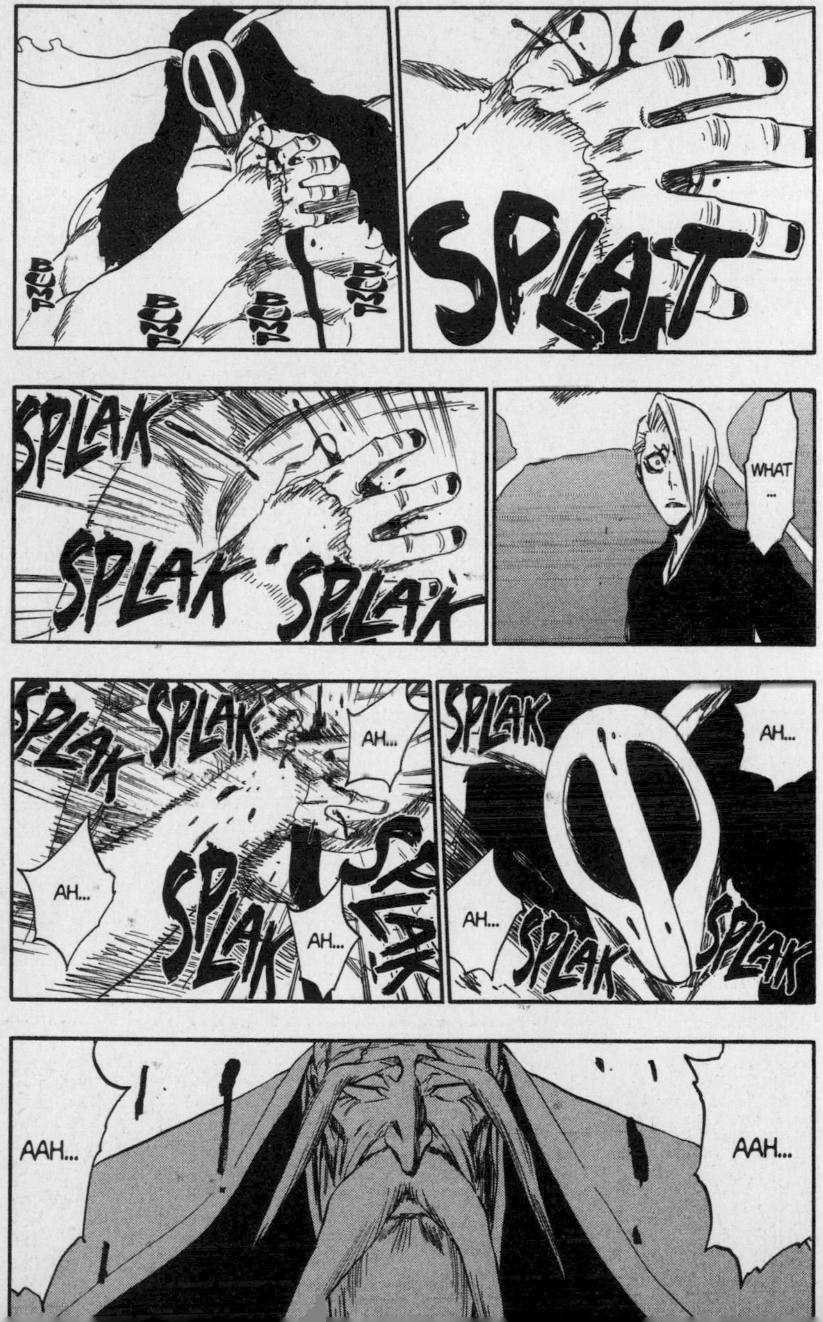
SPLAT
BUMP
BUMP
BUMP
BUMP
WHAT...
SPLAK
SPLAK
SPLAK
SPLAK
AH...
AH...
SPLAK
SPLAK
SPLAK
SPLAK
AH...
AH...
AH...
SPLAK
SPLAK
AAH...
AAH...

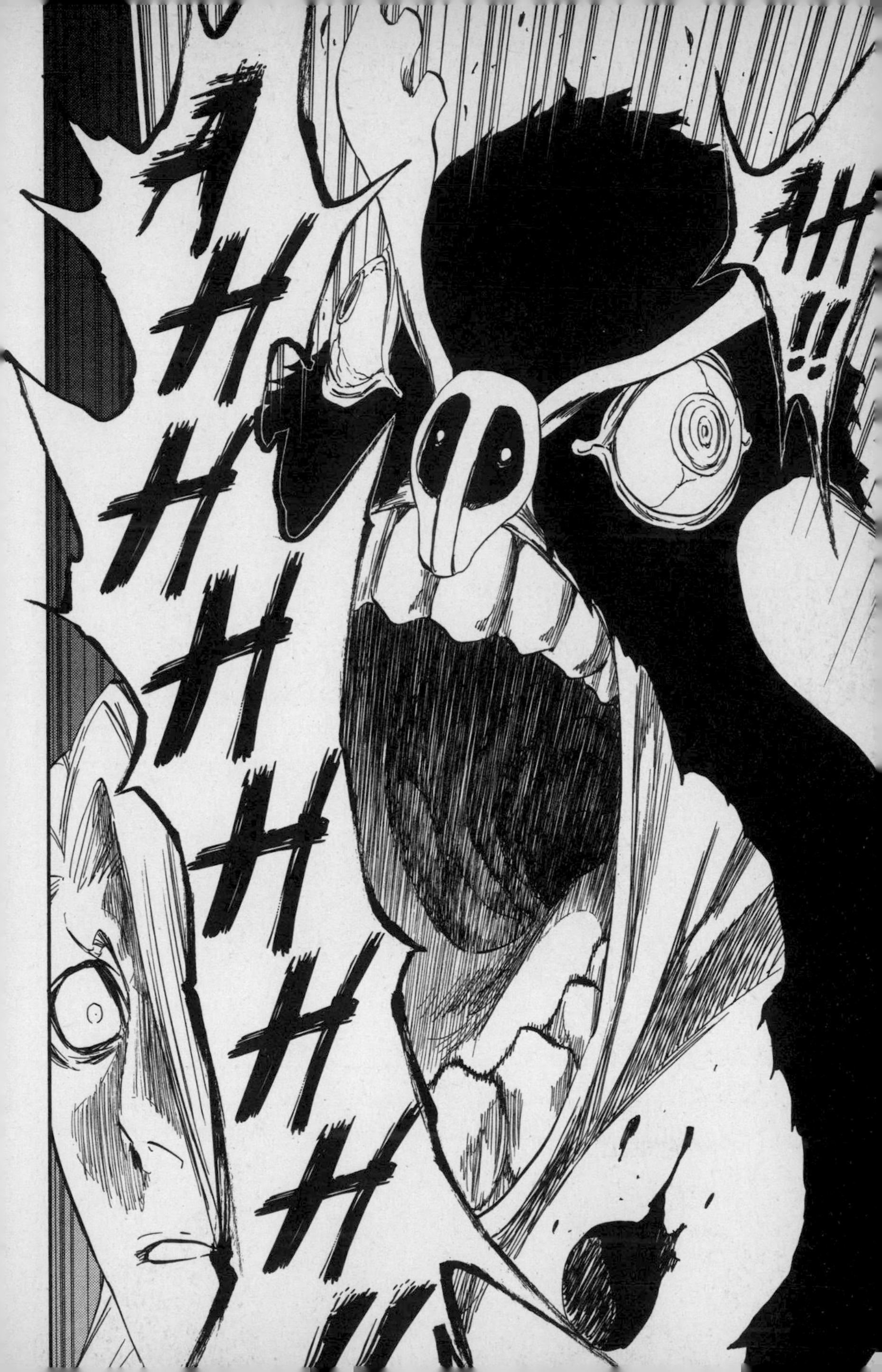
AH!!
AHHHHHHH

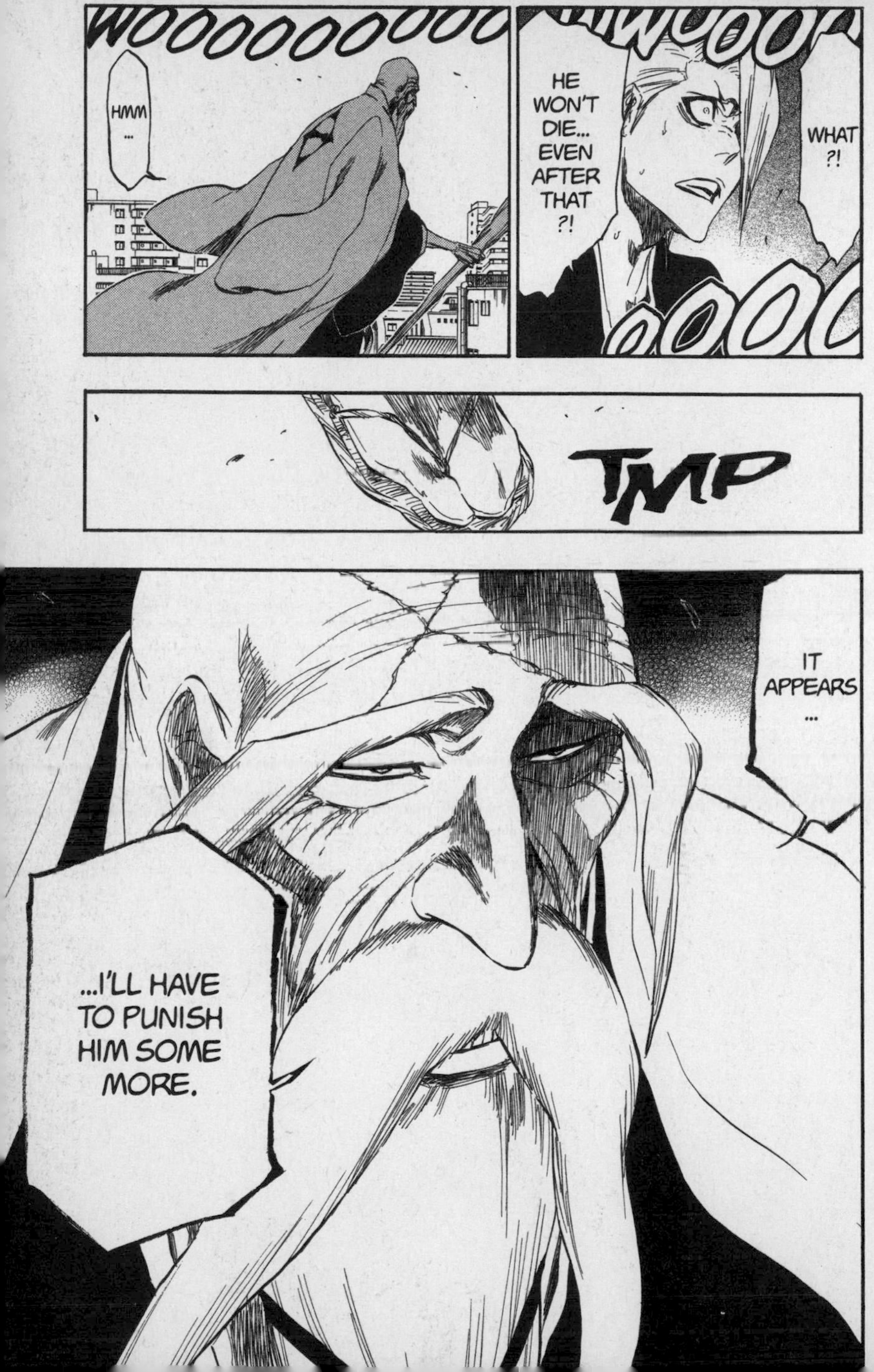
WHAT ?!
HE WON'T DIE... EVEN AFTER THAT ?!
WOOOOOOOOOOO
HMM ...
TMP
IT APPEARS ...
...I'LL HAVE TO PUNISH HIM SOME MORE.

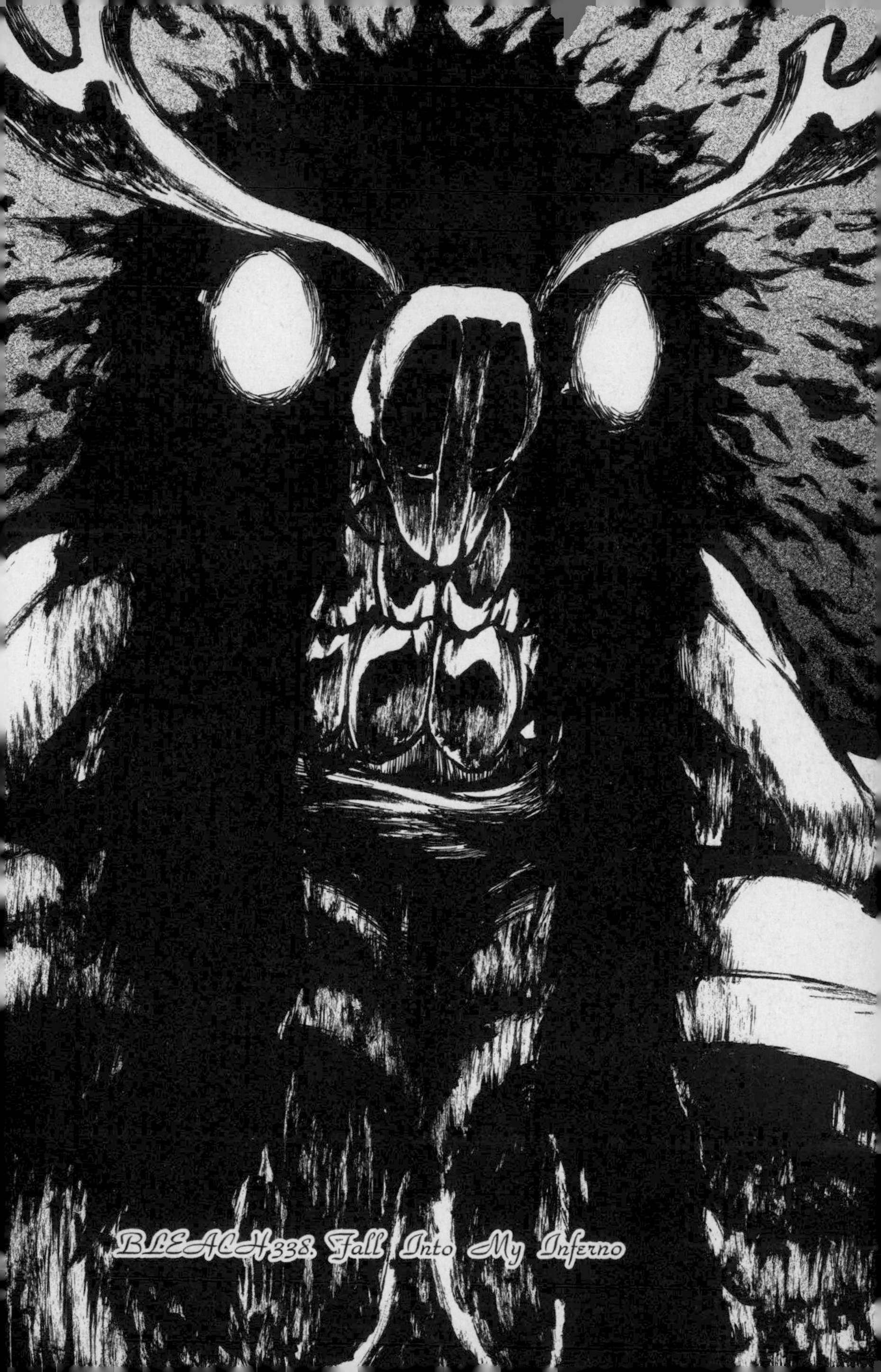
BLEACH 338. Fall Into My Inferno

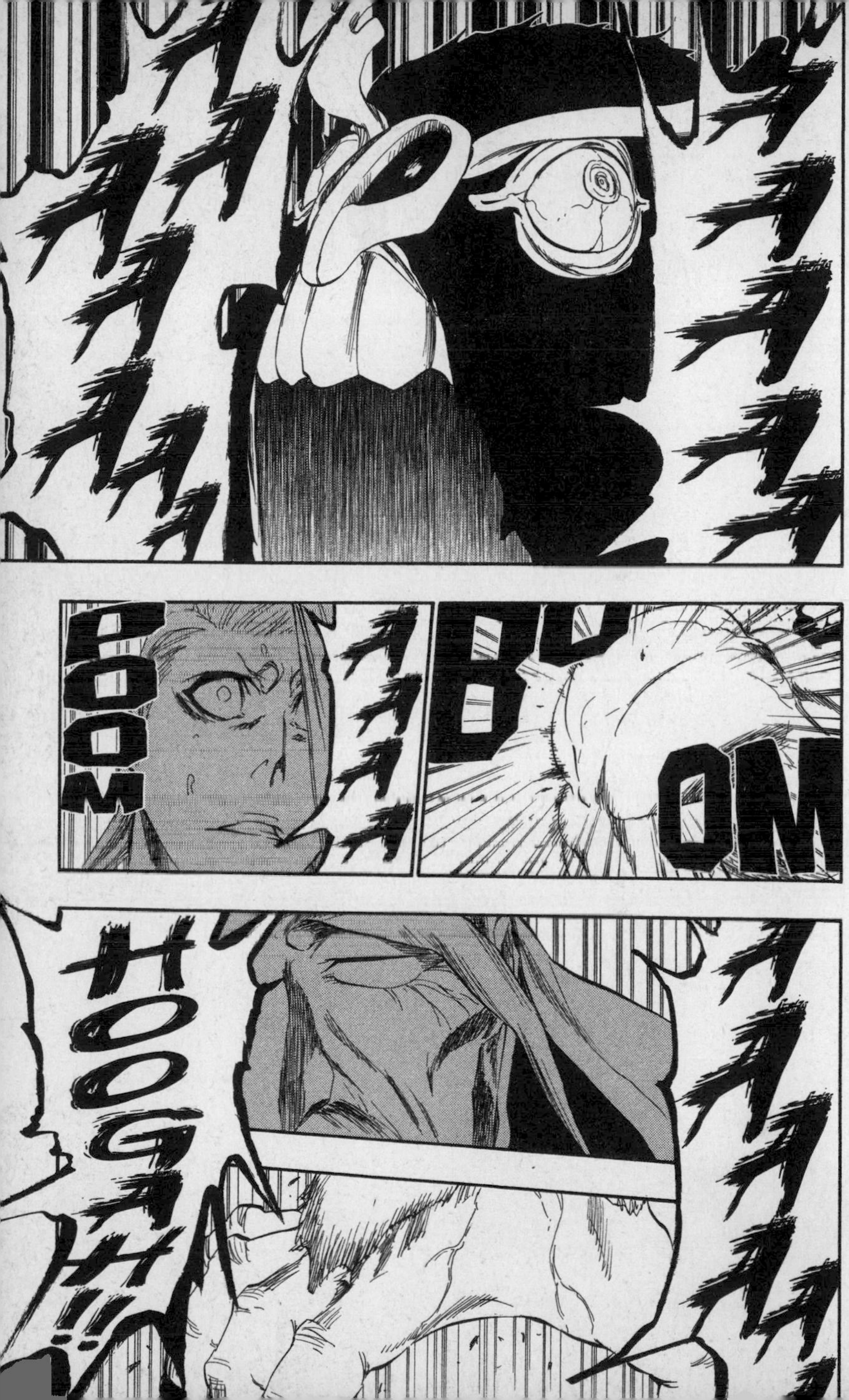

AAAAAAAA
AAAAAAA
BOOM
AAAA
BOOM
AAAAAAA
HOOGH!!

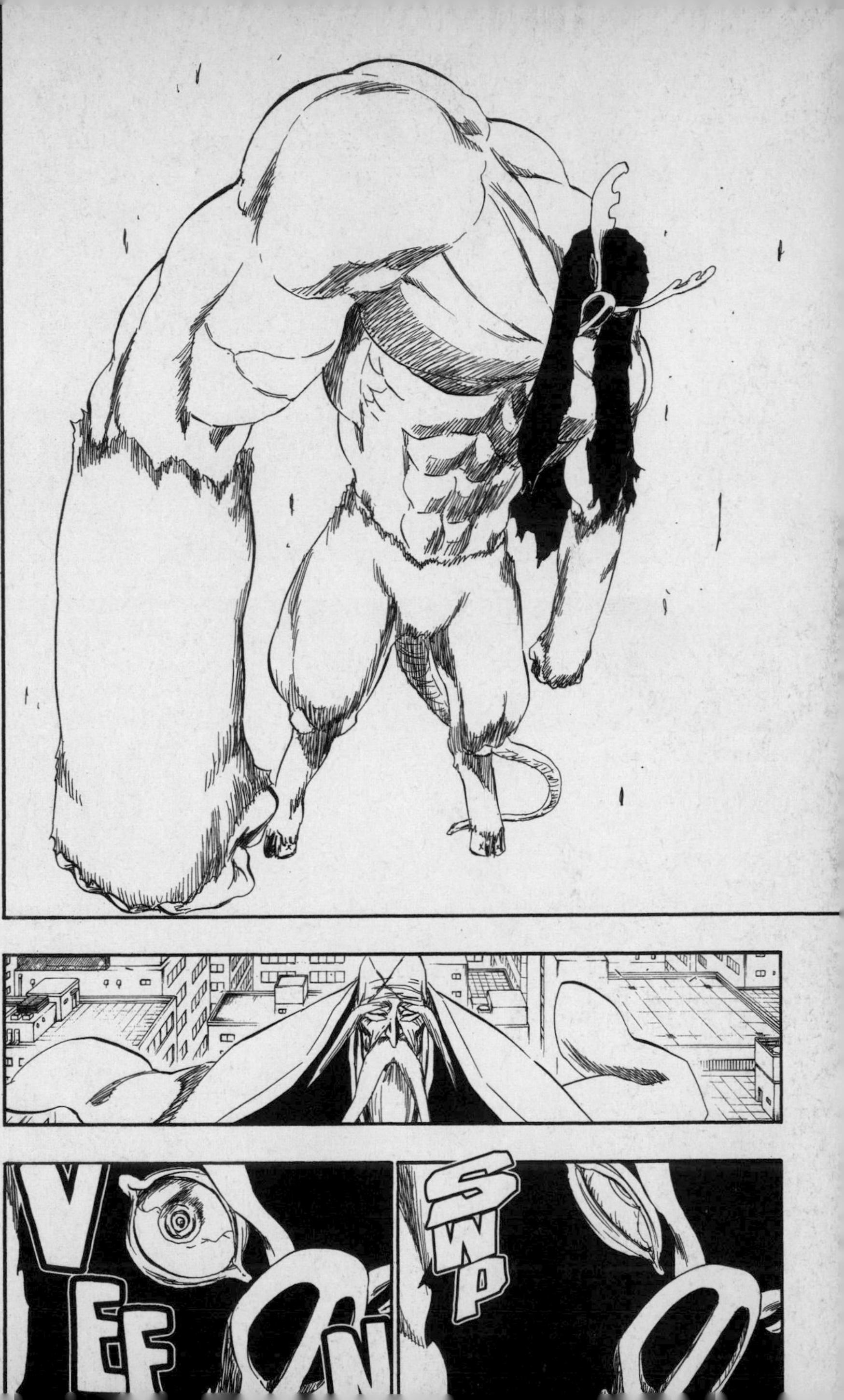
SWP
V
EF
ON

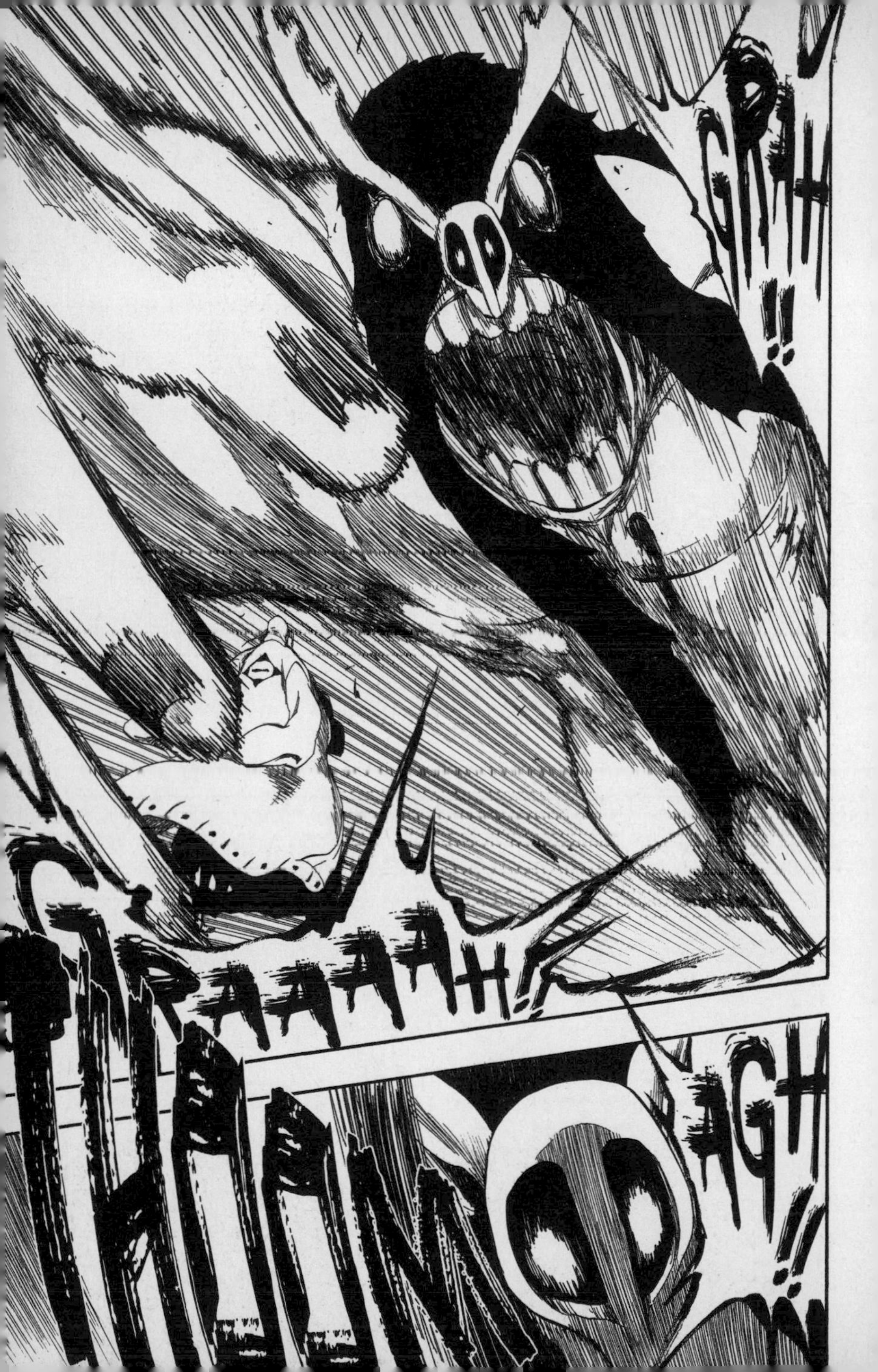
GRAH!!
GRAAAAAH!?
AGH!!

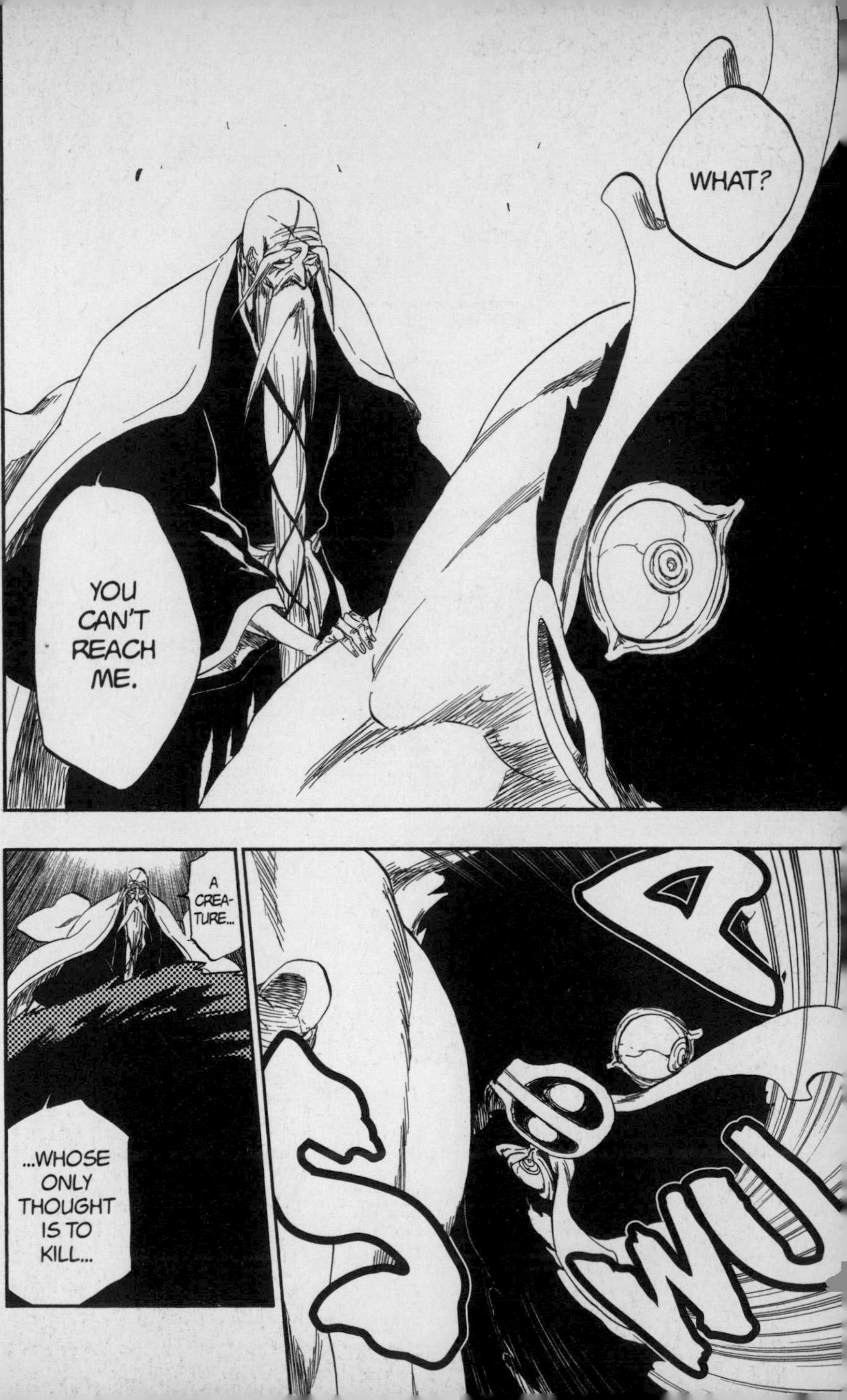
WHAT?
YOU CAN'T REACH ME.
A CREATURE...
...WHOSE ONLY THOUGHT IS TO KILL...

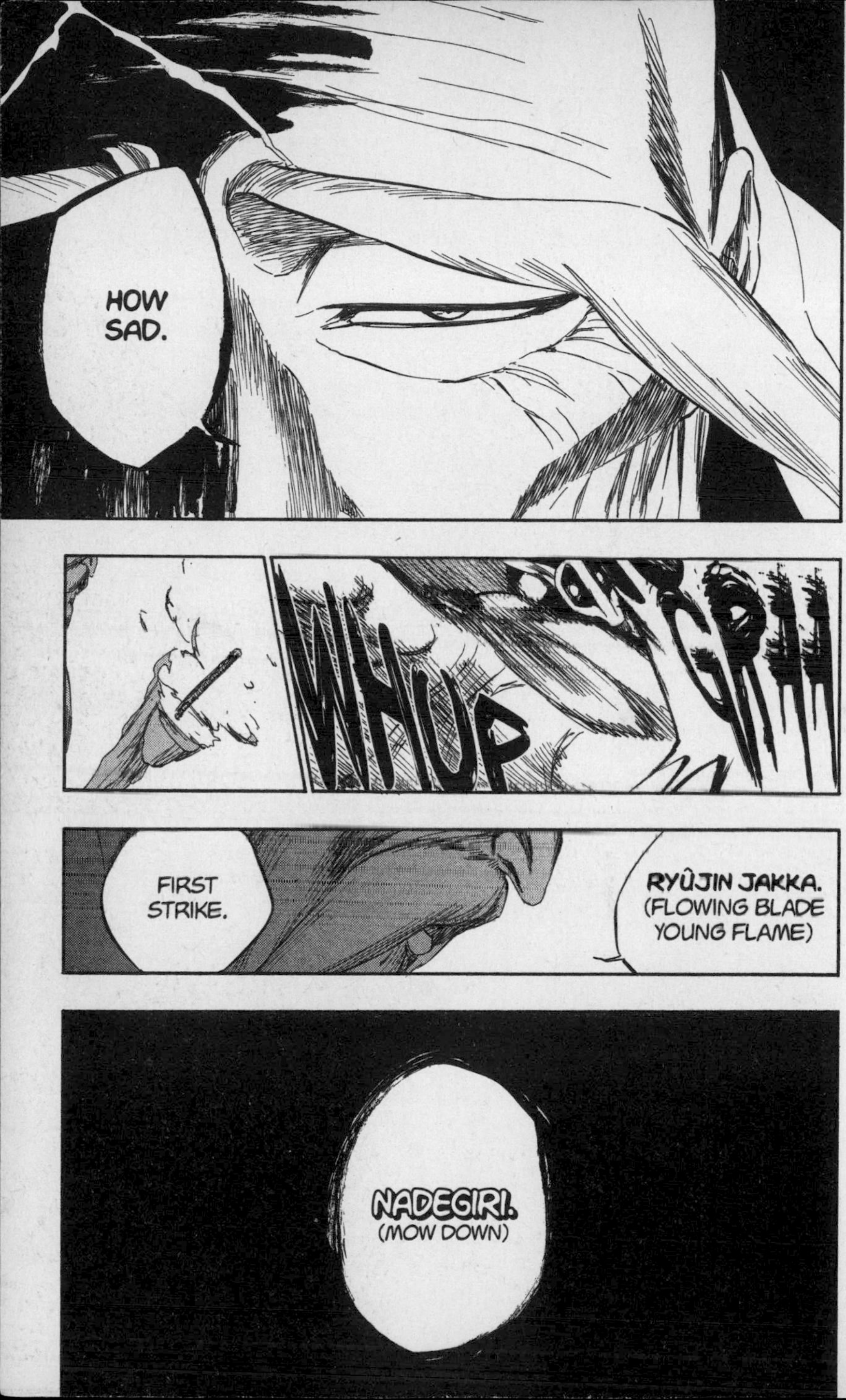
HOW SAD.
WHUP
RYÛJIN JAKKA. (FLOWING BLADE YOUNG FLAME)
FIRST STRIKE.
NADEGIRI. (MOW DOWN)

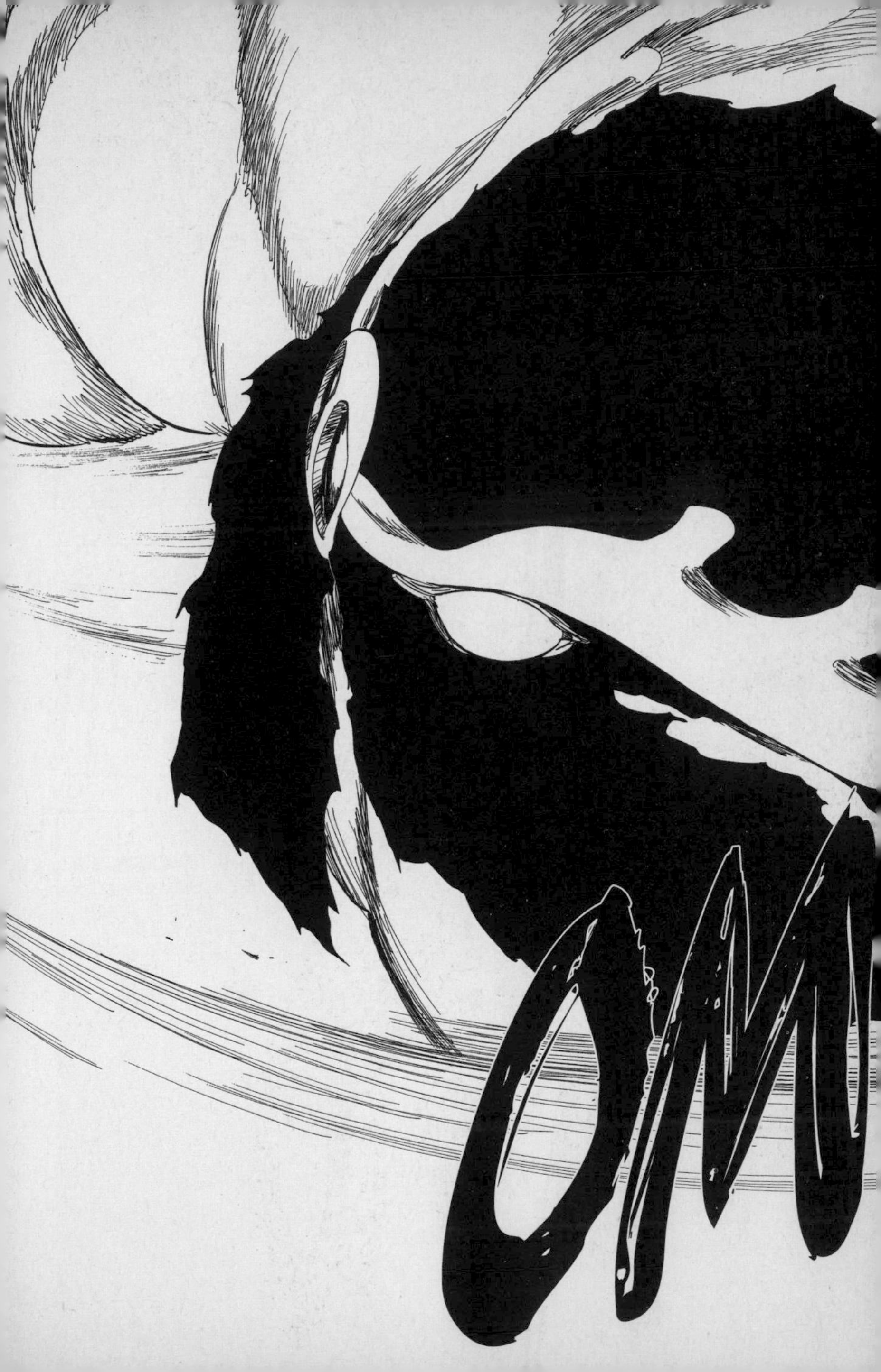
OM

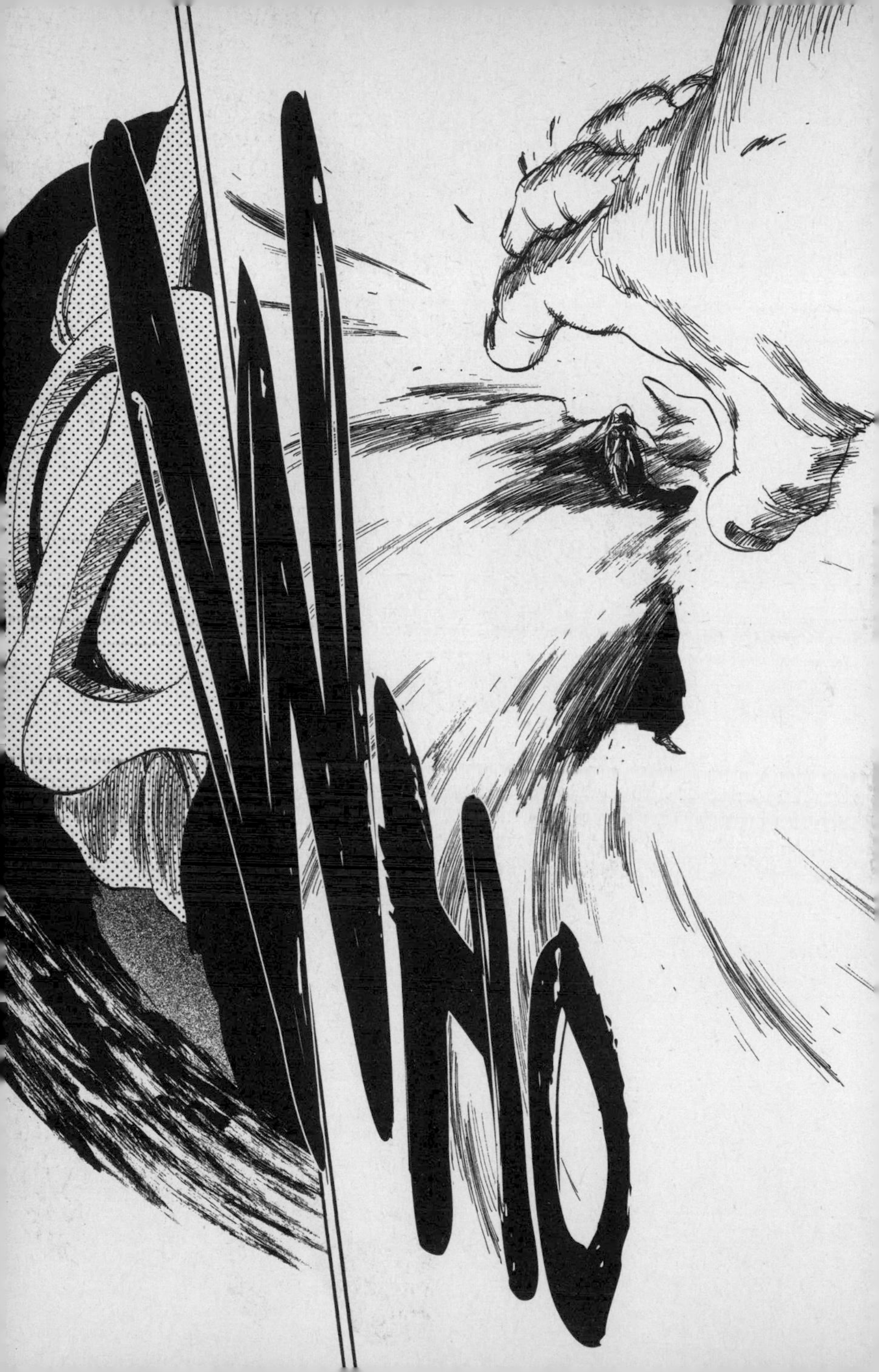

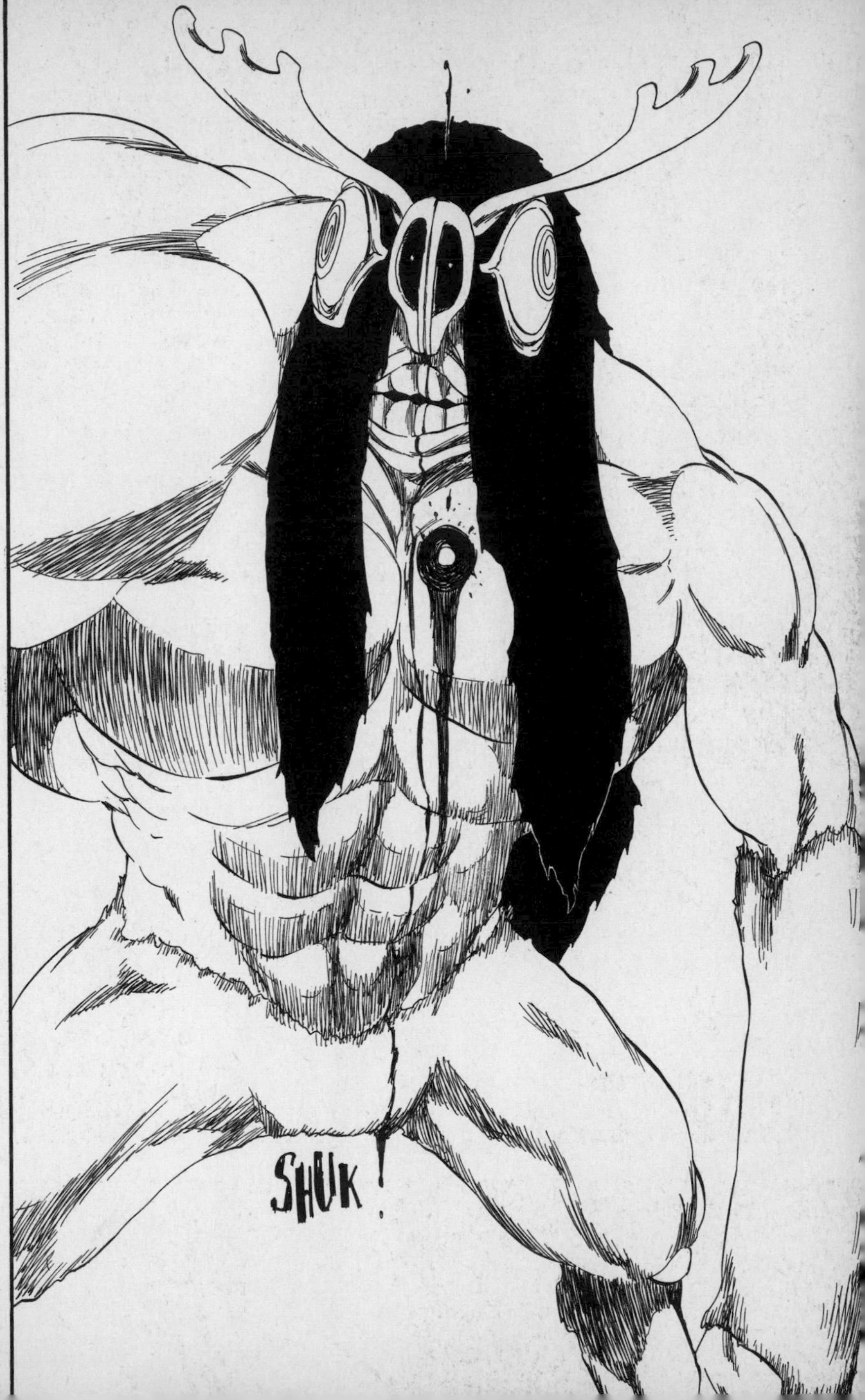
SHUK

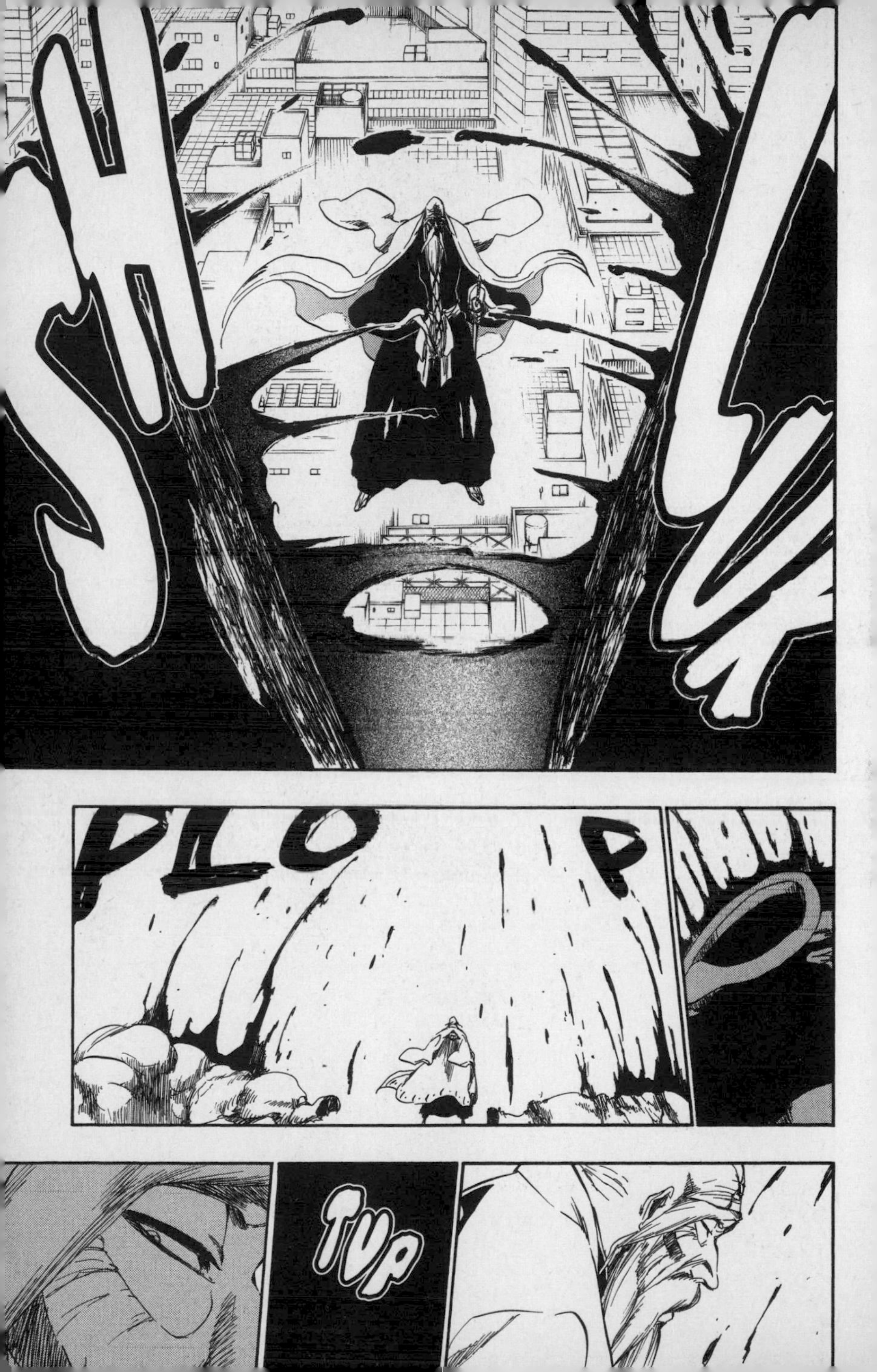
PLOP
TUP

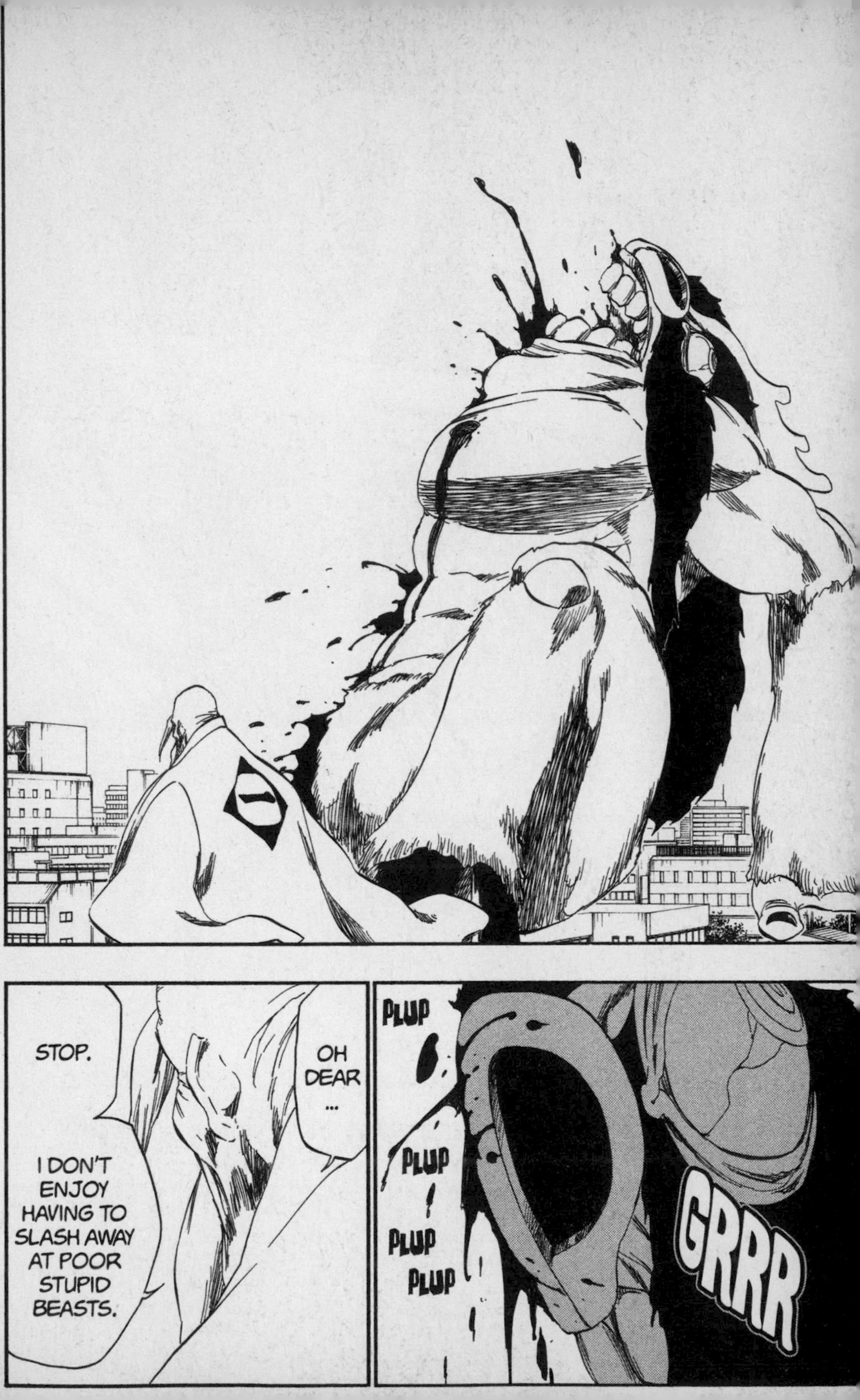
PLUP
PLUP
PLUP
PLUP
GRRR
OH DEAR ...
STOP.
I DON'T ENJOY HAVING TO SLASH AWAY AT POOR STUPID BEASTS.

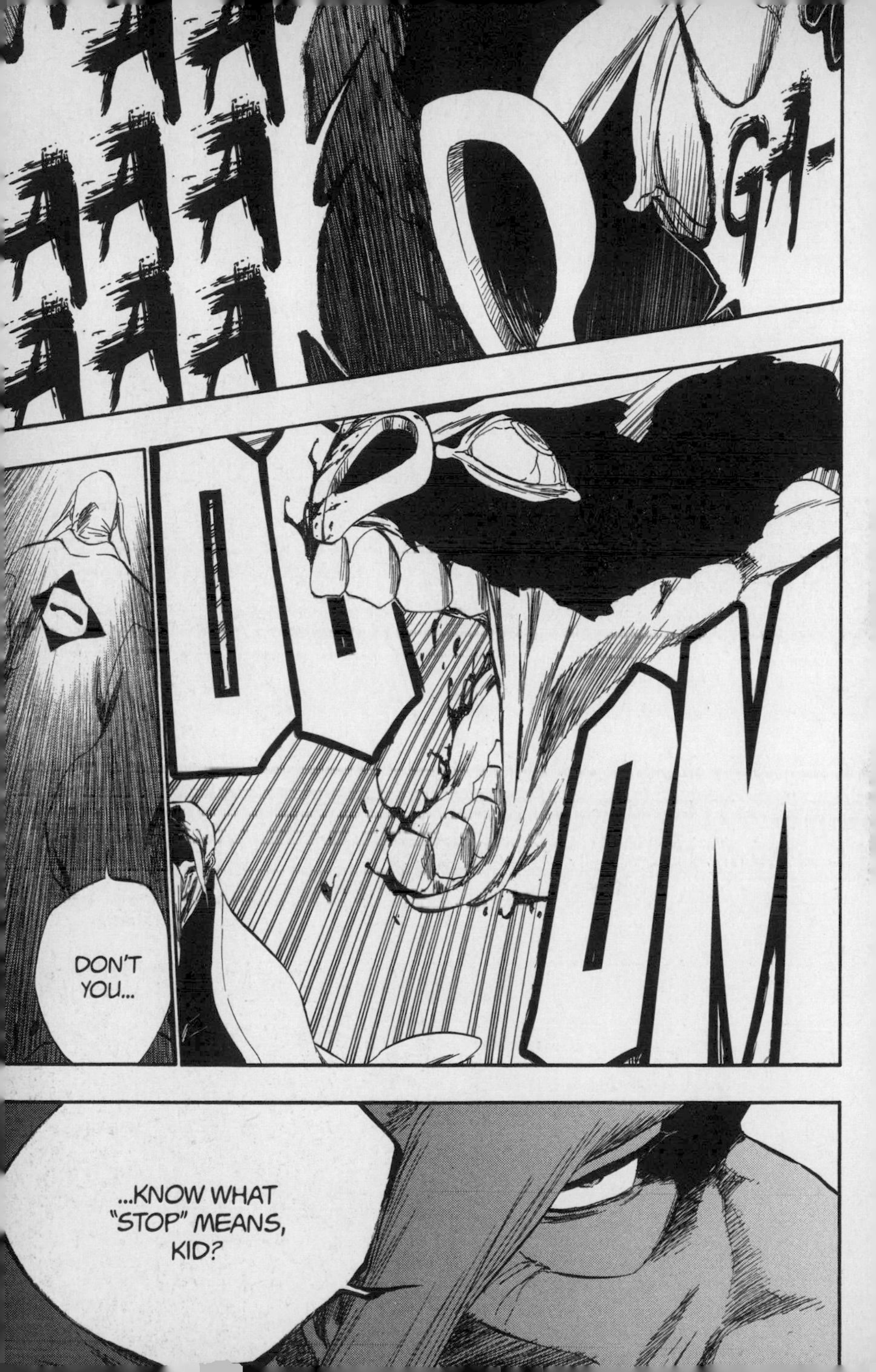
GA-
AAAAAAAAAAAA
DOOM
DON'T YOU...
...KNOW WHAT "STOP" MEANS, KID?

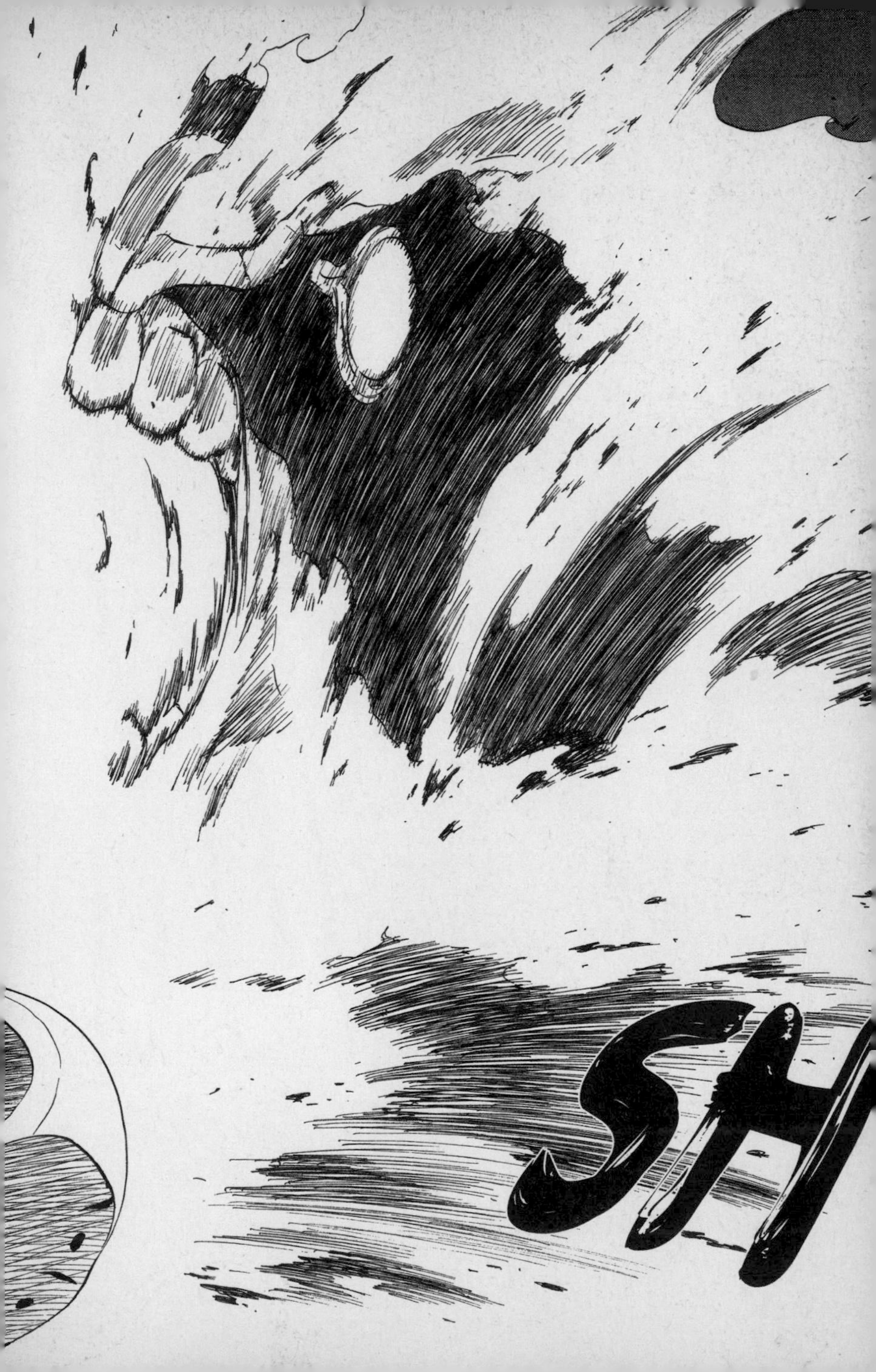
SH

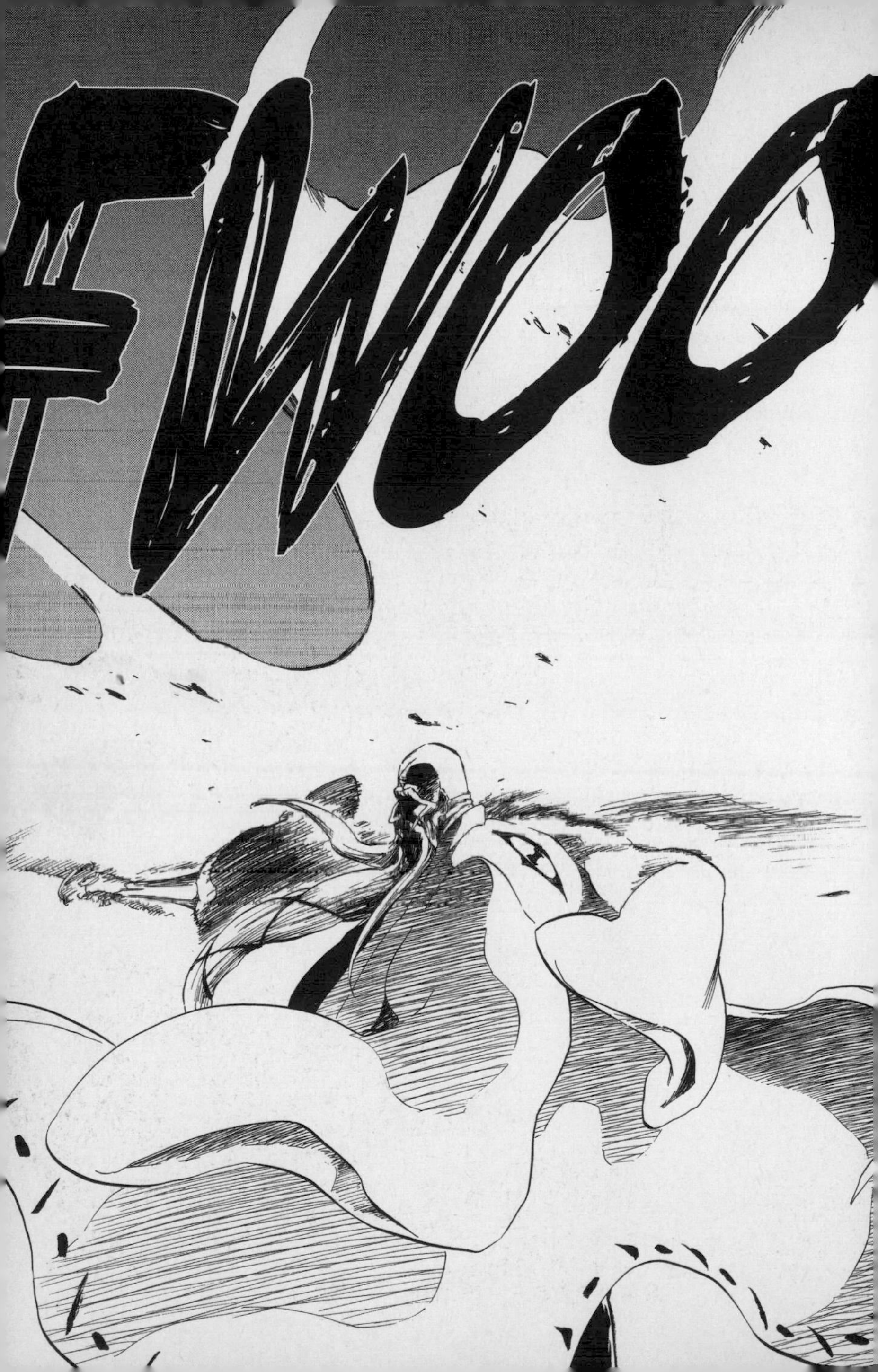
FWOO

BASHFUL
AYON

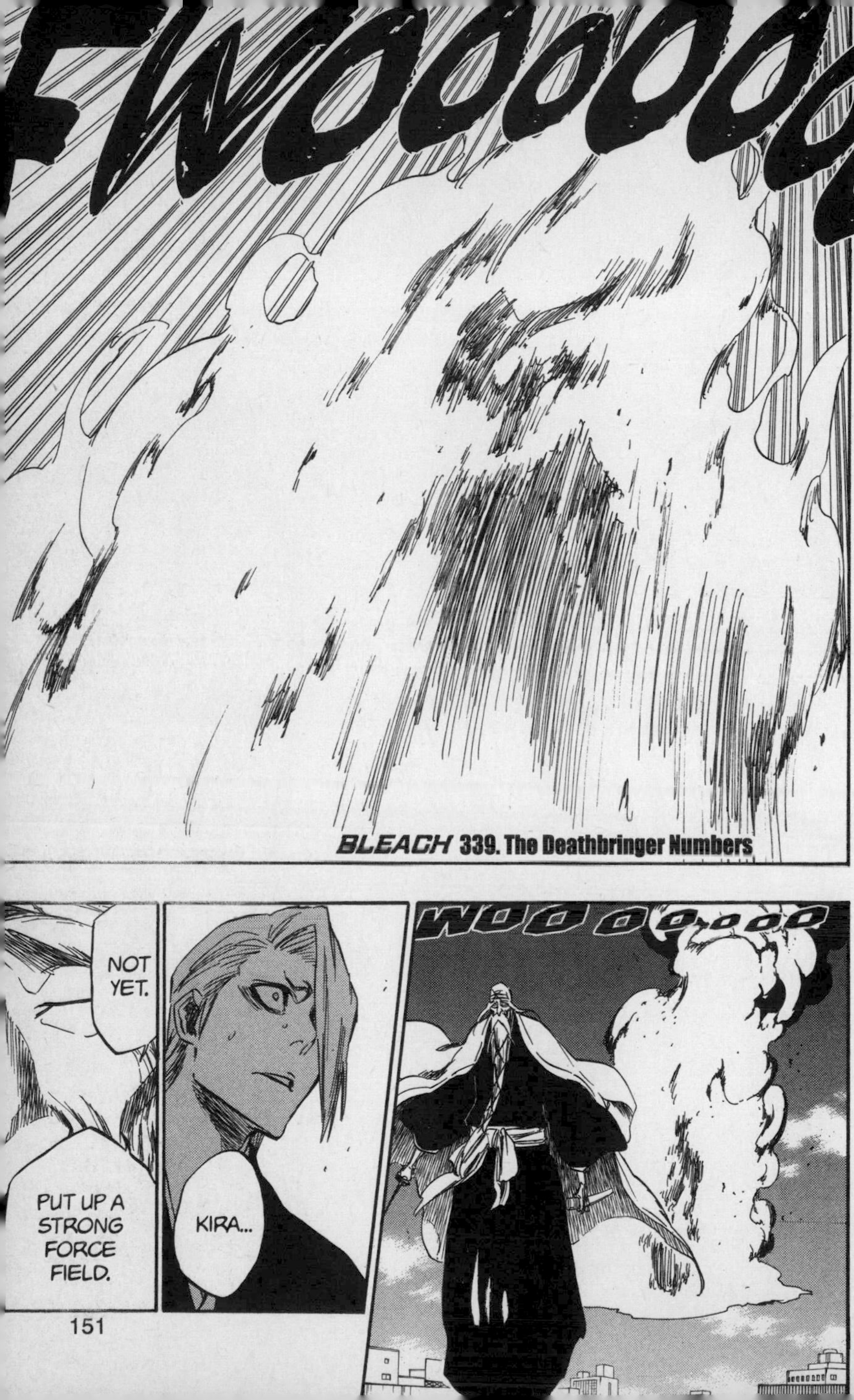
BLEACH 339. The Deathbringer Numbers
KIRA...
NOT YET.
PUT UP A STRONG FORCE FIELD.

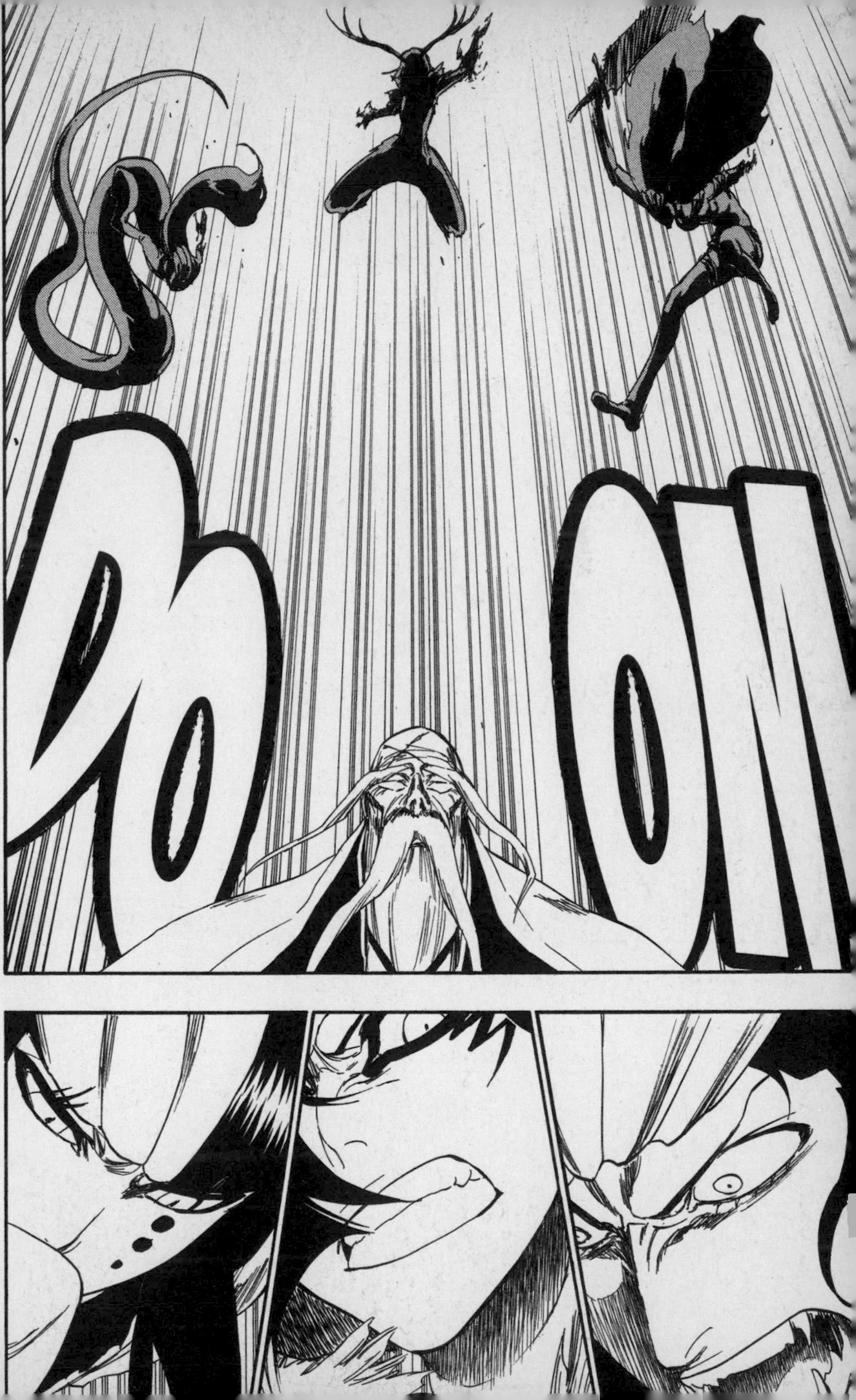
BOOM

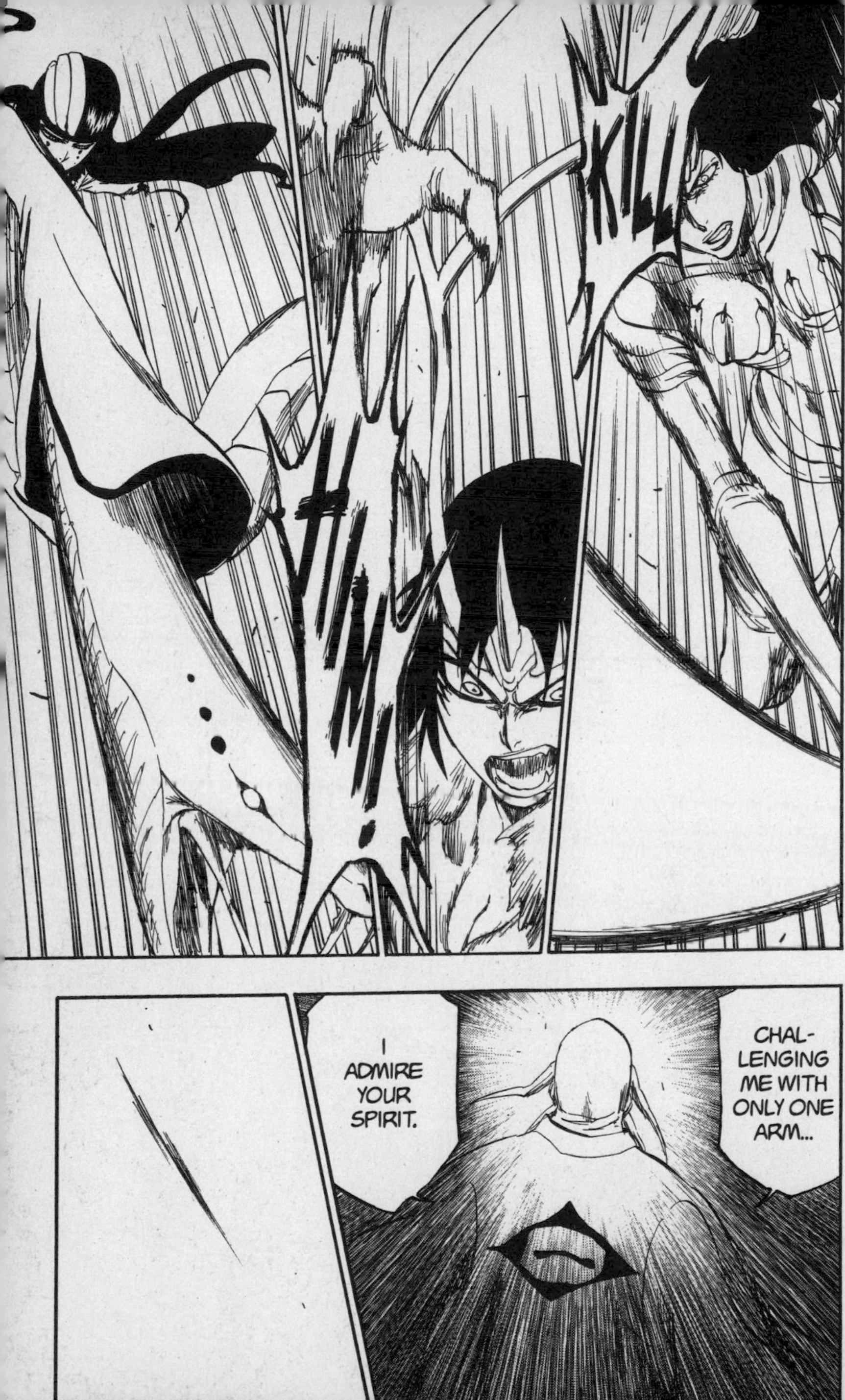
KILL
CHAL-
LENGING
ME WITH
ONLY ONE
ARM...
I
ADMIRE
YOUR
SPIRIT.

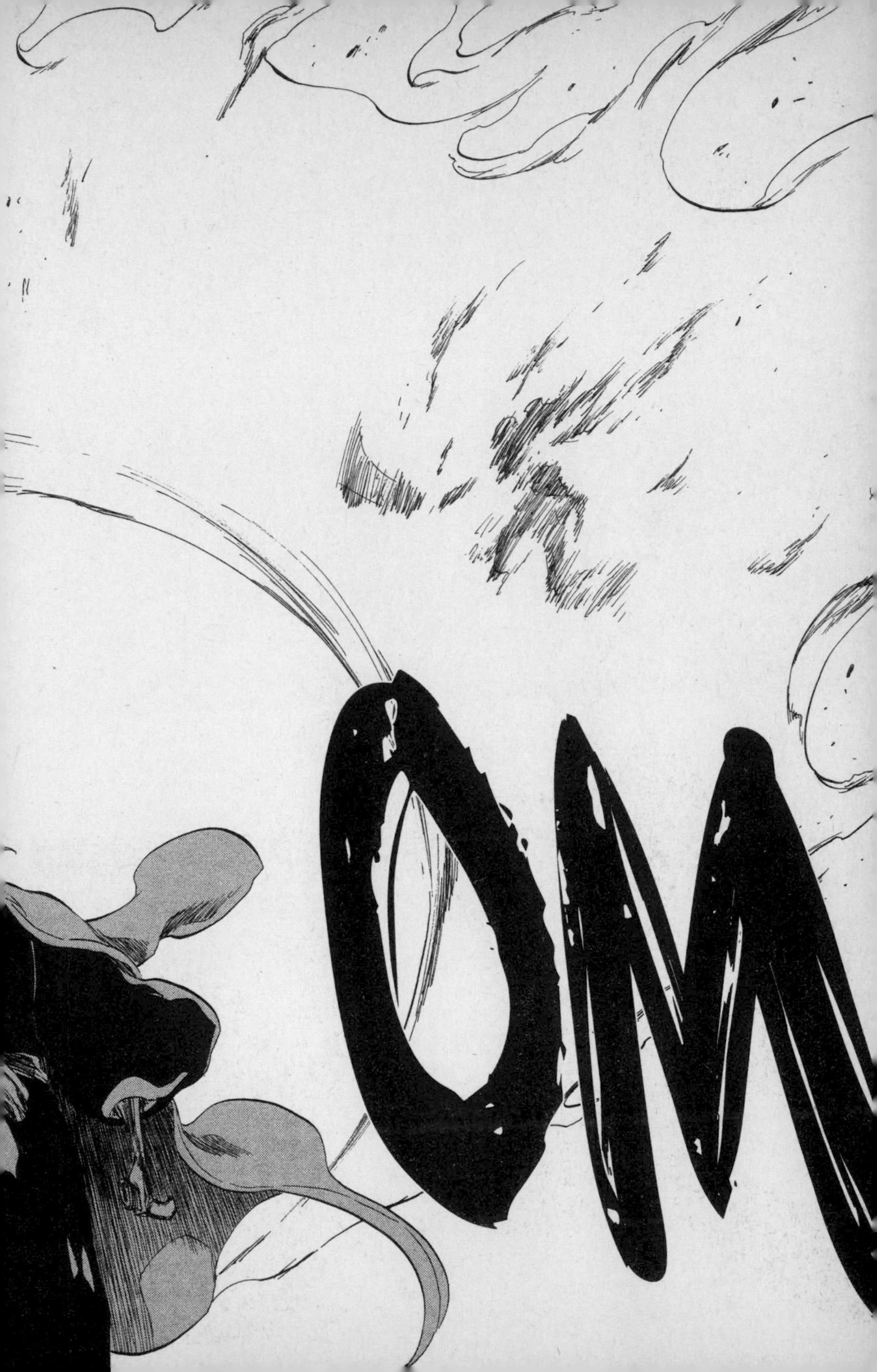
OM

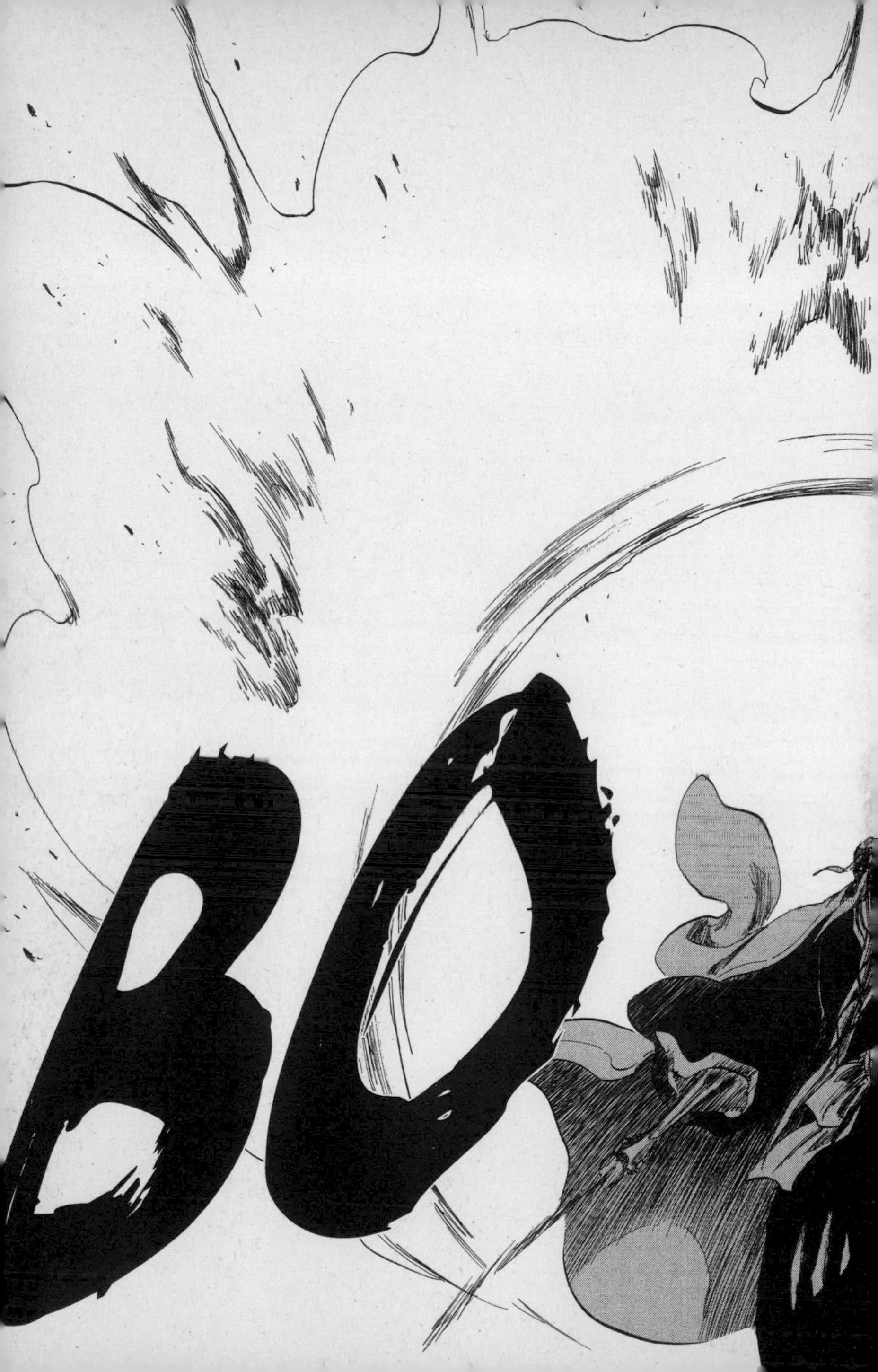
BOO

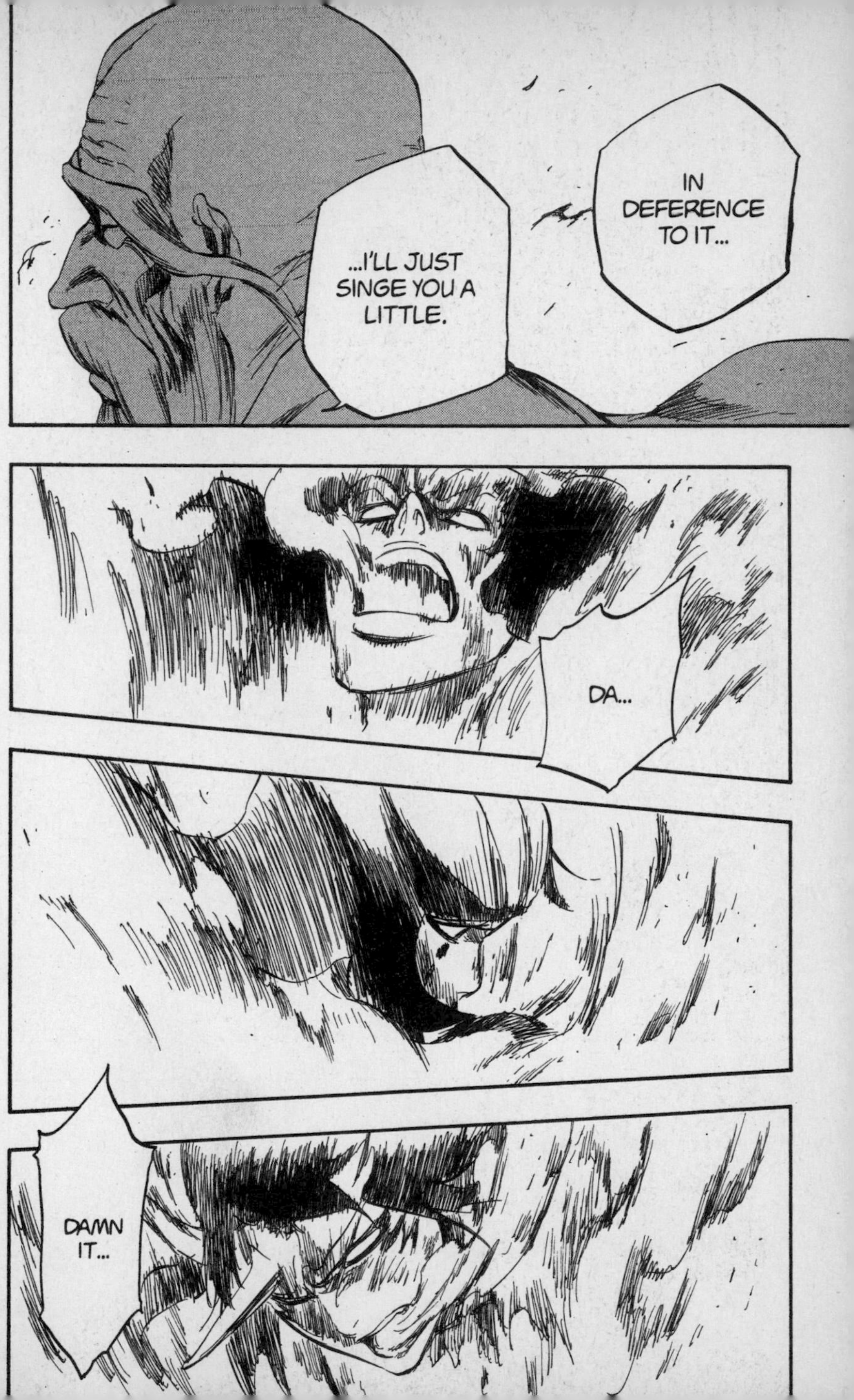
IN DEFERENCE TO IT...
...I'LL JUST SINGE YOU A LITTLE.
DA...
DAMN IT...

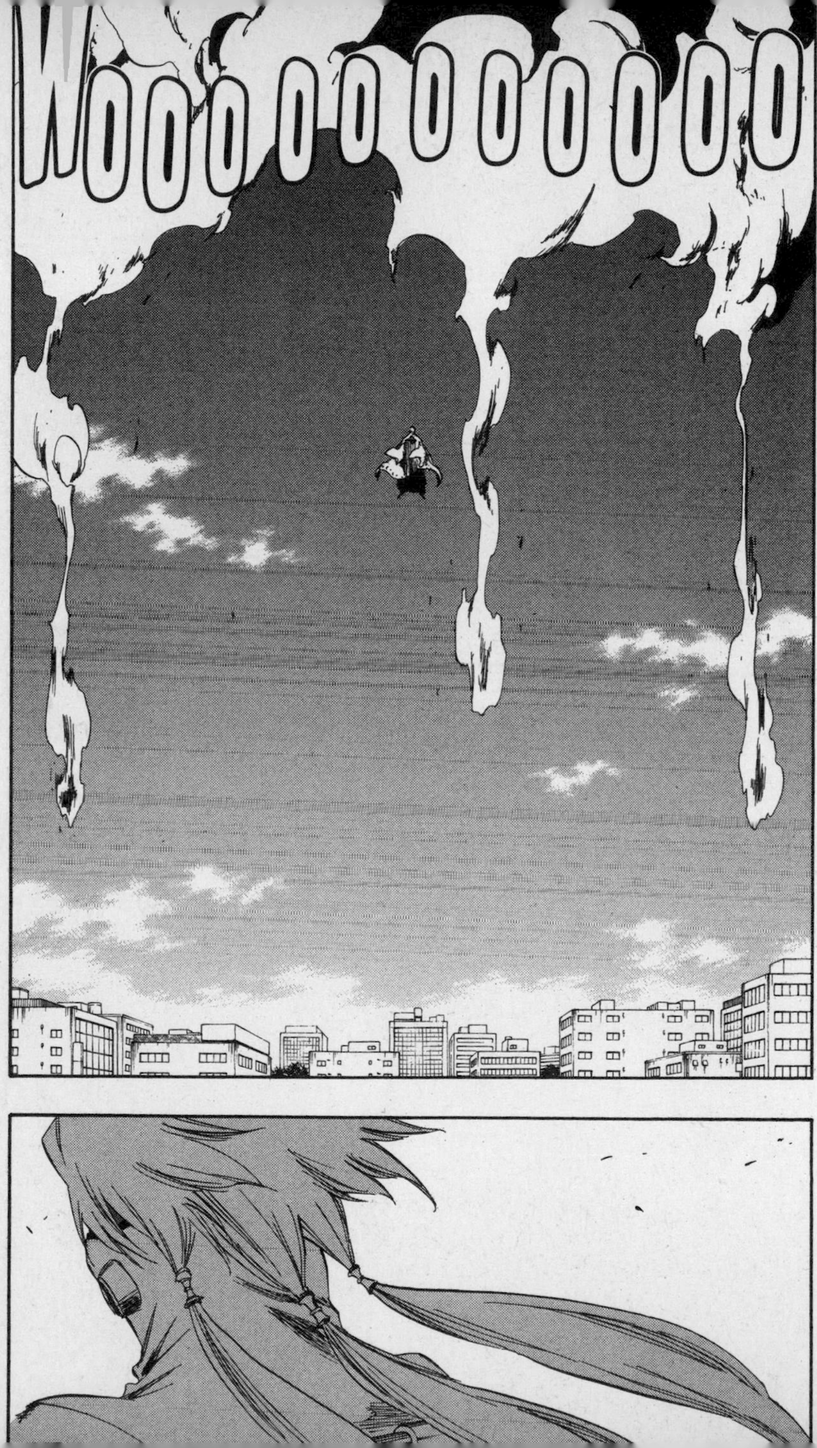
WOOOOOOOOOOOO

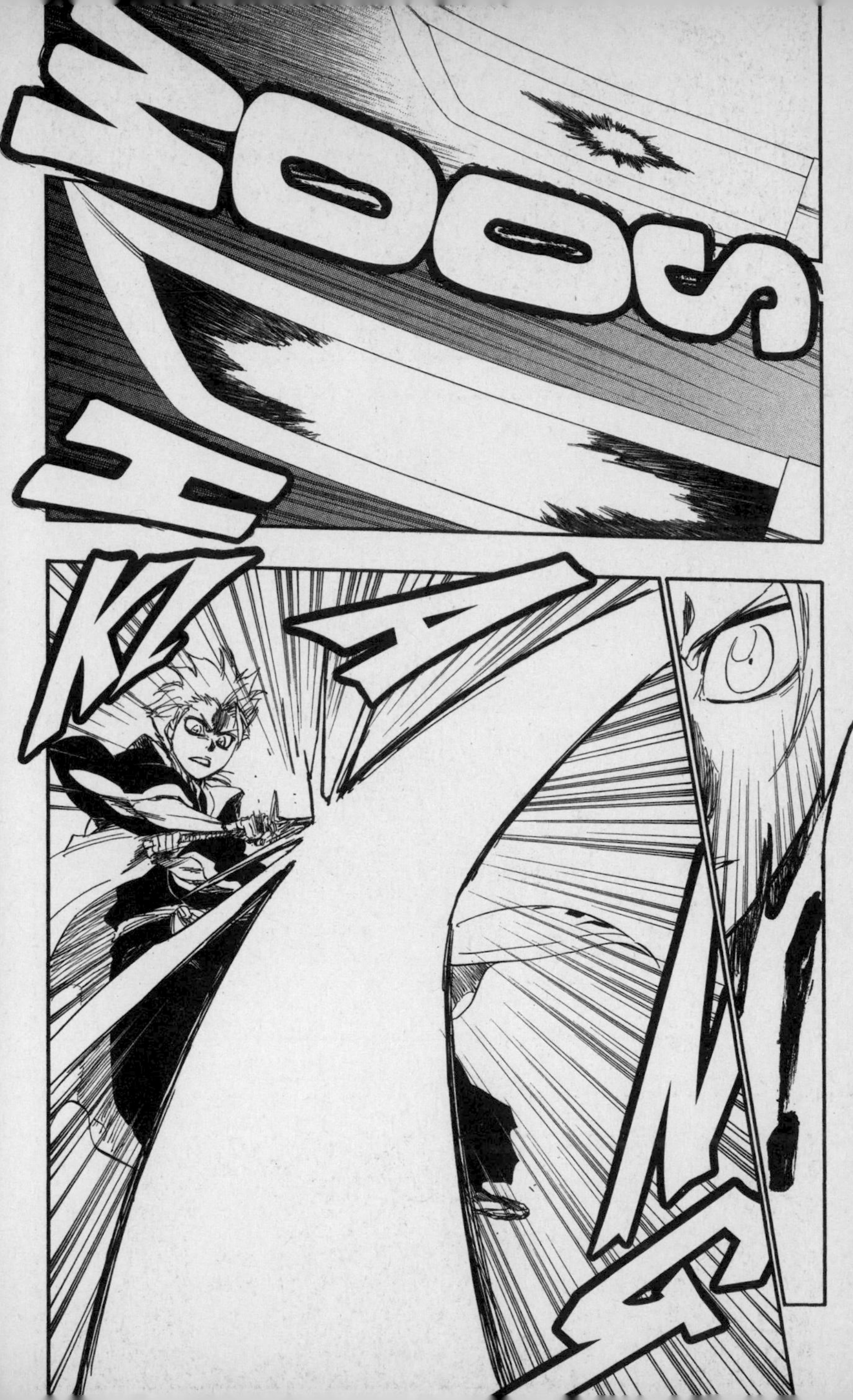
WOOSH
KANG!

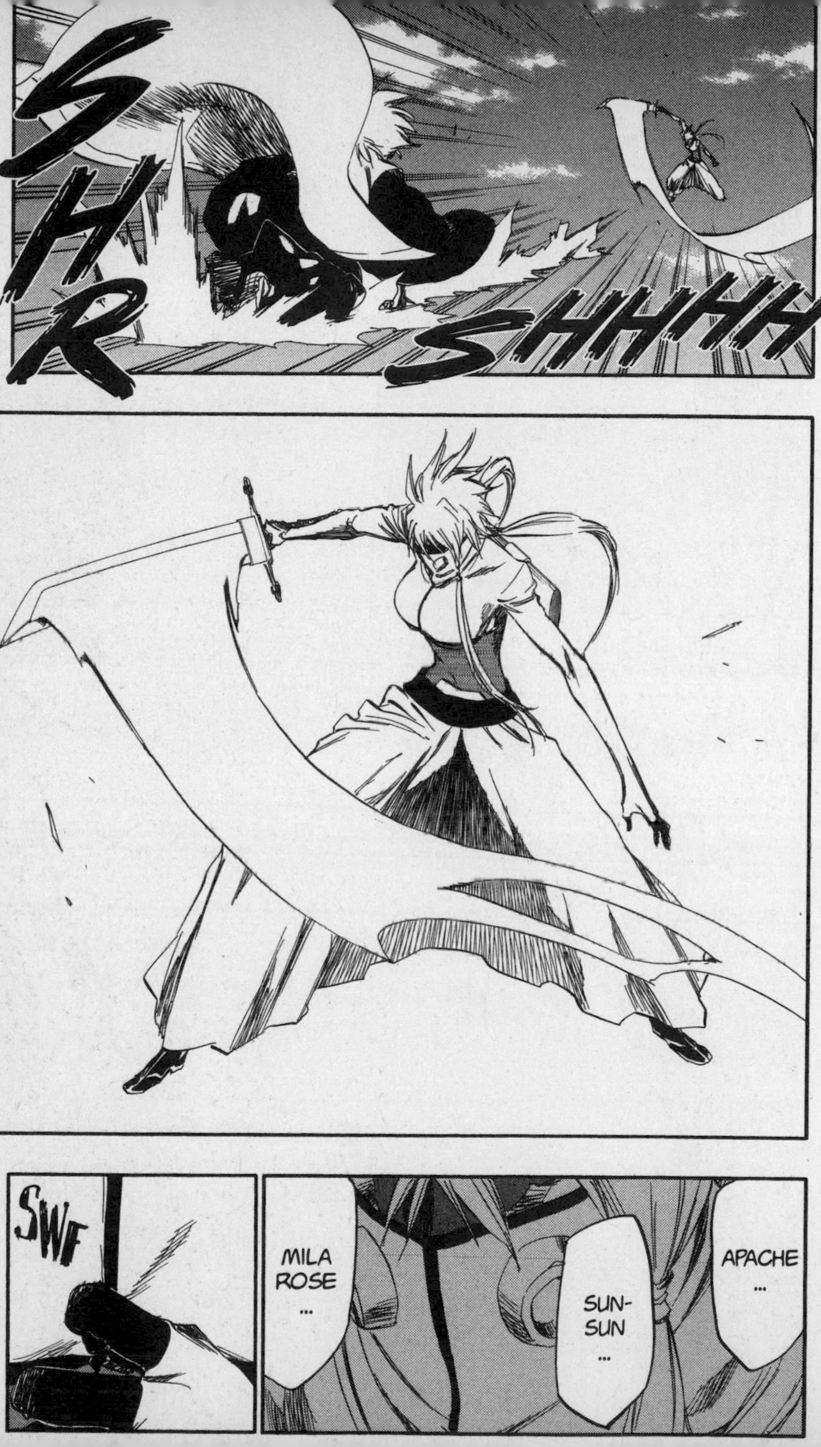
SHR
SHHHHH
APACHE...
SUN-SUN...
MILA ROSE...
SWF

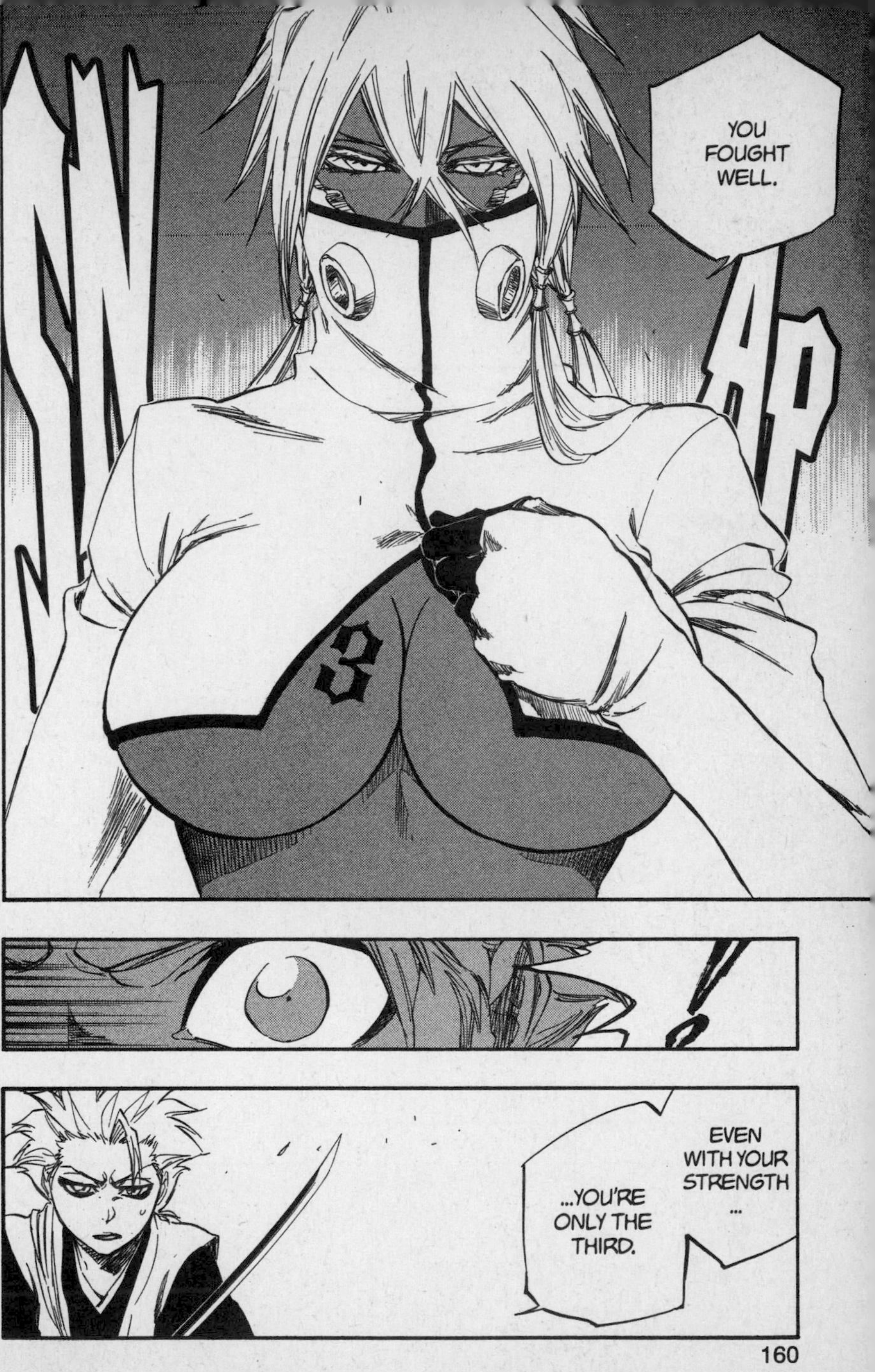
YOU FOUGHT WELL.
!
EVEN WITH YOUR STRENGTH ...
...YOU'RE ONLY THE THIRD.

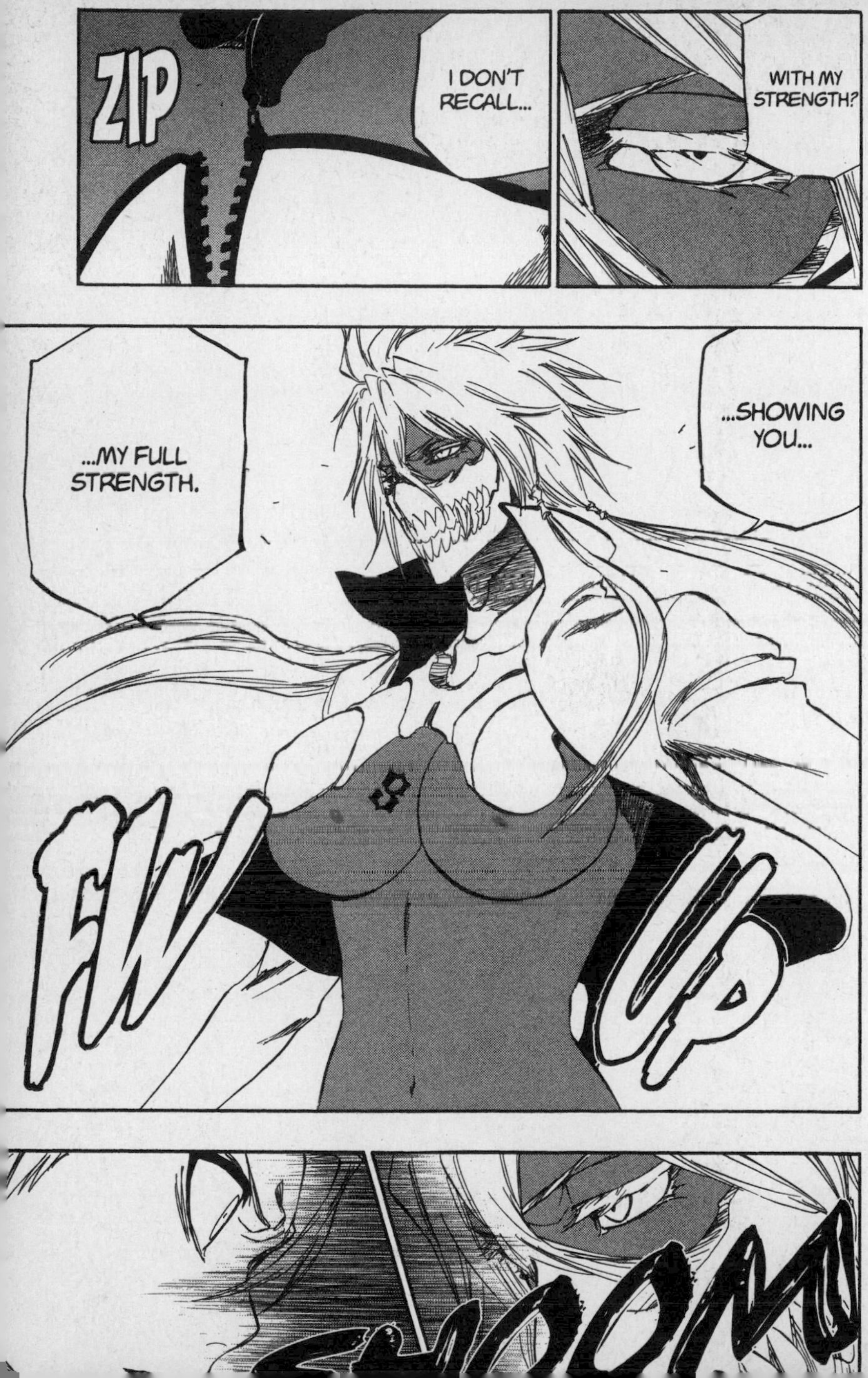
WITH MY STRENGTH?
I DON'T RECALL...
ZIP
...SHOWING YOU...
...MY FULL STRENGTH.
FW
UP

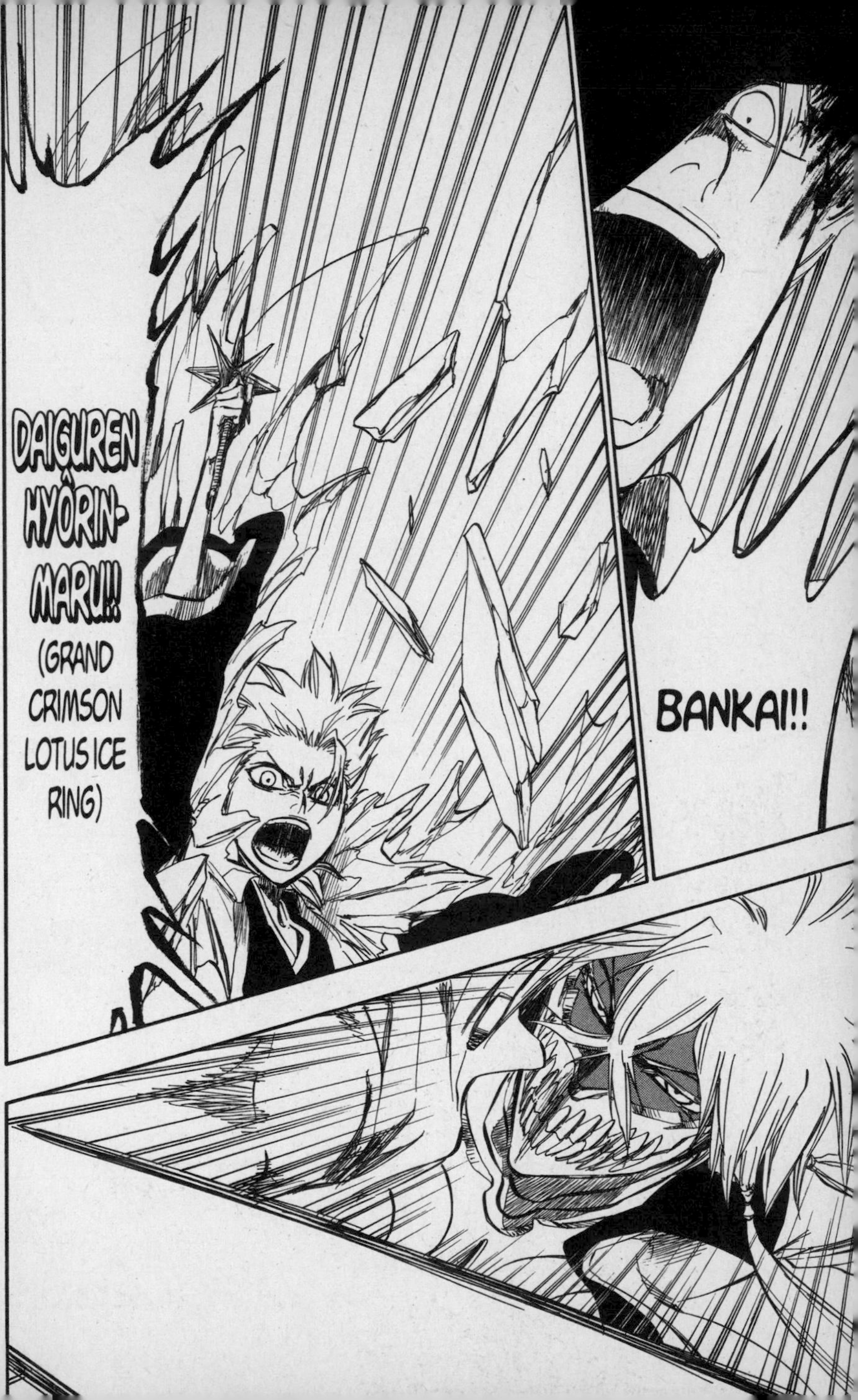
BANKAI!!
DAIGUREN HYÔRINMARU!!
(GRAND CRIMSON LOTUS ICE RING)

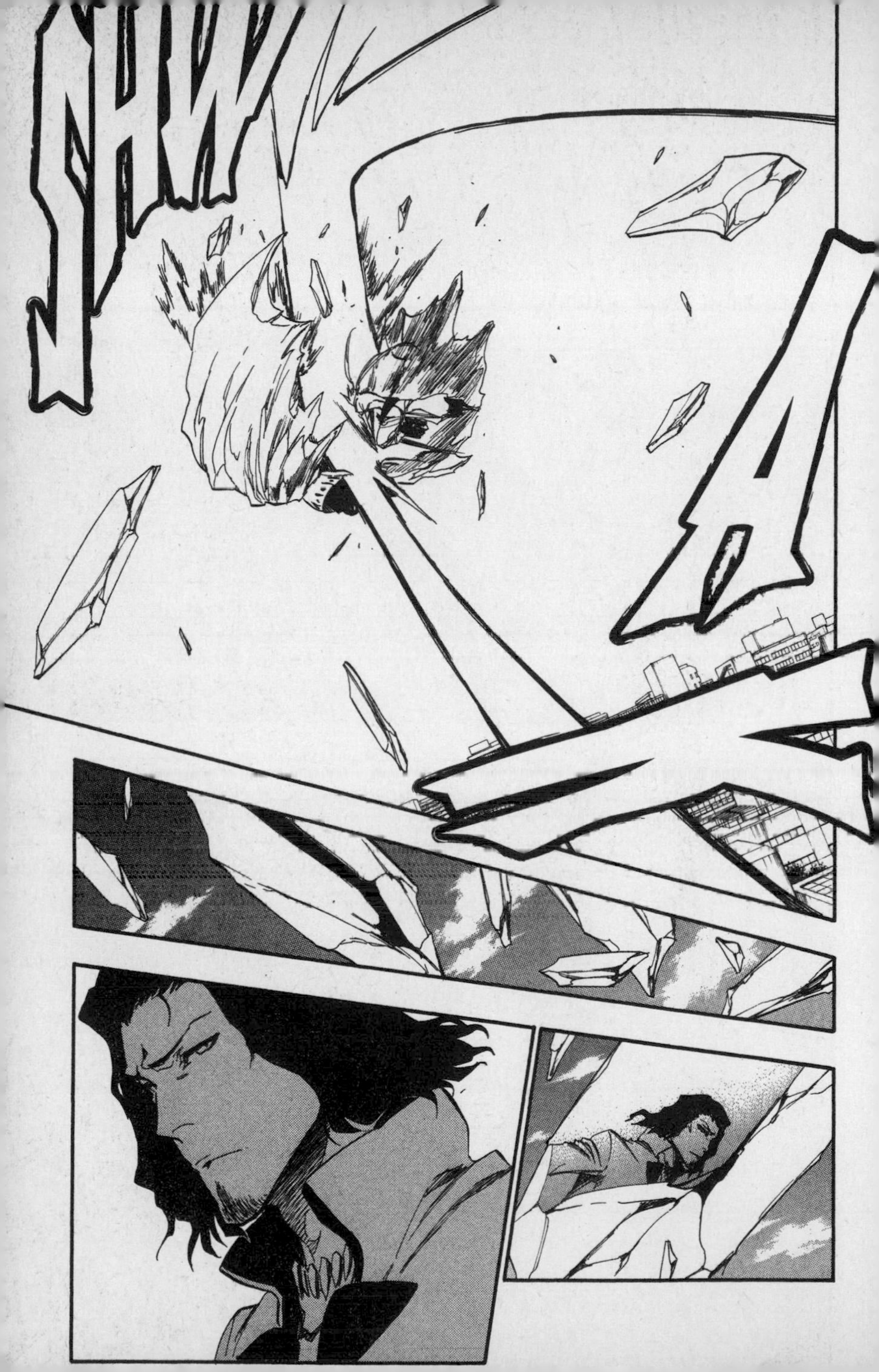
SHAA

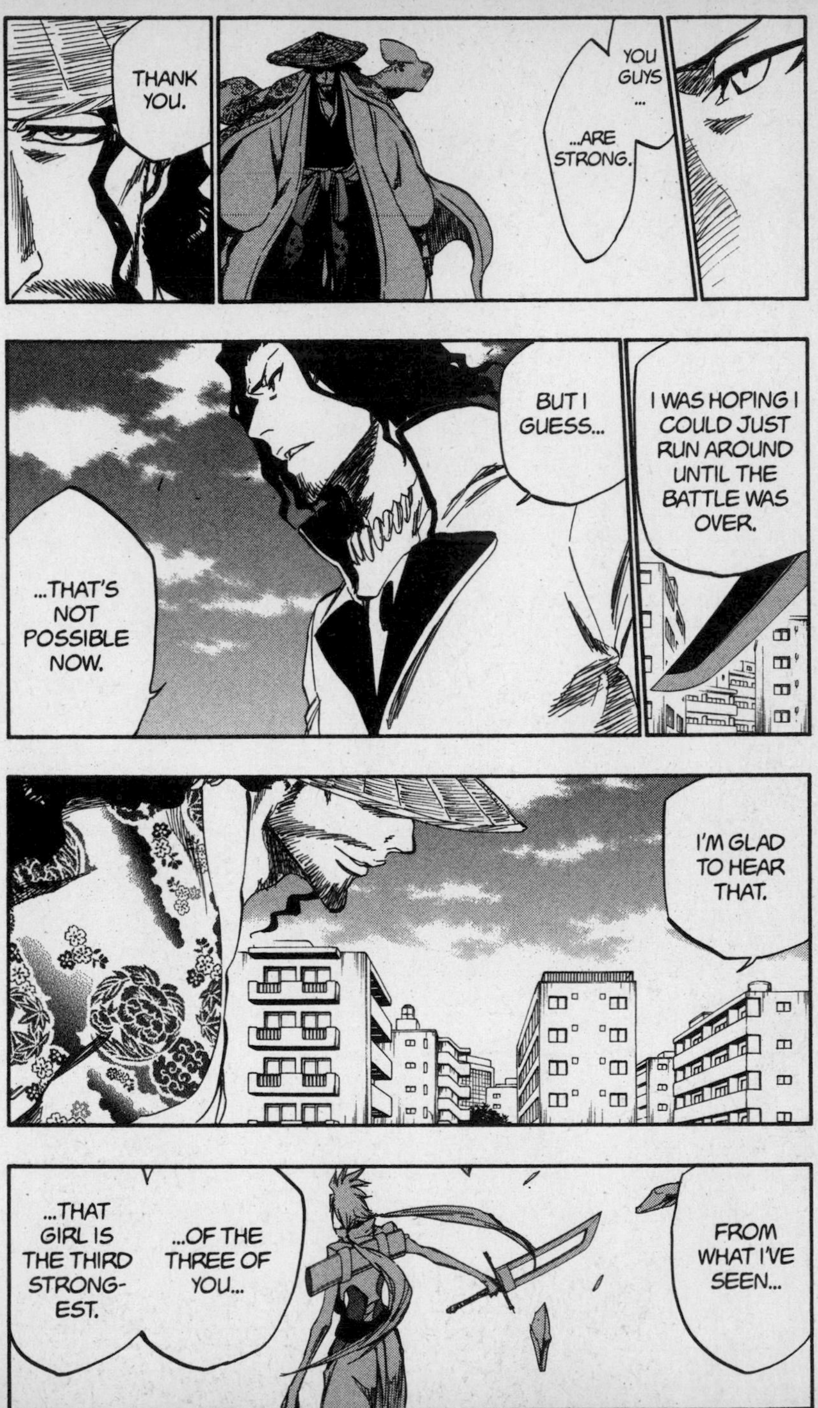
YOU GUYS ...
...ARE STRONG.
THANK YOU.
I WAS HOPING I COULD JUST RUN AROUND UNTIL THE BATTLE WAS OVER.
BUT I GUESS...
...THAT'S NOT POSSIBLE NOW.
I'M GLAD TO HEAR THAT.
FROM WHAT I'VE SEEN...
...OF THE THREE OF YOU...
...THAT GIRL IS THE THIRD STRONG-EST.

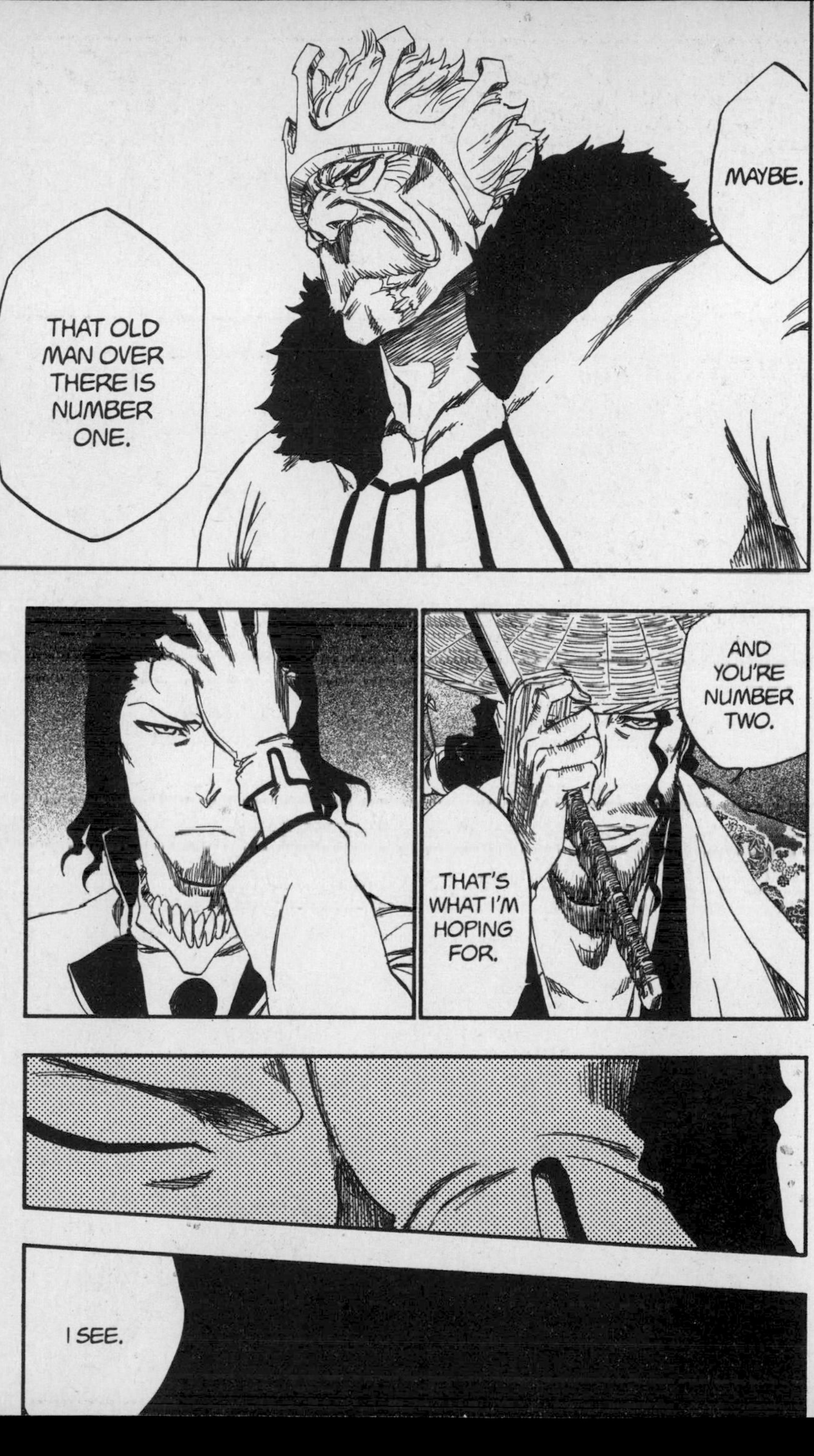
MAYBE.
THAT OLD MAN OVER THERE IS NUMBER ONE.
AND YOU'RE NUMBER TWO.
THAT'S WHAT I'M HOPING FOR.
I SEE.

SORRY.

I'M THE PRIMERA ESPADA.

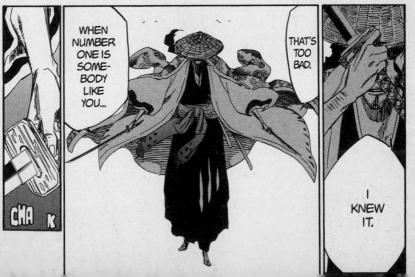

WHEN NUMBER ONE IS SOMEBODY LIKE YOU...

THAT'S TOO BAD.

I KNEW IT.

CHA K

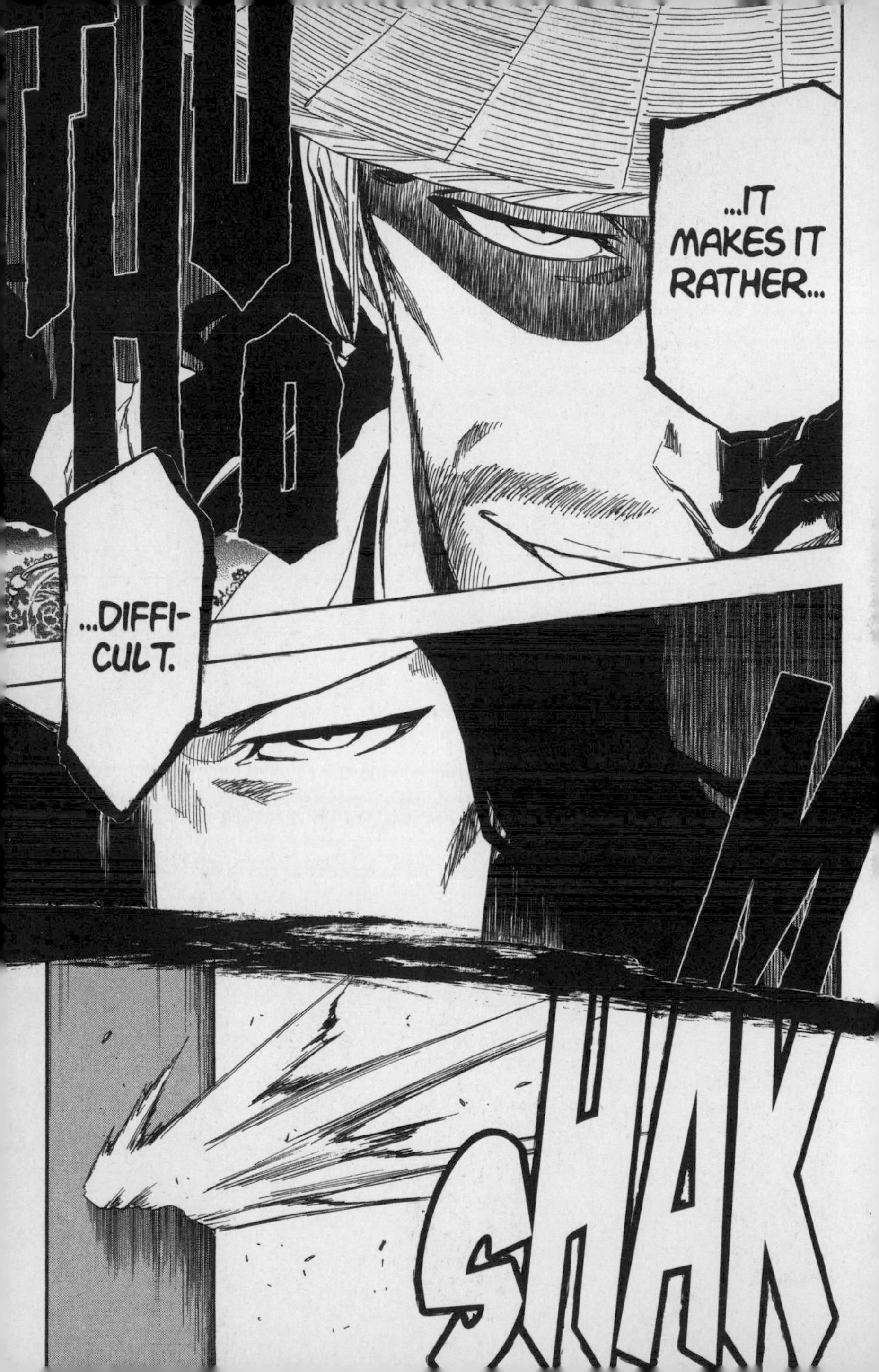

THUD
...IT MAKES IT RATHER...
...DIFFICULT.
SHAK

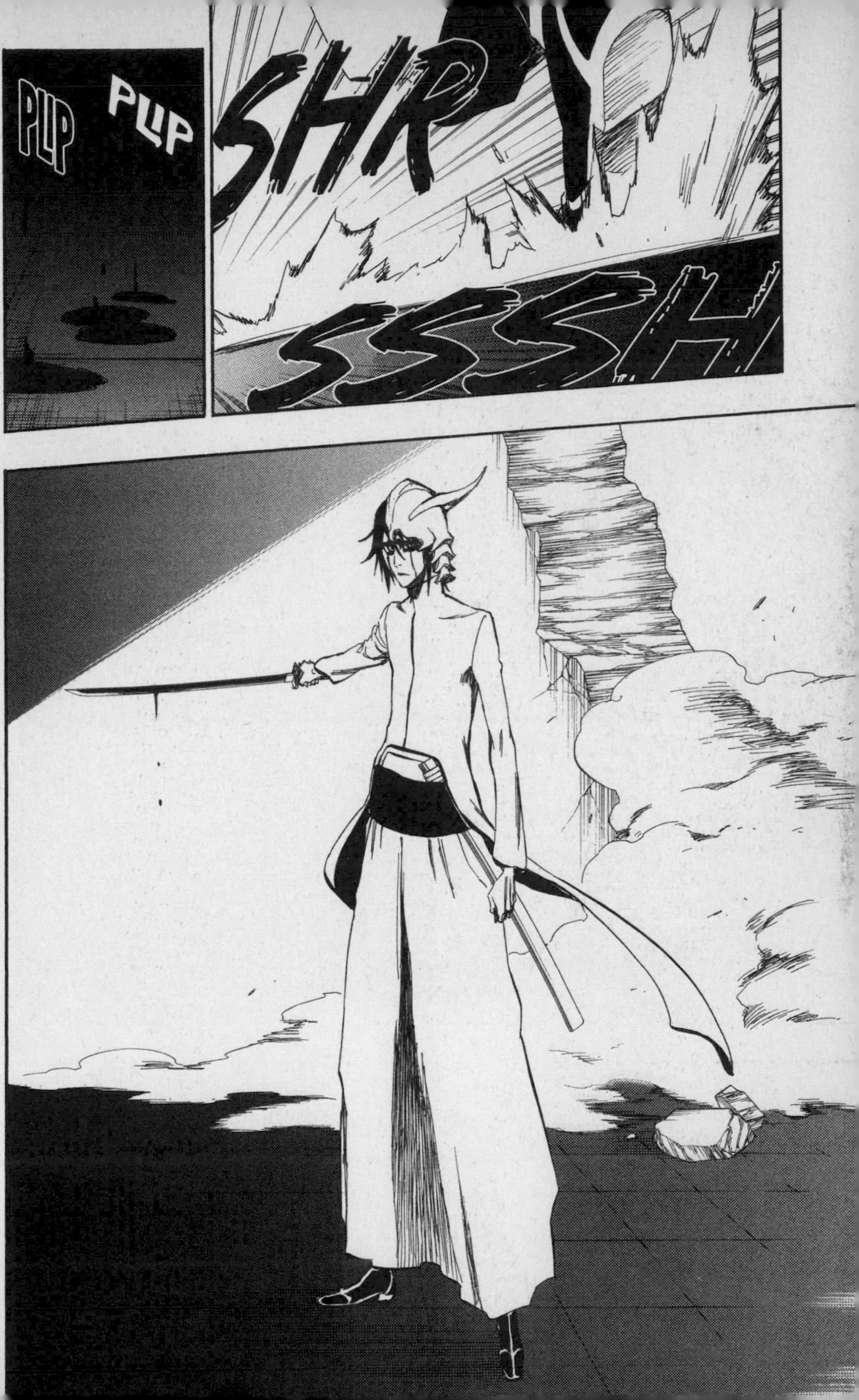
SHR
SSSH
PLIP
PLIP

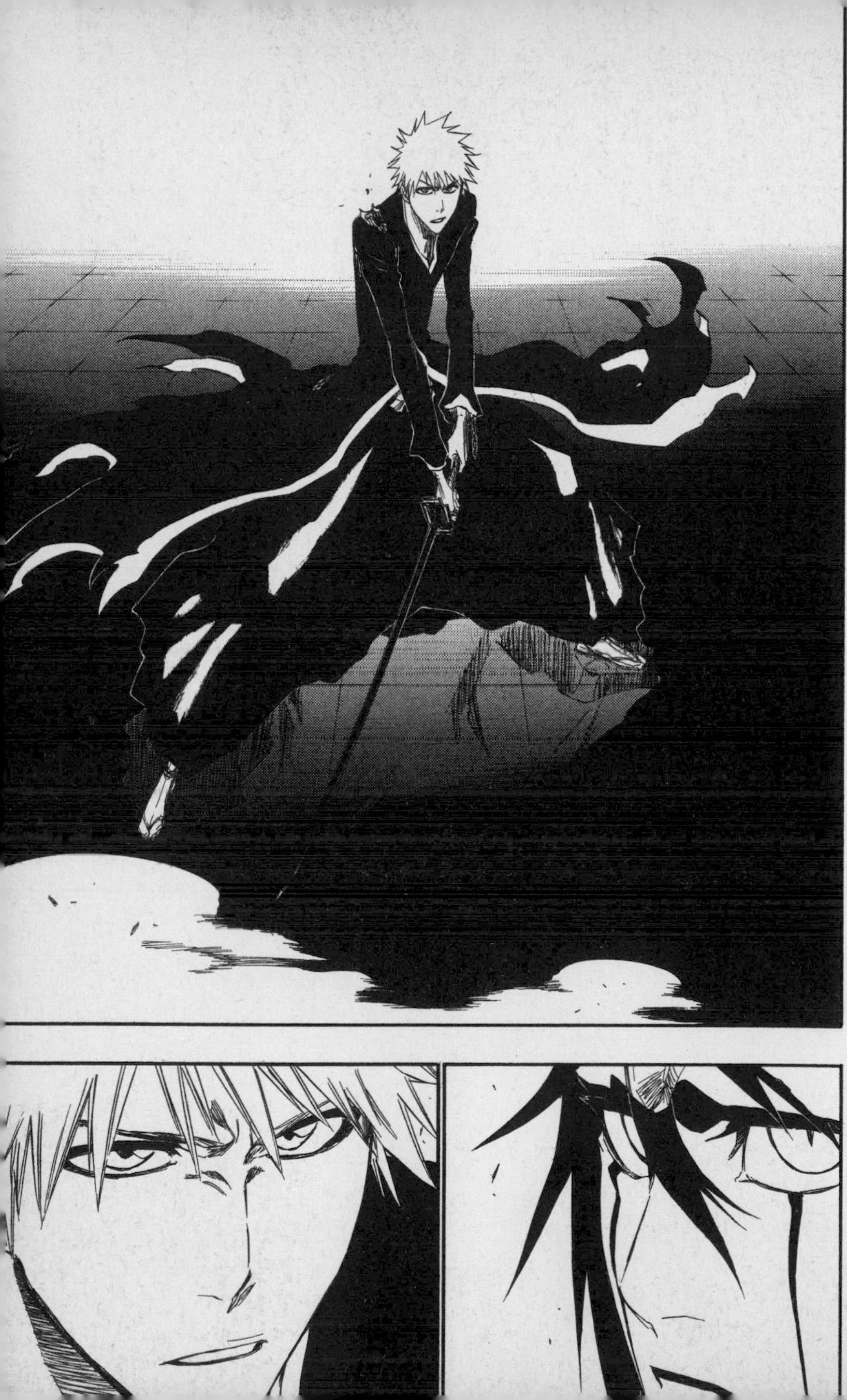

AYON THINKING,
"I HOPE WE HAVE
HAMBURGERS
FOR DINNER
TONIGHT."

WOOOOOOO

340. The Antagonizer

CRRRAAAKK

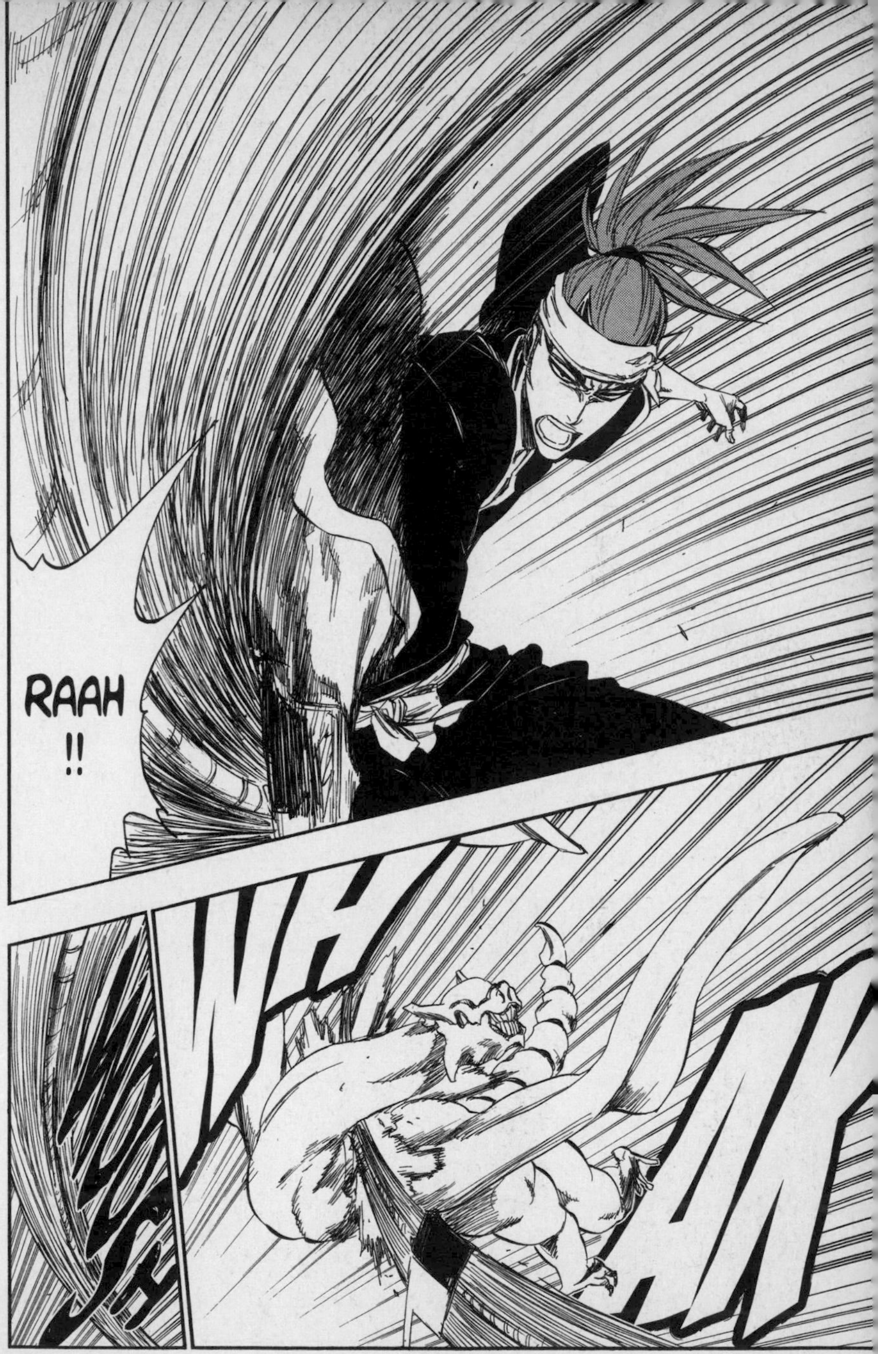
RAAH
!!

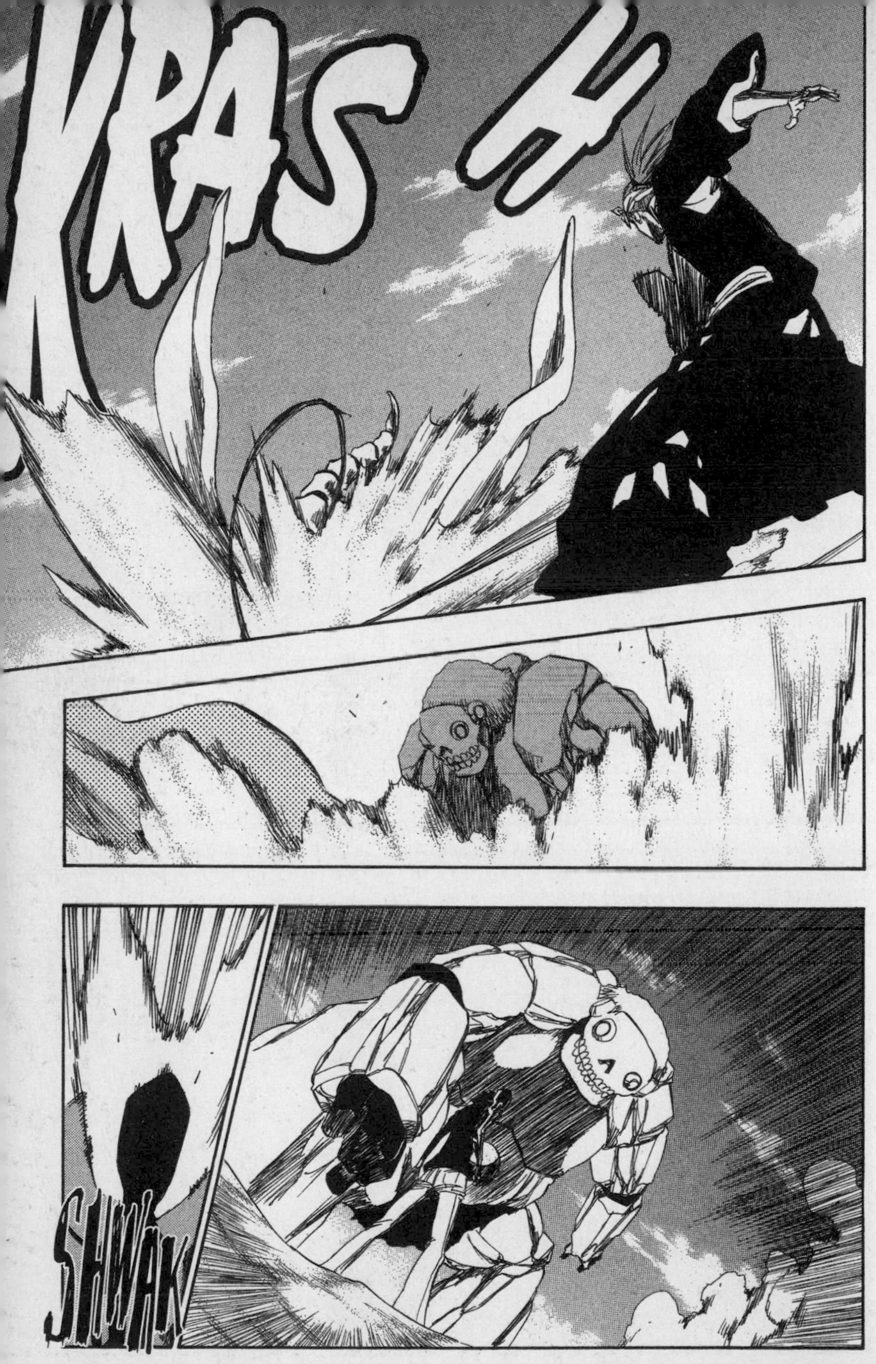
KRASH
SHWAK!

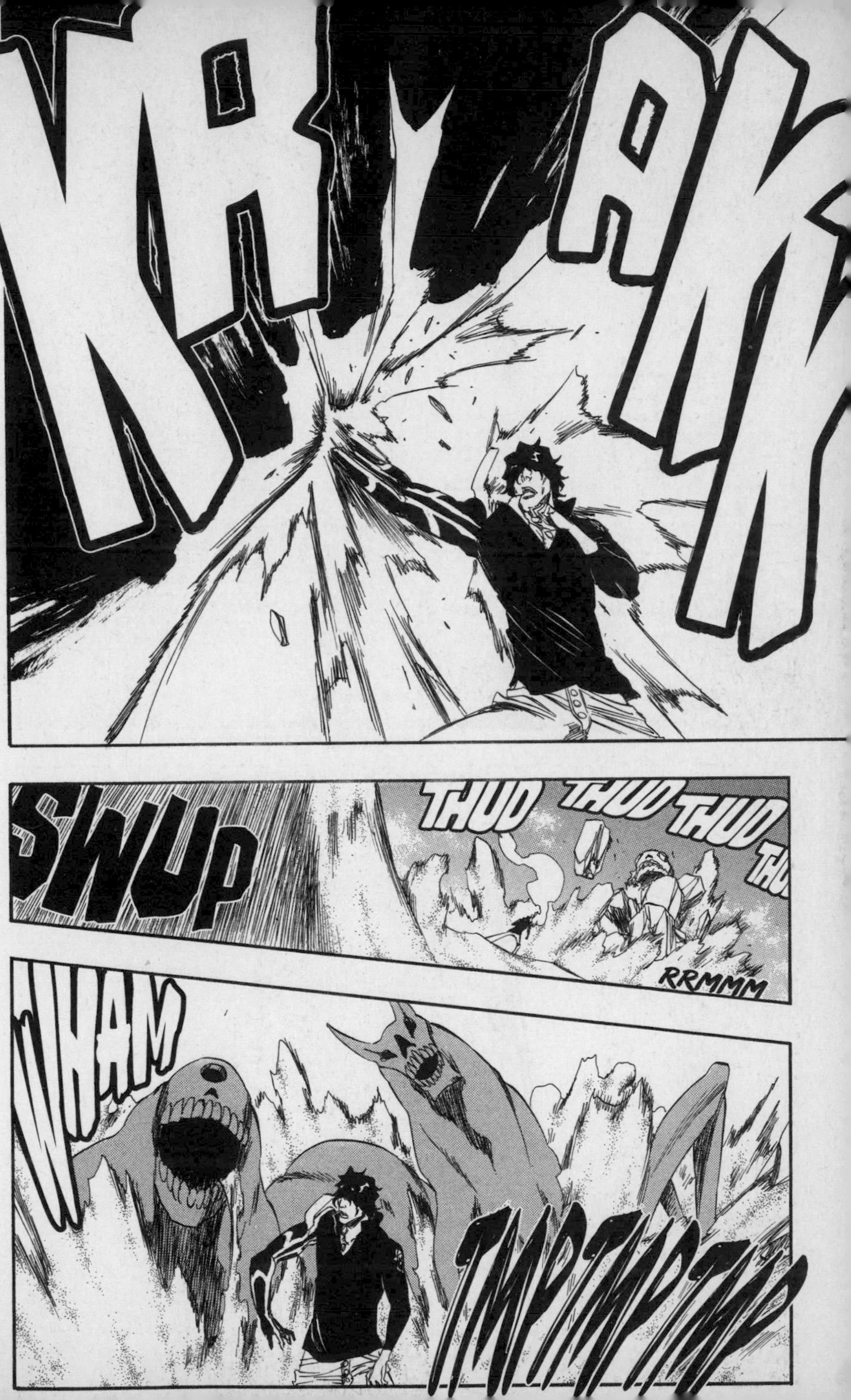
THUD THUD THUD
THU
RRMMM
SWUP
WHAM

READ THIS WAY

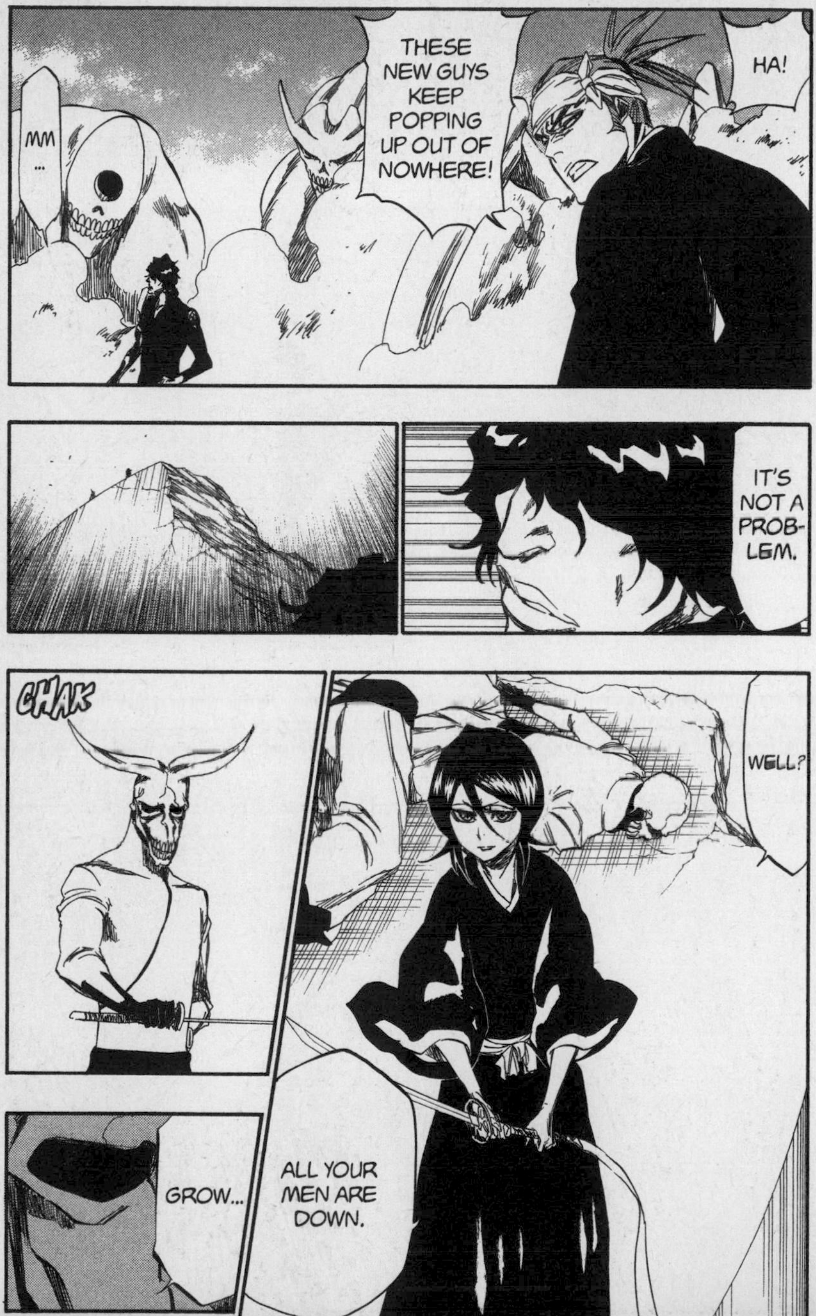
HA!
THESE NEW GUYS KEEP POPPING UP OUT OF NOWHERE!
MM ...
IT'S NOT A PROB-LEM.
WELL?
ALL YOUR MEN ARE DOWN.
CHAK
GROW...

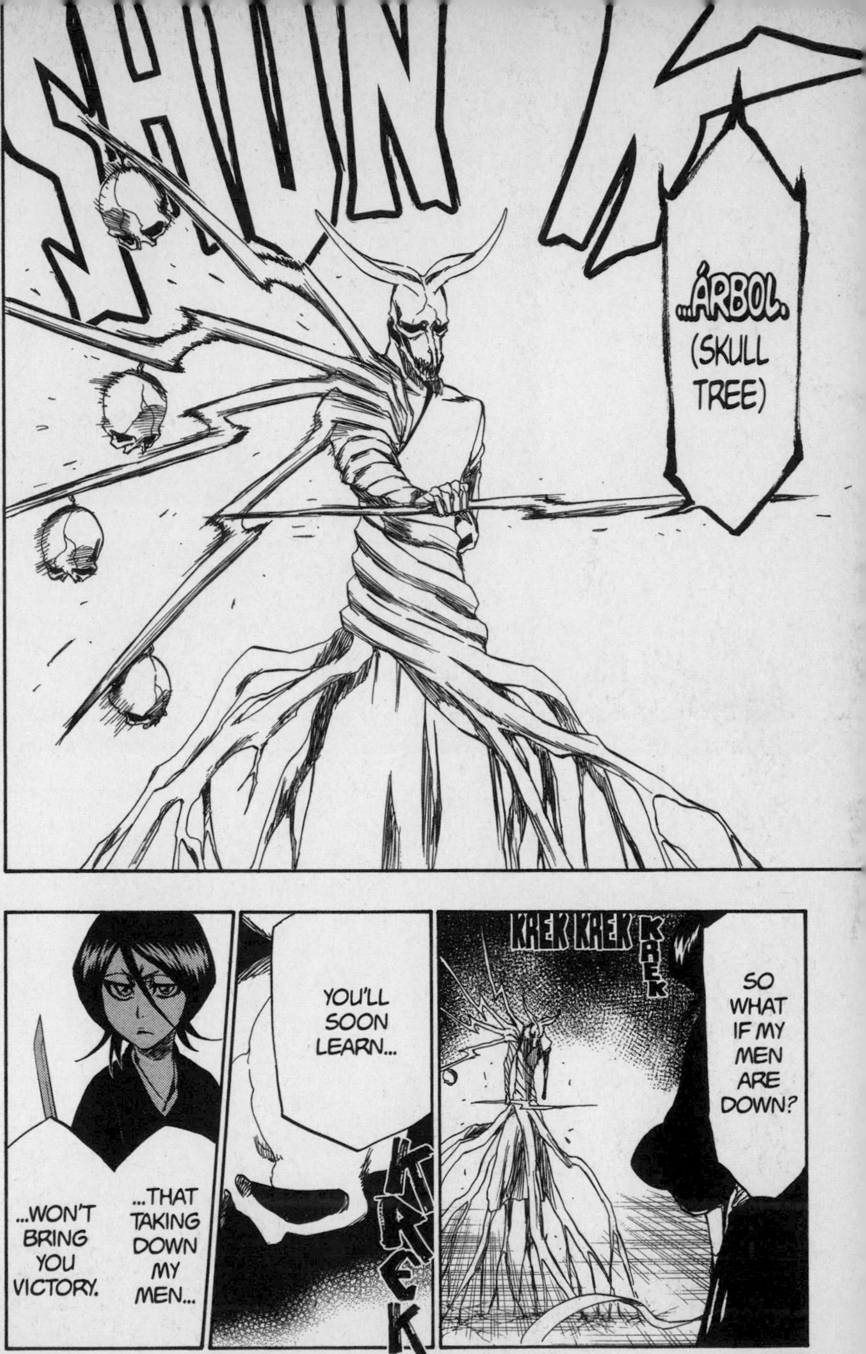
...ÁRBOL.
(SKULL TREE)
KREK KREK KREK
SO WHAT IF MY MEN ARE DOWN?
YOU'LL SOON LEARN...
...THAT TAKING DOWN MY MEN...
KREK
...WON'T BRING YOU VICTORY.

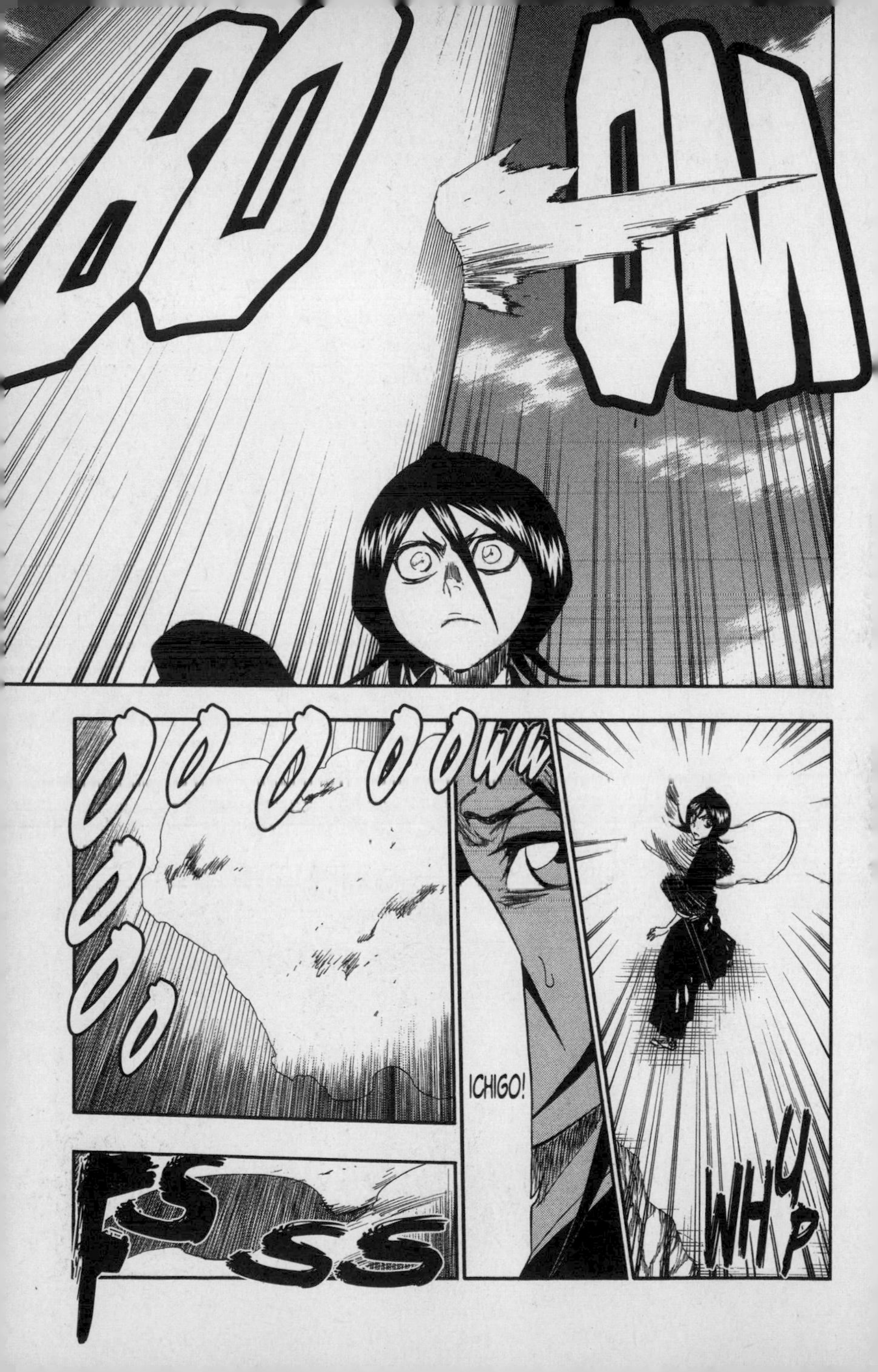
BOOM
WHUP
ICHIGO!
OOOOOOOOOOOWA
FSSS

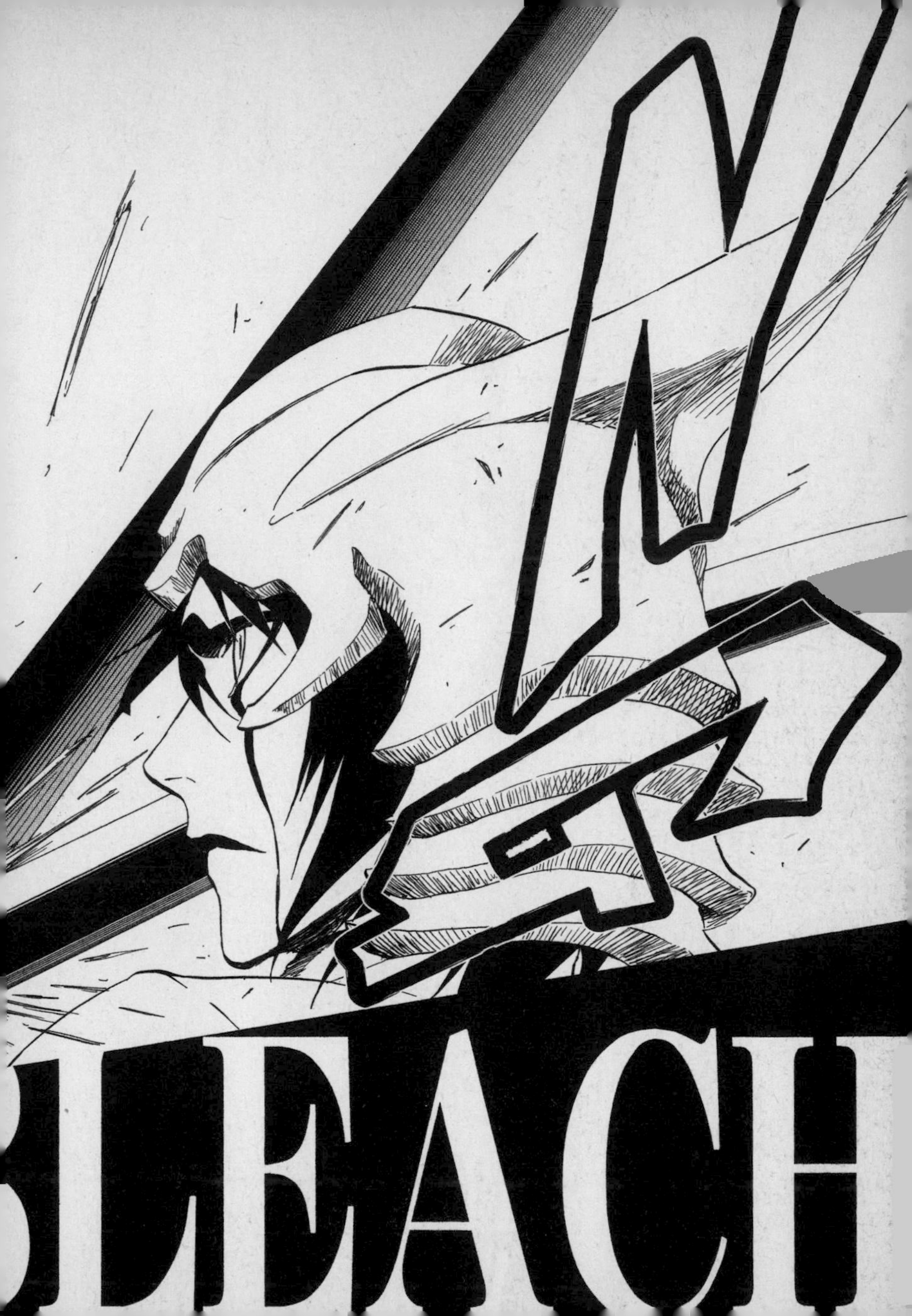

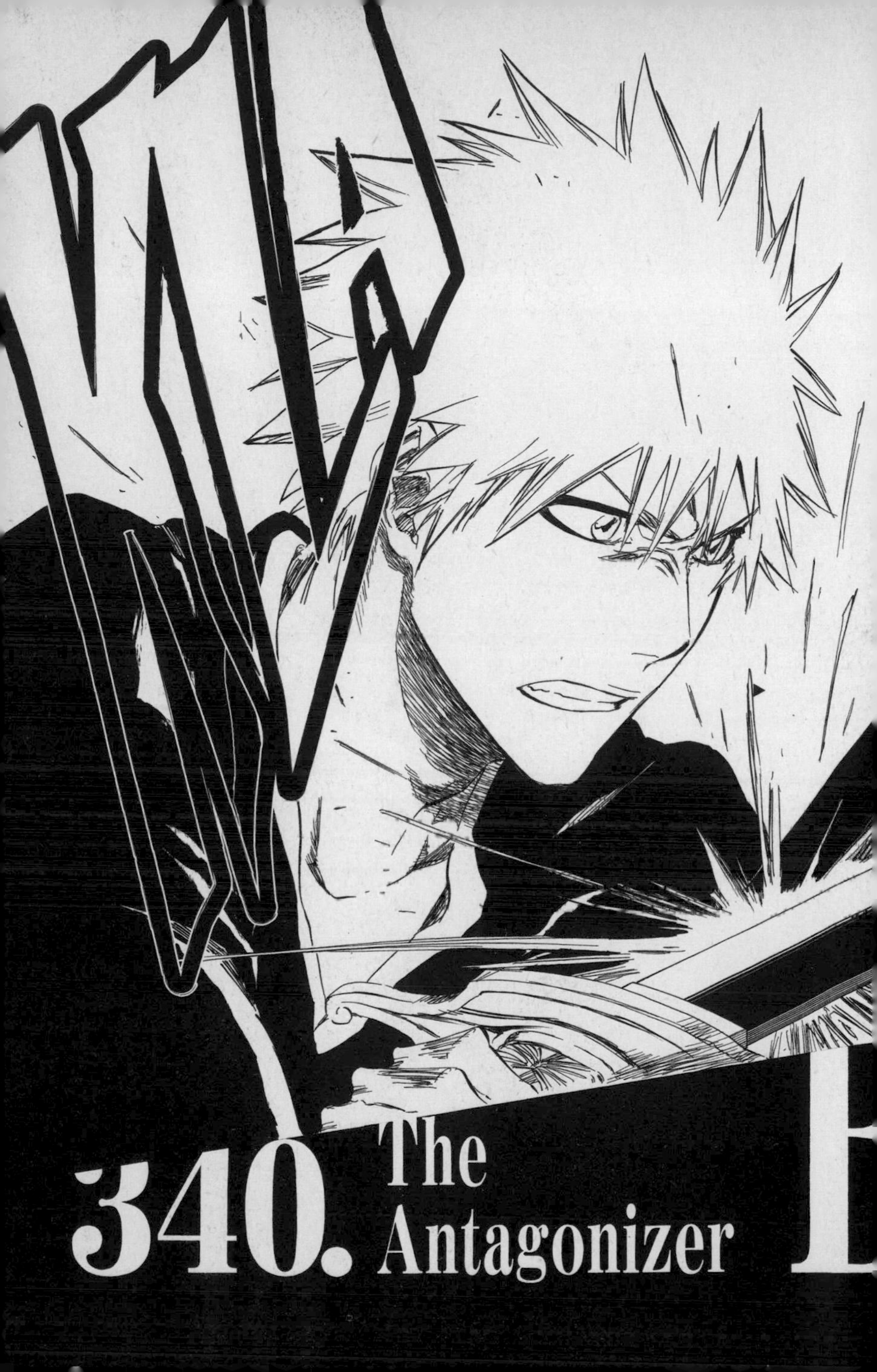
340. The Antagonizer

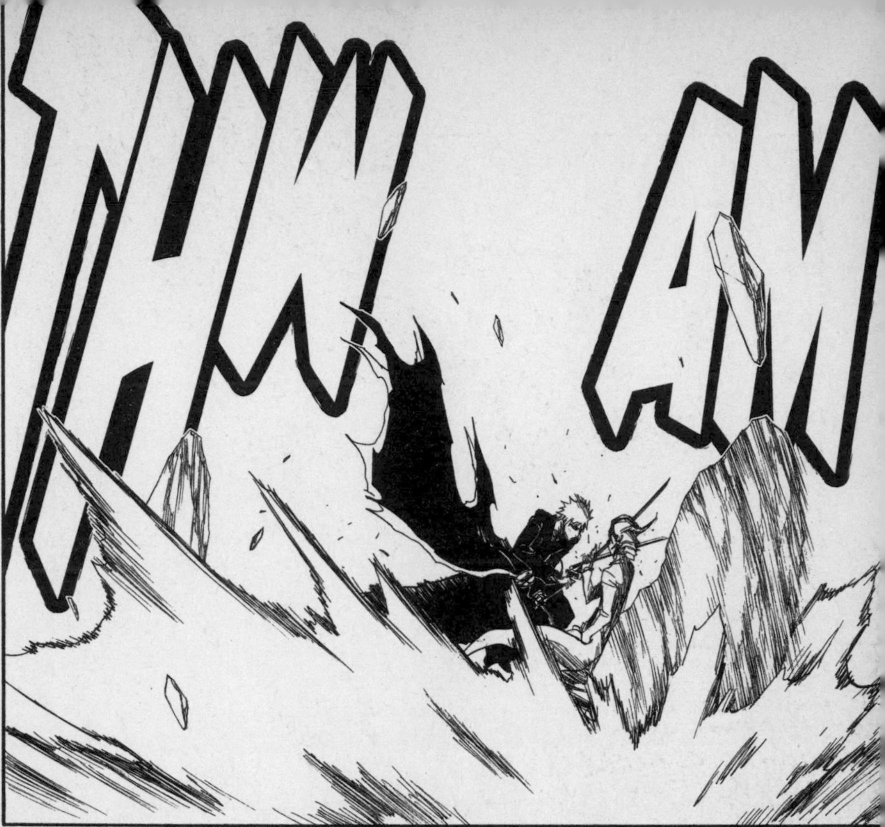

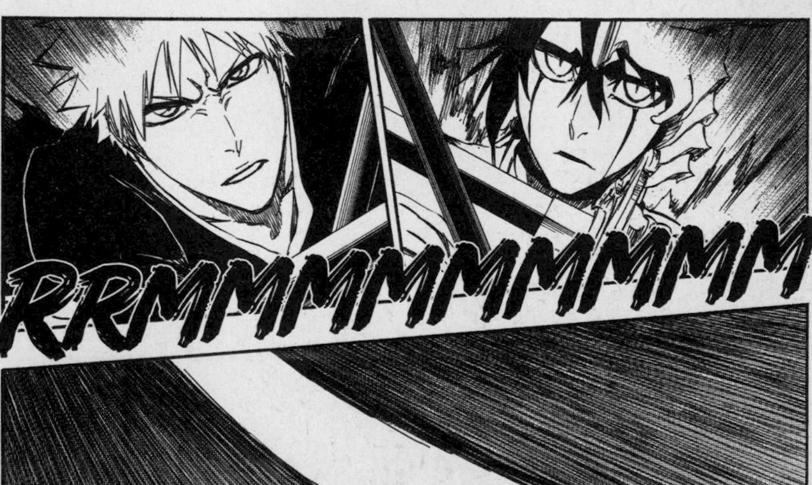
RRMMMMMMMMM

READ THIS WAY

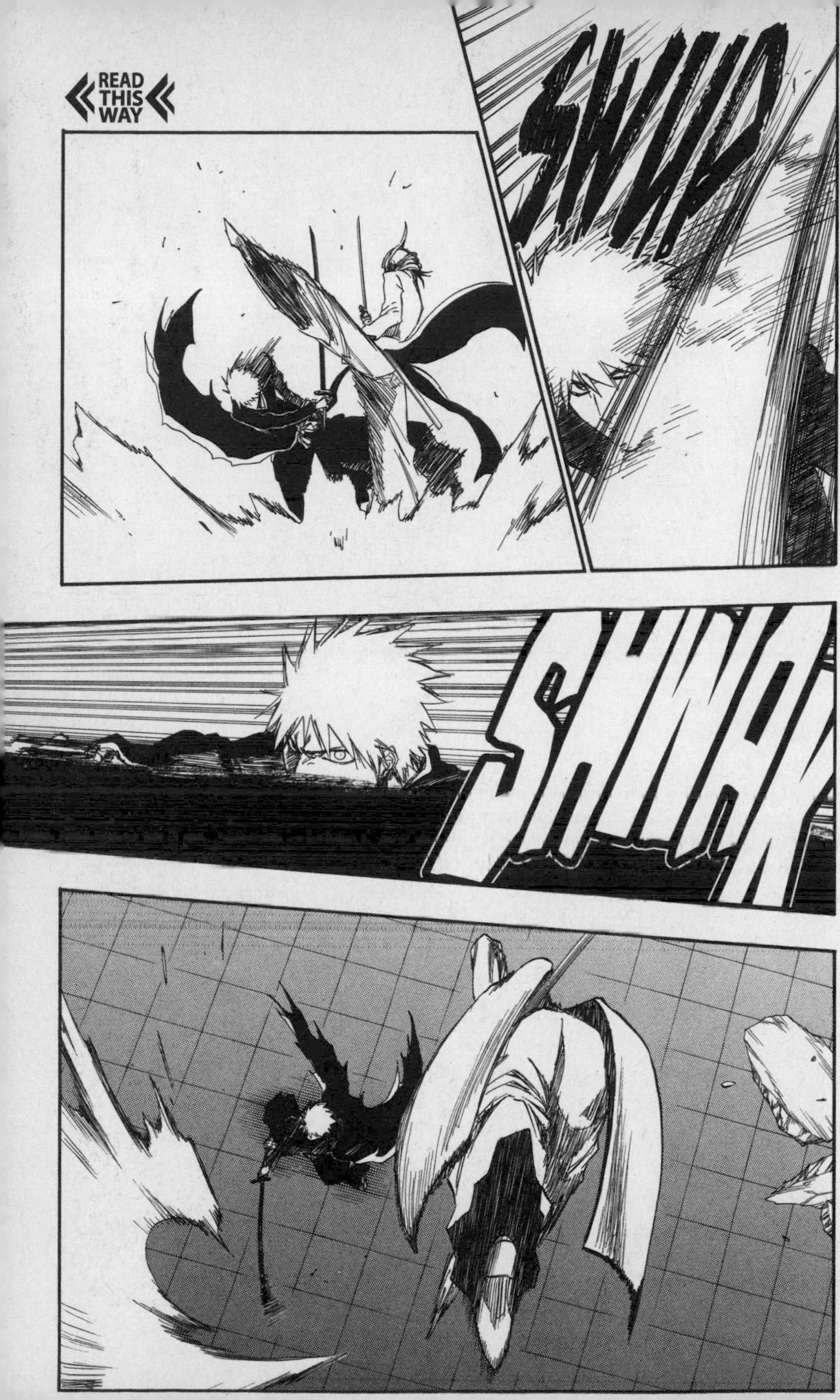
SHWAK

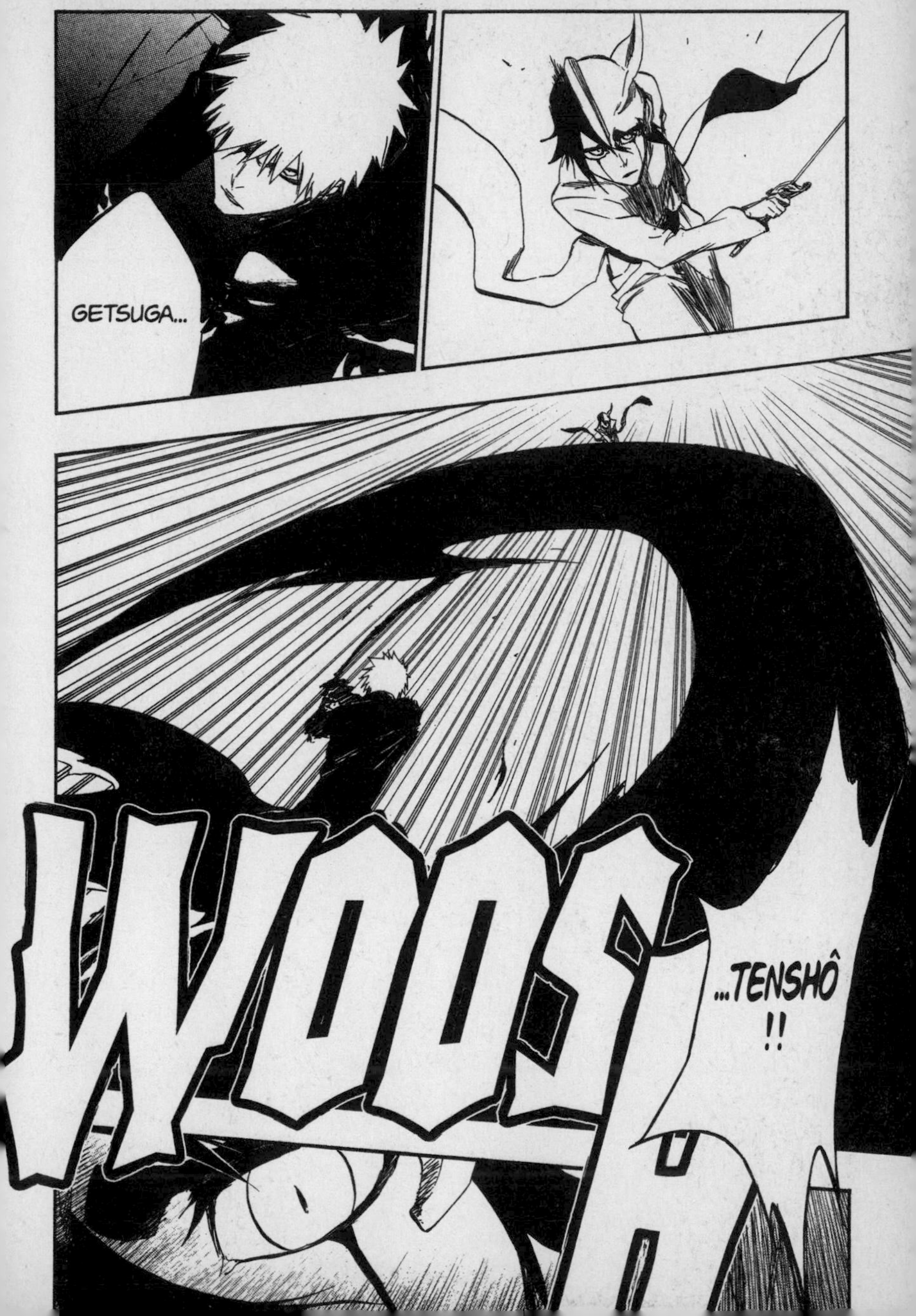
GETSUGA...
WOOSH
...TENSHÔ !!

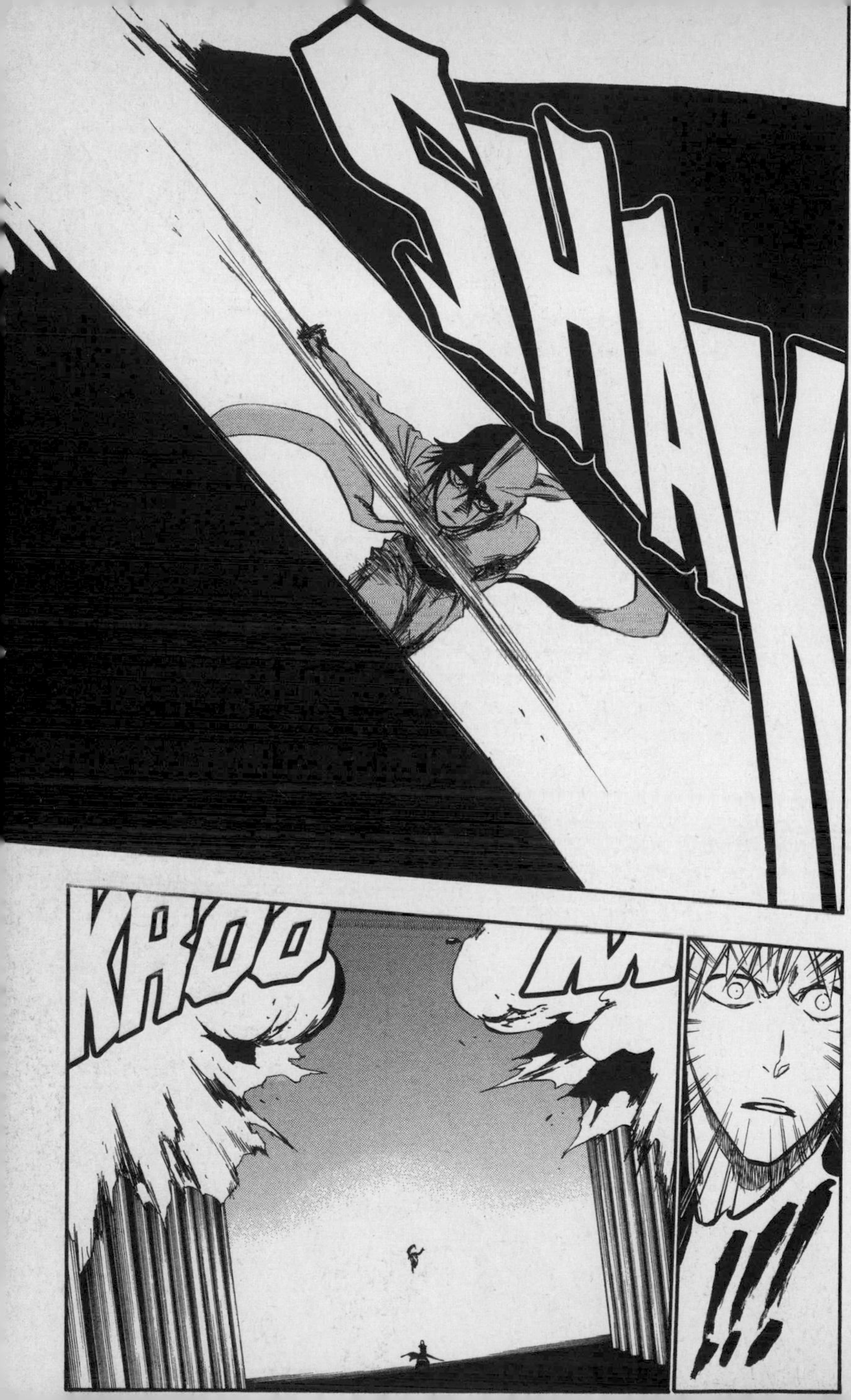
SHAK
!!
KADOOM

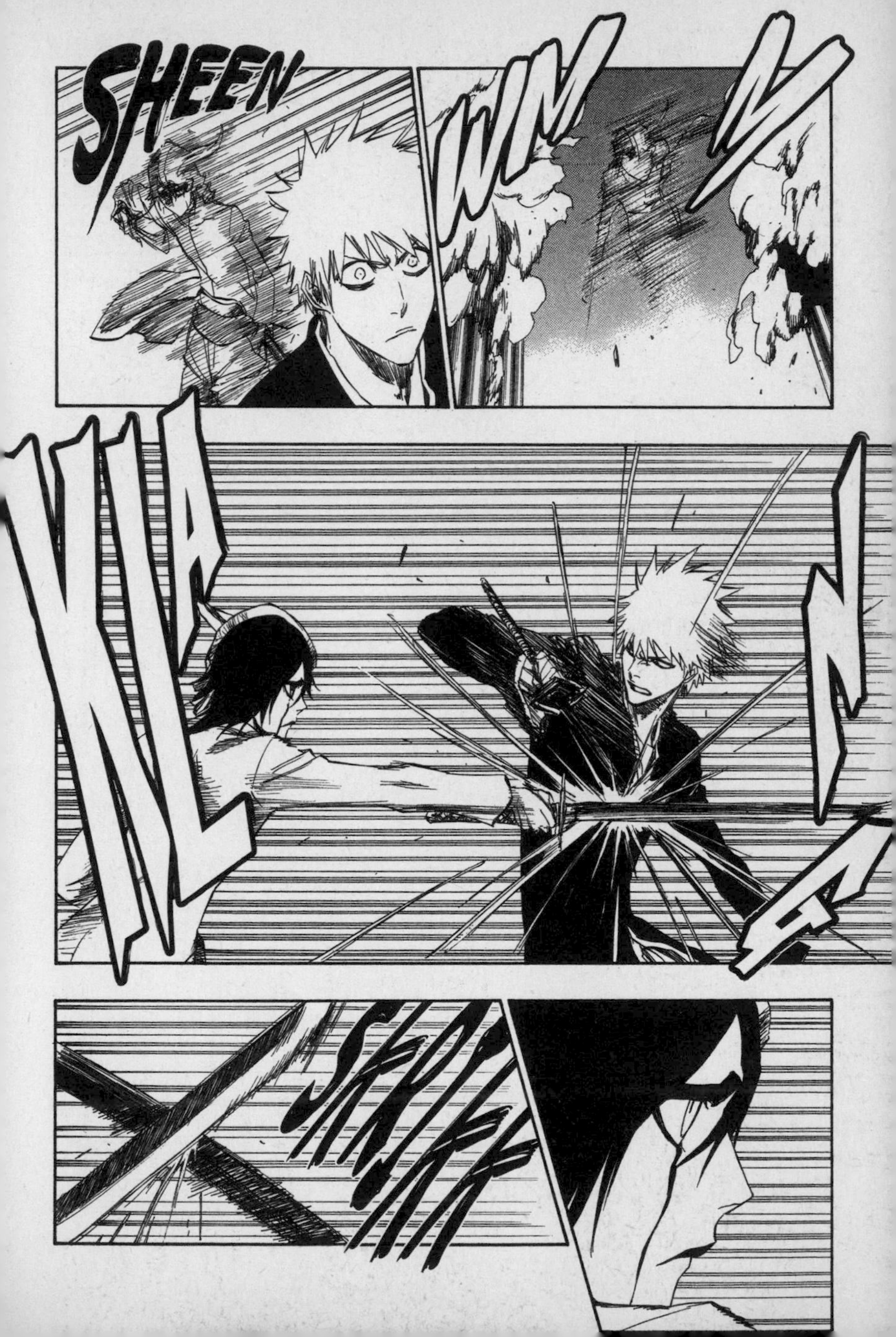
SHEEN

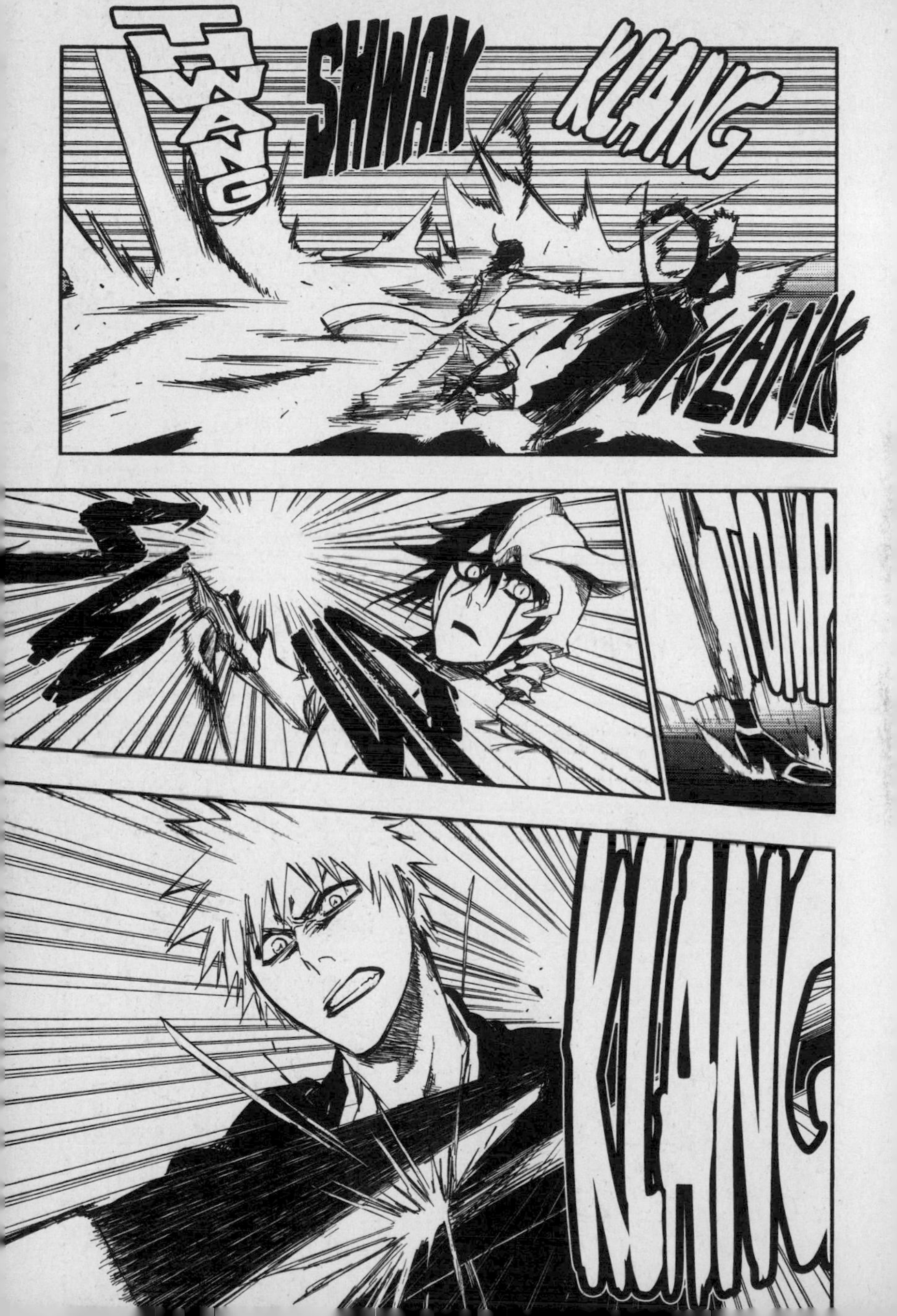
KLANG
SHWAK
TWANG
KLANK
TOMP
KLANG

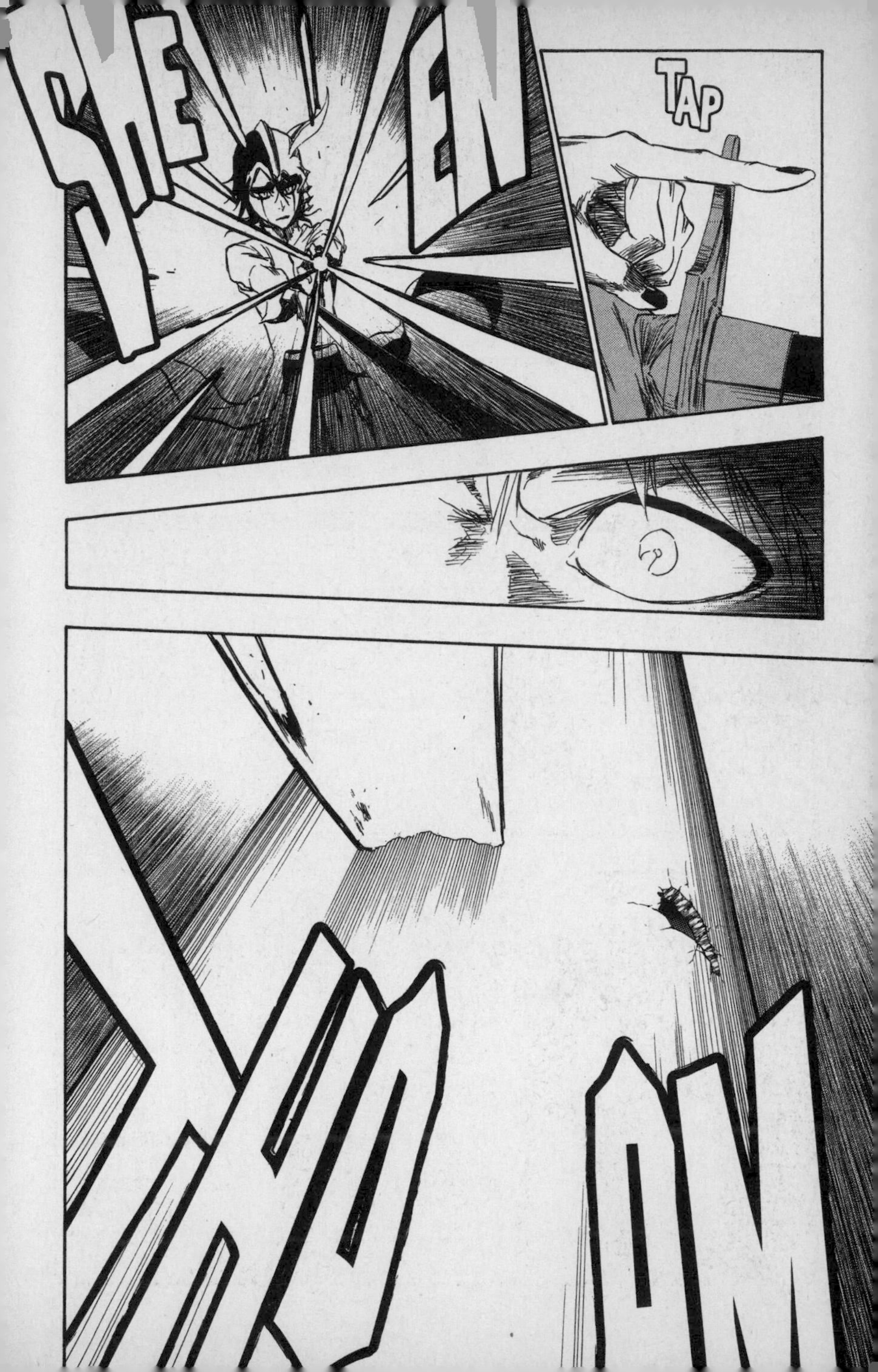
TAP
SHE EN

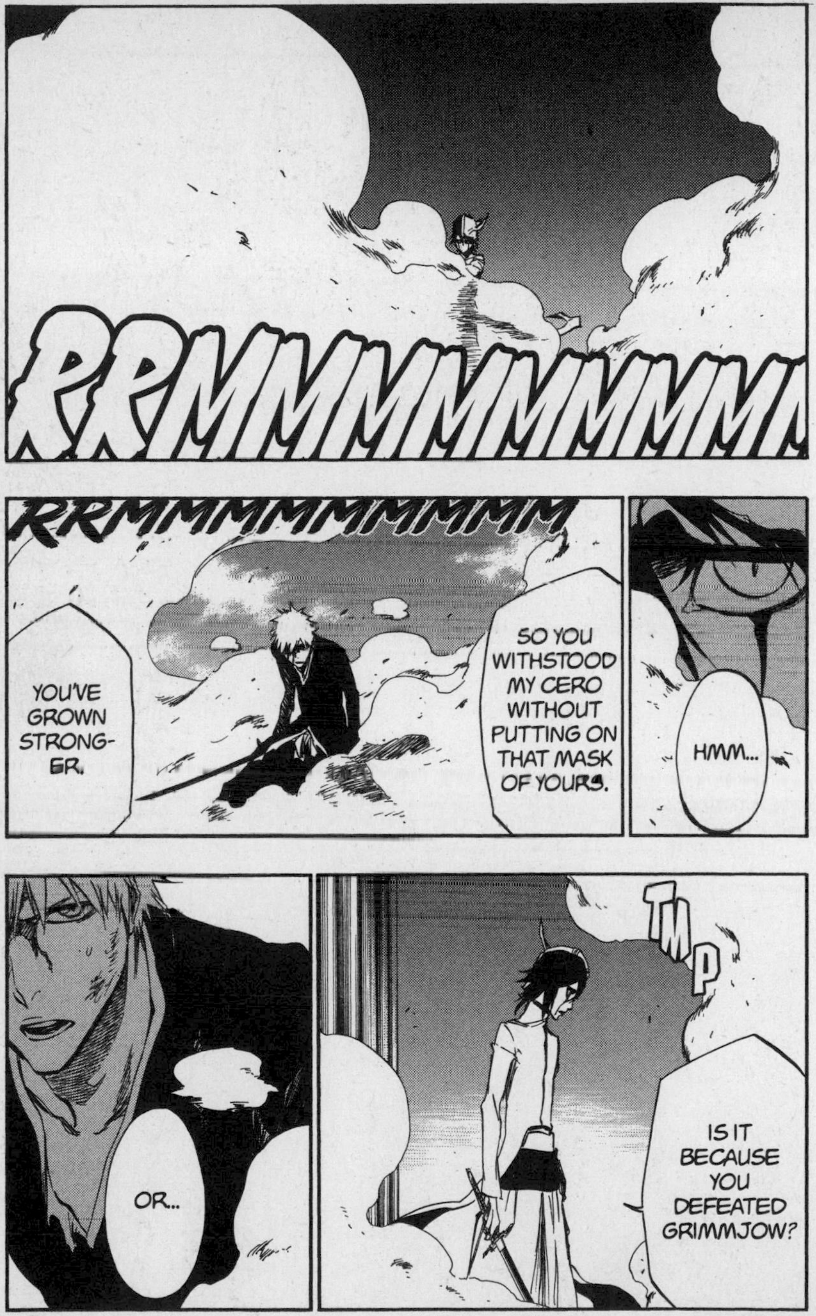
RRMMMMMMMMMM
HMM...
RRMMMMMMMMMMM
SO YOU WITHSTOOD MY CERO WITHOUT PUTTING ON THAT MASK OF YOURS.
YOU'VE GROWN STRONG-ER.
TMP
IS IT BECAUSE YOU DEFEATED GRIMMJOW?
OR...

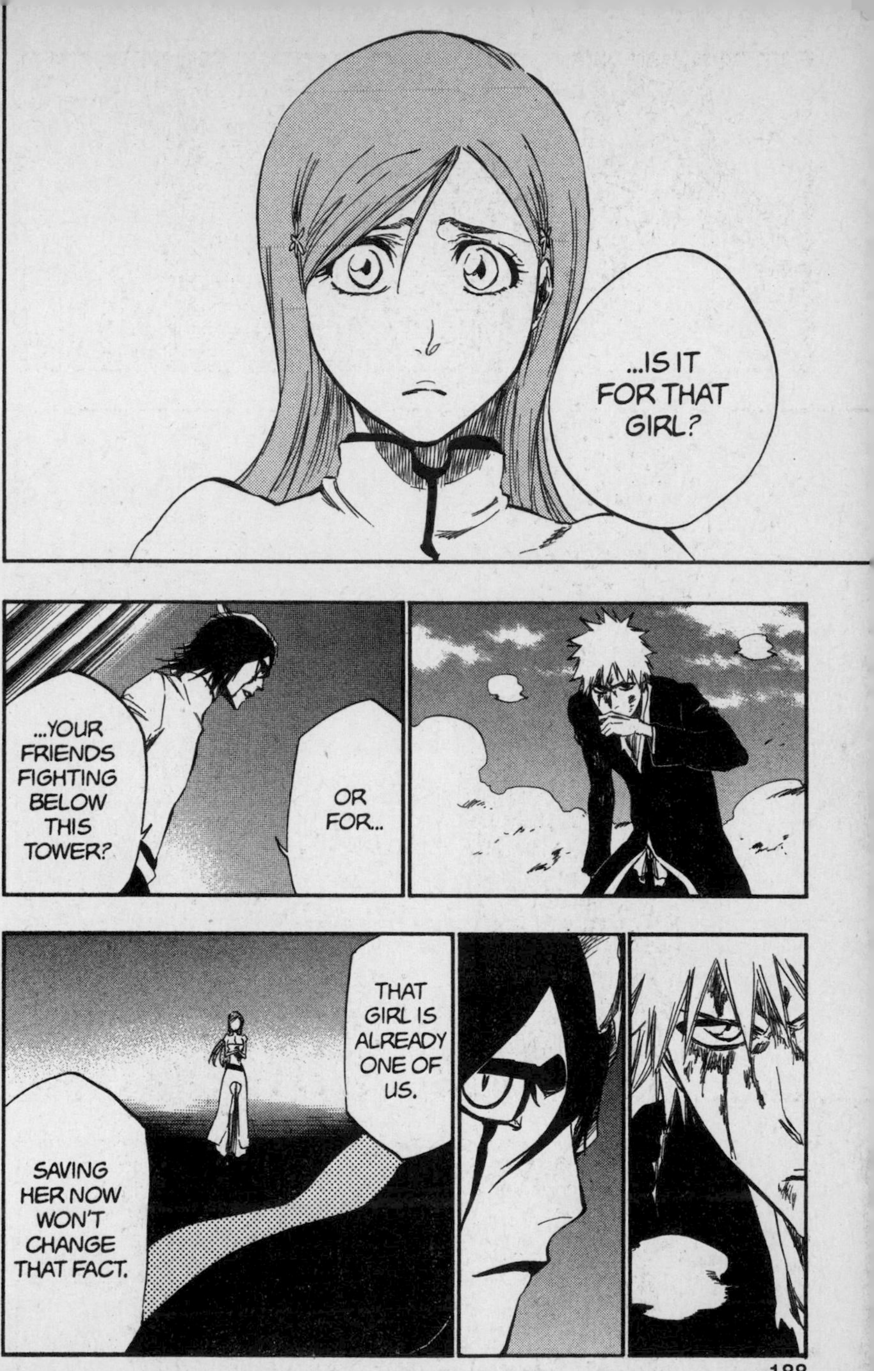
...IS IT FOR THAT GIRL?
OR FOR...
...YOUR FRIENDS FIGHTING BELOW THIS TOWER?
THAT GIRL IS ALREADY ONE OF US.
SAVING HER NOW WON'T CHANGE THAT FACT.

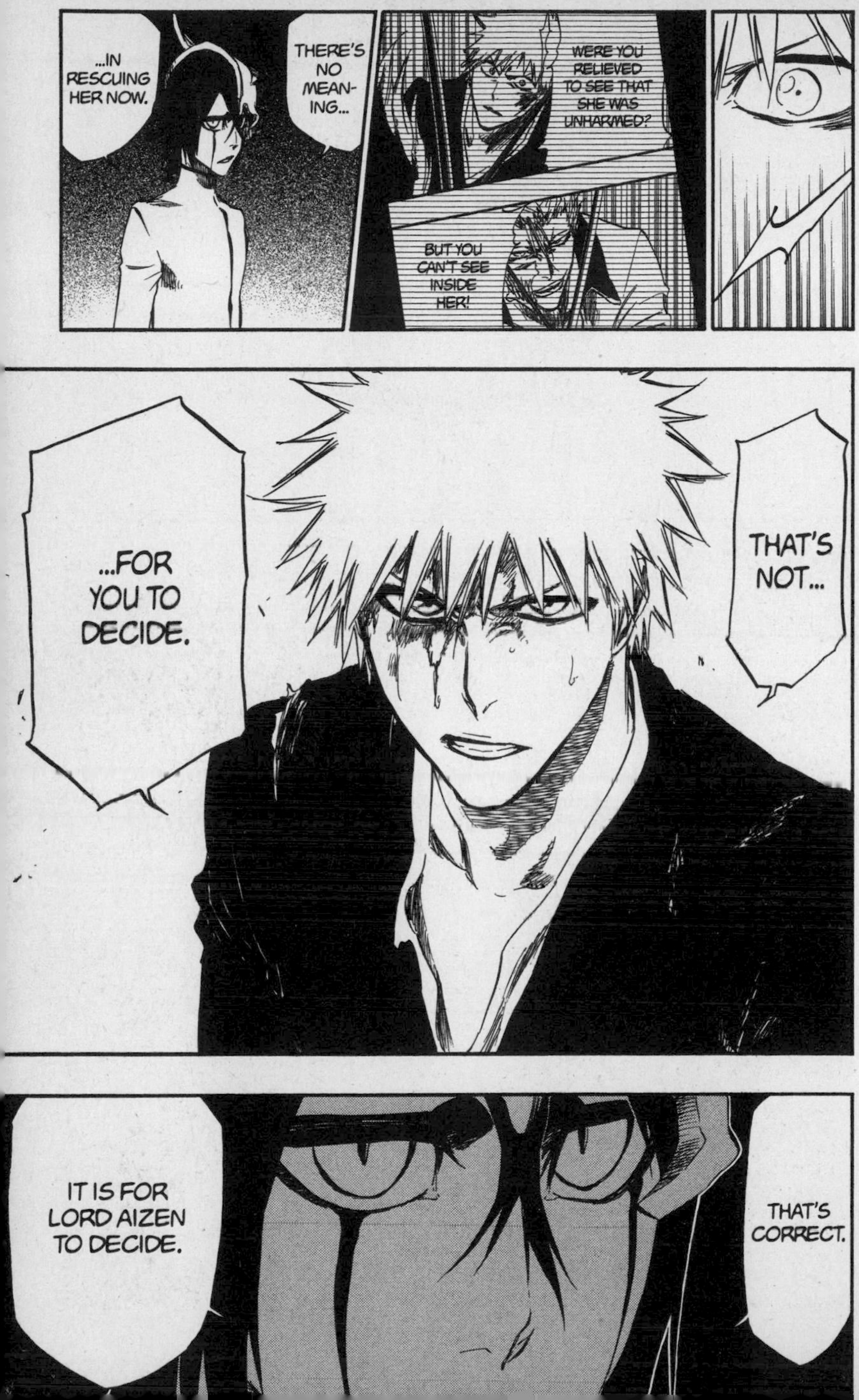
WERE YOU RELIEVED TO SEE THAT SHE WAS UNHARMED?
BUT YOU CAN'T SEE INSIDE HER!
THERE'S NO MEAN-ING...
...IN RESCUING HER NOW.
THAT'S NOT...
...FOR YOU TO DECIDE.
THAT'S CORRECT.
IT IS FOR LORD AIZEN TO DECIDE.

CONTI
NUED
IN
BLEACH
40

AYON THINKING,
"W-WHAT?!
YOU'RE MY OLDER
BROTHER?!"

Next Volume Preview

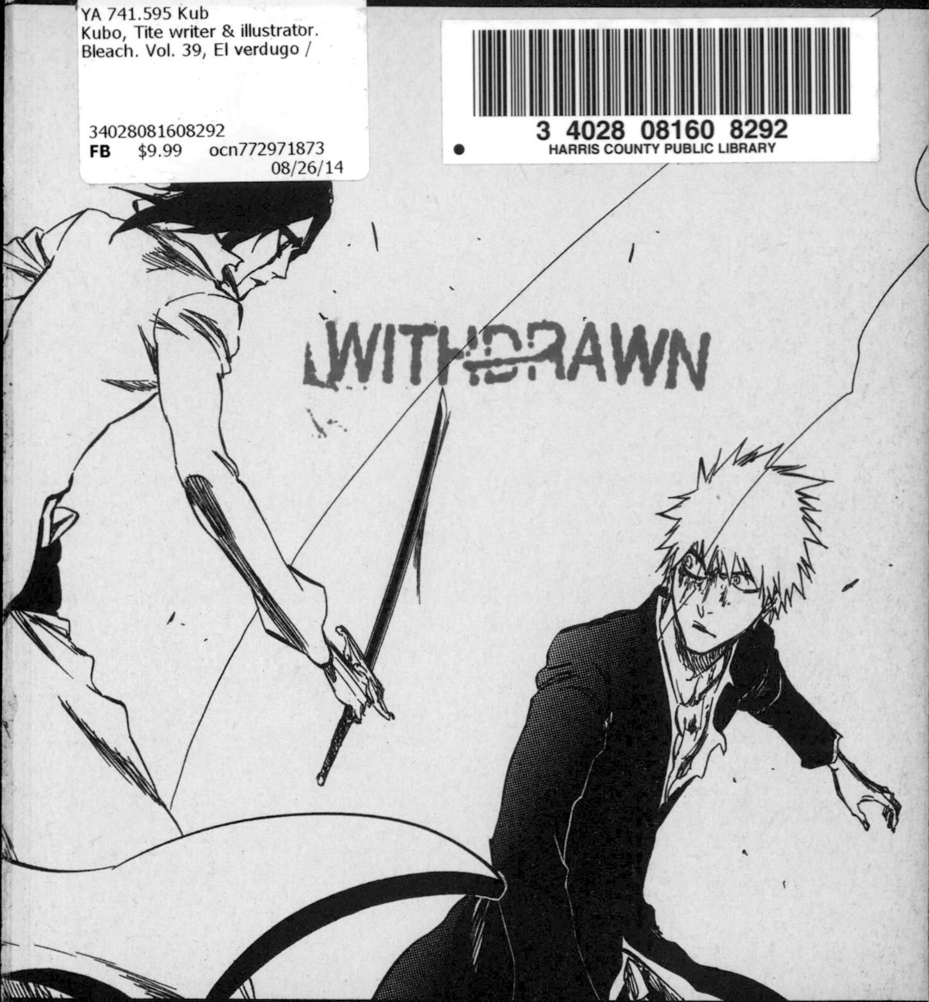

The battle between Ichigo and Ulquiorra heats up as both fighters release the full extent of their powers. Can Ichigo maintain control in his Hollow form long enough to grasp victory?

Coming June 2012!!